2012

alan rogers

the best campsites in Spain & Portugal

over 280 independent reviews

alan rogers publishing
experts in camping for over 40 years

Compiled by: Alan Rogers Guides Ltd

Designed by: Vine Design Ltd

Additional photography: T Lambelin, www.lambelin.com
Maps created by Customised Mapping (01769 540044)
contain background data provided by GisDATA Ltd

Published by: Alan Rogers Guides Ltd,
Spelmonden Old Oast, Goudhurst, Kent TN17 1HE
www.alanrogers.com Tel: 01580 214000

British Library Cataloguing-in-Publication Data:
A catalogue record for this book is available
from the British Library.

ISBN 978-1-906215-80-4

Printed in Great Britain by Stephens & George Print Group

Contents

Alan Rogers - in search of 'the best'

Alan Rogers Guides were first published over 40 years ago. Since Alan Rogers published the first campsite guide that bore his name, the range has expanded and now covers 27 countries in six separate guides. No fewer than 20 of the campsites selected by Alan for the first guide are still featured in our 2012 editions.

There are many thousands of campsites in Spain and Portugal of varying quality: this guide contains impartially written reports on almost 300, including many of the very finest, each being individually inspected and selected. We aim to provide you with a selection of the best, rather than information on all – in short, a more selective, qualitative approach. New, improved maps and indexes are also included, designed to help you find the choice of campsite that's right for you.

We hope you enjoy some happy and safe travels – and some pleasurable 'armchair touring' in the meantime!

" ...the campsites included in this book have been chosen entirely on merit, and no payment of any sort is made by them for their inclusion."

Alan Rogers, 1968

How do we find the best?

The criteria we use when inspecting and selecting campsites are numerous, but the most important by far is the question of good quality. People want different things from their choice of site so we try to include a range of campsite 'styles' to cater for a wide variety of preferences: from those seeking a small peaceful campsite in the heart of the countryside, to visitors looking for an 'all singing, all dancing' site in a popular seaside resort. Those with more specific interests, such as sporting facilities, cultural events or historical attractions, are also catered for.

The size of the site, whether it's part of a chain or privately owned, makes no difference in terms of it being required to meet our exacting standards in respect of its quality and it being 'fit for purpose'. In other words, irrespective of the size of the site, or the number of facilities it offers, we consider and evaluate the welcome, the pitches, the sanitary facilities, the cleanliness, the general maintenance and even the location.

Expert opinions

We rely on our dedicated team of Site Assessors, all of whom are experienced campers, caravanners or motorcaravanners, to visit and recommend campsites. Each year they travel some 100,000 miles around Europe inspecting new campsites for the guide and re-inspecting the existing ones. Our thanks are due to them for their enthusiastic efforts, their diligence and integrity.

We also appreciate the feedback we receive from many of our readers and we always make a point of following up complaints, suggestions or recommendations for possible new campsites. Of course we get a few grumbles too – but it really is a few, and those we do receive usually relate to overcrowding or to poor maintenance during the peak school holiday period. Please bear in mind that, although we are interested to hear about any complaints, we have no contractual relationship with the campsites featured in our guides and are therefore not in a position to intervene in any dispute between a reader and a campsite.

Independent and honest

Whilst the content and scope of the Alan Rogers guides have expanded considerably since the early editions, our selection of campsites still employs exactly the same philosophy and criteria as defined by Alan Rogers in 1968.

'telling it how it is'

Firstly, and most importantly, our selection is based entirely on our own rigorous and independent inspection and selection process. Campsites cannot buy their way into our guides – indeed the extensive Site Report which is written by us, not by the site owner, is provided free of charge so we are free to say what we think and to provide an honest, 'warts and all' description. This is written in plain English and without the use of confusing icons or symbols.

Looking for the best

Highly respected by site owners and readers alike, there is no better guide when it comes to forming an independent view of a campsite's quality. When you need to be confident in your choice of campsite, you need the Alan Rogers Guide.

- Sites only included on merit
- Sites cannot pay to be included
- Independently inspected, rigorously assessed
- Impartial reviews
- Over 40 years of expertise

Written in plain English, our guides are exceptionally easy to use, but a few words of explanation regarding the layout and content may be helpful. In Spain we have used the 16 official administrative regions, whilst in Portugal we use the five regions defined by the Portugal Tourist Board. A full page introduction to each region highlights its main areas of interest, places to visit and the local cuisine.

Region

Index town

Site name

Postal address (including area) T: telephone number. E: email address

alanrogers.com web address (including Alan Rogers reference number)

A description of the site in which we try to give an idea of its general features – its size, its situation, its strengths and its weaknesses. This section should provide a picture of the site itself with reference to the facilities that are provided and if they impact on its appearance or character. We include details on pitch numbers, electricity (with amperage), hardstandings etc. in this section as pitch design, planning and terracing affects the site's overall appearance. Similarly we include reference to pitches used for caravan holiday homes, chalets, and the like. Importantly at the end of this column we indicate if there are any restrictions, e.g. no tents, no children, naturist sites.

Facilities

Lists more specific information on the site's facilities and amenities and, where available, the dates when these facilities are open (if not for the whole season). Off site: here we give distances to various local amenities, for example, local shops, the nearest beach, plus our featured activities (bicycle hire, fishing, horse riding, boat launching). Where we have space we list suggestions for activities and local tourist attractions.

Open: Site opening dates.

Directions

Separated from the main text in order that they may be read and assimilated more easily by a navigator en-route. Bear in mind that road improvement schemes can result in road numbers being altered.

GPS: references are provided in decimal format. All latitudes are North. Longitudes are East unless preceeded by a minus sign e.g. 48.71695 is North, 0.31254 is East and -0.31254 is West.

Charges 2012 (or a general guide)

Maps, campsite listings and indexes

For this 2012 guide we have changed the way in which we list our campsites and also the way in which we help you locate the sites within each region.

We now include a map immediately after our Introduction to that region. These maps show the towns near which one (or more) of our featured campsites is located.

Within each regional section of the guide, we list these towns and the site(s) in that vicinity in alphabetical order.

You will certainly need more detailed maps for navigation, for example the Michelin atlas. We provide GPS coordinates for each site to assist you. Our three indexes will also help you to find a site by region and site name, by reference number or by the town where the site is situated.

Understanding the entries

Facilities

Toilet blocks

We assume that toilet blocks will be equipped with WCs, washbasins with hot and cold water and hot showers with dividers or curtains, and will have all necessary shelves, hooks, plugs and mirrors. We also assume that there will be an identified chemical toilet disposal point, and that the campsite will provide water and waste water drainage points and bin areas. If not the case, we comment. We do mention certain features that some readers find important: washbasins in cubicles, facilities for babies, facilities for those with disabilities and motorcaravan service points. Readers with disabilities are advised to contact the site of their choice to ensure that facilities are appropriate to their needs.

Shop

Basic or fully supplied, and opening dates.

Bars, restaurants, takeaway facilities and entertainment

We try hard to supply opening and closing dates (if other than the campsite opening dates) and to identify if there are discos or other entertainment.

Children's play areas

Fenced and with safety surface (e.g. sand, bark or pea-gravel).

Swimming pools

If particularly special, we cover in detail in our main campsite description but reference is always included under our Facilities listings. We will also indicate the existence of water slides, sunbathing areas and other features. Opening dates, charges and levels of supervision are provided where we have been notified. There is a regulation whereby Bermuda shorts may not be worn in swimming pools (for health and hygiene reasons). It is worth ensuring that you do take 'proper' swimming trunks with you.

Leisure facilities

For example, playing fields, bicycle hire, organised activities and entertainment.

Dogs

If dogs are not accepted or restrictions apply, we state it here. Check the quick reference list at the back of the guide.

Off site

This briefly covers leisure facilities, tourist attractions, restaurants etc. nearby.

Charges

These are the latest provided to us by the sites. In those cases where 2012 prices have not been provided to us by the sites, we try to give a general guide.

Reservations

Necessary for high season (roughly mid-July to mid-August) in popular holiday areas (i.e. beach resorts). You can reserve many sites via our own Alan Rogers Travel Service or through other tour operators. Or be wholly independent and contact the campsite(s) of your choice direct, using the phone or e-mail numbers shown in the site reports, but please bear in mind that many sites are closed all winter.

Telephone Numbers

All numbers assume that you are phoning from within Spain or Portugal. To phone Spain from outside that country, prefix the number shown with the relevant International Code '00 34' and then the number indicated. To phone Portugal prefix the number shown with the International Code '00 351'.

Opening dates

These are advised to us during the early autumn of the previous year – sites can, and sometimes do, alter these dates before the start of the following season, often for good reasons. If you intend to visit shortly after a published opening date, or shortly before the closing date, it is wise to check that it will actually be open at the time required. Similarly some sites operate a restricted service during the low season, only opening some of their facilities (e.g. swimming pools) during the main season; where we know about this, and have the relevant dates, we indicate it – again if you are at all doubtful it is wise to check.

Sometimes, campsite amenities may be dependent on there being enough customers on site to justify their opening and, for this reason, actual opening dates may vary from those indicated.

Some campsite owners are very relaxed when it comes to opening and closing dates. They may not be fully ready by their stated opening dates – grass and hedges may not all be cut or perhaps only limited sanitary facilities open. At the end of the season they also tend to close down some facilities and generally wind down prior to the closing date. Bear this in mind if you are travelling early or late in the season – it is worth phoning ahead.

The Camping Cheque low season touring system goes some way to addressing this in that many participating campsites will have all key facilities open and running by the opening date and these will remain fully operational until the closing date.

You're on your way!

Whether you're an 'old hand' in terms of camping and caravanning or are contemplating your first trip, a regular reader of our Guides or a new 'convert', we wish you well in your travels and hope we have been able to help in some way.

We are, of course, also out and about ourselves, visiting sites, talking to owners and readers, and generally checking on standards and new developments.

Our Accommodation section

180

Over recent years, more and more campsites have added high quality mobile home and chalet accommodation. In response to feedback from many of our readers, and to reflect this evolution in campsites, we have now decided to include a separate section on mobile homes and chalets.

If a site offers this accommodation, it is indicated above the site report with a page reference where full details are given. We have chosen a number of sites offering some of the best accommodation available and have included full details of one or two accommodation types at these sites. Please note however that many other campsites listed in this guide may also have a selection of accommodation for rent.

We wish all our readers thoroughly enjoyable Camping and Caravanning in 2012 – favoured by good weather of course!

The Alan Rogers Team

Cantabria
page 129
Pais Vasco-Euskadi
page 135
La Rioja
page 139
Galicia
page 119
Asturias
page 123
Navarra
page 143
Porto & North
page 176
Castilla y Léon
page 113
Lisbon &
ale do Tejo
page 166
Beiras & Centre
page 171
Aragón
page 147
Catalunya
page 18
Madrid
page 109
Extremadura
page 101
Castilla-La Mancha
page 105
Balears
page 153
Alentejo
page 161
Comunidad
Valenciana
page 60
Andalucia
page 81
Murcia
page 77
Algarve
page 155

The Alan Rogers Awards

The Alan Rogers Campsite Awards were launched in 2004 and have proved a great success.

Our awards have a broad scope and before committing to our winners, we carefully consider more than 2,000 campsites featured in our guides, taking into account comments from our site assessors, our head office team and, of course, our readers.

Our award winners come from the four corners of Europe, from southern Portugal to Slovenia, and this year we are making awards to campsites in 10 different countries.

Needless to say, it's an extremely difficult task to choose our eventual winners, but we believe that we have identified a number of campsites with truly outstanding characteristics.

In each case, we have selected an outright winner, along with two highly commended runners-up. Listed below are full details of each of our award categories and our winners for 2011.

Alan Rogers Progress Award 2011

This award reflects the hard work and commitment undertaken by particular site owners to improve and upgrade their site.

Winner

IT62290	Camping Lago di Levico *Italy*

Runners-up

ES87430	Marjal Camping & Bungalows Resort *Spain*
CR6731	Naturist Camping Valalta *Croatia*

Alan Rogers Welcome Award 2011

This award takes account of sites offering a particularly friendly welcome and maintaining a friendly ambience throughout readers' holidays.

Winner

ES80500	Camping Aquarius *Spain*

Runners-up

DE3670	Camping Hopfensee *Germany*
IR9650	Woodlands Park Touring Caravan & Camping Park *Ireland*

Our warmest congratulations to all our award winners and our commiserations to all those not having won an award on this occasion.

The Alan Rogers Team

Alan Rogers Active Holiday Award 2011

This award reflects sites in outstanding locations which are ideally suited for active holidays, notably walking or cycling, but which could extend to include such activities as winter sports or watersports.

Winner

FR24060 Camping le Paradis *France*

Runners-up

ES86250 Kiko Park Rural *Spain*

IT62030 Caravan Park Sexten *Italy*

Alan Rogers Innovation Award 2011

Our new Innovation Award acknowledges campsites with creative and original concepts, possibly with features which are unique, and cannot therefore be found elsewhere. We have identified innovation both in campsite amenities and also in rentable accommodation.

Winner

AU0265 Park Grubhof *Austria*

Runners-up

IT60370 Camping Jesolo International *Italy*

SV4200 Camping Bled *Slovenia*

Alan Rogers Small Campsite Award 2011

This new award acknowledges excellent small campsites (less than 75 pitches) which offer a friendly welcome and top quality amenities throughout the season to their guests.

Winner

FR38040 Camping à la Rencontre du Soleil *France*

Runners-up

UK0065 Wayfarers Camping & Caravan Park *England*

DE3750 Camping Schloss Issigau *Germany*

Alan Rogers Seaside Award 2011

This award is made for sites which we feel are outstandingly suitable for a really excellent seaside holiday.

Winner

IT60200 Camping Union Lido Vacanze *Italy*

Runners-up

NL6948 Camping Strandpark De Zeeuwse Kust *Netherlands*

FR66560 Camping la Sirène *France*

Alan Rogers Country Award 2011

This award contrasts with our former award and acknowledges sites which are attractively located in delightful, rural locations.

Winner

FR37140 Huttopia Rillé *France*

Runners-up

UK3430 Kelling Heath Holiday Park *England*

FR19200 Les Hameaux de Miel *France*

Alan Rogers Family Site Award 2011

Many sites claim to be child friendly but this award acknowledges the sites we feel to be the very best in this respect.

Winner

NL5985 Vrijetijdspark Beerze Bulten *Netherlands*

Runners-up

IT60450 Camping Marina di Venezia *Italy*

FR40060 Club Camping International Eurosol *France*

Alan Rogers Readers' Award 2011

We believe our Readers' Award to be the most important. We simply invite our readers (by means of an on-line poll at www.alanrogers.com) to nominate the site they enjoyed most.

The outright winner for 2011 is:

Winner

FR17010 Camping Bois Soleil *France*

Book with us for the best holidays
on the best campsites

The Alan Rogers Travel Service was originally set up to provide a low cost booking service for readers. We pride ourselves on being able to put together a bespoke holiday, taking advantage of our experience, knowledge and contacts. We can even arrange low cost ferry crossings – ask us about our famous Ferry Deals!

FREE 2012 Brochure

call 01580 214000

Over 100 campsites in France, Italy and Spain hand picked for you

www.alanrogers.com/travel

alan rogers travel

The aims of the Travel Service are simple

- **To provide convenience - a one-stop shop to make life easier.**
- **To provide peace of mind - when you need it most.**
- **To provide a friendly, knowledgeable, efficient service – when this can be hard to find.**
- **To provide a low cost means of organising your holiday – when prices can be so complicated.**

When you book with us, you will be allocated an experienced Personal Travel Consultant to provide you with personal advice and manage every stage of your booking. Our Personal Travel Consultants have first-hand experience of many of our campsites and access to a wealth of information. They can check availability, provide a competitive price and tailor your holiday arrangements to your specific needs.

- Discuss your holiday plans with a friendly person with first-hand experience
- Let us reassure you that your holiday arrangements really are taken care of
- Tell us about your special requests and allow us to pass these on
- Benefit from advice which will save you money – the latest ferry deals and more
- Remember, our offices are in Kent not overseas and we do NOT operate a queuing system!

Call us for advice or an instant quote

01580 214000 or visit
www.alanrogers.com/travel

Sant Pere Pescador
Kawan Village L'Amfora
COSTA BRAVA · SPAIN
alanrogers.com

Look for a campsite entry like this to indicate which campsites we can book for you.

The list is growing so please call for up to the minute information.

alan rogers travel

Getting the most from **off peak touring**

There are many reasons to avoid high season, if you can. Queues are shorter, there's less traffic, a calmer atmosphere and prices are cheaper. And it's usually still nice and sunny!

And when you use Camping Cheques you'll find great quality facilities that are actually open and a welcoming conviviality.

Did you know?

Camping Cheques can be used right into mid-July and from late August on many sites. Over 90 campsites in France alone accept Camping Cheques from 20th August.

Camping Cheque

Save up to 60% with Camping Cheques

Camping Cheque is a fixed price scheme allowing you to go as you please, staying on over 600 campsites across Europe, always paying the same rate and saving you up to 60% on regular pitch fees. One Cheque gives you one night for 2 people + unit on a standard pitch, with electricity. It's as simple as that.

Special offers mean you can stay extra nights free (eg 7 nights for 6 Cheques) or even a month free for a month paid! Especially popular in Spain during the winter, these longer-term offers can effectively halve the nightly rate. See Site Directory for details.

Check out our amazing Ferry Deals!

One of the largest countries in Europe, with glorious beaches, a fantastic sunshine record, vibrant towns and laid back sleepy villages, plus a diversity of landscape, culture and artistic traditions, Spain has all the ingredients for a great holiday.

Tourist Office

Spanish Tourist Office
Second Floor, 79 New Cavendish Street
London W1W 6XB

Tel: 020 7486 8077
Fax: 020 7317 2048
E-mail: info.londres@tourspain.es
Internet: www.spain.info

Spain has a huge choice of beach resorts to choose from. With charming villages and attractive towns, the Costa Brava boasts spectacular scenery with towering cliffs and sheltered coves. There are plenty of lively resorts, including Lloret, Tossa and Calella, plus several quieter ones. Further along the east coast, the Costa del Azahar stretches from Vinaros to Almanzora, with the great port of Valencia in the middle. Orange groves abound. The central section of the coastline, the Costa Blanca, has 170 miles or so of silvery-white beaches. Benidorm is the most popular resort. The Costa del Sol lies in the south, home to more beaches and brilliant sunshine, whilst in the north the Costa Verde is largely unspoiled, with clean water, sandy beaches and rocky coves against a backdrop of mountains.

Beaches and sunshine aside, Spain also has plenty of great cities and towns to explore, including Barcelona, Valencia, Seville, Madrid, Toledo and Bilbao, all offering an array of sights, galleries and museums.

Population

46.5 million

Capital

Madrid

Climate

Spain has a very varied climate. The north is temperate with most of the rainfall; dry and very hot in the centre; sub-tropical along the Mediterranean.

Language

Castilian Spanish is spoken by most people with Catalan (northeast), Basque (north) and Galician (northwest) used in their respective areas.

Telephone

The country code is 00 34.

Currency

The Euro (€).

Banks

Mon-Fri 09.00-14.00. Sat 09.00-13.00.

Shops

Mon-Sat 09.00-13.00/14.00 and 15.00/16.00-19.30/20.00.
Many close later.

Public Holidays

New Year; Epiphany; Saints Day 19 March; Maundy Thurs; Good Fri; Easter Mon; Labour Day; Saints Day 25 July; Assumption 15 Aug; National Day 12 Oct; All Saints Day 1 Nov; Constitution Day 6 Dec; Immaculate Conception 8 Dec; Christmas Day.

Flanked by the Pyrenees mountains and bathed by the Mediterranean Sea, Catalunya occupies the northeastern part of the Iberian peninsula. It has a strong identity, with a unique culture and language all of its own.

CATALUNYA IS COMPOSED OF FOUR PROVINCES: BARCELONA, TARRAGONA, LLEIDA AND GIRONA

THE REGIONAL CAPITAL IS BARCELONA

Barcelona is the historical capital of Catalunya and Spain's second leading city in both size and importance, after Madrid. The beautiful city has an impressive architectural heritage that includes the Gothic Quarter, with its cathedral, the old City Hall Building, the Episcopal Palace and the splendid Palace of the Generalitat. The city also boasts the work of the incomparable modernist architect Antonio Gaudí. In the centre of the fertile plain of the River Segre sits Lleida, capital of the province of the same name. Prominent atop a hill in the historic quarter of the city is the old cathedral or Seu Vella. The Costa Brava is the coastal zone that begins about 40 km. north of Barcelona and includes the entire shoreline of the province of Girona. It is an area of great natural beauty, formed by a succession of steep cliffs and small coves with finely grained sand. Some of its towns have been massively exploited for tourism but others, such as Tossa de Mar, still maintain their original size and fishing-village charm. The principal tourist centres on the coast include Roses, Sant Pere Pescador, L'Escala, L'Estartit, Palamós, Palafrugell, Platja d'Aro, S'Agaro, Sant Feliu de Guíxols, Lloret de Mar and Blanes. There are daily boat services which operate along the coast for most of the year.

Places of interest

Empúries: Greco-Roman city.

Figueres: birthplace of Salvador Dali, museum displaying his finest work.

Girona: one of the oldest and most beautiful Catalan cities, 14th-century cathedral.

La Costa Dorada: stretches south from the Costa Brava to Tarragona, with beautiful, open, well maintained beaches.

Parque Natural de Aigüamolls de L'Empordà: park made up of three reserves, with wildlife and over 320 bird species.

Sitges: attractive beach town, museum of Cau-Ferrat featuring paintings by El Greco.

Tarragona: Roman remains of Tarraco, the original Roman city.

Cuisine of the region

Mediterranean influence with lots of tomatoes, garlic, fresh herbs, olive oil, onions, fish. Wild mushrooms in the autumn. Locally produced wines from Penedés, Conca de Barberá, Pla de Bages and Alella.

Calçots: green onions grilled on a barbecue.

Cod esqueixada: cod soaked in cold water then mixed with tomatoes, olives and onion.

Escalivada: vegetable stew with roasted aubergine and peppers.

Fuet, llonganisa, butifarra: local sausages.

Suquet: seafood casserole.

Recao de binefar: rice cooked with white beans, potatoes and chorizo.

For a map of northeast Catalunya, see the next page.

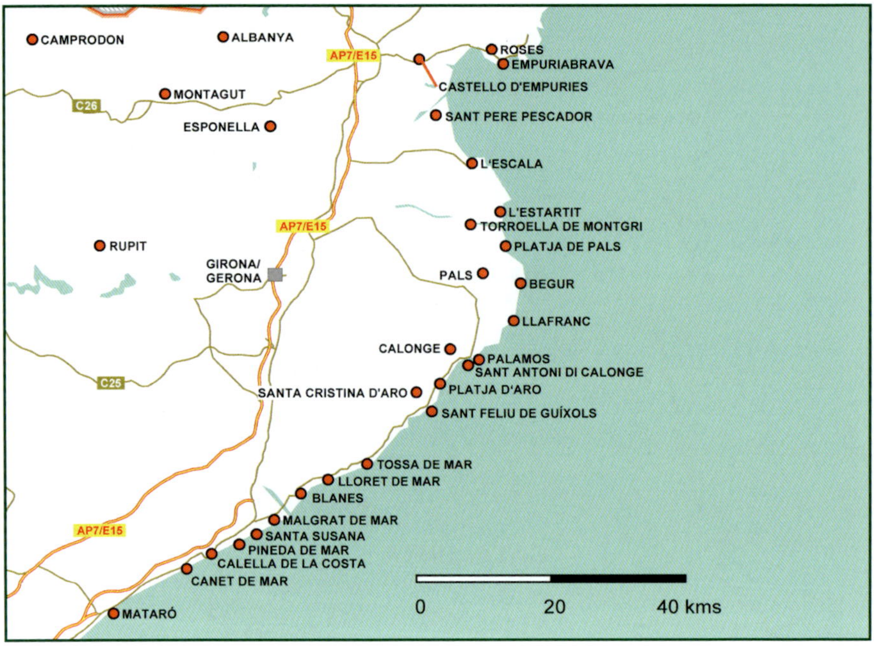

Albanyá

Camping Bassegoda Park

Camí Camp de l'illa, E-17733 Albanyá (Girona) T: 972 542 020. E: info@bassegodapark.com

alanrogers.com/ES80640

Surrounded by mountains alongside the Muga river, Bassegoda Park is a place to experience Spain in a natural environment but with a touch of luxury. This totally rebuilt site is just beyond Albanyá on the edge of the Alta Garrotxa National Park in an area of great beauty. In their own area, the 60 touring pitches are level and shaded, all on hardstanding and with access to electricity, water and drainage. Tents are dotted informally in the terraced forest areas. Particular care has been taken in the landscaping, layout and design of the attractive pool, bar and restaurant, the hub of the site. Regional wines and dishes are available in the reasonably priced restaurant. The enthusiastic young director, Esteve Guerra (Steve) who speaks excellent English, and his assistant Laura have been working hard to make a stay at Bassegoda Park a memorable experience. Two separate areas provide modern, attractive chalets, 15 pitches are occupied by seasonal caravans, whilst walkers engaged in the famous G11 treks camp on the upper terraced slopes. The site is designed with tourers in a separate area, 40 mobile homes in a pretty village setting and specially designed walkers' accommodation in the upper areas for those engaged in the famous G11 treks. The excellent sporting facilities, children's club and a high season programme of activities for adults and children make this an ideal site for a family holiday whilst being in tune with nature.

Facilities

A new spacious and well equipped, main toilet building is centrally located and provides controllable showers and facilities for babies and disabled visitors. It is supplemented by two smaller refurbished blocks. Washing machine and dryer. Gas supplies. Supermarket. Bar, restaurant and takeaway (all season). Swimming pool (1/6-15/9). Playground. New leisure area (5-a-side football, volleyball, basketball). Minigolf. Activities for adults and children, plus weekend entertainment. Bicycle hire. Barbecue areas. WiFi. Torches useful. Air-conditioned bungalows to rent. Off site: Fishing and river 1 km. Sailing 5 km. Riding 15 km. Golf 20 km. Beach 35 km. Limited public transport.

Open: 1 March - 11 December.

Directions

Site is north of Girona, 23 km. west of Figueres. From Barcelona on AP7/E15, take exit 4 and the N11 towards France, then the GI510 to Llers and GI511 to St Llorenc de la Muga and Albanyá. Site is beyond the village (take care with sharp bend), well signed where the road ends. From France take exit 3 then the GI510 to Llers. There is NO exit 3 northbound on the AP7/E15.
GPS: 42.30654, 2.70933

Charges guide

Per unit incl. 2 persons and electricity	€ 29.85 - € 35.40
extra person	€ 5.60 - € 6.85
child (3-10 yrs)	€ 4.60 - € 5.10

Ametlla de Mar

Camping Caravanning Ametlla Village Platja

Apdo 240, Paraje Santes Creus, E-43860 Ametlla de Mar (Tarragona) T: 977 267 784.
E: info@campingametlla.com **alanrogers.com/ES85360**

Occupying a terraced hillside above colourful coves with shingle beaches and two small associated lagoons, this site falls into four areas. The central one with reception and supermarket has a group of 44 touring pitches, below this are chalets for rent and a few touring pitches on ground falling away towards the lagoons and beach. A second larger touring section also has 54 mobile homes owned by tour operators and finally, the bar/restaurant, pool and other leisure facilities are on the hilltop, with glimpses of the sea through the trees. There is some train noise, especially in the front section.

Facilities

Two large toilet blocks, plus a smaller one. Controllable showers and open-style washbasins. Some private cabins with WC and washbasin. En-suite unit for disabled visitors. Baby rooms with bath. Motorcaravan services. Gas supplies. Supermarket (2/4-30/9; small shop incl. bread at other times). Bar/restaurant with TV, snack menu and takeaway, pub/cocktail bar (all 2/4-30/9). Swimming pools (supervised 22/6-15/9). Sub-aqua diving. Kayaking. Fishing. Children's club. Fitness room. Bicycle hire. Entertainment (July/Aug). Barbecue area. WiFi (charged).

Open: All year.

Directions

Ametlla is 50 km. south of Tarragona. From AP7/E15 (Barcelona-Valencia) at exit 39 (or from N340) follow signs for Ametlla de Mar. Bear right before village following numerous white signs and continue for 2 km. Take care on final steep bend to site. GPS: 40.8645, 0.7788

Charges guide

Per unit incl. 2 persons and electricity	€ 20.70 - € 36.50
extra person	€ 3.40 - € 6.50

Amposta

Camping Eucaliptus

Platja Eucaliptus s/n, E-43870 Amposta (Tarragona) T: 977 479 046. E: eucaliptus@campingeucaliptus.com
alanrogers.com/ES85550

Ideally situated in the Parc Natural del Delta del Ebro, a unique area of wetland and a World Heritage site, this campsite is close to the golden sands of Platja Eucaliptus. Arriving here is like finding an oasis after the extraordinary drive through miles of flat marshland and rice fields. There are 264 small, level, shady grass pitches, 156 for touring, all with electricity (6A). The site is very well maintained and has a pleasant bar/restaurant which has a terrace that overlooks both the pleasant pool area and the campsite's own lagoon and its variety of wildlife. The pool has a grassy area for sunbathing and the lagoon (fenced) replicates in miniature the habitat of the Delta, with signs identifying flora and fauna.

Facilities

One clean toilet block includes open style washbasins and good sized shower cubicles. Baby bath. Good facilities for disabled visitors. Laundry facilities. Dog shower. Shop. Gas supplies. Bar with satellite TV. Restaurant and snack bar with takeaway (all season). Play area. Swimming pool with paddling pool (1/6-15/9). Bicycle hire. Barbecue area with covered seating. Large units may require two pitches (no extra charge in low season). Off site: Beach 300 m.

Open: 23 March - 30 September.

Directions

From the AP7 take exit 41 and follow N340 south. Immediately after crossing river Ebro take exit signed Els Muntells and Sant Jaume, then bear right in 4 km. on TV3405 to Els Muntells. Continue 13.5 km. to site on the right. GPS: 40.65658, 0.77978

Charges guide

Per unit incl. 2 persons and electricity	€ 25.55 - € 33.10
extra person	€ 4.90 - € 6.90

Begur

Camping El Maset

Playa de Sa Riera, E-17255 Begur (Girona) T: 972 623 023. E: info@campingelmaset.com
alanrogers.com/ES81030

A delightful little gem of a site in lovely surroundings, El Maset has 107 pitches, of which just 20 are slightly larger for caravans and motorcaravans, the remainder suitable only for tents. The site celebrated its 50th anniversary in 2011 and the owner, Sr Juan Perez is delightful and his staff are very helpful. The site entrance is steep and access to the caravan pitches can be quite tricky. However, the owner's son will tow your caravan to your pitch. Some of the pitches are shaded and all have electricity, 20 also have water and drainage. Tent pitches are more shaded on steep, rock-walled terraces on the hillside.

Facilities

Good sanitary facilities in three small blocks are kept very clean. Baby facilities. Washing machines and dryers. Unit for disabled campers (ground is steep). Bar/restaurant, takeaway and shop. Swimming pool. Solarium. Play area. Excellent games room. Satellite TV. Internet access and free WiFi. Dogs are not accepted. Charcoal barbecues are not permitted. Off site: Fishing and beach 300 m.

Open: 13 March - 13 October.

Directions

From C31 Figueres - Palamos road south of Pals, north of Palafrugell, take GI653 to Begur. Site is 2 km. north of town; follow signs for Playa de Sa Riera and site (steep entrance). GPS: 41.96860, 3.21002

Charges 2012

Per unit incl. 2 persons and electricity	€ 27.70 - € 40.50

Begur

Camping Begur

Ctra d'Esclanya km 2, E-17255 Begur (Girona) T: 972 623 201. E: info@campingbegur.com

alanrogers.com/ES81040

The choice of pitches on this pleasant, wooded site, just three kilometres from the coast, is remarkable; some are on gently-sloping grassland, others on hillside terraces or on the hilltop itself, and one steep slope has terraced tent pitches. Two hundred and thirty-two have electricity (10A), water and drainage, 30 are for tents and various corners are occupied by 45 mobile homes and chalets to rent, and by seasonal caravans. At the centre is a pleasant swimming pool with grassy terrace and a small paddling pool, overlooked by an attractive bar and snack bar. Begur is a pretty village with a choice of seven beaches.

Facilities

Two modern toilet blocks with open style washbasins, large showers, a good unit for disabled visitors. Baby room, hot water to dishwashing and laundry sinks and a private bathroom for hire. Laundry. Motorcaravan services. Bar/snack bar. Swimming and paddling pool. Boules. Gym (free). Play area. Large field for children's and family activities (20/6-11/9). Children's 'huerta' (small market garden). Children's farm. WiFi. Off site: Site's own supermarket just by gate. Village 2 km. Beaches 3-5 km.

Open: 1 April - 26 September.

Directions

From north on AP7 at exit 6 (Girona) take C66 to La Bisbal; before Palafrugell follow signs for Begur. From south on AP7 at exit 9 follow Palamós, Palafrugell, then Begur. Site is 2 km. south of Begur on minor road to Palafrugell. GPS: 41.940216, 3.200079

Charges guide

Per unit incl. 2 persons and electricity € 20.10 - € 41.00

No credit cards.

Bellver de Cerdanya

Camping Solana del Segre

Ctra N260 km 198, E-25720 Bellver de Cerdanya (Lleida) T: 973 510 310. E: sds@solanadelsegre.com

alanrogers.com/ES91420

The Sierra del Cadi offers some spectacular scenery and the Reserva Cerdanya is very popular with Spanish skiers. This site is situated in an open, sunny lower valley beside the River Segre where the far bank is a National Park (unfenced so children will need supervision). The immediate area is ideal for walkers and offers many opportunities for outdoor sports enthusiasts. The site is in two sections, the lower one nearer the river being for tourists, mainly flat and grassy with 200 pitches of 100 sq.m. or more, shaded by trees with 15A electricity. The upper area is taken by permanent units.

Facilities

Modern sanitary facilities are in a central building on the lower level, with extra Portacabin style units (unisex toilets/showers). Facilities for disabled campers are on the upper level (wheelchair users will experience problems). Laundry facilities. Motorcaravan services. Shop, bar and restaurant (1/7-15/9). Swimming and paddling pools (1/7-5/9). Indoor pool. Two play areas. Games room. River fishing. Barbecue areas. Internet. Torches are required.

Open: 1 July - 15 September.

Directions

Bellver de Cerdanya is 18 km. southwest of Puigcerdá, which is on the French border opposite Bourg-Madame. Site is on left at the 198 km. marker on the N260 from Puigcerdá to La Seu d'Urgell. GPS: 42.372697, 1.760484

Charges guide

Per unit incl. 1 person and electricity	€ 28.50
extra person	€ 6.00

Blanes

Camping La Masia

Ctra Colon 44, E-17300 Blanes (Girona) T: 972 331 013. E: info@campinglamasia.com

alanrogers.com/ES82250

A large resort site, La Masia has 757 pitches with 300 for touring units. These pitches are flat, shaded by trees and in rows with some mobile homes inserted here and there. There is something for everyone in La Masia and the resort town is just outside the gate, as is the fine beach. A large, central building houses the main bar and restaurant. The jewel in the crown of the site is below this complex, where you can enjoy an indoor heated pool, spa, massage, plunge pools and exercise pools, and pamper yourself in luxury in a Roman bath type setting (extra charge).

Facilities

Six well maintained toilet blocks have basic facilities with facilities for disabled campers and a baby room (key entry). Motorcaravan services. Laundry facilities. Supermarket. Bakery. Restaurants. Snack bars. Swimming pools. Spa centre. Play areas. Boules. Bicycle hire. Barbecue area. Entertainment programme. Internet access and WiFi. ATM. Security boxes. Torches useful. Off site: Resort town and beach outside the gate. Public transport. Fishing.

Open: 9 January - 9 December.

Directions

La Masia is on the southwest side of Blanes. From exit 9 on AP7 Girona - Barcelona road follow N11 to the B600 towards Blanes. Before Blanes turn southwest following site signs at roundabouts, which will direct you to La Masia avoiding Blanes town which has narrow roads. GPS: 41.66291, 2.78075

Charges guide

Per unit incl. 2 persons and electricity € 24.60 - € 40.50

Camping Cheques accepted.

Blanes

Camping Blanes

Avenida Villa de Madrid 33, Apdo 72, E-17300 Blanes (Girona) T: 972 331 591. E: info@campingblanes.com

alanrogers.com/ES82280

Camping Blanes is the first of the sites which edge the pedestrian promenade here and probably the smallest. Open all year, it is family owned and run and indeed has been in the hands of the Boix family for 40 years. Antonio, the son, runs the site now with pride and care, speaking good English. With only 206 pitches, no bungalows or mobile homes and only five seasonal vans, it has a comfortable family atmosphere. Shade is provided by tall pines and because of this, some of the pitches are a bit irregular in shape and average between 60-80 sq.m.

Facilities

Smart, well equipped sanitary block with provision for disabled visitors (by key). Baby changing unit. Washing machines and dryers. Shop (15/6-15/9). Bar (1/4-12/10). Restaurant (7/7-25/8). Takeaway (7/7-25/8). Swimming pool. Play area. No organised entertainment. Beach alongside site. Car wash. Internet access and WiFi.
Off site: All amenities of the town (500 m). Golf and riding 5 km.

Open: All year.

Directions

Site is south of the town beside the beach before Camping Bella Terra and El Pinar. Follow signs for 'campings' until individual site signs appear.
GPS: 41.65918, 2.77959

Charges guide

Per unit incl. 2 persons and electricity	€ 25.20 - € 35.90

Less 10% in low season. No credit cards in winter.

Blanes

Beach Camp El Pinar

Avenida Vila de Madrid 39, E-17300 Blanes (Girona) T: 972 331 083. E: camping@elpinarbeach.com

alanrogers.com/ES82300

A long established campsite, El Pinar enjoys an excellent location on the southern edge of Blanes with direct access to the superb beach. The site is in two halves, arranged on either side of a large road that terminates just past the site entrance gates where it meets the very clean, sandy beach. One side of the site is more modern than the other. The 300 touring pitches are on level sandy grass and all have 6A electricity. There is a degree of shade with younger trees on the newer side while the very old pine trees on the original, older side are impressive and provide a good deal of shade. The site roads are of fine gravel/coarse sand. The touring pitches are in the centre of the site whilst pitches for 115 bungalows and chalets to rent are placed around the perimeter. The buildings on the older side tend to look their age but are kept clean and whilst we were visiting a lot of work was being done in preparation for the new season. This site offers good value in a friendly, relaxed way with the wonderful beach close at hand.

Facilities

Sanitary facilities in two large blocks include some private washbasins. Facilities for disabled visitors. Baby room. Cleaning is continuous during day. Full laundry facilities. Shop, bar/restaurant and takeaway (all season). Games room. Large swimming pool with adjacent paddling pool on the newer side (1/5-15/9). Multisports area. Bicycle hire. Play area. Miniclub (late June-early Sept). WiFi (free). Beach. Large motorcaravans and twin-axle caravans accepted. Off site: Tourist train into town (10 mins). Bicycle hire 500 m. Water theme park. Marina and harbour. Blanes town with tourist attractions.

Open: 31 March - 30 September.

Directions

From AP7 or C-32 motorways follow signs for Blanes. Site is the last travelling south from Blanes town centre. Follow camping signs in Blanes until you see the El Pinar sign. GPS: 41.6555, 2.77862

Charges 2012

Per unit incl. 2 persons and electricity	€ 28.70 - € 38.70
extra person	€ 5.50 - € 6.60
child (2-10 yrs)	free - € 5.70
dog	free - € 4.50

Blanes

Camping Bella Terra

Avenida Vila de Madrid 35-40, E-17300 Blanes (Girona) T: 972 348 017. E: info@campingbellaterra.com

alanrogers.com/ES82320

Camping Bella Terra is set in a shady pine grove facing a white sandy beach on the Mediterranean coast. There are 797 pitches with 600 for touring units, the rest taken by bungalows to rent (97) and by Spanish residents (200). All pitches have 5/6A electricity and 134 are fully serviced. The site is in two sections, each with its own reception. The main reception is on the right of the road as you approach, with the swimming and paddling pools and new pool bar and restaurant. The other half is older, with direct access to the beach so always fills up first. The older area has a supermarket with its own bakery.

Facilities

The newer side of the site has excellent new sanitary blocks. The older side has older blocks which are clean, but dated. Provision for disabled visitors and laundry on both sides. The blocks on the newer side have superb facilities for children and a baby room. Shop, restaurant, bar and takeaway. Outdoor swimming and paddling pools (from May). Playground. Fishing. Bicycle hire. Internet café and WiFi. Miniclub. For dogs, contact site first.
Off site: Blanes within walking distance. Road train.

Open: 31 March - 30 September.

Directions

Site is on southwest side of Blanes. From exit 9 on AP7 Girona - Barcelona road follow N11 to B600 towards Blanes. Before entering Blanes turn southwest following site signs at roundabouts which will avoid Blanes town with its narrow roads, best avoided by large units. GPS: 41.6616, 2.77612

Charges guide

Per unit incl. 2 persons and electricity	€ 25.60 - € 56.60
extra person	€ 4.50 - € 6.20

Borredá

Camping Campalans

Ctra Sant Jaume de Frontanyá km 1,5, E-08619 Borredá (Barcelona) T: 938 239 163.
E: campalans@campalans.net **alanrogers.com/ES91380**

With its wonderful location in a quiet river valley with views of the surrounding mountains, Camping Campalans is an excellent site for enjoying this beautiful area. Combining camping with chalets and a hostel, the site has 40 small, grass touring pitches (with 5A electricity). The terraced pitches are below an old, stone built building housing reception, a comfortable bar, a restaurant and a small shop. The approach is by a steep, narrow, gravel mountain track and the site is 5 km. from the nearest village. However, for all but the largest units, the trip is worth making. The site can assist with a 4x4 vehicle.

Facilities

One new toilet block, heated and with well equipped showers, washbasins and en-suite cabins. Laundry room and drying room. Motorcaravan services. Shop (1/6-31/8). Bar (all season). Swimming pool (1/6-15/9). Play area. Large adventure trail for three age groups next to site. Wooden bungalows and lodges to rent. Off site: Small shops in Borredá 5 km. Supermarket in Berga 22 km.

Open: 1 July - 31 August,
weekends only 31 December - 1 February.

Directions

From France via Puigcerda on the C-16, just before Berga turn left towards Ripoll. After Borredá turn left to Sant Jaume de Frontanyá. Site is east of the village, 1.5 km. on the left. GPS: 42.14583, 1.99954

Charges guide

Per person	€ 5.35
pitch incl. car	€ 12.84
electricity (5A)	€ 4.07

Calella de la Costa

Camping Botánic Bona Vista Kim

Ctra NII km 665,8, E-08370 Calella de la Costa (Barcelona) T: 937 692 488. E: info@botanic-bonavista.net

alanrogers.com/ES82400

While Calella itself may conjure up visions of mass tourism, this site is set on a very steep hillside some 3 km. out of the town. Any noise from the nearby coast road and railway gets lost as you gain height and it is a quite delightful setting with an abundance of flowers, shrubs and roses (1,700, all planted by the knowledgeable owner Kim, who has won prizes for his roses). The design of the site successfully marries the beautiful botanic surrounds with the wonderful views over the bay. Of the 160 pitches, 130 are for tourers, all with electricity and on flat terraces on the slopes, with some shade.

Facilities

The standard of design in the three sanitary blocks is quite outstanding for a small site. Some washbasins in cabins in the newest block. Baby room. Washing machines. Motorcaravan services. Bar/restaurant, takeaway and shop (all year). Outdoor pool (1/5-30/9). Large play area. Recreation park. Satellite TV. Internet point. Games room. Barbecue and picnic area. Entertainment for adults and children (11/7-26/8). No cycling on site. Off site: Fishing 100 m. Bicycle hire 1 km.

Open: All year.

Directions

From N11 coast road, site is signed south of Calella (km. 665), and give ample warning of the entrance (shared ES82420 on coastal side). Entrance is very steep. From Barcelona direction you must pass the entrance and turn at the roundabout in some 800 m. GPS: 41.606667, 2.639167

Charges guide

Per unit incl. 2 persons and electricity	€ 38.75 - € 40.65

Calella de la Costa

Camping Roca Grossa

Ctra NII km 665, E-08370 Calella de la Costa (Barcelona) T: 937 691 297. E: rocagrossa@rocagrossa.com

alanrogers.com/ES82420

Roca Grossa's owners, the Bachs family, are very friendly and there is a very happy atmosphere in the campsite. Very steep slopes predominate at this site and there is a challenging 1 in 3, 100 m. climb from reception to the swimming pool set at the top of the site. In high season a road train runs all day to ferry you up to the amenities, but the site is unsuitable for disabled campers. The bonus is some great views over the sea from most of the terraced, but flat and reasonably sized pitches. Landrovers may be used to site your unit.

Facilities

An amazing array of clean sanitary blocks means there is not far to walk from any area of the site. Large and small, all blocks are well kept with hot water throughout. Washing machines. Gas supplies. Shop. Pleasant bar (with internet access) and restaurant. Swimming pools (1/5-30/9). Playground. Road train. Tennis. Recreation programme including children's entertainment. Excursions. WiFi. ATM. Torches useful. Off site: Beach 50 m. Town 100 m. Indoor pool and riding 1 km. Golf 2 km.

Open: 1 April - 15 October.

Directions

From A7 (Girona - Barcelona) take exit 9 or 10 for Malgrat del Mar on the N11. Turn south towards Calella and site is at 665 km. marker sharing an entrance with another campsite. GPS: 41.60632, 2.63892

Charges guide

Per unit incl. 2 persons and electricity	€ 34.40
extra person	€ 7.10

No credit cards.

Calonge

Camping Internacional de Calonge

Ctra San Feliu/Guixols - Palamós km 7.6, E-17251 Calonge (Girona) T: 972 651 233.
E: info@intercalonge.com **alanrogers.com/ES81300**

This spacious, well laid out site has access to a fine beach via a footbridge over the coast road, or you can take the little road train as the site is on very sloping ground. Calonge is a family site with two good sized pools on different levels, a paddling pool and large sunbathing areas. A great restaurant, bar and snack bar are by the pool. The site's 793 pitches are on terraces and all have electricity (5A), with 84 being fully serviced. The pitches are set on attractively landscaped terraces (access to some may be challenging). There is good shade from the tall pine trees and some views of the sea through the foliage. The views from the upper levels are taken by a tour operator and mobile home pitches. The pools are overlooked by the restaurant terraces which have great views over the mountains. A nature area within the site is used for walks and picnics. A separate area within the site is set aside for visitors with dogs. The beach is accessed over the main road by 100 steps and is shared with another site (ES81400).

Facilities

Generous sanitary provision in new and renovated blocks includes some washbasins in cabins. No toilet seats. Laundry facilities. Motorcaravan services. Gas supplies. Shop (26/3-30/10). Restaurant (1/2-31/12). Bar, patio bar with pizzas and takeaway (27/3-24/10, then weekends). Swimming pools (26/3-16/10). Playground. Electronic games. Noisy disco two nights a week (but not late). Bicycle hire. Tennis. Hairdresser. ATM. WiFi. Torches necessary in some areas. Road train on site (high season). Off site: Supermarket 500 m. Golf 3 km.

Open: All year.

Directions

Site is on inland side of coast road between Palamós and Platja d'Aro. Take C31 south to 661 at Calonge. At Calonge follow signs to C253 towards Platja d'Aro and on to site. GPS: 41.83333, 3.08417

Charges guide

Per unit incl. 2 persons and electricity	€ 20.25 - € 47.70
extra person	€ 3.70 - € 8.35

No credit cards.

Calonge

Camping Treumal

182

Ctra 253 km 47.5, E-17250 Calonge (Girona) T: 972 651 095. E: info@campingtreumal.com

alanrogers.com/ES81400

This very attractive terraced site has been developed on a hillside around the beautiful gardens of a large, spectacular estate house which is close to the sea. The house is the focus of the site's excellent facilities, including a superb restaurant with terraces overlooking two tranquil beaches, protected in pretty coves. The site has 551 pitches on well shaded terraces. Of these, 409 are accessible to tourers and there are some 50 pitches on flat ground alongside the sea – the views are stunning and you wake to the sound of the waves. Electrical connections (6/10/16A) are available in all parts. Cars may not park by tents or caravans in high season, but must be left on car parks or the site roads. There are 140 pitches occupied by mobile homes and chalets to rent. In summer the gardens around the house area are a blaze of colour and very appealing. A multi-coloured, flower bedecked and landscaped hillside leads down to the sea from the house with pretty paths and fishponds. There is a small (10 m) round swimming pool in the lower areas of the gardens, if you prefer fresh water. The two beaches are connected by a tunnel carved through solid rock through which you may safely walk.

Facilities

Four well maintained sanitary blocks have free hot water in the washbasins (some private cabins) and controllable showers, and a tap to draw from for the sinks. New beach block. Washing machines. Motorcaravan services. Gas supplies. Supermarket, bar and takeaway (all season). Restaurant (1/6-15/9). Beach bar. Fishing. Play area. Sports area. Games room. Satellite TV. Internet access and WiFi (charged). ATM. Dogs are not accepted. Charcoal barbecues are not permitted. Off site: Public transport 300 m. Bicycle hire 2 km. (delivered to site). Riding and golf 5 km.

Open: 31 March - 30 September.

Directions

Site is southeast of Girona on the coast 3 km. south of Palamós. It is best to avoid the town centre by using C31 (Girona - Palomós) road, leave at km. 320, and take road south to Sant Anthoni de Calonge. Take C253 south towards Platja d'Aro. Site is well signed. GPS: 41.83642, 3.08725

Charges 2012

Per unit incl. 2 persons and electricity	€ 23.70 - € 49.30
extra person	€ 4.30 - € 8.50
child (4-10 yrs)	€ 2.60 - € 4.70

Discounts in low seasons. No credit cards.

Calonge

Camping Cala Gogo

Avenida Andorra 13, E-17251 Calonge (Girona) T: 972 651 564. E: calagogo@calagogo.es

alanrogers.com/ES81600

Cala Gogo is a large traditional campsite with a pleasant situation on a wooded hillside with mature trees giving shade to most pitches. The 578 shaded touring pitches, which vary in size, are in terraced rows, some with artificial shade, all have 10A electricity and water, and most have drainage. There may be road noise in eastern parts of the site. Some pitches are now right by the beach, the remainder are up to 800 m. uphill, but the 'Gua gua' tractor train, operating almost all season, takes people between the centre of the site and the beach and adds to the general sense of fun. The small cove of considerable natural beauty has a coarse sand beach and there is access to a further two small beaches along the sand. If you prefer fresh water there are two heated pools on the site.

Facilities

Seven toilet blocks (one new) are of a high standard and are continuously cleaned. Some washbasins in private cabins. Two private cabins for hire. New baby rooms. Facilities for disabled visitors. Laundry room. Motorcaravan services. Gas supplies. Supermarket, shop, restaurants/takeaway and bars, two heated swimming pools (lifeguards) and paddling pool (all open all season). Playground and crèche. Sports centre. Programme of sports and entertainment. Bicycle hire. Kayaks (free). Fishing. Internet access and WiFi (free). Medical service. Bus to local disco. Dogs are not accepted in high season. Off site: Huge Aqua Park nearby with bus from site. Golf 5 km. Riding 10 km.

Open: 28 April - 16 September.

Directions

Sant Antoni de Calonge is southeast of Girona. Leave the AP7/E15 at exit 6. Take the C66 towards Palamós which becomes the C31. Use the C31 (Girona - Palamós) road to avoid Palamós town. Take the C253 coast road. Site is at km. 46.5, which is 4 km. south of Palamós. GPS: 41.83083, 3.08247

Charges 2012

Per unit incl. 2 persons and electricity	€ 22.80 - € 52.00
extra person	€ 3.90 - € 8.30
child (3-12 yrs)	€ 1.35 - € 4.10
dog	€ 2.00

Discounts for longer stays and for cash payments.

Cambrils

Camping La Llosa

Camí de les Lloses, Ctra. N-340, km. 1143, E-43850 Cambrils (Tarragona) T: 977 362 615.
E: info@camping-lallosa.com **alanrogers.com/ES84770**

La Llosa is situated close to the attractive seafront town of Cambrils. You will meet three generations of this family about the site, the younger members speak good English. We were met by a bustle of happy noise from the bar/restaurant area and this atmosphere was evident throughout our stay. The site is hidden in a residential area 100 m. from the excellent beach and promenade of Cambrils and has a pleasant pool with separate paddling area. The 300 touring pitches with 6A electricity, are level, shaded by trees (watch the overheads) and are traditional, as are most of the facilities here. This site will appeal to campers who do not wish for the glitz and brashness of modern sites.

Facilities

The four sanitary blocks have a variety of clean facilities. Separate facilities for disabled campers. Baby bath. Washing machines. Restaurant and bar (all year) Supermarket. Outdoor pool with separate paddling pool. Bicycle hire. Multisports pitch. Limited entertainment in high season. WiFi (code). Internet access. Pets accepted. Accommodation for hire. Torches useful. Off site: Beach 100 m. Train and bus 500 m. Cambrils town 1 km.

Open: All year.

Directions

From A7 Valencia/Barcelona autoroute take exit 37 for Cambrils and the N340 to Cambrils. Site is near the 1143 km. marker on the N340 – well signed. GPS: 41.065339, 1.044585

Charges guide

Per unit incl. 2 persons and electricity	€ 24.00 - € 46.00
extra person	€ 4.70 - € 7.00

Cambrils

Camping Joan

Passeig Maritim 88, E-43850 Cambrils (Tarragona) T: 977 364 604. E: info@campingjoan.com
alanrogers.com/ES84780

Camping Joan is a very friendly, family run site to the south of the popular resort of Cambrils and with direct access to a fine sandy beach. There are 220 touring pitches, most between 60-90 sq.m and all with 5A electrical connections. There is good shade. Access can be tight and large motorcaravans are not accepted. There are 84 chalets to rent and separate areas are devoted to seasonal caravans. This is a lively site in high season with a varied and comprehensive programme of entertainment and activities for adults and children. The Palmera bar/restaurant serves authentic Spanish food.

Facilities

Three sanitary blocks (one refurbished) serve the touring pitches. Controllable showers and open-style washbasins. Baby rooms and unit for disabled visitors. Motorcaravan service point planned. Bar, restaurant and takeaway meals (1/3-15/10). Supermarket (all season). Small swimming and paddling pools. Playground. Entertainment programme and children's club in high season, Bicycle and kayak hire. WiFi throughout (charged). Direct access to beach. Discounted tickets for Port Aventura theme park (8 km). Off site: Sailing 1 km. Cambrils 2 km. Golf 2 km.

Open: 25 February - 4 November.

Directions

Cambrils is 25 km. west of Tarragona. From north on the AP7, leave at exit 37 (Cambrils) and join the southbound N340. From south on AP7 leave at exit 38 (L'Hospitalet) join free motorway A7, leave at first exit and follow signs for Cambrils. Site is signed at the service station in La Dorada. Turn right after railway, following signs. GPS: 41.05789, 1.02669

Charges guide

Per unit incl. 2 persons and electricity	€ 20.45 - € 36.25
extra person	€ 3.95 - € 7.20

Cambrils

Camping Playa Cambrils Don Camilo

Ctra Cambrils - Salou km 1,5, Avenida Oleastrum, E-43850 Cambrils (Tarragona) T: 977 361 490.
E: info@playacambrils.com **alanrogers.com/ES84790**

This is a smart, well kept site with a canopy of mature shading trees, 300 m. from the beach across a busy road. The small (60 or 80 sq.m) pitches are on flat ground, divided by hedges. There are many permanent pitches and a quarter of the site is given up to chalet style accommodation, which is generally separate from the touring pitches. Large units are placed in a dedicated area where the trees are higher. The very pleasant pool complex includes a smart glassed restaurant and bar with a distinct Spanish flavour reflected in the menu and tapas available throughout the day.

Facilities

Three modern sanitary buildings, offer clean facilities with British style WCs and showers in separate buildings. Excellent facilities for disabled campers. Laundry facilities. Supermarket (April-Sept). Bar/snacks and separate restaurant (April-Sept). Swimming pools. Playground. Entertainment in high season. Miniclub. Huge electronic games room. Bicycle hire. Torches useful. WiFi (free).

Open: 15 March - 14 October.

Directions

Leave AP7 autopista at exit 37, go to Cambrils and then to the beach. Turn left along beach road. Site is 1 km. east of Cambrils Playa and is well signed as you leave Cambrils marina. GPS: 41.06487, 1.08368

Charges 2012

Per unit incl. 2 persons and electricity	€ 19.10 - € 55.90

Camping Cheques accepted.

Cambrils

Cambrils Park Resort

Avenida Mas Clariana s/n, E-43850 Cambrils (Tarragona) T: 977 351 031. E: mail@cambrilspark.es

alanrogers.com/ES84810

Close to the Cambrils beaches, this is a wonderful holiday destination for the whole family. Lawns lined with palm trees and flowers lead to 330 fully equipped chalets (touring units are no longer taken here). The accommodation is divided between three themed areas: the Polynesian Village with Aloha bungalows – 158 authentic wooden chalets in an exotic landscape; the Caribbean Village offering luxury Villa Bonitas – 172 coloured wooden chalets; and the Mediterranean Village (ready for 2013) with 170 new units in the style of a Mediterranean coastal town. There are three themed swimming pools and an entertainment team provide activities all day for adults and children.

Facilities

Quality indoor and outdoor restaurant. Takeaway. Several themed bars. Huge supermarket, souvenir shop and bakery. Laundry. Themed swimming pools with lifeguards. Minigolf. Tennis. Multisports court. Pétanque. Entertainment all season. Miniclub. WiFi (free). Medical centre. Pets are not accepted. Off site: Fishing and bicycle hire 400 m. Beach 500 m. Riding 3 km. Port Aventura theme park 4 km. Golf 7 km.

Open: 26 March - 12 October.

Directions

On west side of Salou about 1.5 km. from the centre, site is well signed from the coast road to Cambrils and from the other town approaches. Caution as there are many campsites with similar names off this road. GPS: 41.076463, 1.109238

Charges guide

Per person	€ 6.00
pitch incl. electricity	€ 15.00 - € 52.00
incl. water and waste water	€ 17.00 - € 55.00

Camprodon

Camping Vall de Camprodon

Ctra C38 Ripoll a Camprodon, E-17867 Camprodon (Girona) T: 972 740 507. E: info@valldecamprodon.net

alanrogers.com/ES91225

This large holiday village is attractively situated in a wooded valley with cows grazing to one side, their pleasant bells often to be heard. A stream runs below the site between it and the road. There are 200 grass and gravel pitches some with shade, others without. Most are occupied by seasonal caravans (some rather scruffy) and private chalets, with just 40 pitches for touring units, all with 4/10A electricity. There are 26 modern chalets for rent. Only 20 km. away is the mountain and ski resort of Vallter 2000 and to the southwest is the historical town of Ripoll. Camprodon is a very pleasant old town with a magnificent ancient bridge at its centre.

Facilities

One centrally placed, fully equipped and well maintained toilet block with controllable showers, washbasins with dividers, and a large en-suite unit for disabled visitors. Baby/toddler baths. Washing machines, dryers and ironing board. Shop and bar/restaurant with local menus (July/Aug plus holiday periods and weekends in low season). Swimming and paddling pools (July/Aug). Adventure play area. Tennis. Multisports court. Boules. Miniclub (July/Aug). Riding (July/Aug). WiFi throughout (free). Separate motorcaravan park by entrance (€20-26).

Open: All year.

Directions

From north leave AP7 at Figueres, join N11 south and turn west signed Olot to join N260/A26. At exit 84 follow signs for Camprodon on C26 via Valley of Bianya. After tunnels turn north on C38 to Camprodon. Site is between Sant Pau de Seguries and Camprodon. GPS: 42.29033, 2.36242

Charges guide

Per unit incl. 2 persons and electricity	€ 35.60

Camping Cheques accepted.

Canet de Mar

Camping Globo Rojo

Ctra NII km 660.9, E-08360 Canet de Mar (Barcelona) T: 937 941 143. E: camping@globo-rojo.com

alanrogers.com/ES82430

Camping Globo Rojo is cleverly laid out in a semi-circular fashion. Within the various sectors, permanent campers and touring units stay alongside each other. The restaurant which serves authentic food and tapas, is within a sensitively restored farmhouse and is superb. The site is located on the beach road (N11) so is subject to some traffic noise, but the full shading of mature trees also absorbs the noise. The 170 flat pitches include 100 touring pitches, all with 10A electricity and with an average size of 70 sq.m. An excellent elevated pool and paddling pool are waiting for you to enjoy and the beach is close by.

Facilities

Two sanitary blocks have clean, modern equipment. Baby room. Facilities for disabled campers. Washing machines. Motorcaravan service areas. Shop. Bar. Restaurant. Takeaway. Swimming and paddling pools (with lifeguards). Miniclub. WiFi (free) in restaurant area. Playground. Pétanque. Electronic games. Dog bath. Car wash. Safes.

Open: 1 April - 30 September.

Directions

Site is at the 660.9 km. marker on the N11. Leave the C-32 autoroute at exit 20 (AP7 exit 120) and follow signs to Canet de Mar. Site is well signed on the N11. GPS: 41.590903, 2.591951

Charges guide

Per unit incl. 2 persons and electricity	€ 22.50 - € 45.75

Castelló d'Empúries

Camping Caravaning La Laguna

Apdo 55, E-17486 Castelló d'Empúries (Girona) T: 972 450 553. E: info@campinglaguna.com

alanrogers.com/ES80150

La Laguna is a relaxed, spacious site on an isthmus within a Catalan national maritime park, on the migratory path of many different birds. It has direct access to an excellent sandy beach and the estuary of the River Muga (also a beach). The owners continue to spend much time and effort on improvements. The double lagoons are a most attractive feature. The 756 pitches (with just 46 mobile homes) are shaded and clearly marked on grass and sand, all with 6/10A electricity. There are also 51 fully serviced pitches. A very attractive bar/restaurant and sitting room overlook the lagoons and there are two swimming pools (one is heated in low season). A disco operates across the road from reception, keeping the noise away from the main site. A large riding school operates (May-Sept) and there are many other activities. The beach frontage is large and has a sailing school. It is said to be possible to cross over to Empuriabrava when the tide is out. There are many walks locally and this a good site for family holidays.

Facilities

Five superb toilet blocks, placed to avoid long walks, have solar heated water. Laundry room. Bar, restaurant and takeaway. Comprehensive supermarket. Swimming pools (15/5-31/10). Football. Tennis (free in low seasons). ATM. Minigolf. Windsurfing and sailing schools (July/Aug). Fishing. Miniclub. Play areas. Bicycle hire. Riding. Entertainment programme and competitions. Satellite TV. Internet access. WiFi throughout (charged). Off site: Boat launching. Birdwatching (Ramsar area). Golf 15 km.

Open: 29 March - 24 October.

Directions

Castelló d'Empúries is north of Girona and east of Figueras on the coast. From AP7/E15 take exit 3 south or exit 4 north (there is no exit 3 north) and then N11 to the C260 towards Roses. At Castelló d'Empúries roundabout follow signs to Depuradora (2 km) and 'camping' for 4 km. on a hard track road to the site. GPS: 42.2374, 3.121

Charges 2012

Per unit incl. 2 persons and electricity € 26.25 - € 51.15

No credit cards.

Castelló d'Empúries

Kawan Village Mas Nou

Mas Nou no. 7, E-17486 Castelló d'Empúries (Girona) T: 972 454 175. E: info@campingmasnou.com

alanrogers.com/ES80120

Some two kilometres from the sea on the Costa Brava, this is a pristine and surprisingly tranquil site in two parts, split by the access road. One part contains the pitches and toilet blocks, the other houses the impressive leisure complex. There are 450 neat, level and marked pitches on grass, a minimum of 70 sq.m. but most 80-100 sq.m, and 300 with electricity (10A). The leisure complex is across the road from reception and features a huge L-shaped swimming pool with a paddling area. A formal restaurant has an adjoining bar/café, pleasant terrace and rotisseria under palms.

Facilities

Three absolutely excellent, fully equipped sanitary blocks include baby baths, good facilities for disabled visitors. Washing machines. Motorcaravan services. Supermarket and other shops. Baker in season. Bar/restaurant, rôtisserie and takeaway. Swimming pool with lifeguard (1/5 - 30/9). Tennis. Minigolf. Miniclub (July/Aug). Play areas. Electronic games. Internet access and free WiFi. Car wash. Off site: Public transport 1 km. Riding 1.5 km. Fishing and bicycle hire 2 km. Beach 2.5 km.

Open: 31 March - 30 September.

Directions

From A7 use exit 3. Mas Nou is 2 km. east of Castelló d'Empúries, on the Roses road, 10 km. from Figueras. Do not turn left across the main road but continue to the roundabout and return. Site is clearly marked. GPS: 42.26558, 3.1025

Charges 2012

Per unit incl. 2 persons and electricity € 24.20 - € 43.60

Camping Cheques accepted.

Castelló d'Empúries

Camping Nautic Almata

Ctra GIV- 6216 km 11,6, E-17486 Castelló d'Empúries (Girona) T: 972 454 477. E: info@almata.com

alanrogers.com/ES80300

In the Bay of Roses, south of Empuriabrava and beside the Parc Natural dels Aiguamolls de l'Empordá, this is a high quality site of particular interest to nature lovers (especially birdwatchers). Beautifully laid out, it is arranged around the river and waterways, so will suit those who like to be close to water or who enjoy watersports and boating. It is worth visiting because of its unusual aspects and the feeling of being on the canals, as well as being a superb beachside site. A large site, there are 1,109 well kept, large, numbered pitches, all with electricity and on flat, sandy ground.

Facilities

Toilet blocks of a high standard include some en-suite showers with basins. Good facilities for disabled visitors. Washing machines. Gas supplies. Excellent supermarket. Restaurants and bar. Beach bars and snack bars with discos (main season). Water-skiing, diving and windsurfing schools. 300 sq.m. swimming pool. New tennis court. Squash. Fronton. Minigolf. Games room. Riding tuition. New children's play park. Fishing (licence required). Car, motorcycle and bicycle hire. Hairdresser. WiFi. ATM.

Open: 14 May - 18 September (with all services).

Directions

Site is signed at 26 km. marker on C252 between Castello d'Empúries and Vildemat, then 7 km. to site. Alternatively, on San Pescador - Castello d'Empuries road head north and site is well signed. GPS: 42.206077, 3.10389

Charges guide

Per unit incl. 2 persons and electricity	€ 28.30 - € 56.60
extra person (over 3 yrs)	€ 2.65 - € 5.30

No credit cards.

Castelló d'Empúries

Camping Castell Mar

Platja de la Rubina, E-17486 Castelló d'Empúries (Girona) T: 972 450 822. E: cmar@campingparks.com

alanrogers.com/ES80100

This traditional and pricey site is a 450 m. walk from one of the very pleasant Gulf of Roses beaches (one of the closest beach gates is not used), and within the large Aiguamolls de l'Empordá Nature Reserve. It is also convenient for (but quite separate from) the latest tourist development and facilities at Empuriabrava. With some 310 pitches (160 for touring), it is smaller than many sites in this part of Spain and may be suitable for some families. The pitches, most with electricity, are of average size for the Costa Brava and are on level ground with some artificial shade added to the shade from the trees.

Facilities

The large, well maintained, modern toilet block is kept clean but there are no toilet seats. Some washbasins in cabins. Facilities for disabled visitors. Laundry facilities. Bar, restaurant/pizzeria and takeaway. Supermarket. Play area. Swimming pools. Many activities and limited entertainment over a long season. ATM. Security boxes. Torches required in some areas. WiFi (charged).
Off site: Boat launching 500 m. Riding 1 km. Bicycle hire 3 km. Golf 10 km. Discounts at local attractions.

Open: 19 May - 23 September.

Directions

From motorway AP7 take exit 3 south or exit 4 north (note there is no exit 3 north). Do not go into Castello d'Empuries or Empuriabrava, but continue on N11 to the C260 towards Roses. At km 40 La Rubina, turn and pass by La Llar restaurant, site is 1.5 km further. GPS: 42.25517, 3.1366

Charges 2012

Per unit incl. 2 persons and electricity	€ 19.00 - € 50.00

No credit cards.

Cubelles

Camping La Rueda

Ctra C31 km 146,2, E-08880 Cubelles (Barcelona) T: 938 950 207. E: larueda@la-rueda.com

alanrogers.com/ES83930

La Rueda is a pleasant, no frills site with 370 pitches, including up to 70 occupied by seasonal caravans. Some pitches are in a small pine wood. The circular central area has flat, grassy pitches set amongst mature trees with bamboo canopies providing extra shade; the final area has grassy pitches without electricity and with little shade. From the far corner, a road takes you under the railway (some noise) to a long sandy beach. An elevated bar and snack bar serving simple, inexpensive fare overlooks the swimming pool. Beneath is a well stocked shop.

Facilities

Two traditional sanitary blocks are kept very clean and provide controllable showers and open style washbasins. Baby cubicle. Facilities for disabled visitors in one block (on demand in low season). Washing machines and dryer. Shop, bar and snack bar with takeaway (15/6-11/9, weekends in low season). Swimming pool (23/6-11/9). Basic children's playground. WiFi over site (charged).

Open: 16 April - 11 September.

Directions

Cubelles is 50 km. southwest of Barcelona. From C32 coastal motorway leave at exit 13 for Cubelles and join C31 west. Site is a short distance on left (at 146.2 km). GPS: 41.19987, 1.64335

Charges guide

Per unit incl. 2 persons and electricity	€ 24.84 - € 45.34
extra person	€ 4.14 - € 6.90

El Vendrell

Camping Vendrell Platja

Avenida del Sanatori s/n, E-43880 Coma-ruga - El Vendrell (Tarragona) T: 977 694 009.
E: vendrell@camping-vendrellplatja.com **alanrogers.com/ES84020**

In the popular Calafell area, this site is set back from the sea across a beach road. Popular with tourists for many years, the area has apartment buildings, bars and restaurants, and is popular with families. The pitches (70 sq.m) are fairly close together, partially shaded by trees, and all have 6A electricity. Access to all the pitches is through one narrow central avenue of palms which is busy with foot and vehicle traffic. The pleasant pool area with more tall palms and grassy areas, has very wide slides that delight children and adults alike. There is a railway line at the western end of the site.

Facilities

Two well located and modern toilet blocks provide clean facilities with a unit for disabled campers and well equipped baby rooms. Washing machines. Car wash. Supermarket. Restaurant. Snack bar. Swimming pools and pool bar. Play areas. Boules. Bicycle hire. Entertainment and activity programmes. ATM. Security boxes. Torches useful. Internet access and WiFi.
Off site: Town and beach nearby. Bicycle hire 200 m.

Open: 1 April - 12 October.

Directions

From A7 or A16 take exit 31 for El Vendrell. Then go east to Sant Salvador, and north on coast road towards Platja Calafell. Site is well signed on this road west of the town centre. GPS: 41.1856, 1.5554

Charges guide

Per person	€ 4.50 - € 9.00
child (3-11 yrs)	€ 2.50 - € 8.50
pitch incl. electricity	€ 12.00 - € 23.50

Empuriabrava

Camping Rubina Resort

Playa de la Rubina, E-17487 Empuriabrava (Girona) T: 972 450 507. E: info@rubinaresort.com
alanrogers.com/ES80200

Situated in the 'Venice of Spain', Empuriabrava is interlaced with inland waterways and canals, where many residents and holidaymakers moor their boats directly outside their expensive homes on the canal banks. Camping Rubina Resort is a large friendly site 200 m. from the wide, sandy beach, which is bordered on the east and west by the waterway canals. It is a surprisingly pretty and hospitable site where people seem to make friends easily and get to know other campers and the staff. The site has 600 touring pitches, most enjoying some shade from strategically placed trees. All have 10A electricity and water connections.

Facilities

Toilet facilities are in five fully equipped blocks. Washing machines. Motorcaravan services. Modern supermarket, bakery and shop. Restaurant/bar. Disco bar. Large takeaway/pizzeria. Watersports with windsurfing school. Organised sports activities, children's programmes and entertainment. Swimming pool (15/4-10/10). Bicycle hire. Playground. Pétanque. Tennis. Very smart Internet café. WiFi over part of site (charged). Dog shower. Apartments.
Off site: Beach 200 m. Fishing 300 m. Riding 1 km.

Open: 1 April - 15 October.

Directions

Empúriabrava is north of Girona and east of Figueras on the coast. From AP7/E15 take exit 3 south or exit 4 north (note there is no exit 3 north) and then N11 to the C260 towards Roses. At Empuriabrava follow 'camping area' signs to site. GPS: 42.25267, 3.1317

Charges 2012

Per person (over 3 yrs)	€ 4.00
pitch incl. electricity and water (85 sq.m)	€ 16.00 - € 36.00

No credit cards.

Esponellá

Camping Caravaning Esponellá

Ctra de Banyoles a Figueres km 8, E-17832 Esponellá (Girona) T: 972 597 074.
E: informa@campingesponella.com **alanrogers.com/ES80360**

This large campsite has a lovely setting alongside a slow flowing river. There are 240 small to medium sized pitches, 140 for touring, all with 5A electricity and shaded by trees. Many are fully serviced (water, waste water drain and electricity). The older part of the campsite houses a well stocked shop and a bar/restaurant adjacent to the swimming pools. One smaller pool is heated and partly covered. A small stream runs along the lower side which can be seen from the pool and restaurant area, which faces the swimming pool complex, which runs children's club activities in high season.

Facilities

Two old toilet blocks, a smaller one with only toilets and washbasins near the rental accommodation, and a newer one at the front part of the site. Some washbasins with only cold water. Small shop (Easter-Sept). Attractive restaurant with terrace, bar and takeaway. Three heated swimming pools. Play area. Boules. Minigolf. Tennis. Children's activities. Small disco. Bicycle and kayak hire. WiFi in bar area (free). Communal barbecue area.

Open: All year.

Directions

From N260 Figueres-Olot road, 4 km. west of Navata turn south on Gip512 to Esponellá. After factory on left, cross river and on left-hand bend turn sharp right to site. GPS: 42.18166, 2.79499

Charges guide

Per unit incl. 2 persons and electricity	€ 25.55 - € 33.85
extra person	€ 5.35 - € 6.95

Farga de Moles

Frontera Park

Ctra Seo d'Urgell - Andorra N145 km 8, E-25799 Farga de Moles (Lleida) T: 973 355 830.

E: info@fronterapark.com **alanrogers.com/ES91190**

Frontera Park lives up to its name, as it is situated on the border with Andorra and makes an ideal base for visiting this small principality. The site is strung out along the banks of a small river with no reported problems with flooding. There are 230 fairly small grass pitches, 50 for touring, with mountain views, trees giving some shade and 10A electricity. Spacious chalets are situated in the northern part of the site, away from the camping area. During the winter this is a good area for skiing in the Pyrenees. In summer there are hiking trails plus lakes and rivers, with many possibilities for wild water canoeing and swimming in this picturesque region.

Facilities

Two very clean toilet blocks have separate areas for women and men. Baby washroom but no facilities for campers with disabilities. Small bar with terrace. Cosy restaurant (open all year, closed Wed). Swimming pool and paddling pool (July/Aug) with grassy sunbathing area. Multisports field. Play area. Off site: Fishing. Riding. Golf. Lake with beach and sailing 8 km. Hiking trails. During the ski season many pistes 13 km.

Open: All year.

Directions

Site lies south of Andorra. From Seu d'Urgell take N145 towards Andorra. After 8 km. sign look out for site sign on the left mountain wall. Turn right to make a sharp left turn across the main road into the access road of the site. GPS: 42.42809, 1.4633

Charges guide

Per unit incl. 2 persons and electricity (10A)	€ 20.00
extra person	€ 4.10

Camping Cheques accepted.

Guardiola de Bergueda

Camping El Bergueda

Ctra B400 a Saldes km 3,5, E-08694 Guardiola de Bergueda (Barcelona) T: 938 227 432.

E: info@campingbergueda.com **alanrogers.com/ES91390**

The short, scenic drive through the mountains to reach this site is breathtakingly beautiful. Situated under trees, this terraced campsite in the area of the Cadi-Moixer Natural Park, is not far from the majestic Pedraforca mountain. A favourite for Catalan climbers and walkers, its amazing rugged peak in the shape of a massive stone fork gives it its name. Access to the site is quite easy for large units. Of the 73 small grass gravel pitches there are 40 for touring, all with 6A electricity. The campsite owners will do all in their power to make your stay here enjoyable.

Facilities

Two clean, well equipped, heated modern toilet blocks. Facilities for campers with disabilities. Three private cabins with washbasin, toilet and bidet. Washing machines and dryer. Small shop, restaurant, bar and takeaway (w/ends only then 1/7-1/9). Outdoor pools (24/6-31/8). Play areas. WiFi over part of site (free). Barbecues are not permitted except in communal area. Off site: Mountain biking. Artigas gardens designed by Gaudí. Picasso Museum.

Open: Easter - 30 October.

Directions

Guardiola de Bergueda is 125 km. north of Barcelona. From C16 Manresa-Berga road 2 km. south of Guardiola de Bergueda turn west towards Saldes. Site is on right after 3.5 km. GPS: 42.21642, 1.83692

Charges 2012

Per unit incl. 2 persons and electricity	€ 28.45
extra person	€ 5.70
child (1-10 yrs)	€ 4.55

Guils de Cerdanya

Camping Pirineus

Ctra Guils de Cerdanya km 2, E-17528 Guils de Cerdanya (Girona) T: 972 881 062. E: guils@stel.es

alanrogers.com/ES91430

On entering this well organised site close to the French border, high in the Pyrenees, you gain an immediate impression of space, green trees and grass – there is always someone watering and clearing up to maintain the high standards here. The pitches are neat, marked, of average size and organised in rows. Generally flat with some on a gentle incline, a proportion have water at their own sink on the pitch. Many trees offer shade but watch for overhanging branches if you have a high unit. From the restaurant terrace you have fine views of the mountains in the background and the pool in the foreground.

Facilities

One brand new, central and well equipped sanitary block is kept spotlessly clean and can be heated. Good laundry facilities. Motorcaravan service point. Shop, bar and restaurant. Heated swimming pool and circular paddling pool. Boules. Tennis. Outdoor sports. TV and games room. Snooker. Play area and supervised clubhouse for youngsters. Entertainment (high season). WiFi. Dogs are not accepted. Off site: Bicycle hire 2 km. Riding 4 km.

Open: 22 June - 11 September.

Directions

From Perpignan take N116 to Prades and Andorra. Exit at Piugcerdá taking N250 signed Le Seu d'Urgell and almost immediately take second right for Guils de Cerdanya. Follow for 2 km. to site on right. GPS: 42.44312, 1.90583

Charges 2012

Per unit incl. 2 persons and electricity	€ 35.30 - € 42.80

Hospitalet del Infante

Camping-Pension Cala d'Oques

Via Augusta s/n, E-43890 Hospitalet del Infante (Tarragona) T: 977 823 254. E: info@caladoques.com

alanrogers.com/ES85350

This peaceful and delightful, family run site has a lot going for it: its situation beside the sea with a wide beach of sand and pebbles, its amazing mountain backdrop, the views across the bay to the town and the friendly, relaxed atmosphere created by its owner of 40 years, Elisa Roller, her family and her staff. There are 152 mosty level pitches, some beside the beach, others on wide, informal terracing. Electricity (10A) is available throughout (although long leads may be needed in places). Pine and olive trees are an attractive feature and provide some shade. The restaurant with its homely touches has a good local menu and a reputation extending well outside the site. Gates provide access to the pleasant beach with useful cold showers to wash the sand away. Torches are needed at night. For those interested, there is a naturist beach of fine sand around the little headland just south of the site. This is a pretty place to stay. Kim and Joost give a pleasant personal service and the entertainment too is geared to the family, in total contrast with that provided at the larger, brasher sites of the Costa Daurada.

Facilities

Toilet facilities are in the central part of the main building. Clean, neat and recently refurbished with some en-suite units. Hot water to showers by token but free to campers. New heated unit with toilets and washbasins for winter use. Unit for disabled visitors. Additional small block at far end of site. Motorcaravan service point. Restaurant/bar and shop (1/4-30/10). Play area. Kids' club and family entertainment (high season). Fishing. Sailing. Internet access and WiFi. Torches required in some areas. Mobile home and apartments to rent. Off site: Village facilities, incl. shop and restaurant 1.5 km.

Open: All year.

Directions

Hospitalet del Infante is 35 km. southwest of Tarragona, accessed from A7 (exit 38) or N340. From north take first exit to Hospitalet del Infante at 1128 km. marker. Follow 'Campings' signs before the village, then signs to site for 1.5 km. GPS: 40.97777, 0.90338

Charges guide

Per unit incl. 2 persons and electricity	€ 24.75 - € 42.95
extra person	€ 4.95 - € 9.50

No credit cards.

Hospitalet del Infante

Camping Naturista El Templo del Sol

E-43890 Hospitalet del Infante (Tarragona) T: 977 823 434. E: info@eltemplodelsol.com

alanrogers.com/ES85370

El Templo del Sol is a large, luxurious terraced naturist site with a distinctly Arabesque style and superb buildings in Moorish style. The owner has designed the magnificent main turreted building at the entrance with fountains and elaborate Moorish arches. The site has over 400 pitches of two different sizes, some with car parking alongside and 85 with full services. There is shade and the pitches are on terraces giving rewarding views over the sea. Attractive steps give ready access to the sandy beach. There is some daytime rail noise especially in the lower areas, where the larger pitches are located.

Facilities

The sanitary blocks provide everything you could require. Extensive facilities for disabled campers. Washing machines. Well stocked supermarket. Health shop. Bars. Restaurant and snack bar (1/4-10/10). Swimming pools (20/3-15/10). Jacuzzi. Cinema. Games area. Miniclub. Library. Entertainment. Hairdresser. Bicycle hire. ATM. Dogs not accepted. No jet skis. Off site: Fishing 100 m.

Open: 22 March - 22 October.

Directions

From N340 south of Tarragona, exit at km. 1126 towards L'Hopitalet Plaja and follow signs. Heading north, near km. 1124, turn right immediately after a modern railway bridge and site is just 400 m. on the right. GPS: 40.97723, 0.90093

Charges guide

Per unit incl. 2 persons	€ 18.70 - € 47.65
extra person	€ 3.30 - € 9.00

L'Escala

Camping Neus Tent-Lodge

Cala Montgó, E-17130 L'Escala (Girona) T: 972 770 403. E: info@campingneus.com

alanrogers.com/ES80690

Camping Neus is set on the edge of a forest under mature pines with 190 pitches arranged on sets of terraces, all with 6A electricity. This mature site is being thoughtfully renovated. It is fenced from the road and facilities are mainly close to the reception building. A small pool with a circular paddling pool is welcome after a hot day's sightseeing; other site amenities include a tennis court and small bar/restaurant. A new play area and a volleyball court have been added (2010) and gardens planted.

Facilities

Renovated sanitary blocks offer sound and clean facilities along with baby rooms and facilities for disabled campers. Motorcaravan service point. Shop. Bar. Restaurant. Takeaway. Swimming pool. Paddling pool. Tennis. Volleyball. Play area. TV room. Entertainment and activities in peak season. Club for children. WiFi over part of site (free). Bicycle hire. Mobile homes and chalets to rent. Only electric barbecues are permitted. Off site: Resort of Cala Montgó with beach 850 m. Fishing. Kayaking. Diving.

Open: 25 May - 16 September.

Directions

Take exit 5 from the AP7 and the GI623 to L'Escala. Continue to Riells and Montgó. Site is on the right shortly before reaching Cala Montgó.
GPS: 42.1049, 3.15816

Charges 2012

Per unit incl. 2 persons and electricity	€ 21.70 - € 44.70
extra person	€ 3.00 - € 5.00
child (4-12 yrs)	€ 1.00 - € 3.50

L'Escala

Camping L'Escala

Cami Ample, E-17130 L'Escala (Girona) T: 972 770 084. E: info@campinglescala.com

alanrogers.com/ES80700

Under the same ownership as Las Dunas (no. ES80400), but a complete contrast in terms of size and location. It is a small site with all the amenities of the town within easy reach and the beach within 100 m. and fabulous sanitary facilities. The site has a canopy of fir trees giving excellent shade. There are 140 pitches of which 90 are for touring units, so reservation is essential. Unusually for a small site, all pitches have electricity, water and drainage. In season there is a bar and pizza oven. There is some road noise despite the very high wall between the site and the busy road alongside.

Facilities

New central toilet block of the highest quality with underfloor heating for cooler seasons and sliding glass doors. Wonderful facilities for children featuring tiled pirate ships. Laundry sinks with hot water. Shop, bar and pizza oven (all high season). Simple play area. Satellite TV. WiFi. No pets allowed. Modern bungalow apartments to rent. Off site: Beach 100 m. Bicycle hire and public transport 500 m. Riding 3 km. Golf 15 km.

Open: Easter - last Sunday in September.

Directions

L'Escala is northeast of Girona. From A7/E15 autostrada take exit 5 towards L'Escala on GI623. Turn north 2 km. before L'Escala towards Sant Marti d'Ampurias. Site well signed on north side of town and beach. GPS: 42.121, 3.13478

Charges guide

Per person	€ 3.00 - € 5.00
pitch incl. electricity	€ 18.00 - € 31.00

No credit cards. Discounts for longer stays.

L'Escala

Camping Illa Mateua

Avenida de Montgó 260, E-17130 L'Escala (Girona) T: 972 770 200. E: info@campingillamateua.com

alanrogers.com/ES80740

If you prefer a quieter site out of the very busy resort of L'Escala, then this site is an excellent option. This large, family run site has a dynamic owner Marti, who speaks excellent English. The site is divided by the beach access road and has its own private access to the very safe and unspoilt beach. There are 358 pitches on the two parts of the site, all with 10A electricity, some on sloping ground, although the pitches in the second part are flat. Established pine trees provide shade for most places with more coverage on the western side. Non-stop improvement and maintenance ensure that all facilities at this site are of a high standard.

Facilities

Very modern, fully equipped sanitary blocks are kept spotlessly clean. Facilities for children. Washing machines and dryers. Shop. Modern complex of restaurants, bars and takeaways. Swimming pools (20/4-12/10). Pool bar. Play areas. Kayak hire. Organised activities for children in high season. Diving school. Sports centre. Internet access and WiFi. ATM. Private access to beach. Off site: Road train to town centre from outside site. Cala Montgó beach with pretty restaurants and a disco in season 100 m.

Open: 21 March - 12 October.

Directions

Leave autopista A7 at exit 5 heading for Viladimat, then L'Escala. Site is well signed from town centre. Follow signs for Montgó and site is south of town by the coast. Some signs may show the site's old name of Paradis. GPS: 42.11051, 3.16542

Charges guide

Per unit incl. 2 persons and electricity	€ 22.80 - € 44.00

No credit cards.

L'Estartit

Camping Castell Montgri

Ctra Toroella - l'Estartit km 4,7, E-17258 L'Estartit (Girona) T: 972 751 630. E: cmontgri@campingparks.com

alanrogers.com/ES80070

This is a large, noisy, bustling, expensive site with all the modern paraphernalia of holiday-making. Over 50 per cent of this site is dedicated to catering for tour operators, and obviously so, but there are three designated areas for independent campers. These provide 590 terraced and flat pitches, some shaded but all with electricity. On arrival you are processed by rather impersonal staff. The site could be of interest to families with teenagers, offering the possibility for parents to rest whilst the youngsters enjoy their own type of holiday within the confines of the site.

Facilities

Toilet facilities are adequate, each area having its own block. Cleaning is continual (06.00-22.00) but with the numbers on site, queuing and litter can be a problem. Bars and restaurants. Pizzeria. Takeaway. Swimming pools. Supermarket and souvenirs. Tennis. Minigolf. Playground. Large screen TV. Disco. Entertainment programme and excursions. Free bus to L'Estartit. WiFi (charged). Torches required in some areas.

Open: 15 May - 26 September.

Directions

L'Estartit is on the coast northeast of Girona. Leave the AP7/E15 and take the C66 towards Palamós. Then take the GI642 towards Parlava and the GI643 towards Torroella de Montgri. Site is well signed on the GI641 Torroella de Montgri - L'Estartit road just north of the town on the left. GPS: 42.0511, 3.1827

Charges guide

Per person	€ 5.00
pitch incl. car and electricity	€ 9.00 - € 56.00

L'Estartit

Camping Les Medes

Paratge Camp de L'Arbre, E-17258 L'Estartit (Girona) T: 972 751 805. E: info@campinglesmedes.com

alanrogers.com/ES80720

Les Medes is different from some of the 'all singing, all dancing' sites so popular along this coast, and the friendly family of Pla-Coll are rightly proud of their award-winning site and provide a very warm welcome. With just 170 pitches, the site is small enough for the owners to know their visitors and, being campers themselves, they have been careful in planning their top class facilities and are aware of environmental issues. The level, grassy pitches range in size from 70-80 sq.m. depending on your unit. All have electricity (5/10A) and 155 also have water and drainage. All are clearly marked in rows, but with no separation other than by the deciduous trees which provide summer shade.

Facilities

Two modern sanitary blocks can be heated and are well maintained. Washbasins in cabins, good facilities for disabled visitors. Baby baths. Washing machines and dryer. Motorcaravan services. Shop. Bar with snacks and pizza. Restaurant (1/4-31/10). Swimming and paddling pools (1/5-15/9). Indoor pool with sauna, solarium and massage (15/9-15/6). Play area. TV room. Entertainment (July/Aug). Diving. Multisports. Boules. Bicycle hire. WiFi.

Open: All year excl. November.

Directions

Site is signed from the main Torroella de Montgri - L'Estartit road GI641. Turn right after Camping Castel Montgri, at Joc's hamburger/pizzeria and follow signs. GPS: 42.048, 3.1881

Charges 2012

Per unit incl. 2 persons and electricity	€ 22.80 - € 41.75

Dogs not accepted July/Aug. No credit cards.

La Bordeta

Camping Caravaning Bedurá Park

Era Bordeta - Val d'Aran CN230 km 174,4, la Bordeta, E-25551 Lleida (Lleida) T: 973 648 293.
E: info@bedurapark.com **alanrogers.com/ES91240**

Bedurá Park lies in the Val d'Aran at a height of 900 metres, surrounded by wonderful panoramic views. The surrounding woods are alive with a wide variety of wildlife, including deer, wild boar, capercaillies and pine martens. This is a perfect place for a quiet, yet active holiday. On site you can unwind around the swimming pool or take a leisurely drink in the bar. There are 173 small, well shaded, stony/grass pitches set out on terraces with 150 for touring, all with 5A electricity. Access for large units may be difficult due to the low trees. This is a haven for nature lovers and photographers.

Facilities

One large and one small toilet block provide some washbasins in cabins plus facilities for disabled campers. Shop (1/6-15/9). Bar and restaurant (24/6-15/9) and takeaway (1/6-15/9). Heated swimming and paddling pools (15/6-15/9). Miniclub (July/Aug). Games/TV room. Play area. Communal barbecues only. Animals are not accepted. Off site: Adventure sports, cycling, hiking, fishing. Vielha ice palace with ice rink, indoor pool, sauna 10 km. Riding 12 km. Skiing 20 km. Lourdes.

Open: All year.

Directions

Site is on N230, 12 km. from French border, 10 km. north of Vielha. Leave A60 (French) autoroute at exit 17 and take N125 south to the border. Continue on N230 through Bossost then 4 km. to site at la Bordeta. GPS: 42.74969, 0.69804

Charges 2012

Per person	€ 5.60
pitch	€ 13.50 - € 18.70

No credit cards.

La Pineda

Camping La Pineda de Salou

Ctra Costa Tarragona - Salou km 5, E-43481 La Pineda (Tarragona) T: 977 373 080.
E: info@campinglapineda.com **alanrogers.com/ES84820**

La Pineda is a clean, neat site north of Salou, just 300 m. from an aquapark and 2.5 km. from Port Aventura, to which there is an hourly bus service from outside the site entrance. There is some noise from the road. The site has two swimming pools; the smaller is heated. A colourful themed paddling pool and outdoor spa are also here, behind tall hedges close to the entrance. A large terrace has sun loungers, and various entertainment aimed at young people is provided in season. The 366 flat pitches (all with 5A electricity) are shaded by mature trees in attractive gardens.

Facilities

Sanitary facilities have been completely refurbished and are excellent with baby bath, dishwashing and laundry sinks. Facilities for disabled visitors. Washing machines. Gas supplies. Shop (1/7-31/8). Restaurant and snacks (1/7-31/8). Swimming pools, paddling pool and outdoor spa (1/7-31/8). Bar. New community room with satellite TV. Bicycle and road cart hire. Games room. Playground (3-12 yrs). Entertainment (1/7-30/8). Torches may be required. No pets in August. WiFi. Bus from gate.

Open: All year.

Directions

From A7 just southwest of Tarragona take exit 35 and follow signs to La Pineda and Port Aventura then campsite signs appear. GPS: 41.08921, 1.1837

Charges guide

Per unit incl. 2 persons and electricity (6A)	€ 29.00 - € 51.50
extra person	€ 5.40 - € 8.30
child (1-10 yrs)	€ 3.70 - € 6.20

Llafranc

Kim's Camping

Font d'en Xeco 1, E-17211 Llafranc - Palafrugell (Girona) T: 972 301 156. E: info@campingkims.com
alanrogers.com/ES81200

This attractive, terraced site (to which the owner has been welcoming guests for 54 years) is arranged on the wooded slopes of a narrow valley leading to the sea and there are many trees including huge eucalyptus. There are 350 grassy and partly shaded pitches (70-120 sq.m), 240 used for touring units, all with electricity (5A). Many of the larger pitches are on a plateau from which great views can be enjoyed. The terraced pitches are connected by winding drives, narrow in places. This is a pleasant place for holidays where you can enjoy the bustling atmosphere of the village and beach, while staying in a quieter environment. English and Dutch are spoken by the very friendly management and staff.

Facilities

All sanitary facilities are spotlessly clean and include excellent facilities for disabled visitors. Laundry facilities. Motorcaravan services. Gas supplies. Shop. Bar. Bakery. Café/restaurant (15/6-15/9). Swimming pools. Play areas and children's club. TV room. Excursions arranged – bus calls at site. Visits arranged to sub-aqua schools (high season). Torches required. WiFi. Pets accepted. Gas only barbecues. Mobile homes to rent. Off site: Beach, fishing and bicycle hire 500 m. Llafranc 1 km. Riding 3.5 km.

Open: Easter - 2 October.

Directions

Llafranc is southeast of Palafrugell. Turn off the Palafrugell - Tamariu road at turn (GIV 6542) signed Llafranc. Site is on right 1 km. further on. GPS: 41.90053, 3.18935

Charges guide

Per unit incl. 2 persons and electricity	€ 18.15 - € 41.20
extra person	€ 2.65 - € 6.55

Lloret de Mar

Camping Tucan

Ctra de Blanes - Lloret, E-17310 Lloret de Mar (Girona) T: 972 369 965. E: info@campingtucan.com
alanrogers.com/ES82100

Situated on the busy Costa Brava near Lloret de Mar, Camping Tucan is well placed to access all the attractions of the area. Views of the mountains are mixed with views of the nearby town. Of the 307 good sized pitches, 48 are fully serviced (60-100 sq.m) and most have electricity (3/6/10A). Laid out in a herring-bone pattern, there are areas dedicated to singles, families with young children and couples who enjoy the quiet. Pitches are on terraces, flat surfaced with gravel and many are shaded. Tucan is a lively site with many activities including an activity programme for children and modest entertainment at night.

Facilities

Two modern toilet blocks include washbasins with hot water and facilities for disabled visitors, although access can be difficult. Washing machines. Gas supplies. Shop. Bar and good restaurant. Takeaway. Swimming pools and indoor solarium. Playground and fenced play area for toddlers. TV in bar. Bicycle hire. Entertainment in high season. Miniclub. WiFi (charged). Only charcoal and gas barbecues permitted. Off site: Town 500 m. Beach 600 m.

Open: 1 April - 25 September.

Directions

From A7/E4, A19 or N11 Girona - Barcelona roads take an exit for Lloret de Mar. Site is 1 km. west of the town, well signed and is at the base of the hill off the roundabout. The entrance can get congested in busy periods. GPS: 41.6972, 2.8217

Charges 2012

Per unit incl. 2 persons and electricity	€ 25.70 - € 55.40

Malgrat de Mar

Camping La Tordera

182

Cami de la Tordera s/n, E-08380 Malgrat de Mar (Barcelona) T: 937 612 778. E: camping@latordera.com

alanrogers.com/ES82330

With direct access to a beach and to a small nature reserve on the nearby river delta of La Tordera, the site is between Malgrat and Blanes. At present there are about 60 touring pitches, all with electricity (10A), either close to the beach in an open area to be developed for 2012, or in a new section with 30 larger serviced pitches. There are many more under the trees scattered among the seasonal pitches which dominate this site and give it a very Spanish feel. There is a pleasant swimming pool, a well stocked supermarket and a bar/restaurant with covered terrace. The site is lively in peak season with a varied programme of entertainment and activities for all ages. Nearby Blanes is a popular resort with fine beaches. There are also some steep rocky cliffs and surprisingly quiet little coves.

Facilities

Large sanitary block with spacious controllable showers, open style washbasins (cold water), baby baths and en-suite units for disabled visitors. Smaller block has controllable showers and open-style washbasins (cold water). Washing machines. Motorcaravan services. Swimming pool with children's section and grassy terrace (15/6-30/9). Supermarket and bar/restaurant with takeaway (1/6-11/9, weekends in low season). Children's play areas. Sports field. Games/Internet room. Activity and entertainment programme (high season and weekends). Bicycle hire. Chalets for rent. WiFi (charged). Note: access to the central pitches can be difficult, with narrow roads and high kerbs; staff will site vans. Off site: Blanes 2 km. Malgrat de Mar 3 km. Sailing and boat-launching 4 km. Riding 5 km. Golf 7 km.

Open: 18 February - 13 November.

Directions

Malgrat de Mar is 60 km. northeast of Barcelona and site is 3 km. northeast of town. From Barcelona on C32 motorway, leave at Malgrat de Mar exit and join N11 from Girona. Take right fork towards town centre until you pick up signs for 'Zona de Campings', then signs for site which is approached across flat agricultural land.
GPS: 41.652304, 2.775483

Charges guide

Per unit incl. 2 persons and electricity	€ 22.15 - € 36.00
extra person	€ 4.00 - € 6.40
child (5-10 yrs)	€ 3.30 - € 5.40
dog	€ 3.20 - € 4.95

Malgrat de Mar

Camping del Mar

Avenida Pomareda s/n, E-08380 Malgrat de Mar (Barcelona) T: 937 653 767. E: info@campingdelmar.com

alanrogers.com/ES82340

With such a wide choice of campsites along this part of the coast, standards have to be kept high and that is just what you get at Camping del Mar. Beautifully manicured lawns and a well designed site help to create a relaxed atmosphere. All the facilities are kept immaculately clean. The 120 flat, grassy pitches all have electricity (6A) and easy access to a water point. The site is surrounded by a high hedge providing privacy and some shade to those pitches alongside. In time the many young trees and shrubs on the site will give plenty of shade. A central modern building houses all the facilities, including the reception, shop, bar and restaurant with access to a terrace overlooking the pleasant swimming and paddling pools. With the sandy beach just across the road, this site fulfils the needs of the whole family. The owners and their staff take great pride in their campsite and rightly so.

Facilities

Modern, clean sanitary facilities are in the central building. Showers in large cubicles, open style washbasins and controllable hot water. Separate laundry room with washing machines. Small shop. Bar with TV and separate restaurant with varied menu. Games room. Swimming pool with separate children's pool. Multisports court. Tennis. Large play area. Minigolf. Children's club and entertainment (July/Aug). Fishing. Internet access and WiFi. Car wash. Off site: Public transport in high season. Boat launching and watersports 4 km. Riding 5 km.

Open: 1 April - 16 October.

Directions

From Malgrat de Mar town centre follow signs to 'zona campings'. Cross railway line and head north along beach front. Site is the second campsite on the left. GPS: 41.64726, 2.76378

Charges guide

Per unit incl. 2 persons and electricity	€ 21.00 - € 37.00
extra person	€ 4.50 - € 6.50
child (4-10 yrs)	€ 3.50 - € 4.50
dog	€ 3.00

Mataró

Camping Barcelona

Ctra NII km 650, E-08304 Mataró (Barcelona) T: 937 904 720. E: info@campingbarcelona.com

alanrogers.com/ES82450

Camping Barcelona has a pleasant Spanish flavour, evident in the restaurant which serves authentic food and tapas. Like other sites in this area, it is on the beach road (N11) which means it is subject to train and traffic noise. However, the 250 touring pitches, which are separated from the permanent areas, do allow you to avoid the problem. Pitches vary in size and most have electricity (6/10A Europlug). An excellent pool is provided in which to cool off and reception will assist in arranging many off site activities. There is a rocky coastline 100 m. away, but we recommend you to use the free shuttle to Mataró for serious sunning. An area containing several types of animals and fowl is on site for your enjoyment, and the management takes a pride in making sure you have fun whilst staying here. Entertainment is provided in high season for both adults and children. The wonderful city of Barcelona is just 40 minutes away by bus or train. This is a pleasant, family owned site where English is spoken.

Facilities

Three clean sanitary blocks provide fine facilities. Baby room. Facilities for disabled campers. Washing machines. Freezer. Motorcaravan service areas. Supermarket. Bar. Restaurant. Takeaway. Pool bar. Swimming pool with lifeguard (30/5-30/9). Pétanque. Playground. Children's farm. Miniclub and entertainment (high season). Disco. WiFi (charged). Picnic area. Electronic games. Free daily bus to Barcelona (small charge, Jul/Aug) and free shuttle to Mataró beach club, train station and wellness centre.

Open: 2 March - 8 November.

Directions

Site is east of Mataró at the 650 km. marker on the N11. Leave the C-32 autoroute at exits 104 or 108 and follow signs for the sea and Mataró. Site is well signed on both carriageways.
GPS: 41.55055, 2.48338

Charges 2012

Per unit incl. 2 persons and electricity	€ 25.95 - € 52.30
extra person	€ 5.50 - € 9.50
dog	€ 2.00 - € 3.00

Miami-Playa

Els Prats Village Beach & Camping Park

Ctra N340 km 1137, E-43892 Miami-Playa (Tarragona) T: 977 810 027. E: info@campingelsprats.com

alanrogers.com/ES85330

This Costa Daurada beach resort is constantly developing with excellent facilities and many more improvements planned. This is a very popular area, not far from Tarragona and the Port Aventura theme park. There are now 444 pitches, all with 5A electricity. They are fairly close together, mostly flat and shaded, and a few are next to the pleasant narrow, white sand/shingle beach. There is a separate area of bungalows to rent and an apartment block in one corner. A feature is the tropical style beach bar, whilst attractive plants adorn the site. There is some road and rail noise on one side of the site.

Facilities

Three blocks provide clean facilities with controllable showers and some washbasins in cubicles. A fourth, modern unit has WCs and open style washbasins. En-suite unit for disabled visitors. Baby rooms with bath for children. Washing machines. Motorcaravan services. Supermarket. Restaurant, takeaway and three bars. Swimming pool (3/4-17/10). Play area. Bicycle hire. Sailing, windsurfing, canoeing and diving (free try dive Sat am). Activities, excursions and evening entertainment. Dogs are accepted in one area. Torches useful. WiFi (free for 5 hrs). Off site: Golf 3 km. Riding 5 km. Cambrils 7 km.

Open: 5 March - 1 November.

Directions

Miami-Playa is 35 km. southwest of Tarragona. Site is between the town and Cambrils on the N340. Take exit at 1138 from the A7 (Mont-roig del Camp), then turn south on N340. Site is on the left.
GPS: 41.03611, 0.975

Charges guide

Per unit incl. 2 persons and electricity	€ 24.20 - € 44.00
extra person	€ 6.50 - € 7.50
child (1-10 yrs)	€ 1.20 - € 5.20
dog	€ 2.10 - € 4.20

Montagut

Camping Montagut

Ctra Montagut - Sadernes km 2, E-17855 Montagut (Girona) T: 972 287 202. E: info@campingmontagut.com

alanrogers.com/ES91220

This is a delightful, small family site where everything is kept in pristine condition. Jordi and Nuria, a brother and sister team, work hard to make you welcome and maintain the superb appearance of the site. Flowers and shrubs abound, with 90 pitches on attractively landscaped and carefully constructed terraces or on flat areas overlooking the pool. All but ten are for touring units and 5A electricity is available throughout. A tranquil atmosphere pervades the site and it is a delight to enjoy drinks on the pleasant restaurant terrace, or to sample the authentic menu as you enjoy the views over the Alta Garrotxa.

Facilities

The modern sanitary block has controllable hot showers, open style washbasins, a pleasant baby room and an en-suite unit for disabled visitors. Washing and laundry facilities. Motorcaravan services. Supermarket (all season). Restaurant and bar (1/7-28/8, snacks and bar at weekends in low season). Medium sized swimming pool with large sunbathing area and children's pool (1/5-30/9). Playground. Sports field. Pétanque. Barbecue area. WiFi area (free). Torches useful in some areas. Off site: Riding 1 km. Shop and restaurant in village 2 km. Beach 60 km.

Open: 1 April - 16 October.

Directions

From north leave AP7 at Figueres, join N11 south and turn west signed Olot to join N260/A26. Take exit 75, turn right towards Montagut. At end of village turn left towards Sadernes and site entrance is on the left in 2 km. GPS: 42.2469, 2.5971

Charges guide

Per unit incl. 2 persons and electricity	€ 20.35 - € 33.00
extra person	€ 5.10 - € 7.10
child (2-10 yrs)	€ 4.30 - € 5.90

Montblanc

Camping Caravaning Montblanc Park

Ctra Prenafeta km 1,8, E-43400 Montblanc (Tarragona) T: 977 862 544. E: montblancpark@franceloc.fr

alanrogers.com/ES85020

Purpose designed, Montblanc Park has 290 terraced pitches of which 160 are ostensibly for touring units, although well over 100 are occupied by permanently installed seasonal caravans; they are grassless, all have electricity (20A) and vary in size, with hedging and young trees (so little shade). Water taps are scarce. The upper terraces are taken up by 130 wooden chalets for rent. The bar/restaurant and terrace overlook a large, lagoon-style pool with views across the valley, beyond the busy railway line and the autopista, to the town of Montblanc and the mountains of the Serra del Prades.

Facilities

Two toilet blocks feature en-suite units but no separate WCs or showers, so they will be under pressure in high season. Good unit for disabled visitors. Baby room. Washing machines and dryers. Supermarket (June-Oct). Bar/restaurant and snack bar with takeaway (weekends only in low season). Swimming pool and paddling pool. Games room. Gym. Bicycle hire. Entertainment for children (weekends and main season). Chalets for hire. Free WiFi in leisure area. Off site: Amenities in town 2 km.

Open: 1 April - 30 November.

Directions

Montblanc is between Barcelona and Lleida on the AP2 motorway. Leave at exit 9 and join N240 (Reus-Tarragona); take first exit towards Prenafeta and site stands out on the hillside ahead. GPS: 41.3787, 1.1826

Charges guide

Per unit incl. 2 persons and electricity	€ 19.00 - € 34.00
extra person	€ 4.00 - € 6.00

Montroig

Playa Montroig Camping Resort

Ctra N340 km 1136, E-43300 Montroig (Tarragona) T: 977 810 637. E: info@playamontroig.com

alanrogers.com/ES85300

What a superb site! Playa Montroig is about 30 kilometres beyond Tarragona set in its own tropical gardens with direct access to a very long, narrow, soft sand beach. The main part of the site lies between the sea, road and railway (as at other sites on this coast, there is some train noise) with a huge underpass. The site is divided into spacious, marked pitches with excellent shade provided by a variety of lush vegetation including very impressive palms set in wide avenues. There are 1,177 pitches, all with electricity and 564 with water and drainage. Some 47 pitches are directly alongside the beach.

Facilities

Very good quality sanitary buildings with washbasins in private cabins and separate WCs. Facilities for disabled campers and for babies. Launderettes. Motorcaravan services. Good shopping centre. Restaurants and bars. Fitness suite. Hairdressers. TV lounges. Beach bar. Playground. Tennis. Minigolf. Organised activities. Pedalo hire. Bicycle hire. Internet café. WiFi in all bars. Dogs are not accepted. Off site: Public transport 100 m. from gate.

Open: 23 March - 4 November.

Directions

Site entrance is off main N340 nearly 30 km. southwest from Tarragona. From motorway take Cambrils exit and turn west on N340 at 1136 km. marker. GPS: 41.03292, 0.96921

Charges 2012

Per unit incl. 2 persons and electricity	€ 19.00 - € 50.00

Montroig

Camping La Torre del Sol

182

Ctra N340 km 1136, E-43300 Montroig (Tarragona) T: 977 810 486. E: info@latorredelsol.com

alanrogers.com/ES85400

A pleasant banana tree-lined approach road gives way to avenues of palms as you arrive at Torre del Sol. This is a very large site occupying a good position in the south of Catalunya with direct access to the soft sand beach. The site is exceptionally well maintained by a large workforce. There is good shade on a high proportion of the 1,500 individual, numbered pitches. All have electricity and are mostly of about 70-80 sq.m. Strong features here are 800 m. of clean beachfront with a special Mediterranean type of pitch, and the entertainment that is provided all season. Part of the site is between the railway and the sea, so there is some occasional train noise.

Facilities

Five well maintained, fully equipped, toilet blocks include units for disabled visitors and children. Washing machines. Gas supplies. Supermarket, bakery and souvenir shops. Restaurant. Takeaway. Bar with terrace for daily entertainment. Beach bar. Pizzeria. Cinema. 3 TV lounges. Soundproofed disco. Swimming pools. Two jacuzzis. Tennis. Squash. Minigolf. Sub-aqua diving (first dive free!). Bicycle hire. Fishing. Windsurfing school. Crèche and Happy Camp. Fridge hire. WiFi. No animals permitted.

Open: 15 March - 31 October.

Directions

Entrance is off main N340 road by 1136 km. marker, about 30 km. from Tarragona towards Valencia. From motorway take Cambrils exit and turn west on N340. GPS: 41.03707, 0.97478

Charges 2012

Per unit incl. 2 persons and electricity	€ 20.30 - € 66.55
extra person	€ 3.35 - € 9.90

Camping Cheques accepted.

Palamós

Camping Internacional de Palamós

Apdo 100, E-17230 Palamós (Girona) T: 972 314 736. E: info@internacionalpalamos.com

alanrogers.com/ES81500

This is an uncomplicated, comfortable site which is clean, welcoming and useful for exploring the local area from a peaceful base. Traditional in style, it is open for a long season and has a range of facilities. It might have space when others are full and has over 453 moderate sized pitches. The majority are level and terraced with some less defined under pine trees on a gentle slope. All pitches have a sink and variable shade, with electrical connections (6A) available in most parts. Some access roads are gravel and may suffer in the case of heavy rain.

Facilities

Two refurbished toilet blocks and one smart new one are fully equipped. Some washbasins in cabins. Facilities for disabled campers. Laundry room. Small shop. Bar (1/4-29/9). Snack bar serving simple food and takeaway (from 1/6). Swimming pool (36x16 m) with paddling pool. Play area. Car wash. ATM. Torches necessary. Off site: Nearest beach 400 m. Fishing 500 m. Town 1 km. with hourly bus service. Riding 1.5 km.

Open: 30 March - 30 September.

Directions

Central Palamós streets are too narrow for caravans which should turn off C255 road just outside Palamós. Continue north by large garage signed Kings Camping and La Fosca. Turn right just before Kings and follow Camping 'Internacional' Palamós signs. GPS: 41.85722, 3.13805

Charges guide

Per unit incl. 2 persons and electricity	€ 30.30 - € 47.10

No credit cards. Camping Cheques accepted.

Pineda de Mar

Camping Caballo de Mar

Passeig Maritim 52-54, E-08397 Pineda de Mar (Barcelona) T: 937 671 706. E: info@caballodemar.com

alanrogers.com/ES82380

This is a site for lovers of the seaside with its direct access to a lovely, sandy beach. Divided into two parts by the railway and dual-carriageway, the main part of the site is arranged off a central access road with plenty of colourful shrubs and trees providing shade. In total there are 450 pitches, 300 taken by seasonal visitors and a few bungalows. On the beach side of the site the pitches are generally smaller (60-70 sq.m), all with shade and 5/6A electricity, and there is a bar, snack bar and a toilet block here.

Facilities

Two toilet blocks are fully equipped and well maintained. En-suite units to rent (main side) with units for disabled visitors. Facilities for babies. Washing machines. Motorcaravan services. Shop and baker (15/6-31/8). Main bar and restaurant. Bar and snacks at the beach in high season. Swimming pool. Play area. Entertainment organised. Miniclub. Fitness room. Internet access. ATM. Fishing. Off site: Beach. Town within walking distance.

Open: 1 April - 30 September.

Directions

Site is off N11 coast road, southwest of Pineda de Mar. Leave the C32 at exit 122 and head for Pineda de Mar. Site is well signed off the beach road on the outskirts of the town. GPS: 41.61664, 2.64997

Charges guide

Per unit incl. 2 persons and electricity	€ 22.25 - € 36.65

Pals

Camping-Resort Mas Patoxas Bungalow-Park

Ctra C31 Palafrugell - Pals km 339, E-17256 Pals (Girona) T: 972 636 928. E: info@campingmaspatoxas.com

alanrogers.com/ES81020

This is a mature, lush and well laid out site for those who prefer to be apart from, but within easy travelling distance of, the beaches (5 km) and town (1 km). It has a very easy access and is set on a slight slope with wide avenues on level terraces providing 376 grassy pitches of a minimum of 72 sq.m. All have 6A electricity and some share water taps. There are some very pleasant views and shade from a variety of mature trees. Both bar and restaurant terraces give views over the pools and distant hills. The air-conditioned restaurant/bar provides both waiter- and self-service meals. A good value takeaway operates close by (weekends only mid Sept-April) and entertainment takes place on a stage below the terraces during high season. The restaurant menu is varied and very reasonable. We were impressed with the children's miniclub activity when we visited. There is a large, supervised, irregularly shaped swimming pool with triple flume, a separate children's pool and a generous sunbathing area at the poolside and on the surrounding grass.

Facilities

Three modern sanitary blocks provide controllable hot showers, some washbasins with hot water. Baby bath and three cabins for children. No specific facilities for disabled campers. Laundry facilities. Fridges for rent. Gas supplies. Supermarket, restaurant/bar, pizzeria and takeaway (all 1/4-30/9). Swimming pool with a new bar (1/5-30/9). Tennis. Entertainment in high season. Fitness area with games. Massage. Bicycle hire. Internet access. WiFi (charged). Torches useful in some areas. Off site: Bus service from site gate. Bicycle hire and riding 2 km. Fishing and golf 4 km.

Open: 13 January - 16 December.

Directions

Site is east of Girona and about 1.5 km. south of Pals at km. 339 on the C31 Figueres - Palamós road, just north of Palafugel. GPS: 41.9568, 3.1573

Charges 2012

Per unit incl. 2 persons and electricity	€ 18.50 - € 52.00
extra person	€ 4.20 - € 7.00
child (1-7 yrs)	€ 3.60 - € 5.00
dog	€ 2.60 - € 4.20

Special low season offers.

Platja d'Aro

Camping Valldaro

Apdo de correos 57, Cami Vell 63, E-17250 Platja d'Aro (Girona) T: 972 817 515. E: info@valldaro.com

alanrogers.com/ES81700

Valldaro is 600 m. back from the sea at Platja d'Aro, a small, bright resort with a long, wide beach and plenty of amusements. It is particularly pleasant during off-peak weeks and is popular with Spanish, Dutch and British visitors. Valldaro has been extended and many pitches have been made larger, bringing them up to 85 sq.m. There are now almost 1,200 pitches with 544 for touring units. The site is flat, with pitches in rows divided up by access roads. You will probably find space here even at the height of the season. The newer section has its own vehicle entrance (the nearest point to the beach) and can be reached via a footbridge; it is brought into use at peak times. It has some shade and its own toilet block, as well as a medium sized swimming pool of irregular shape with a grassy sunbathing area and adjacent bar/snack bar and takeaway. The original pool (36x18 m) is next to the attractive, Spanish style restaurant, which also offers takeaway fare.

Facilities

Four sanitary blocks are of a good standard and are well maintained. Child size toilets. Washbasins (no cabins) and adjustable showers. Two supermarkets and general shops. Two restaurants. Large bar. Swimming pools. New outdoor jacuzzi. Minigolf with snack bar. Playgrounds. Sports ground. Tennis. Children's club. Organised entertainment in season. Hairdresser. Internet. WiFi area (code). Satellite TV. Gas supplies. Off site: Fishing and bicycle hire 1 km. Beach 1.5 km. Riding 4 km. Golf 5 km.

Open: 1 April - 25 September.

Directions

From Girona on AP7/E15 take exit 7 to Sant Feliu on C65. At km. 313 take exit to Platja d'Aro (the road no. changes here to C31). In 200 m. at roundabout take GI662 towards Platja d'Aro. Site is at km. 4. GPS: 41.81427, 3.0437

Charges guide

Per unit incl. 2 persons and electricity	€ 20.00 - € 45.90

No credit cards. Camping Cheques accepted.

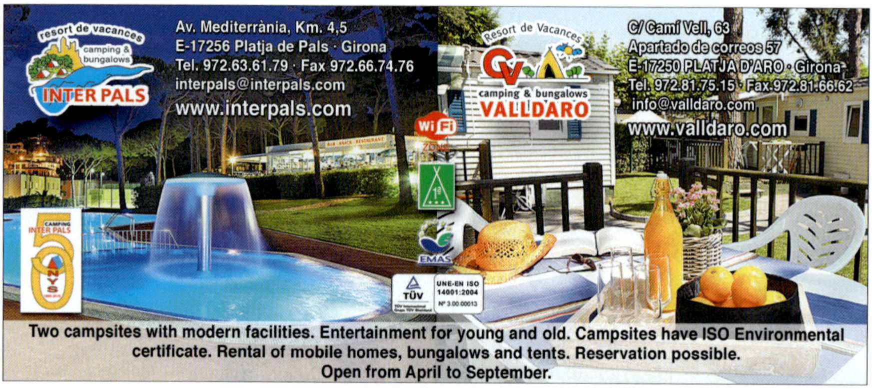

We can book this site for you! alan rogers travel
Call 01580 214000

Platja de Pals

Camping Inter-Pals

Avenida Mediterrania, E-17256 Platja de Pals (Girona) T: 972 636 179. E: interpals@interpals.com

alanrogers.com/ES81000

Set on sloping ground with tall pine trees providing shade and about 500 metres from the beach, Inter-Pals has 450 terraced pitches. It is sister site to no. ES81700 Valldaro. Arranged on level terraces, mostly with shade, some of the terraced pitches have views of the sea through the trees. The main entrance and its drive resembles a pretty village street as the bungalows are set on both sides of the street which is lined with traditional lamp posts. Continuing the village theme is a row of shops where you will find most campers' needs. The formal restaurant with good value menu and choice of takeaway overlooks the pools. The site is close to Platja de Pals, which is a long sandy unspoilt stretch of beach; a discreet area, reached by a very hard climb, is now an official naturist beach. The pretty town of Pals is nearby.

Facilities

Three well maintained toilet blocks include facilities for disabled campers. Motorcaravan service point. Laundry facilities. Gas supplies. Shops. Restaurant/bar. Pizzeria entertainment area. Café/bar by entrance. Swimming pool. Jacuzzi. Playground. Bicycle hire. Activities and entertainment in high season. Excursions. Watersports. Mini-adventure park. Medical centre. ATM. Internet and WiFi. Some breeds of dog are excluded. Torch useful.

Open: 31 March - 25 September.

Directions

Site is on the road leading off the Torroella de Montgri - Bagur road north of Pals and going to Platja de Pals (Pals beach). GPS: 41.97533, 3.19317

Charges 2012

Per unit incl. 2 persons and electricity	€ 29.80 - € 51.80
extra person	€ 4.50 - € 6.90

No credit cards. Camping Cheques accepted.

Platja de Pals

Camping Playa Brava

Avenida del Grau 1, E-17256 Platja de Pals (Girona) T: 972 636 894. E: info@playabrava.com

alanrogers.com/ES81010

This is an extremely pleasant site with an open feel, having direct access to an excellent soft sand beach and a freshwater lagoon where you can enjoy watersports and launch your own boat (charged). The ground is level and very grassy with shade provided for many of the 706 spacious touring pitches by a mixture of conifer and broad-leaf trees. All the pitches have 10A electricity and about a third have water and drainage. The spaciousness continues around the superb large swimming pool with its huge grass sunbathing areas, overlooked by the terrace of the restaurant and bar. The restaurant is very pleasant and offers a most reasonable menu of the day including wine. An energetic entertainment programme runs during July and August. There are many interesting things to explore in the area, including La Bisbal (famous for ceramics), Dali's museum, the Roman ruins at Empúries and much more.

Facilities

Five modern, fully equipped toilet blocks include facilities for disabled visitors. Washing machines and dryers. Motorcaravan service point. Supermarket. Bar/restaurant. Takeaway. Swimming pool. Tennis. Minigolf. Beach volley-ball. Football. Basketball. Play area on grass. Bicycle hire. Watersports on river and beach, including sheltered lagoon for windsurfing novices. New stage show. Internet. WiFi over site (charged). Satellite TV. Gas supplies. Torches required in some areas. Dogs are not accepted. Off site: Two 18-hole golf courses 300 m.

Open: 12 May - 12 September.

Directions

Platja de Pals is southeast of Girona on the coast. From the AP7/E15 at Girona take exit 6 towards Palamós on the C66. 7.5 km. past La Bisbal, exit to Pals on the GIV-6502. Follow signs for Platja de Pals - Golf Platja de Pals. Site is on left just before road ends at beach car park. GPS: 42.001130, 3.193800

Charges 2012

Per unit incl. 2 persons and electricity	€ 32.60 - € 55.80
extra person	€ 2.30 - € 3.40

Platja de Pals

Camping Cypsela

Ctra de Pals - Platja de Pals, E-17256 Platja de Pals (Girona) T: 972 667 696. E: info@cypsela.com

alanrogers.com/ES80900

This impressive, deluxe site with lush vegetation and trees is very efficiently run. The main part of the camping area is pinewood, with 688 clearly marked touring pitches of varying categories on sandy gravel, all with electricity and 552 with full facilities. The 267 élite pitches of 120 sq.m. are impressive. Cypsela is a busy, well administered site, only 2 km. from the sea, which we can thoroughly recommend, especially for families. The site has good quality fixtures and fittings, all kept clean and maintained to a high standard. All your needs will be catered for here. The site has many striking features, one of which is the sumptuous complex of sports facilities and amenities near the entrance.

Facilities

Four sanitary blocks are of excellent quality. Three have washbasins in cabins and three have amazing children's rooms. Private sanitary facilities to rent. Superb facilities for disabled visitors. Serviced launderette. Supermarket and other shops. Restaurant, caféteria and takeaway. Bar. Hairdresser. Swimming pools. Tennis. Squash. Minigolf. Skating rink. Fitness room. Solarium. Air-conditioned social/TV room. Entertainment in season. Games room. Bicycle hire. WiFi over site (charged). Gas supplies. ATM. Dogs are not accepted. Off site: Golf 1 km.

Open: 18 May - 16 September.

Directions

From the AP7/E15 at Girona take exit 6 towards Palamós on the C66. This road changes to C31 near La Bisbal. 7.5 km. past La Bisbal, exit to Pals on GI652. Follow signs for Platja de Pals. At El Masos take 6502 for 1 km. Main entrance for Cypsela is on left between white fencing. GPS: 41.98608, 3.18105

Charges 2012

Per unit incl. 2 persons and electricity	€ 36.78 - € 58.12
extra person	€ 6.40
child (2-10 yrs)	€ 4.80

Poboleda

Camping Poboleda

Placa de les Casetes s/n, E-43376 Poboleda (Tarragona) T: 977 827 197. E: poboleda@campingsonline.com

alanrogers.com/ES85080

Time stands still at this unique site, watched over by La Morera de Montsant, a peak of the Serra del Montsant. Situated among olive groves, on the edge of the lovely old village of Poboleda, it is an idyllic site for tents, small caravans and motorcaravans. Large units would have problems negotiating the narrow village streets and even small caravans might find it tricky. The 151 average sized pitches (70 with 4A electricity) are set on broad grassy terraces under olive and almond trees in a peaceful haven broken only by bird song or the peal of church bells.

Facilities

One small block, open all year, is fully equipped, as is a larger block open for high season. Shower for children. Facilities for disabled visitors (key). Laundry service. Breakfast to order. Bar. Swimming pool (24/6-11/9). Tennis. Boules. Reception has tourist information, postcards and basic items. WiFi area (free). Off site: Bars, restaurants and shops in village. Bicycle hire 10 km. Fishing and boat launching 12 km. Gaudí Centre in Reus 30 km. Beach and Port Aventura theme park 40 km.

Open: All year.

Directions

Poboleda is best approached from the south. From AP7 at exit 34, take T11 (Reus then Falset) and continue on N420. After Borges del Camp turn north on C242 for 18 km. over Coll d'Alforja. Take T702 west for 6 km to Poboleda. Watch for tent signs and follow carefully through narrow village streets. Not suitable for large units. GPS: 41.23231, 0.84316

Charges guide

Per unit incl. 2 persons and electricity	€ 32.32
extra person	€ 6.48

Puigcerdá

Camping Stel

Ctra N152 Ramal - Llivia s/n, E-17520 Puigcerdá (Girona) T: 972 882 361. E: puigcerda@stel.es

alanrogers.com/ES91440

High in the Pyrenees, right on the French border, this is an extremely efficient site. Part of a large, attractive building, the spacious entrance houses a modern reception (English is spoken). From here you will quickly be on your way to one of the flat, terraced pitches. Many of the pitches have shade and all are marked, clean and organised in rows with a water tap for each row. There is some road noise so, in order to avoid this and have views of the Cerdanya valley and the eastern Pyrenees, take one of the pitches on the upper terraces. It is worth the trouble.

Facilities

Sanitary facilities in the main building are of very high standard and are kept clean. Facilities for disabled campers. Laundry facilities. Shop. Bar/restaurant (all season). Swimming pool (June-Sept). Boules. Adventure style play frame (supervision needed). Adventure club (watersports and outdoor activities). Bicycle hire. Entertainment. Barbecues are not permitted. Large motorcaravans and twin-axle caravans are not accepted.

Open: 1 June - 11 September.

Directions

From Perpignan take N116 to Prades and Andorra. At roundabout at border crossing at Puigcerdá take first right for Llivia (almost a turn back on yourself). Site is on left after 1 km. GPS: 42.44153, 1.94128

Charges 2012

Per unit incl. 2 persons and electricity	€ 35.30 - € 42.80

Camping Cheques accepted.

Roda de Bará

Kawan Village Stel

Ctra N340 km 1182, E-43883 Roda de Bará (Tarragona) T: 977 802 002. E: rodadebara@stel.es

alanrogers.com/ES84200

Camping Stel is situated between mountains and the sea with direct access to an excellent beach, via a passage under the railway, which runs along the entire coast (so expect some rail noise, especially on the lower pitches). The 800 pitches are generally in rows separated by hedges, all have electricity (5A) and many have individual sinks. In one area, radios and TVs are not allowed. The impressive central area contains a large bar/restaurant with terrace and snack bar overlooking the attractive pool complex, which includes a wonderful fun pool for children, a flume and a grass area carefully set out with palms.

Facilities

Three clean sanitary blocks provide spacious controllable showers, washbasins in cabins, excellent facilities for children and disabled visitors and four private bathrooms for rent. Baby baths. Launderette. Motorcaravan service area. Supermarket and tourist shop. Bar/restaurant and snack bar. Swimming pool with children's section (heated in low season). Sports complex. Tennis courts and padel court. Gym. Hairdresser. Internet room with free WiFi. ATM. Bicycle hire. Miniclub. Dogs are not accepted.

Open: Easter - 30 September.

Directions

Roda de Bará is 22 km. east of Tarragona. From east on AP7 leave at exit 31 and take motorway link to join N340 west. From west take exit 32 onto N340 east. Site is at 1182 km. marker on the N340 near Arc de Bará. GPS: 41.16969, 1.46469

Charges guide

Per unit incl. 2 persons and electricity	€ 23.60 - € 30.60

Camping Cheques accepted.

Roses

Camping Salatá

Port Reig s/n, Platja Salatá, E-17480 Roses (Girona) T: 972 256 086. E: info@campingsalata.com

alanrogers.com/ES80090

Situated in the heart of Roses, in one of the most attractive areas of the Costa Brava, Salatá is a short walk from the magnificent seafront promenade with its bars, restaurants and shops. Opposite the site entrance there is a pretty landscaped sea inlet. There are 288 grass pitches with 16A electricity and some shade (80-110 sq.m). Buildings and amenities are very well maintained. The campsite is part of a complex that includes apartments and the Hotel Terraza where a spa centre, indoor pool and other amenities can be enjoyed by campers in low season (extra charge).

Facilities

Very clean toilet blocks have British style toilets and good showers. Facilities for disabled visitors, babies and children. Washing machines. Gas supplies. Bar with snacks. Swimming pool. Playground. Entertainment for adults and children (15/6-15/9). Internet. WiFi. Barbecue area. Bicycle hire. Minigolf. No animals in high season. Off site: Extra facilities at hotel nearby (under the same ownership). Public transport. Beach and bicycle hire 130 m.

Open: 1 March - 30 November.

Directions

From the AP7/E15, take exit 3 south or exit 4 north (there is no exit 3 northbound) and then the N11 to the C260 and on to Roses. Site is well signed before you enter the town. GPS: 42.26588, 3.15762

Charges guide

Per person	€ 4.65 - € 7.75
pitch	€ 10.00 - € 28.00
dog	free - € 2.75

Rupit

Camping Rupit

Ctra de Vic - Olot km 31,5, E-08569 Rupit (Barcelona) T: 938 522 153. E: info@rupit.com

alanrogers.com/ES83400

The last 15 kilometres of the approach road to this site are not for the faint hearted, but if a remote rural setting is what you are looking for, then this could be the site for you. The main area is attractive: on the right is a beautiful stone building housing reception, a bar and restaurant, to the left an avenue of modern chalets for rent. The toilet block is also of traditional stone. There are 60 touring pitches, all with electricity (3/7A), most at the far end of the site, on level grass but with no shade and rather featureless.

Facilities

The central toilet block has open-style washbasins, some with hot and cold water. There is no door to the changing area. Baths for babies. WCs for disabled visitors but no showers. Washing machine. No shop (essentials at the bar). Bar with takeaway and separate restaurant (all season, restricted opening in low season). Outdoor swimming pool and children's pool (June-Aug). Games room. Play area. Communal barbecue area. Chalets and tents for hire. Site unsuitable for long vehicles.
Off site: Rupit town 1 km. Riding 5 km. Bicycle hire 15 km.

Open: 27 March - 8 December.

Directions

Rupit is 30 km. south of Olot. From south on the AP7 leave at exit 6 (Girona), take C66/A26 to Olot. From north leave AP7 at Figueres, join N11 south and turn west signed Olot to join N260/A26. From Olot head south on C152, then C153 for 31.5 km. This road climbs steadily and is very winding in places. Site is 1 km. before Rupit. Site entrance is on a sharp bend. GPS: 42.02516, 2.45883

Charges guide

Per unit incl. 2 persons and electricity	€ 24.80 - € 33.20

Saldés

Camping Repos del Pedraforca

Ctra B400 km 13.5, E-08697 Saldes (Barcelona) T: 938 258 044. E: pedra@campingpedraforca.com

alanrogers.com/ES91400

Looking up through the trees in this steeply terraced campsite in the area of the Cadi-Moixero Natural Park, you see the majestic Pedraforca mountain. A favourite for Catalan climbers and walkers, its amazing rugged peak in the shape of a massive stone fork gives it its name. Access to the site is via a steep, curving road which could challenge some units. There are 200 pitches, including 100 for touring, all with electricity (3-10A) and 15 with connection to water and waste water. They vary in size and accessibility, although there are excellent pitches for larger units. The long scenic drive through the mountains to reach the site is breathtakingly beautiful.

Facilities

Two clean, modern sanitary blocks are fully equipped (at peak periods expect queues). Facilities for disabled visitors. Separate family room with baby baths. Washing machines and dryer. Shop and bar (1/4-31/10). Restaurant and takeaway (24/6-10/9). Heated indoor swimming pool, gym and spa. Outdoor pool (15/6-10/9). Entertainment for all in high season. Games and social rooms. WiFi (free). Only charcoal barbecues permitted. Torches required.

Open: 1 April - 31 October.

Directions

Saldes is west of Guardiola de Bergueda, 125 km. north of Barcelona. From the C16 Manresa-Berga road 2 km. south of Guardiola de Bergueda turn west towards Saldes. Site is in 13.5 km. and is well signed. GPS: 42.23078, 1.75245

Charges 2012

Per unit incl. 2 persons and electricity	€ 27.05 - € 32.35

Camping Cheques accepted.

Salou

Camping La Siesta

Calle Norte 37, E-43840 Salou (Tarragona) T: 977 380 852. E: info@campinglasiesta.es

alanrogers.com/ES84700

La Siesta occupies a remarkable location close to the heart of the thriving resort of Salou, yet only two blocks from the fine sandy beach. The 470 pitches, all with 10A electricity, vary in size, some suitable for larger units, others for tents. There is considerable shade from the trees and shrubs that contribute to the site's attractive appearance. Considerable recent investment has seen the creation of a pleasant, grassy play area for children and impressive new sports provision. For 2012, an extensive new leisure pool complex is being built, overlooked by the existing bar/restaurant offering comprehensive and competitively priced menus, and entertainment in high season. A surprisingly large supermarket caters for most needs in season, and close by are all the shops, bars, restaurants and nightlife of Salou. The town is popular with British and Spanish holidaymakers and has just about all that a highly developed Spanish resort can offer, including miles of sandy beaches.

Facilities

Three bright and clean sanitary blocks provide very reasonable facilities including controllable showers and open style washbasins. Unit for disabled visitors. Motorcaravan services. Supermarket. Vending machines. Self-service restaurant and bar with takeaway. Children's club (June-Aug). Entertainment (July/Aug). Playground. Multisports and short tennis courts. New pool complex planned for 2012. Medical service daily in season. ATM point. Torches may be required. Off site: Many shops, restaurants and bars nearby. Port Aventura is close.

Open: 14 March - 3 November.

Directions

Salou is 10 km. southwest of Tarragona. Leave AP7 at exit 35 or A7 motorway at exit for Salou. Follow Tarragona-Salou road (dual-carriageway) until you pass the side of the site on the right. Site is signed (narrow turning). Follow further small signs through the one way system. GPS: 41.0777, 1.1389

Charges guide

Per unit incl. 2 persons and electricity	€ 27.00 - € 47.00
extra person	€ 5.00 - € 10.00
child (4-9 yrs)	€ 3.60 - € 5.00

Salou

Camping Resort Sangulí Salou

183

Passeig miramar - Plaça Venus, Apdo 123, E-43840 Salou (Tarragona) T: 977 381 641. E: mail@sanguli.es

alanrogers.com/ES84800

Sanguli is a superb site boasting excellent pools and entertainment. Owned, developed and managed by a local Spanish family, it has something for all the family with everything open when the site is open. There are 1,067 pitches of varying size (75-100 sq.m) and all have electricity. Mobile homes occupy 58 pitches and there are fully equipped bungalows on 147. A wonderful selection of trees, palms and shrubs provides natural shade and an ideal space for children to play. The good sandy beach is little more than 100 metres across the coast road and a small railway crossing. Although large, Sanguli has an open feel and a quality family atmosphere due to the efforts of the very keen and efficient staff.

Facilities

The six sanitary blocks are constantly cleaned and are always exceptional, including many individual cabins with en-suite facilities. Some blocks have excellent facilities for babies. Launderette with service. Motorcaravan services. Car wash (charged). Gas supplies. Snack bars. Indoor and outdoor restaurants with takeaway. Swimming pools. Sports complex. Fitness room (charged). Playgrounds. Miniclub. Minigolf. WiFi (free). Security bracelets. Medical centre. Off site: Activities on the beach. Bus at gate.

Open: March - November.

Directions

On west side of Salou about 1 km. from centre, site is signed from the coast road to Cambrils and from other town approaches. GPS: 41.075, 1.116

Charges guide

Per unit incl. 2 persons and electricity	€ 27.00 - € 71.00
extra person	€ 6.00
child (4-12 yrs)	€ 4.00

Reductions outside high season for longer stays.

Sant Antoni di Calonge

Eurocamping

Avinguda Catalunya 15, E-17252 Sant Antoni di Calonge (Girona) T: 972 650 879. E: info@euro-camping.com

alanrogers.com/ES81350

This large campsite on the Costa Brava near Girona is attractively landscaped, with lawns, flowers and pretty features around the site. It has 615 pitches of varying sizes, with 475 for touring, of which 100 are fully serviced. Older areas of the campsite are shaded by tall trees creating a cooler zone, while the new areas have reasonably sized trees but are not yet under the same shade canopy. There are two pool complexes, one near the entrance with an unusual feature where one large pool cascades into another at a slightly lower level. Alongside is a paddling pool, an outdoor chess game and a large grassy area.

Facilities

Four clean toilet blocks vary in size and are well sited. Almost all WCs are British style (but no seats) in cabins with shower and basin. Two private cabins for rent. Good facilities for disabled visitors. Rooms for babies and families. Washing machines. Gas supplies. Supermarket just outside gate. Pleasant bars and good restaurant. Swimming and paddling pools. Playgrounds. Tennis. TV in bar. Weight training room. Full activities programme. ATM. Internet and WiFi. Excursions. Beach train (July/Aug).

Open: 21 April - 23 September.

Directions

Sant Antoni di Calonge is southeast of Girona. Leave AP7/E15 at exit 6. Take C66 towards Palamós which becomes the C31. Use C31 (Girona - Palamós) road to avoid Palamós town. Take the C253 coast road. Site well signed at northern end of Sant Antoni di Calogne. GPS: 41.8470, 3.0986

Charges 2012

Per person	€ 3.00 - € 7.55
pitch	€ 21.00 - € 35.10

Sant Feliu de Guíxols

Camping Sant Pol

Carrer del Doctor Fleming No.1, E-17220 Sant Feliu de Guíxols (Girona) T: 972 327 269.
E: info@campingsantpol.cat **alanrogers.com/ES81800**

Sant Pol is a small, family owned site and the owners have a firm understanding of campers' needs, as do the friendly staff. On the Costa Brava, this hillside site is on the edge of Sant Feliu, only 350 m. from the beach (there may be some road noise on one side of the site) and the resort town. An attractive solar-heated pool and a paddling pool, bar and restaurant are the focus of the site, with shaded terraces and pitches of differing sizes curving down the slope. There are 100 pitches for tourers (19 fully serviced) and the small terraces take 37 tents. The on-site restaurant features regional dishes based on local produce.

Facilities

The clean and modern sanitary block has British style WCs and hot water throughout. WC for disabled campers, but no shower (terrain is difficult for wheelchairs). Washing machines and dryer. Small supermarket. Restaurant/bar. Solar heated swimming pools. Play area. Entertainment for children in high season. Minigolf. Internet point and WiFi (code). Excursions. Torches needed in some areas. Dogs allowed (no dangerous breeds). Off site: Large supermarket, restaurants 300 m. Beach 350 m.

Open: 30 March - 4 November.

Directions

Sant Feliu is southeast of Girona, reached via theC65 (Girona - Palamós) road. Leave this at km. 312 signed to S'Agaró. Go on towards Sant Feliu to outskirts of village. Site signed from first roundabout and directly off third roundabout. Entrance is up very steep slope. GPS: 41.78633, 3.04122

Charges 2012

Per unit incl. 2 persons and electricity (6A)	€ 26.00 - € 55.00
extra person	€ 4.00 - € 7.00

Sant Pere Pescador

Camping La Gaviota

Ctra de la Platja s/n, E-17470 Sant Pere Pescador (Girona) T: 972 520 569. E: info@lagaviota.com

alanrogers.com/ES80310

La Gaviota is a delightful, small, family run site at the end of a cul-de-sac with direct beach access. This ensures a peaceful situation with a choice of the pleasant L-shaped pool or the fine clean beach with slowly shelving access to the water. Everything here is clean and smart and the Gil family are very keen that you enjoy your time here. There are 165 touring pitches on flat ground with shade and 8A electricity supply. A lush green feel is given to the site by many palms and other semi-tropical trees and shrubs.

Facilities

One smart and clean toilet block is near reception. All WCs are British style and the showers are excellent. Superb facilities for disabled visitors. Two family rooms plus two baby rooms. Washing machine. Gas supplies. Supermarket (fresh bread), pleasant bar and small, restaurant (all Mar-Oct). Swimming pool (May-Oct). Playground. Games room. Limited entertainment. Beach sports and windsurfing. WiFi over site (charged). Torches useful. ATM. Off site: Boat launching 2 km. Riding 4 km.

Open: 23 March - 28 October.

Directions

From AP7/E15 take exit 3 onto N11 north towards Figueras and then C260 towards Roses. At Castello d'Empúries take GIV 6216 and continue to Sant Pere Pescador. Site is well signed in the town. GPS: 42.18901, 3.10843

Charges guide

Per unit incl. 2 persons and electricity	€ 23.95 - € 51.95

No credit cards. Discounts for longer stays.

Sant Pere Pescador

Camping Las Palmeras

Ctra de la Platja, E-17470 Sant Pere Pescador (Girona) T: 972 520 506. E: info@campinglaspalmeras.com

alanrogers.com/ES80330

A very polished site, the pleasant experience begins as you enter the palm bedecked site and are welcomed at the airy reception building. The 230 pitches are flat, very clean and well maintained, with some shade and 10A electricity. A few pitches are complete with water and drainage. Thirty smart mobile homes are placed unobtrusively around the site. A very pleasant pool complex has a lifeguard and the brightly coloured play areas are clean and safe. A great beach is just a 200 m. walk through a gate at the rear of the site. A full activities programme for children allows parents a break during the day and there is organised fun in the evenings in high season. Full recreational facilities include a gym. The very Spanish style restaurant serves high quality food. The owner, Juan Carlos Alcantara, and his wife have many years experience in the campsite business which is clearly demonstrated. You will enjoy your stay here as there is a very happy atmosphere.

Facilities

Two excellent, clean, solar powered toilet blocks include first class facilities for disabled campers. Baby rooms. Facilities may become a little busy at peak periods. Washing machines. Motorcaravan services. Supermarket, restaurant/bar/takeaway open all season (children's menu). Swimming pools (heated). Play areas. Tennis. five-a-side. Fronton. Boules. Gym. Barbecue. Bicycle hire. Miniclub. Entertainment. Satellite TV. Internet access. WiFi throughout (charged). ATM. Torches useful. Off site: Beach and fishing 200 m. Sailing and boat launching 2 km.

Open: 31 March - 20 October.

Directions

Sant Pere Pescador is south of Perpignan between Roses and L'Escala. From the AP7/E15 take exit 4 onto N11 north towards Figueres and then the C31 towards Torroella de Fluvia. Take Vilamacolum road east and continue to Sant Pere Pescador. Site signed in town. GPS: 42.18805, 3.1027

Charges 2012

Per unit incl. 2 persons and electricity	€ 24.30 - € 52.90
extra person	€ 3.20 - € 4.60

No credit cards.

Sant Pere Pescador

Kawan Village L'Amfora

Avenida Josep Tarradellas, 2, E-17470 Sant Pere Pescador (Girona) T: 972 520 540.
E: info@campingamfora.com **alanrogers.com/ES80350**

This super, spacious site is family run and friendly. A Greek theme is evident, mainly in the restaurant and around the pool areas. The site is spotlessly clean and well maintained and the owner operates in an environmentally friendly way. There are 830 level, grass pitches (741 for touring units) laid out in a grid system, all with 10A electricity. Attractive trees and shrubs have been planted around each pitch. There is good shade in the more mature areas which include 64 large pitches (180 sq.m), each with an individual sanitary unit (toilet, shower and washbasin). The newer area is more open with less shade and you can choose which you would prefer. Three excellent sanitary blocks (one heated) are fully equipped and offer free hot water, each with staff on almost permanent duty to ensure very high standards are maintained. Access is good for disabled visitors. At the entrance a terraced bar and two restaurants overlook a smart pool complex that includes three pools for children, one with two water slides. In high season (from July) there is ambitious evening entertainment (pub, disco, shows) and an activity programme for children. Alongside the site, the magnificent sandy beach on the Bay of Roses offers good conditions for children and a choice of high season watersport activities.

Facilities

Three main toilet blocks, one heated, provide washbasins in cabins and roomy free showers. Baby rooms. Laundry facilities and laundry service. Motorcaravan services. Supermarket. Terraced bar, self-service and waiter-service restaurants. Pizzeria/takeaway. Restaurant and bar on the beach with limited menu (high season). Disco bar. Swimming pools (1/5-30/9). Pétanque. Tennis. Bicycle hire. Minigolf. Play area. Miniclub. Entertainment and activities. Windsurfing. Boat launching and sailing. Fishing. Exchange facilities. Games and TV rooms. Internet room and WiFi. Car wash. Torches required in beach areas. Barbecues are not permitted. Off site: Riding 4 km. Golf 15 km.

Open: 2 April - 29 September.

Directions

Sant Pere Pescador is north of Girona between Roses and L'Escala. From north on A17/E15 take exit 3 onto N11 towards Figueres and then shortly onto the C260 towards Roses. At Castello d'Empúries turn right onto GIV6216 to Sant Pere. From south on A17 use exit 5 (L'Escala) and turn to Sant Pere in Viladamat. Site is well signed in town towards the beach. GPS: 42.18147, 3.10405

Charges 2012

Per unit incl. 2 persons and electricity	€ 25.00 - € 56.20
extra person	€ 4.50 - € 6.20
child (2-9 yrs)	€ 2.50 - € 4.20
dog	€ 2.60 - € 4.95

No credit cards. Camping Cheques accepted.

Sant Pere Pescador

Camping Las Dunas

Ctra San Marti - Sant Pere, E-17470 Sant Pere Pescador (Girona) T: 972 521 717.
E: info@campinglasdunas.com **alanrogers.com/ES80400**

Las Dunas is an extremely large, impressive and well organised resort style site with many on-site activities and an ongoing programme of improvements. It has direct access to a superb sandy beach that stretches along the site for nearly a kilometre with a windsurfing school and beach bar. There is also a much used, huge swimming pool, plus a large double pool for children. Las Dunas is very large, with 1,700 individual hedged pitches (1,479 for tourers) of around 100 sq.m. laid out on flat ground in long, regular parallel rows. All have electricity (6/10A) and 180 also have water and drainage. Shade is available in some parts of the site. Pitches are usually available, even in the main season. Much effort has gone into planting palms and new trees here and the results are very attractive. The large restaurant and bar have spacious terraces overlooking the swimming pools or you can enjoy a very pleasant, more secluded, cavern style pub. A magnificent disco club is close by in a soundproofed building (although people returning from this during the night can be a problem for pitches in the central area of the site). With free quality entertainment of all types in season and positive security arrangements, this is a great site for families with teenagers. Everything is provided on site so you don't need to leave it during your stay. A member of Leading Campings Group.

Facilities

Five excellent large toilet blocks with electronic sliding glass doors (resident cleaners 07.00-21.00). British toilets but no seats, controllable hot showers and washbasins in cabins. Excellent facilities for youngsters, babies and disabled campers. Laundry facilities. Motorcaravan services. Extensive supermarket, boutique and other shops. Large bar with terrace. Large restaurant. Takeaway. Ice cream parlour. Beach bar in main season. Disco club. Swimming pools. Playgrounds. Tennis. Archery. Minigolf. Sailing/windsurfing school and other watersports. Programme of sports, games, excursions and entertainment, partly in English (15/6-31/8). Exchange facilities. ATM. Safety deposit. Internet café. WiFi (charged). Dogs taken in one section. Torches required in some areas. Off site: Resort of L'Escala 5 km. Riding and boat launching 5 km. Water park 10 km. Golf 30 km.

Open: 19 May - 2 September.

Directions

L'Escala is northeast of Girona between Palamós and Roses. From A7/E15 autostrada take exit 5 towards L'Escala on GI623. Turn north 2 km. before L'Escala towards Sant Marti d'Ampúrias. Site well signed. GPS: 42.16098, 3.13478

Charges guide

Per unit incl. 2 persons and electricity	€ 21.00 - € 59.20
extra person	€ 3.50 - € 5.75
child (3-10 yrs)	€ 3.00 - € 3.25
dog	€ 3.20 - € 4.50

Sant Pere Pescador

Camping Riu

Ctra de la Platja s/n, E-17470 Sant Pere Pescador (Girona) T: 972 520 216. E: info@campingriu.com
alanrogers.com/ES80320

Camping Riu is an established campsite which has been purchased and upgraded by the Senia group. The pool and gym areas are brilliant for such a small site. There are 200 pitches of which 190 are for tourers with electricity (5/10A mostly Europlug) on flat ground and are shaded by mature trees. The bungalows are in a separate area away from the touring pitches. The pleasant bar/restaurant and terrace overlook the floodlit pool and children's area, where some entertainment is held in high season. Riu is on the Fluvia river, 1.5 km. from the sea.

Facilities

Two toilet blocks are clean and well positioned with good showers. Almost all WCs are British style. Facilities for disabled visitors. Baby room. Washing machines. Gas supplies. Motorcaravan service point. Supermarket, pleasant bar and restaurant, takeaway. Swimming pool and new pool for children. Adventure playground. Internet. Gym. Bicycle hire. Activities programme (high season). Kayaking (rental at reception). Tennis. Fishing. Barbecue area. Satellite TV in bar. Torches useful. Off site: Public transport 400 m. Road train to beach (high season).

Open: 31 March - 16 September.

Directions

Sant Pere Pescador is between Roses and L'Escala. From AP7/E15 exit 4 take N11 north towards Figueres and then C31 towards Torroella de Fluvia. Take Vilamacolum road east and continue to Sant Pere Pescador. Site is well signed in the town. GPS: 42.18757, 3.08914

Charges guide

Per unit incl. 2 persons and electricity	€ 20.90 - € 45.00
extra person	€ 3.00 - € 4.70

Sant Pere Pescador

Camping La Ballena Alegre

183

Ctra Sant Marti d'Empuries s/n, E-17470 Sant Pere Pescador (Girona) T: 902 510 520.
E: info@ballena-alegre.com **alanrogers.com/ES80600**

La Ballena Alegre is partly in a lightly wooded setting, partly open, and has almost 2 km. of frontage directly onto an excellent beach of soft golden sand (which is cleaned daily). They claim that none of the 966 touring pitches is more than 100 m. from the beach. The grass pitches are individually numbered and there is a choice of size (up to 120 sq.m). Electrical connections (5/10A) are available in all areas and there are 670 fully serviced pitches. A recent addition is a resort village area within the site with holiday homes and its own small pool and play area. This is a great site for families. There are restaurant and bar areas beside the pleasant terraced pool complex (four pools including a pool for children). For those who wish to drink and snack late there is a pub open until 03.00. The well managed, soundproofed disco is popular with youngsters. A little train ferries people along the length of the site and a road train runs to local villages. Plenty of entertainment and activities are offered, including a well managed watersports centre, with sub-aqua, windsurfing and kite-surfing, where equipment can be hired and lessons taken. You can also use a comprehensive open-air fitness centre near the beach. A full entertainment programme is provided all season. An overflow area across the road provides additional parking and sports activities. The site has won Spanish tourist board awards and is keen on ecological fitness.

Facilities

Seven well maintained toilet blocks are of a very high standard. Facilities for children, babies and disabled campers. Launderette. Motorcaravan services. Gas supplies. Supermarket. 'Linen' restaurant. Self-service restaurant and bar. Takeaway. Pizzeria and beach bar in high season. Swimming pool complex. Jacuzzi. Tennis. Watersports centre. Fitness centre. Bicycle hire. Playgrounds. Soundproofed disco. Dancing twice weekly and organised activities, sports, entertainment, etc. ATM. In high season dogs only allowed in one zone (26/6-22/8). Internet access and WiFi. Torches useful in beach areas. Off site: Go-karting nearby with bus service. Fishing 300 m.

Open: 12 May - 24 September.

Directions

From A7 Figueres - Girona autopista take exit 5 to L'Escala GI623 for 18.5 km. At roundabout take sign to Sant Marti d'Empúries and follow site signs. GPS: 42.15323, 3.11248

Charges 2012

Per unit incl. 2 persons and electricity	€ 25.60 - € 57.00
extra person	€ 4.00 - € 5.00
child (3-10 yrs)	€ 2.80 - € 3.30
dog	€ 2.30 - € 4.80

Discount of 10% on pitch charge for pensioners all season. No credit cards.

Sant Pere Pescador

Camping Aquarius

Playa s/n, E-17470 Sant Pere Pescador (Girona) T: 972 520 003. E: camping@aquarius.es

alanrogers.com/ES80500

A smart and efficient family site, Aquarius has direct access to a quiet sandy beach that slopes gently and provides good bathing (the sea is shallow for quite a long way out). Watersports are popular, particularly windsurfing (a school is provided). One third of the site has good shade with a park-like atmosphere. There are 430 touring pitches, all with electricity (6A). Markus Rupp and his wife are keen to make every visitor's experience a happy one and even issue flags to denote the number of years they have stayed at the site. The site is ideal for those who really like sun and sea, with a quiet situation. Mr Rupp has a background in architecture and a wealth of knowledge on the whole Catalan area and culture. He has written a booklet of suggested tours (available from reception). The family is justifiably proud of their most attractive and absolutely pristine site which they continually upgrade and improve.

Facilities

Fully equipped, large toilet blocks provide some cabins for each sex. Excellent facilities for disabled visitors, and baths for children. Superb new block has underfloor heating and family cabins with showers and basins. Laundry facilities. Gas supplies. Motorcaravan services. Refrigerators. Supermarket. Restaurant and bar with terrace. Takeaway. Play centre (with qualified attendant), playground and separate play area for toddlers. TV room. Surf Center. Minigolf. Bicycle hire. Barbecue and dance once weekly when numbers justify. ATM. Internet and WiFi (charged). Dogs are accepted in one section. (Note: no pool). Off site: Fishing and boat launching 3 km. Riding 6 km.

Open: 15 March - 31 October.

Directions

Recommended route is from AP7 exit 3 (Figueres Nord) direction Roses on C-68. At roundabout Castello d'Empuries take second right to Sant Pere Pescador, cross town and river bridge. From there site is well signed. GPS: 42.18092, 3.09425

Charges 2012

Per person	€ 3.15 - € 4.35
pitch	€ 9.40 - € 46.90
electricity	€ 3.80

No credit cards.

Santa Cristina d'Aro

Yelloh! Village Mas Sant Josep

Ctra Santa Cristina - Platja d'Aro km 2, E-17246 Santa Cristina d'Aro (Girona) T: 972 835 108.
E: info@campingmassantjosep.com **alanrogers.com/ES81750**

This is a very large, well appointed, open site in two parts. There are 1025 pitches with 327 for tourers in a separate area, with shade from established trees. These level pitches with some shade are in two sizes, access is good with well maintained gravel and tarmac roads. The main side of the site is centred around charming historic buildings, including a beautiful, but mysterious, locked and long unused chapel. Nearby is a huge, irregular lagoon-style pool with a bridge to a palm decorated island (lifeguards) and an excellent, safe paddling pool. A large complex including a bar, restaurant, takeaway and entertainment areas overlooks the pool.

Facilities

Two toilet blocks for tourers, ignore the block for the permanent pitches. Facilities for disabled visitors and pleasant baby rooms. Washing machines and dryers. Motorcaravan service point. Large supermarket, bars, restaurant, snack bar and takeaway, swimming pools. Playgrounds. Games room. Tennis. Squash. Minigolf. 5-a-side football. Spa room and gym. Entertainment. Hairdresser. Internet. WiFi (charged). ATM. Bicycle hire.

Open: 6 April - 11 September.

Directions

Site is at Santa Christiana d'Aro, 5 km. from the sea. From AP7 E15 (Girona - Barcelona) take exit 7 and C65 San Filiu road. Site is well signed at S. Christina d'Aro roundabout. GPS: 41.811167, 3.018217

Charges guide

Per unit incl. 2 persons and electricity	€ 15.00 - € 47.00
extra person (over 7 yrs)	€ 6.00 - € 8.00

Santa Susana

Camping Bon Repos

Malgrat de Mar, E-08398 Santa Susana (Barcelona) T: 937 678 475. E: info@campingbonrepos.com

alanrogers.com/ES82350

If you enjoy the hustle and bustle of the Costa Brava in summer, then Bon Repos is ideal, if a little expensive. It is a long, narrow coastal site with many pitches along the length of the attractive fine sandy beach with direct access and no fence. The 500 pitches are of reasonable size, flat with a sand surface and lots of shade, and with 10A electricity. The railway runs close along one side of the site, which is good for train spotters but does create a noise problem. The beach is the strong point of the site, having rocky outcrops and close by is the bar/restaurant with huge terrace.

Facilities

The two sanitary blocks are dated but clean. The number of showers is low and may be busy at peak periods. Cold water to washbasins. Units for disabled visitors. Baby room. Washing machines and dryers. Motorcaravan services. Supermarket. Restaurant. Chicken bar. Swimming pools (with lifeguard). Play area. Barbecue area. Tennis. Bicycle hire. Entertainment and happy hour. Internet and WiFi. ATM. Torches useful. Off site: Resort town nearby. Boat launching 200 m. Bicycle hire 1 km.

Open: All year.

Directions

From A7 exit 9 (A19 exit 22) take road to Malgrat de Mar, then turn south on coast road for S. Susanna. Campsite signs lead to site through high tunnel under the railway line. GPS: 41.6314, 2.7199

Charges guide

Per unit incl. 2 persons and electricity	€ 16.41 - € 46.90
extra person	€ 1.82 - € 5.20

Sitges

Camping El Garrofer

Ctra 246 km 39, E-08870 Sitges (Barcelona) T: 938 941 780. E: info@garroferpark.com

alanrogers.com/ES83920

This large, pine-covered site beside fields of vines is 900 m. from the beach, close to the pleasant town of Sitges. This is an attractive resort with seaside entertainments and is well worth exploring. The site has over 500 pitches, many of which are occupied by seasonal caravans or chalets. A central area on dusty, baked earth beneath the trees is devoted to touring caravans and a corner of the site has 28 pitches with water mainly used for large motorcaravans. All have electricity (6A). There is an open field for tents. A cosy restaurant with a small terrace offers a varied menu.

Facilities

One of the three sanitary blocks has been refurbished and provides roomy showers and special bright facilities for children. Separate baby room with bath. Good facilities for disabled campers. Laundry. Bar/restaurant and small supermarket (all season). Saltwater swimming and paddling pools (30/4-31/09). Football pitch. Tennis. Play area for older children and fenced play area for toddlers. Bicycle hire. Boules. WiFi (charged). Off site: Bus from outside site to Barcelona. Golf 500 m. Beach 900 m.

Open: 27 January - 16 December.

Directions

From north on AP7 leave at exit 29, take C15/C158 (Sitges) to join C32 motorway east. Leave at exit 26 (Sitges). From Tarragona on AP7 leave at exit 31 to join C32 motorway; continue to exit 26. Follow signs for Sitges and site along C246a to km. 39; site is on right - look for the flags. GPS: 41.23352, 1.78112

Charges guide

Per unit incl. 2 persons and electricity	€ 23.75 - € 35.40
extra person	€ 3.30 - € 5.80

Solsona

Camping El Solsones

Ctra Sant Llorenc km 2, E-25280 Solsona (Lleida) T: 973 482 861. E: info@campingsolsones.com

alanrogers.com/ES91230

Situated on a hillside, 2 km. from Solsona, this all year site has pleasant views of the hills on three sides and lots of mature trees giving a pleasant green shady appearance. With a lovely Spanish feel, it would be a pleasant spot for a short stay during any season. There are many weekend units here, and although only 72 of the 269 pitches are for touring (22 for caravans and motorcaravans and 50 for tents), we were told that finding a pitch was unlikely to be a problem. They are in separate sections of the site and are slightly sloping, with shade and 6/10A electricity.

Facilities

Modern sanitary facilities are in two buildings, with free hot water. Motorcaravan services. Supermarket. Restaurant and bar (23/6-11/9 and winter weekends). Simple meals and snacks served indoors and on the terrace. Swimming pool with lifeguard (24/6-12/9). Sports complex. Minigolf. Tennis. Bicycle hire. Play area. Miniclub. Pétanque. Aviary. Picnic area. Free WiFi over site. Dogs are not accepted. Off site: Golf, riding and skiing nearby.

Open: 8 January - 8 December.

Directions

Solsona is 45 km. northwest of Manresa, along the C55 and is on the C26 Lleida/Andorra - Barga road. Site is 2 km. out of town on the LV4241 signed to Sant Llorenc de Morunys. GPS: 42.01294, 1.51585

Charges guide

Per unit incl. 2 persons and electricity	€ 29.00 - € 37.60

Credit cards now accepted.

Tarragona

Camping Las Palmeras

Ctra N340 km 1168, E-43080 Tarragona (Tarragona) T: 977 208 081. E: laspalmeras@laspalmeras.com

alanrogers.com/ES84850

Situated amongst pine, poplar and palm trees, running parallel to a fine, white sandy beach, Camping Las Palmeras has a wonderful location. The final approach is under the railway (3.5 m) with a sharp turn into the parking area. The site is very long and thin (1.5 km. so bicycles are handy) along the shore. Most of the 700 pitches are on grass with plenty of shade. All have access to 5A electricity, although long leads may be necessary in places. For its beachside location alone, Las Palmeras is worthy of a visit and, with so many facilities on offer, it is a lively site offering something for the whole family. There is some noise from the frequent trains, which run 24 hours. The air-conditioned reception is smart and efficiently managed by helpful and welcoming staff. There are two swimming pools by the sea (12/6-15/9), one for children, and they are surrounded by a large, lawned area for sunbathing with views of the beach. This is a popular site with all nationalities.

Facilities

Four large toilet blocks attractively tiled in a traditional style, are evenly located and maintained to a high standard. Open style washbasins and good sized shower cubicles. Baby rooms. Laundry in each block. Shop, bar and beach restaurant (all season). Smaller bar and snack bar (high season only). Two swimming pools (15/6-15/9). Tennis. Two large play areas. Children's club in high season. Internet terminals and WiFi (code). Gas barbecues only in high seson. Off site: Town 4 km. Riding 6 km. Golf 5 km.

Open: 1 April - 12 October.

Directions

Las Palmeras is easily accessed from the N340 (Barcelona - Tarragona) and is signed after the 1169 km. marker. Beware of the sharp bend at the entrance. GPS: 41.13019, 1.3117

Charges guide

Per unit incl. electricity	€ 12.00 - € 29.00
person	€ 6.00 - € 10.50
child (under 10 yrs)	€ 5.00 - € 7.50
dog	€ 3.00 - € 5.00

Camping Cheques accepted.

Tarragona

Camping Torre de la Mora

Ctra N340 km 1171, E-43080 Tarragona (Tarragona) T: 977 650 277. E: campmora@tinet.fut.es

alanrogers.com/ES84860

Located on a promontory in a pleasant corner of the Costa Daurada with a village like atmosphere, Torre de la Mora takes advantage of its wonderful location, offering some pitches with beautiful views over the white sandy beaches and rocky promontories of the coastline. The hinterland is pine forest and there are areas where you can pitch a tent, access electricity (6A) and feel close to nature. The 200 touring pitches vary in just about every way, some are on the lower flat area, including a few with beach frontage, others are on steep terraces around the promontory. Many of the higher pitches around the old coastal defence fort and building have amazing views. It is important to select a pitch related to your level of fitness as the higher pitches and some of the lower terraces require an energetic approach (children should be supervised). Some areas of the site reflect its age, the sports area is across a small road, which has a pleasant large pool in a garden-like setting.

Facilities

Two large and three small sanitary blocks have been refurbished and are kept clean. There is a mixture of washing facilities, which have hot water, but this fades at peak periods. Facilities for disabled campers (careful selection of pitch is required). Washing machine. Motorcaravan services. Supermarket. Restaurant. Swimming pool and sports area. Play area. Entertainment. WiFi (code). Torches useful. Barbecues are not permitted. Pets welcome. Off site: Pretty beach town outside the gate. Fishing. Bicycle hire 1 km. Golf 2 km. Riding 3 km. Boat launching 8 km.

Open: 18 March - 31 October.

Directions

From A7 (Barcelona - Tarragona) take exit 32, then N340 towards Tarragona. Turn off for Punta del la Mora and site is well signed approaching the village. The final approach is via some narrow streets so watch for one way signs and there is an unusual entry through a high wire fence alongside road. GPS: 41.128, 1.344

Charges guide

Per unit incl. 1 person and electricity	€ 20.35 - € 38.40
extra person	€ 4.60 - € 9.30
child (3-11 yrs)	€ 3.40 - € 5.35
dog	€ 1.80 - € 3.00

Tarragona

Camping Tamarit Park Resort

N340a km 1172, Tamarit, E-43008 Tarragona (Tarragona) T: 977 650 128. E: resort@tamarit.com

alanrogers.com/ES84830

This is a marvellous, beach-side site, attractively situated at the foot of Tamarit castle at one end of a superb one kilometre long beach of fine sand. It is landscaped with lush Mediterranean shrubs, studded with pines and palms, and home to mischievous red squirrels. The 470 good sized pitches have 10A electricity (most with water) and 50 are virtually on the beach, so are very popular. On hard sand and grass, some are attractively separated by hedging and shaded by trees. The management and staff here are very keen to please and standards are very high. The charming restaurant and snack bar both serve typical Spanish dishes whilst enjoying superb views of the sandy beach and castle. The vast, lagoon-type swimming pool and paddling pool boasts a restaurant, snack bar, two bars, and sun terraces. It is excellent. The site boundary with the beach has three controlled accesses. Tamarit would be a good choice for watersport enthusiasts or a family holiday by the sea. The early morning sun shining on the blue sea and the golden stone of Tamarit castle high above is a memorable sight!

Facilities

The high quality sanitary blocks (two heated) are modern and tiled. Hot water is available throughout. Private bathrooms to rent. Laundry facilities. Motorcaravan services. Fridge hire. Gas supplies. Supermarket, boutique, bars, restaurant and takeaway. Bakery. Wellness area. Swimming pool (all season). Tennis and Padel courts. Pétanque. Bicycle hire. Minigolf. Playground. Sports zone. Club room with bar. Miniclub. Entertainment programme all season. Fishing. Internet access and WiFi (code). Pets allowed. Gas only barbecues. Off site: Village 1.5 km. along beach. Golf 8 km. Tarragona 9 km. Riding 15 km. Port Aventura 16 km.

Open: 15 April - 16 October.

Directions

From A7 take exit 32 towards Tarragona and continue for 4.5 km. At roundabout (km. 1172) turn back towards Atafulla/Tamarit and after 200 m. turn right to Tamarit (beside Caledonia Bungalow Park). Take care over railway bridge, then immediately sharp left. Site is on left after 1 km. having passed another campsite (Trillas Tamarit).
GPS: 41.1316, 1.3610

Charges guide

Per unit incl. 2 persons	€ 12.00 - € 80.00
extra person	€ 6.00
child (6-12 yrs)	free - € 4.00
dog	free - € 5.00

Discounts for students, pensioners, large families and longer stays in low season. Minimum stay 7 nights 1/7-29/8.

Torroella de Montgrí

Camping El Delfin Verde

Ctra de Torroella de Montgrí, E-17257 Torroella de Montgrí (Girona) T: 972 758 454.
E: info@eldelfinverde.com **alanrogers.com/ES80800**

A popular and high quality site in a quiet location, El Delfin Verde has its own long beach stretching along its frontage where activities such as scuba diving are organised. A prime feature of this site is an attractive large pool in the shape of a dolphin with a total area of 1,800 sq.m. This is a large site with 1,265 touring pitches and around 6,000 visitors at peak times. It is well managed by friendly staff. Level grass pitches are 100-110 sq.m. and marked, with many separated by small fences and hedging. All have electricity (5/6A) and access to water points. A stream runs through the centre of the site. There is shade in some of the older parts and a particularly pleasant area of pine trees in the centre provides marked but not separated pitches (sandy and not so level). The pool has two island areas, one containing a huge fountain which can be lit at night. In the main season an elevated area with a large bar, full restaurant and a separate takeaway give wonderful views over the huge pool. There is a further restaurant with slightly cheaper, good value food in the main complex with an open-air arena for entertainment. El Delfin Verde is a large and happy holiday site with many good facilities, sports and a free family entertainment programme in season. It is well worth considering for a Costa Brava holiday. Used by British tour operators (60 pitches).

Facilities

Six excellent large and refurbished toilet blocks plus a seventh smaller block, all with resident cleaners, have showers using desalinated water and some washbasins in cabins. Laundry facilities. Motorcaravan services. Supermarket and shops. Swimming pools with lifeguard (from 1/5). Two restaurants, grills and pizzerias. Three bars. 'La Vela' barbecue and party area. Large sports area. 2 km. exercise track. Dancing and entertainment weekly in season. Excursions. Bicycle hire. Minigolf. Extensive new playground. Trampolines. Beach access. Scuba diving. Fishing. Hairdresser. Car servicing. Gas supplies. Internet café. WiFi. Dogs are not accepted in high season (11/7-14/8). Off site: Golf (20% discount) and riding 4 km.

Open: 28 April - 23 September.

See advertisement on the back cover.

Directions

Torroella de Montgrí is close to the coast, east of Girona. From A7/E15 take exit 6 and C66 (Palafrugell). Then the GI642 east to Parlava and turn north on C31 (L'Escala). Cross River Ter and turn east on C31 (Ulla and Torroella de Montgrí). Site signed off the C31 and has a long approach road. Watch for white dolphin marker and flags on the left. GPS: 42.01197, 3.18807

Charges guide

Per unit incl. 2 persons and electricity	€ 30.50 - € 55.00
extra person	€ 4.75 - € 5.50
child (2-9 yrs)	€ 4.00 - € 5.00
dog (excl. 10/7-14/8)	€ 4.00

Special offers on long stays in low season.

Tossa de Mar

Camping Cala Llevadó

Ctra GI-682 de Tossa a Lloret pk. 18,9, E-17320 Tossa de Mar (Girona) T: 972 340 314.
E: info@calallevado.com **alanrogers.com/ES82000**

For splendour of position, Cala Llevadó can compare with almost any in this guide. A beautifully situated cliff-side site, enjoying fine views of the sea and coast below. It is shaped something like half a bowl with steep slopes. High up on the site, with a superb aspect, is the attractive restaurant/bar with a large terrace overlooking the pleasant swimming pool directly below. There are terraced, flat areas for caravans and tents (with 10/16A electricity) on the upper levels of the two slopes, with a great many individual pitches for tents scattered around the site. Some of these pitches have fantastic settings and views. The site is unsuitable for campers with disabilities. In some areas cars may be required to park separately. Many of the 577 touring pitches are available for caravans. There are a few tour operator pitches (45) and 26 bungalows. The steepness of the site would make access difficult for disabled visitors or those with limited mobility. One beach is for all manner of watersports within a buoyed area and there is a sub-aqua diving school. Some other pleasant little coves can also be reached by climbing down on foot (with care!).

Facilities

Four very well equipped toilet blocks are immaculately maintained and well spaced around the site. Baby baths. Laundry facilities. Motorcaravan services. Gas supplies. Fridge hire. Large supermarket. Restaurant/bar (5/5-28/9). Swimming and paddling pools. Three play areas. Botanic garden. New amphitheatre (2011) with entertainment for children and adults. Sailing, water skiing and windsurfing school. Fishing. Excursions. Internet access and WiFi. Torches definitely needed in some areas. Off site: Bicycle hire 3 km. Riding 10 km.

Open: 1 May - 30 September.

Directions

Cala Llevadó is southeast of Girona on the coast. Leave the AP7/E15 at exit 7 to the C65 Sant Feliu road and then take C35 southeast to the GI681 to Tossa de Mare. Site is signed off the GI682 Lloret - Tossa road at km. 18.9, about 3 km. from Tossa. Route avoids difficult coastal road.
GPS: 41.71282, 2.90623

Charges 2012

Per unit incl. 2 persons and electricity (6A)	€ 29.90 - € 49.90

Vilanova de Prades

Camping & Bungalow Park Serra de Prades

Sant Antoni s/n, E-43439 Vilanova de Prades (Tarragona) T: 977 869 050. E: info@serradeprades.com
alanrogers.com/ES85060

On the edge of the village of Vilanova, nestling in granite foothills with superb views from its elevation of 950 m, this is a welcoming and peaceful site. The 215 pitches are on terraces formed with natural stone and with good access. With 120 for touring units (all with 6A electricity), the remainder are occupied by seasonal caravans. The upper tent pitches have wonderful views. Hedges and trees separate pitches providing a pleasant green environment and some shade. From here it is possible to enjoy the wonderful Prades mountains or a day on the beach an hour's drive away.

Facilities

The modern, heated toilet block has washbasins in cabins. Facilities for disabled visitors and babies. Laundry facilities. Motorcaravan service point. Shop. Bar and restaurant with takeaway. Heated outdoor swimming pool (24/6-15/9). Gym. Archery. Quad bike and 4x4 hire. Paintball. Tennis. Riding with guided treks. Bicycle hire. Entertainment in season. Gas supplies. Chalets for rent. Torches required in some areas. WiFi throughout (charged).

Open: All year.

Directions

From east, leave AP2 (Barcelona/Lleida) at exit 9 (Montblanc) and join N240 towards Lleida. At km. 48 west of Vimbod, turn south towards Vallclara, then Vilanova de Prades. Site on right after roundabout at entrance to village. GPS: 41.3497, 0.95852

Charges guide

Per unit incl. 2 persons and electricity	€ 33.00

Camping Cheques accepted.

Vilanova i la Geltrú

Vilanova Park

184

Ctra de l'Arboc km 2.5, E-08800 Vilanova i la Geltrú (Barcelona) T: 938 933 402. E: info@vilanovapark.es

alanrogers.com/ES83900

Sitting on the terrace in front of the restaurant – a beautifully converted Catalan farmhouse dating from 1908 – it is difficult to believe that in 1982 this was still a farm with few trees and known as Mas Roque (Rock Farm). Since then, imaginative planting has led to there being literally thousands of trees and gloriously colourful shrubs making this large campsite most attractive. It has an impressive range of high quality amenities and facilities open all year. There are 336 marked pitches for touring units in separate areas, all with 6/10A electricity, 168 larger pitches also have water and, in some cases, drainage. They are on hard surfaces, on gently sloping ground and with plenty of shade. A further 1,000 or so pitches are mostly occupied by chalets to rent, and by tour operators. The amenities include an excellent pool with water jets and at night time a coloured, floodlit fountain, which complements the dancing and entertainment taking place in the courtyard above. Nearby is a pleasant nature park with picnic tables. A second pool higher up the site has marvellous views across the town to the sea; here also is an indoor pool and wellness complex and in high season a second, more intimate restaurant, for a special romantic dinner overlooking the twinkling evening lights.

Facilities

All toilet blocks are of excellent quality, can be heated and have controllable showers and washbasins in cabins. Hot water to dishwashing and laundry sinks. Baby rooms. Units for disabled visitors. Serviced and self-service laundry. Motorcaravan services. Supermarket. Souvenir shop. Restaurants. Bar with simple meals and tapas. Outdoor pools (1/4-15/10), indoor pool (all year, charged). Wellness centre with sauna, jacuzzi and gym. Play areas. Sports field. Games room. Excursions and activity and entertainment for all ages. Bicycle hire. Tennis. ATM and exchange facilities. WiFi (charged). Caravan storage can be arranged. Off site: Golf and riding 1 km. Fishing, sailing and boat launching 3 km. Shops, restaurants and bars in Vilanova 3 km. (local buses). Excursions arranged to Barcelona, Monserrat and Bodegas Torres (wine-tasting).

Open: All year.

Directions

Vilanova i la Geltrú is 45 km. southwest of Barcelona. Site is 3 km. northwest of town towards L'Arboc (BV2115). From AP7 from Tarragona take exit 31 onto C32 motorway and leave at exit 16 for Vilanova. Site is on left in 2 km. (use loop on right to cross road). On AP7 from Barcelona take exit 29 onto C15 Vilanova, then C31 west to km. 153, and turn north on BV2115. Site is on right. GPS: 41.23237, 1.69092

Charges guide

Per unit incl. 2 persons and electricity	€ 27.20 - € 46.70
extra person	€ 5.60 - € 10.10
child (4-11 yrs)	€ 3.20 - € 6.10
dog	€ 6.00 - € 12.00

Camping Cheques accepted.

We can book this site for you! alan rogers travel
Call 01580 214000

This Mediterranean region is famous for its magnificent orange groves and beautiful long, sandy beaches. Centuries of Moorish presence have resulted in a profound Hispano-Moorish heritage.

VALENCIANA IS MADE UP OF THE PROVINCES OF CASTELLON, VALENCIA AND ALICANTE

THE CAPITAL OF THE REGION IS VALENCIA

La Costa del Azahar (Orange-blossom Coast) stretches from Vinaros to Almanzora, with the great port of Valencia in the centre. Orange groves grow right down to the coast, particularly in the northern section. Good beaches can be found around Benicassim and Peñíscola. South of Valencia, the Costa Blanca derives its name from its 170 miles or so of silvery-white beaches – some of the best beaches are to be found on this coast, especially between Gandía and Benidorm. As a result, it is one of the most popular tourist areas in Spain. The capital city of Valencia boasts a great nightlife and plays host to numerous festivals held throughout the year, including the unique fiesta of Las Fallas de Saint Joseph, when enormous papier-mâché sculptures are set ablaze. Throughout it all are bullfights, music and fireworks. Alicante, the capital of the province of the same name, is dominated by the great Moorish castle of Santa Barbara, which offers marvellous views of the entire city. It also has several beaches in and around the town.

Places of interest

Castellón de la Plana: Santa Maria cathedral.

El Puig: monastery, Museum of Print and Graphics (world's smallest book).

La Albufera: vast lagoon, home to 250 species of bird.

Morella: medieval fortress town, dinosaur museum.

Oropesa: 16th-century Tower of the King.

Peñiscola: medieval castle.

Cuisine of the region

Rice is the dominant ingredient, grown locally in paddy fields; the most famous dish is the *Paella Valenciana*. Soups and stews known locally as *ollas* are popular and seafood is readily available. Tiger nut milk is a soft drink exclusive to this region, usually accompanied by *fartons* (local pastries).

Arnadí: dessert with pumpkin and sweet potato.

Arroz al horno: rice baked with chickpeas.

Arroz con costra: meat based paella topped with baked egg crust.

Arroz negro: rice cooked with squid.

Bajoques farcides: stuffed peppers.

Olla recapte: with potatoes and pork.

Turrón: made of nuts and honey, either soft and flaky or hard like nougat.

0
25
50
75
100 kms
CATALUNYA
ARAGON
MORELLA
VINAROS
TERUEL
A7/E15
ALCOSSEBRE
RIBERA DE CABANES
BENICASIM
CASTELLON DE LA PLANA
NAVAJAS
MONCOFA
CASTILLA-
LA MANCHA
COMUNIDAD
VALENCIANA
VILLARGORDO DEL CABRIEL
VALENCIA
A3/E901
CULLERA
A7/E15
ALBACETE
GANDIA
OLIVA
CAMPELL
JAVEA
BOCAIRENT
MORAIRA
BENIDORM
VILLAJOYOSA
EL CAMPELLO
ALICANTE
A7/E15
MURCIA
CREVILLENTE
LA MARINA
CARAVACA DE LE CRUZ
MURCIA
GUARDAMAR DEL SEGURA
A37
SAN MIGUEL DE SALINAS
PILAR DE LA HORADADA
SAN PEDRO DEL PINATAR

Alcossebre

Camping Playa Tropicana

Playa Tropicana, E-12579 Alcossebre (Castelló) T: 964 412 463. E: info@playatropicana.com

alanrogers.com/ES85600

Playa Tropicana is a unique site which will strike visitors immediately as being very different. It has been given a tropical theme with scores of Romanesque white statues around the site, including in the sanitary blocks. The site has 300 marked pitches separated by lines of flowering bushes under mature trees. The pitches vary in size (50-90 sq.m), most are shaded and there are electricity connections throughout (some need long leads). There are 50 pitches with shared water and drainage on their boundaries. The site has a delightful position away from the main hub of tourism, alongside a good sandy beach which shelves gently into the clean waters. To gain access to this it is necessary to cross a promenade in front of the site, which also has statues. It is in a quiet position and it is a drive rather than a walk to the centre of the village resort. The theme extends into an excellent restaurant where, in high season, you may dine on the upper terrace with uninterrupted sea views.

Facilities

Three sanitary blocks delightfully decorated, fully equipped and of excellent standard, include washbasins in private cabins. Baby baths and facilities for disabled visitors. Washing machine. Motorcaravan services. Gas supplies. Large supermarket. Superb restaurant. (Easter-late Sept). Swimming pools (including new indoor facility) and children's pool. Playground. Bicycle hire. Children's club. Fishing. Torches necessary in some areas. No TVs allowed in July/Aug. Dogs are accepted in one area. WiFi throughout (charged). Off site: Fishing and watersports on the beaches. Riding and boat launching 3 km. Golf 40 km.

Open: All year.

Directions

Alcoceber (or Alcossebre) is between Peñiscola and Oropesa. Turn off N340 at 1018 km. marker towards Alcossebre on CV142. Just before entering town proceed through two sets of traffic lights and turn right immediately after the second set, follow the road to the coast and site is 2.5 km. The entrance sliding gate faces the coast road and incorporates a pedestrian gate. Avoid alternative route given by GPS as that road is very narrow in places and very uneven. GPS: 40.222, 0.267

Charges 2012

Per unit incl. 2 persons and electricity	€ 24.50 - € 48.00
extra person	€ 5.00 - € 7.00
child (1-10 yrs)	€ 4.00 - € 6.00

Alcossebre

Camping Ribamar

Partida Ribamar s/n, E-12579 Alcossebre (Castelló) T: 964 761 163. E: info@campingribamar.com

alanrogers.com/ES85610

Camping Ribamar is tucked away within the National Park of the Sierra de Irta, to the north of Alcossebre, and with direct access to a rugged beach. There are two grades of pitches on offer here. A number of standard pitches are available for small tents. These pitches of around 30 sq.m. have electrical connections. The majority of pitches are larger (90-100 sq.m) and are classed as premium, with electricity and a water supply. A number of chalets (with air conditioning) are available for rent. Leisure facilities here include a large swimming pool plus delightful children's pool and a paddling pool. A main amenities building is adjacent and houses the site's slightly sterile bar/restaurant and shop. The Sierra de Irta is a magnificent landscape of intense colours. Although little over two hours' drive south of Barcelona, this is a very under populated region with some excellent long distance footpaths and cycle paths. Alcossebre is a delightful resort town which has retained its Spanish identity unlike some of the larger resorts to the north. The town has three Blue Flag beaches and a wealth of cafés and restaurants.

Facilities

One spotlessly clean toilet block with facilities for babies and campers with disabilities. Dishwashing and laundry facilities. Bar. Restaurant. Shop. Swimming pool. Paddling pool. Multisports terrain. Tennis. Five-a-side football. Boules. Paddle court. Bicycle hire. Play area. Library/social room. Tourist information. Chalets for rent. Direct access to rocky beach. Fishing. WiFi. Charcoal barbecues are not allowed. Off site: Beach 2 km. Alcossebre 3 km. Riding 10 km. Golf 35 km. Coastal walks.

Open: All year.

Directions

Leave the AP7 motorway at exit 44 and follow signs to Alcossebre using N340 and CV142. The site can be found to the north of the town. Follow signs to Sierra de Irta and then the site, which is 2.5 km. along a dusty, gravel track.
GPS: 40.270282, 0.306729

Charges 2012

Per unit incl. 2 persons and electricity	€ 22.20 - € 47.00
extra person	€ 3.70 - € 5.25
child (3-12 yrs)	€ 2.90 - € 4.50

Benicasim

Bonterra Park

Avenida de Barcelona 47, E-12560 Benicasim (Castelló) T: 964 300 007. E: info@bonterrapark.com

alanrogers.com/ES85800

If you are looking for a town site which is not too crowded and has very good facilities, this one may be for you. It is a 300 m. walk to a good beach – and parking is not too difficult. The site has 320 pitches (70-90 sq.m), all with electricity (6/10A) and a variety of bungalows, some attractively built in brick. There are dedicated 'green' pitches for tents. Bonterra has a clean and neat appearance with tarmac roads, gravel covered pitches, palms, grass and a number of trees which give good shade. Overhead sunshades are provided for the more open pitches in summer. There is a little road and rail noise. The site has an attractive pool complex including a covered pool for the winter months. The beach is good for scuba diving or snorkelling – hire facilities are available at Benicasim. This is a well run, Mediterranean style site, usefully located for visiting attractions such as the Carmelite monastery at Desierto de las Palmas, six kilometres distant, or the historic town of Castellon.

Facilities

Four attractive, well maintained sanitary blocks provide some private cabins, some washbasins with hot water, others with cold. Baby and dog showers. Facilities for disabled campers. Laundry. Motorcaravan services. Restaurant/bar. Shop. Swimming pool (heated Sept-June) and paddling pool. Playground (some concrete bases). Tennis. Multisports court. Gym. Disco. Bicycle hire. Miniclub. Satellite TV. Internet access (WiFi). Dogs are not accepted in July/Aug. Off site: Town facilities. Sandy beach and fishing 500 m. Riding 3 km. Boat launching 4 km. Golf 12 km. Nature Park.

Open: All year.

Directions

Site is on the quiet old main road running through Benicasim. From either direction leave the N340 at km. 987. At roundabout turn left and travel for about 1.5 km. to site on the left (white painted walls). Look for two supermarkets, one 200 m. before site and a second directly opposite. Site is well signed. GPS: 40.05708, 0.07432

Charges 2012

Per unit incl. 2 persons and electricity	€ 28.72 - € 52.26
extra person	€ 4.30 - € 6.26
child (0-9 yrs)	€ 3.65 - € 5.10

Benidorm

Camping Benisol

Avenida de la Comunidad Valenciana s/n, E-03500 Benidorm (Alacant) T: 965 851 673.
E: campingbenisol@yahoo.es **alanrogers.com/ES86830**

Camping Benisol is a well developed and peaceful site with lush, green vegetation and a mountain background. Mature hedges and trees afford privacy to each pitch and some artificial shade is provided where necessary. There are 298 pitches of which around 115 are for touring units (60-80 sq.m). All have electrical hook-ups (4/6A) and 75 have drainage. All the connecting roads are now surfaced with tarmac. Some daytime road noise should be expected. The site has an excellent restaurant with a pretty, shaded terrace overlooking the pool with its palms and thatched pool bar.

Facilities

Modern sanitary facilities, heated in winter and kept very clean, have free, solar heated hot water to washbasins, showers and sinks. Laundry facilities. Gas supplies. Restaurant with terrace and bar (all year, closed 1 day a week). Shop. Swimming pool (Easter-Nov). Small, old style play area. Minigolf. Jogging track. Tennis. Golf driving range. ATM. WiFi. Off site: Riding 1 km. Bicycle hire and sea fishing 3 km. Golf 14 km. Bus route.

Open: All year.

Directions

Site is northeast of Benidorm. Exit N332 at 152 km. marker and take turn signed Playa Levant. Site is 100 m. on left off the main road, well signed. GPS: 38.559, -0.097

Charges guide

Per person	€ 4.95 - € 5.25
pitch	€ 13.25 - € 18.10
electricity	€ 2.80

No credit cards.

Benidorm

Camping Villasol

Avenida Bernat de Sarria no. 13., E-03503 Benidorm (Alacant) T: 965 850 422. E: info@camping-villasol.com

alanrogers.com/ES86810

Benidorm is increasingly popular for winter stays and Villasol is a genuinely good, purpose built modern site. Many of the 309 well separated pitches are arranged on wide terraces which afford views of the mountains surrounding Benidorm. All pitches (80-85 sq.m) have electricity and satellite TV connections, with 160 with full services for seasonal use. Shade is mainly artificial. Reservations are only accepted for winter stays of over three months (from 1/10). There is a small indoor pool, heated for winter use, and a very attractive outdoor pool complex (summer only) overlooked by the bar/restaurant and elevated terrace. This complex features a sheltered pool in a beautifully landscaped, grassy sunbathing area where palm trees, shrubs and flowers create a colourful and exotic atmosphere. The town and Levante beach are within easy walking distance (1.3 km). If you are looking for first class amenities in Benidorm, this site would make an excellent choice. Part of the site will be lost to a road widening scheme.

Facilities

Modern toilet blocks provide free, controllable hot water to showers and washbasins and British WCs. Good facilities for disabled campers. Laundry facilities. Good value restaurant. Bar. Shop. Swimming pools, outdoor and indoor. Satellite TV. Playground. Evening entertainment programme. Safes. Dogs are not accepted.
Off site: Beach, fishing and bicycle hire 1.3 km.
Riding and sailing 3km. Golf 8 km.

Open: All year.

Directions

From autopista exit 65 (Benidorm). Turn left at second set of traffic lights. After 1 km. at lights turn right, then right again at next lights. Site is on right in 400 m. From northern end of N332 bypass follow signs for Benidorm Playa Levante. In 500 m. at traffic lights turn left, then right at next lights. Site is on right after 400 m. GPS: 38.538, -0.119

Charges guide

Per person	€ 5.50 - € 7.20
pitch incl. car	€ 11.20 - € 26.40
electricity	€ 4.15

Benidorm

Camping Caravaning El Raco

Avenida Doctor Severo Ochoa 35, E-03503 Benidorm (Alacant) T: 965 868 552. E: info@campingraco.com

alanrogers.com/ES86850

This purpose built site with good facilities provides about 597 pitches (90 for touring units). There is wide access from the Rincon de Loix road. The site is situated 1.5 km. from the town, Levante beach and promenade. Pitches are 80 sq.m. or more, separated by low cypress hedging and some trees which provide some shade. Satellite TV connections are provided to each pitch and there are 90 with all services including electricity. The restaurant, bar and elegant pools are all at the entrance.

Facilities

Four large toilet blocks are well equipped. Facilities for disabled visitors and babies. Dishwashing sinks. Laundry facilities. Gas supplies. Motorcaravan services. Large restaurant. Bar. Well stocked shop. Busy bar with TV also open to public and restaurant. Outdoor swimming pool, no slides or diving board (1/4-31/10). Indoor heated pool (1/11-31/3). Playground. ATM. WiFi. Off site: Beach 1 km. Bicycle hire 2 km. Golf 6 km. Theme parks.

Open: All year.

Directions

From autopista exit 65 (Benidorm, Levante) at second set of traffic lights turn left on N332 (Altea, Valencia). After 1.5 km. turn right (Playa Levante), then straight on at next lights for 300 m. to site on right. From north on N332 follow signs for Playa Levante (or Benidorm Palace). At lights turn left (Playa Levante). Site signed. GPS: 38.5487, -0.0991

Charges guide

Per person	€ 5.70 - € 6.60
pitch incl. electricity (10A)	€ 17.00 - € 19.00

No credit cards.

Bocairent

Camping Mariola

Ctra Bocairent - Alcoi km 9, E-46880 Bocairent (Valencia) T: 962 135 160. E: info@campingmariola.com
alanrogers.com/ES86450

Situated high in the Sierra Mariola National Park, in a beautiful rural setting but only 12 km. from the old town of Bocairent, this is a real taste of Spain with hilltop views all around. Used mainly by the Spanish, the site is an undiscovered jewel with 170 slightly sloping pitches. These are well spaced and have shade from a mixture of young and mature trees. An orchard area well away from the main site (with no amenities close by) is used for more casual camping. A traditional, stone built restaurant is slightly elevated with views over the site. Accessed by a few steps, this attractive building is covered in roses. It offers a traditional Spanish menu and is open seven days a week in high season. The good sized swimming pool and play area are away from the serviced pitches giving a feeling of spaciousness.

Facilities

Six identical small toilet blocks offer adequate facilities with British style WCs and showers with shared changing area. Open style washbasins. No facilities for disabled visitors. Washing machine. Motorcaravan services. Small shop (weekends only). Bar/restaurant (weekends only in low season). Satellite TV. Outdoor pool with separate paddling pool (June-Sept). Two multisports pitches. Play area. Communal barbecue area. Children's club and entertainment (Aug. only). Off site: Riding and golf 12 km.

Open: All year.

Directions

From the CV40 take exit for Ontinyent and follow the CV81. Pass town of Bocairent heading west and in 2 km. look for camping sign (at textiles factory). Turn south on VV2031 to Alcoy. Turn right at first roundabout and straight on at next through small industrial estate. Persevere onwards and upwards for about 10 km. and site is a turn to left.
GPS: 38.753317, -0.549402

Charges guide

Per person	€ 4.45
child (3-10 yrs)	€ 3.60
pitch	€ 4.45 - € 6.00
electricity	€ 4.20

Campell

Camping Vall de Laguar

Ctra Sant Antonio 24, la Vall de Laguar, E-03791 Campell (Alacant) T: 965 577 490.
E: info@campinglaguar.com **alanrogers.com/ES86750**

Near the pretty mountain-top village of Campell, this new site is perched high on the side of a mountain with breathtaking views of hilltop villages, the surrounding hills and distant sea. With a wholehearted welcome from the owners, the well maintained site promises a real taste of Spain. The pitches, pool, terrace and restaurant all share the views. The 68 average sized gravel pitches are on terraces and all have electricity and water. Trees and hedges have been planted and now give ample shade. This is a great place to get away from the coastal hustle, bustle and high rise of the beaches. Enrique and Consuelo and their children Ivan, Neus and Irene efficiently run this charming country site.

Facilities

Two new sanitary blocks have excellent clean facilities including some for disabled campers. Washing machines and dryers. Restaurant with pretty terrace (closed Sept). Bar and small pool bar. Swimming pool. Small entertainment programme in high season. WiFi over site (free). Charcoal barbecues only (communal area). Torches useful. Off site: Attractive town close by. Golf and beach 18 km.

Open: All year.

Directions

Site is 20 km. west of Xabia/Javea. From A7/E15 exit 62 head to Ondara/Valencia on the N332 and at the roundabout on the Ondara bypass head to Benidoleig/Orba. At Orba turn right and follow the site signs. GPS: 38.7766, -0.105

Charges guide

Per unit incl. 2 persons and electricity	€ 21.75 - € 24.25
extra person	€ 5.00
dog	€ 1.30

Crevillente

Marjal Costa Blanca Eco Resort

AP7. Salida 730 (Catral-Crevillente), E-03330 Crevillente (Alacant) T: 965 484 945.
E: camping@marjalcostablanca.com **alanrogers.com/ES87435**

Marjal Costa Blanca is a brand new site. We will undertake a full inspection in 2012. There will be 1,500 pitches here, ranging in size from 90-180 sq.m. All pitches will have electricity (16A), water and drainage. A number of new mobile homes will also be available. The site is a major new initiative and is sure to become one of the most modern and best equipped campsites in Spain. Leisure amenities will include a tropically themed swimming pool complex and a state-of-the-art wellness centre. The site's principal restaurant, Marjal Plaza, is open all year and, during summer months, will feature a buffet with fresh, local produce. The site has been developed along very strict environmental guidelines. More than 7,000 mulberry trees have been planted and every effort has been made to conserve resources and use sustainable materials. There's plenty going in peak season, including a lively children's club, which will be led by the site's mascot, Marjalita.

Facilities

Tropical swimming pool complex. Supermarket. Bar, snack bar, restaurant and takeaway food. Play areas. Wellness centre. Hairdresser. Library. Tennis. Football. Entertainment and activity programme. Mobile homes and chalets to rent. Business centre. Car hire service. Pet care facilities. Tourist information. Off site: Nearest beach 15 km. El Honda Nature Reserve. Terra Mitica theme park. Cycle and walking tracks.

Open: All year.

See advertisement on page 69.

Directions

Take the southbound A7 coastal motorway until you reach the fork close to Elche - Crevillente. Continue on AP7 towards Cartagena and then take exit 730 (Catral) and follow signs to the site.
GPS: 38.177901, -0.809504

Charges guide

Per unit incl. 2 persons, and services	€ 25.00 - € 32.00
extra person	€ 4.00
child (4-12 yrs)	€ 3.00
dog	€ 1.50 - € 2.20

Cullera

Camping Santa Marta

Ctra de Faro km 2, E-46400 Cullera (Alacant) T: 961 721 440. E: info@santamartacamping.com
alanrogers.com/ES86220

Santa Marta is beautifully located on the slopes of a mountain and is shaded by many old Mediterranean umbrella pine trees. Originally a municipal site, it was recently purchased by a group of four campsites and is being fully renovated and modernised. There are 250 small, terraced pitches, 235 for touring with 16A electricity. Access can be difficult due to the many trees. An olive grove has been bought to make 18 motorcaravan pitches. Marta was a local saint and the campsite is named after her shrine which is located high above on the mountain. This shrine is accessible for good hikers by a trail starting at the ancient village bull ring at the entrance to the campsite.

Facilities

Four toilet blocks, which are very well equipped (although shower cubicles have only one hook and no shelf or soap dish). Separate facilities for women and men. Facilities for campers with disabilities. Separate baby room. Small shop. Bar serving snacks with terrace (all season). Swimming and paddling pools (23/6-16/9). Multisports field. Hiking trails in the site's grounds. Barbecues are not permitted. Off site: Shop facing the site. Town of Cullera with larger supermarkets. Beach 100 m. Kite surfing. Train and bus to Valencia (45 km).

Open: All year excl. 16 December - 14 January.

Directions

From A7/N332 (Valencia - Alicante) take exit for Cullera. Follow signs into Cullera and then signs to Faro or Far, through the centre of town. From the centre follow signs to site. GPS: 39.17694, -0.24333

Charges guide

Per unit incl. 2 persons and electricity (4A)	€ 30.00
extra person	€ 6.00
child (2-10 yrs)	€ 5.50

El Campello

Camping Costa Blanca

Calle Convento 143, N332 km 120,5, E-03560 El Campello (Alacant) T: 965 630 670.
E: info@campingcostablanca.com **alanrogers.com/ES86900**

This small site has 80 pitches with 60 for tourers, some with views of the distant hills. Bungalows line three sides of the white walled rectangular site with a railway (not too busy) on the final side. Reception is efficient with keen staff members speaking several languages. The flat pitches are on gravel and all have 6A electricity. Some are small (40, 60 or 80 sq.m) and will be a challenge for large units. There is natural shade from trees and some artificial shade. A pleasant pool is the centrepiece with a bright poolside bar and a restaurant with a patio. The pool is open to the restaurant and bar area.

Facilities

Four clean refurbished sanitary units offer a variety of facilities including cabins with toilet and basin, toilet and bidet, washbasins with hot water, others with cold. Two baby baths in cabins. Facilities for disabled campers. Washing machines and dryer. Motorcaravan services at entrance (€ 4 per token). Restaurant/bar (all year). Shop (1/7-1/9). Swimming pool. Basic play area (supervision required). Limited live entertainment in season. WiFi. Communal barbecue. Off site: Town facilities. Fishing, sailing, boat launching and watersports 500 m. ATM 1 km. Riding and golf 8 km.

Open: All year.

Directions

From the N332 take exit for El Campello Costa. Go through traffic lights onto the roundabout and take the first exit right. Site is visible from the roundabout although the name is behind the sliding gate! GPS: 38.43611, -0.38806

Charges guide

Per unit incl. 2 persons and electricity	€ 23.93 - € 44.40
extra person	€ 4.11 - € 5.95
child (1-10 yrs)	€ 3.29 - € 4.75

Gandia

Camping L'Alqueria

Avenida del Grau 142, E-46730 Grau de Gandia (Valencia) T: 962 840 470. E: lalqueria@lalqueria.com
alanrogers.com/ES86200

Camping L'Alqueria is situated on the main Gandia to Grau road and, although in an urban location, it is 1 km. from the beaches of Gandia. The 114 touring pitches are of a good size and on level ground, all with 10A electricity (Europlug) and easy access to one of many water points. Some are separated by dividing hedges and there is plenty of shade from mature trees. An orchard area to the rear of the site is designated for casual camping and is adjacent to the football pitch. There is a large swimming pool (caps required) with a sliding cover and a small paddling pool, adjacent but outside. Below the pools are a steam room, hydro-bath, sauna and jacuzzi. When we visited a temporary structure provided a small bar and snack bar whilst a new building at the entrance was being completed. A wooden cabin houses a small shop that is reasonably well stocked.

Facilities

Four toilet blocks, three with British style toilets, placed evenly around the site. Mostly combined shower and washbasin cubicles. Laundry facilities (key from reception). Motorcaravan service point. Shop (all year) and snack bar (1/4-15/10). Swimming pool (covered for 1/10-31/5) and outdoor paddling pool (1/6-15/10). Steam room and spa facilities. Fridge hire. WiFi throughout (charged). Off site: Shops, restaurant etc. within 1 km. Beach, fishing, golf, bicycle hire, riding and boat launching all 1 km.

Open: All year.

Directions

From A7 (Valencia - Alicante) take exit 60 and follow signs to Gandia on the N332. Through the town follow signs for Grau and Platja de Gandia. Site is northwest of Gandia. GPS: 38.98627, -0.16365

Charges 2012

Per unit incl. 2 persons and electricity	€ 23.30 - € 41.85
extra person	€ 3.90 - € 5.75
child (3-10 yrs)	€ 3.20 - € 4.60

Guardamar del Segura

Marjal Camping & Bungalows Resort

Ctra. N332 km 73,4, E-03140 Guardamar del Segura (Alacant) T: 966 727 070.
E: camping@marjal.com **alanrogers.com/ES87430**

alan rogers Runner up 2011 Awards

Marjal is located beside the estuary of the Segura river, alongside the pine and eucalyptus forests of the Dunas de Guardamar Natural Park. A fine sandy beach can be reached through the forest (800 m). This is a very smart site with a huge tropical lake style pool with bar and a superb sports complex. There are 212 pitches on this award-winning site, 168 for touring with water, electricity (16A), drainage and satellite TV points. The ground is covered with crushed marble, making the pitches clean and pleasant. There is some shade and the site has an open feel with lots of room for manoeuvring. Reception is housed within a delicately coloured building complete with a towering Mirador, topped by a weather vane depicting the 'garza real' (heron) bird which frequents the local area and forms part of the site logo. The large restaurant overlooks the pools and the river that leads to the sea in the near distance. The bar has large terraces fringed by trees, palms and pomegranates. The impressive pool/lagoon complex (1,100 sq.m) has a water cascade, an island bar plus bridge, one part sectioned as a pool for children and a jacuzzi. The extensive sports area is also impressive. No effort has been spared here and facilities are of the highest quality. An extensive programme of entertainment is provided for adults and children in season by a professional team.

Facilities

Three excellent heated toilet blocks have free hot water, elegant separators between sinks, spacious showers and some cabins. Each block has high quality facilities for babies and disabled campers, modern laundry and dishwashing rooms. Motorcaravan service point. Car wash. Well stocked supermarket. Restaurants. Bar. Large outdoor pool complex (1/6-31/10). Heated indoor pool (low season). Jacuzzi. Sauna. Solarium. Beauty salon. Superb well equipped gym. Aerobics. Physiotherapy. All activities discounted for campers. Play room. Minigolf. Floodlit tennis and soccer pitch. Bicycle hire. Car rental. Games room. TV room. Full entertainment programme. Hairdresser. ATM. Business centre. Internet access and free WiFi over site. Caravan storage. Off site: Beach 800 m. Fishing 1 km. Riding and golf 4 km. Parc Natural de las Dunas de Guardamar alongside site.

Open: All year.

Directions

On N332 40 km. south of Alicante, site is on the sea side between 73 and 74 km. markers.
GPS: 38.10933, -0.65467

Charges guide

Per unit incl. 2 persons and electricity	€ 38.00 - € 65.00
extra person	€ 7.00 - € 9.00
child (4-12 yrs)	€ 5.00 - € 6.00
dog	€ 2.20 - € 3.20

Low season discounts.

Jávea

Camping Jávea

Ctra Camí de la Fontana 10, Apdo 83, E-03730 Jávea (Alacant) T: 965 791 070. E: info@camping-javea.com
alanrogers.com/ES87540

The final approach to this site emerges from the bustle of the town and is decorated with palms, orange and pine trees, the latter playing host to a colony of parakeets. English is spoken at reception. The neat, boxed hedges and palms within the site, and its backdrop of hills dotted with villas presents an attractive setting. Three hectares provide space for 214 numbered pitches with 183 for touring units. Flat, level and rectangular in shape, the pitches vary in size 60-80 sq.m. All pitches have a granite chip surface and 8A electricity. Some pitches have artificial shade, although for most the pruned eucalyptus and pepper trees suffice. The restaurant provides great food, way above normal campsite standards.

Facilities

Two very clean, fully equipped, sanitary blocks include two children's toilets plus a baby bath. Separate facilities for disabled campers. Two washing machines. Fridge hire. Extensive bar and restaurant with terraces where in high season you purchase bread and milk. Large swimming pool with lifeguard and sunbathing lawns. Play area. Boules. Electronic barriers (deposit for card). Caravan storage. Post. Safes. Five-a-side footaball. Basketball. Tennis. WiFi. Car rental. Off site: Old and New Jávea within easy walking distance with supermarkets and shops catering for all needs. Sandy beach, boat launching, fishing, bicycle hire all 1.5 km. Golf 3 km.

Open: All year.

Directions

Exit N332 for Jávea on A134, continue in direction of Port (road number changes to CV 734). In town the site is well marked with large orange indicators high on posts. Watch carefully for a sudden slip road sign!
GPS: 38.78333, 0.16983

Charges guide

Per unit incl. 2 persons and electricity	€ 28.71 - € 31.40
extra person	€ 5.58 - € 6.20
child	€ 4.68 - € 5.20
dog	€ 1.50 - € 2.00

Moncofa

Camping Monmar

Ctra Serratelles s/n, E-12593 Moncofa (Castelló) T: 964 588 592. E: campingmonmar@terra.es

alanrogers.com/ES85900

This purpose built, very neat site is in the small town of Moncofa, just 200 metres from the sea and right beside a water park with pools and slides. There are 170 gravel based pitches arranged in rows off tarmac access roads. The 100 touring pitches all have 6A electricity, water and drainage. Hedges have been planted to separate the pitches but these are still small so there is little shade (canopies can be rented in high season). The site's facilities and amenities are all very modern but small stone reminders of the area's Roman and Arab history are used to decorate corners of the site. The attractive pool on the site remains open all year and in high season there is a shop, bar and restaurant. Shops and other local amenities are within walking distance. There may be some noise from children enjoying themselves at the water park next door. This would be a good base for touring the beautiful inland region from a seaside base.

Facilities

Three modern toilet blocks are well placed and provide good, clean facilities. Free hot showers. Facilities and good access for disabled visitors. Laundry facilities. Shop (1/7-31/8). Bar and restaurant (weekends and high season). Swimming pool (all year). Good play area. Boules. New library. Internet (on payment). Animals are not accepted. Off site: Beach 200 m. Water complex. Local amenities within walking distance.

Open: All year.

Directions

Turn off N340 Castellon - Valencia road on the CV2250 signed Moncofa. Follow sign for tourist information office in town and then signs for site. Pass supermarket and turn left to site in 600 m. GPS: 39.80884, -0.1281

Charges guide

Per unit incl. 2 persons and electricity	€ 14.00 - € 25.00

Discounts in low season with this guide and for longer stays.

Moraira

Camping Caravanning Moraira

Camino Paellero 50, E-03724 Moraira-Teulada (Alacant) T: 965 745 249.
E: campingmoraira@campingmoraira.com **alanrogers.com/ES87550**

This neat hillside site with some views over the town and marina is quietly situated in an urban area amongst old pine trees and just 400 metres from a sheltered bay. A striking, stilted and glass-fronted reception building gives great views. Ask about the innovative building features and prepare for pleasant design surprises. Terracing provides shaded pitches of varying sizes, some small (access to some of the upper pitches may be difficult for larger units). There are 17 pitches with full services (6/10A electricity). An attractive irregularly shaped pool with paved sunbathing terrace is below the bar/restaurant and terrace. The pool has large observation windows where you can watch the swimmers and divers as this is used for sub-aqua instruction. The site runs a PADI diving school; the diving here is good and the water warm, even in winter. A sandy beach is 1.5 km. away.

Facilities

The high quality toilet blocks, with polished granite floors and marble fittings are built to a unique and ultra-modern design. Facilities for disabled campers. Washing machines and dryers. Motorcaravan services. Bar/restaurant and shop (1/6-30/9). Bread and basics at the bar. Small swimming pool (all year). Sub-aqua with instruction. Tennis. Limited children's entertainment in high season. Torches may be required. WiFi code. Pets welcome. Off site: Shops, bars and restaurants within walking distance. Beach and fishing 400 m. Gym and ATM 600 m. Bicycle hire 1 km. Golf 8 km.

Open: All year.

Directions

Best approach is from Teulada. From A7 exit 63 take N332 and in 3.5 km. turn right (Teulada and Moraira). In Teulada fork right to Moraira. At junction at town entrance turn right signed Calpe and in 1 km. turn right into road to site on bend immediately after Res. Don Julio. Do not take the first right, as the signs seem to indicate, otherwise you will go round in a loop. GPS: 38.692, 0.14

Charges guide

Per unit incl. 2 persons and electricity	€ 37.00
extra person	€ 7.50
child (4-10 yrs)	€ 5.35

Less 15-60% in low season.

La Marina

Camping Internacional La Marina

Ctra N332 km 76, E-03194 La Marina (Alacant) T: 965 419 200. E: info@campinglamarina.com

alanrogers.com/ES87420

Very efficiently run by a friendly Belgian family, La Marina has 381 pitches of three different types and sizes ranging from 50 sq.m. to 150 sq.m. with electricity (10/16A), TV, water and drainage. Artificial shade is provided and the pitches are extremely well maintained on level, well drained ground with a special area allocated for tents in a small orchard. The huge lagoon swimming pool complex is fabulous and has something for everyone (with lifeguards). William Le Metayer, the owner, is passionate about La Marina and it shows in his search for perfection. A new, modern building which uses the latest architectural technology, houses many superb extra amenities. Facilities include a business centre with Internet access, a tapas bar decorated with amazing ceramics (handmade by the owner's mother) and a quality restaurant with a water fountain feature and great views of the lagoon. There is also a conference centre and an extensive computerised library. The whole of the lower ground floor is dedicated to children with a Marina Park play area and a 'cyber zone' for teenagers. With a further bar and a new soundproofed disco, the building is of an exceptional, eco-friendly standard. A superb fitness centre with personal trainers and a covered, heated pool (14x7 m) are incorporated. A pedestrian gate at the rear of the site gives access to the long sandy beach through the coastal pine forest that is a feature of the area. We recommend this site very highly. A member of Leading Campings Group.

Facilities

The elegant sanitary blocks offer the very best of modern facilities. Heated in winter, they include private cabins and facilities for disabled visitors and babies. Laundry facilities. Motorcaravan services. Gas. Supermarket. Bars. Restaurant and café. Ice cream kiosk. Swimming pools (1/4-15/10). Indoor pool. Fitness centre. Sauna. Solarium. Jacuzzi. Play rooms. Activities and entertainment including barbecues and swimming nights. Sports area. Tennis. Huge playgrounds. Hairdresser. Bicycle hire. Road train to beach. Exclusive area for dogs. Internet café (charged) and free WiFi. Off site: Fishing 700 m. Boat launching 5 km. Golf 7 km. Riding 15 km. Theme parks.

Open: All year.

Directions

Site is 2 km. west of La Marina. Leave N332 Guardamara de Segura - Santa Pola road at 75 km. marker if travelling north, or 78 km. marker if travelling south. Site is well signed.
GPS: 38.129649, -0.649575

Charges guide

Per unit incl. 2 persons and electricity	€ 33.28 - € 62.61
extra person	€ 5.35 - € 8.00
child (1-10 yrs)	€ 3.75 - € 5.50
dog	free - € 2.14

Good discounts for longer stays in low season.

Navajas

Camping Altomira

Ctra CV213 Navajas km 1, E-12470 Navajas (Castelló) T: 964 713 211. E: reservas@campingaltomira.com

alanrogers.com/ES85850

Camping Altomira is a terraced site in a rural, hillside setting, on the outskirts of a quiet village and offers superb views across the valleys and hills. There are 80 touring pitches situated on the higher levels of the site with some shade (artificial awnings are allowed). Due to the nature of this site we would not recommend it for people with mobility problems. Access roads to the gravel pitches are steep with some tight turns. All pitches, although not separated, have electricity and share water points with a neighbour. There are four toilet blocks, including a new one on the upper level. The two smaller ones are accessed by stairways from the pitches. The swimming pool, reception building with shop and a bar and separate restaurant are on the lowest level. There is a play area for children and a communal meeting room with TV adjacent to the bar. The famous Via Verde Ojos Negros cycle/walking track runs adjacent to the site and is very popular with campers who bring their bikes. The train station in the vilage offers easy access to Valencia, a 'must see' city.

Facilities

Four modern toilet blocks (see above) have showers in cubicles and open style washbasins. The larger block also housing laundry facilities is on the lowest level. Shop. Bar/restaurant with small terrace next to play area. TV room. Outdoor swimming pool. Communal barbecue area. Internet WiFi. Off site: Village has a range of shops bars and restaurants. Lake fishing 2 km. Beach 20 km. Cycle route.

Open: All year.

Directions

From A23 (Sagunto - Teruel) road take exit 33 (Navajas). Follow CV213 to site which is 1 km. north of Navajas. GPS: 39.87471, -0.51051

Charges guide

Per unit incl. 2 persons and electricity	€ 19.56 - € 25.60
extra person	€ 4.76 - € 5.95
child (1-10 yrs)	€ 3.72 - € 4.65

Camping Cheques accepted.

Oliva

Camping Azul

No. 1, Apartado 96, E-46780 Oliva (Valencia) T: 962 854 106. E: campingazul@ctv.es

alanrogers.com/ES86115

Found behind the beach and sand dunes, Camping Azul can best be described as rustic and relaxed, ideal for those who prefer a quiet, unregimented site. A barrier at the entrance leads to reception on the left where limited English is spoken. From there, firm sandy roads lead to sandy pitches with many low trees which have been sympathetically pruned to afford partial or full shade. Varying in size, some of the pitches are very compact, and pitching could be difficult. The little trees in and around the bar/café area, with its flower pots and trailing plants hanging from the branches, create a very pleasant Mediterranean atmosphere where food and drinks are served. Opposite this lies a small shop. Most of the chalets are in a segregated area with their own more mature facilities. Note: A 'Café' sign on the dunes may well bring the general public through to the bar/café and is therefore not for the exclusive use of campers.

Facilities

Modern, heated sanitary block. Facilities for disabled campers. Launderette. Motorcaravan services. Gas. Small shop selling basic items. Bar and snack bar. Play area. Bicycle and car hire. WiFi. Entertainment in high season. Direct beach access. Chalets for rent. Off site: Good restaurant providing menu of the day within 500 m. Golf and tennis 1 km. Oliva 3 km. with bars, restaurants, supermarkets and banks.

Open: 1 March - 1 November.

Directions

From the north leave AP7 motorway at exit 61 (Oliva) and follow the N332 through Oliva. From the south take exit 62 onto the N332 and turn left for Oliva. At km. 213 (south) or km. 210.8 (north) turn for 'urbanisation' and follow signs to the site. GPS: 38.906944, -0.068611

Charges guide

Per unit incl. 2 persons and electricity	€ 26.80 - € 28.80
extra person	€ 4.75
child (1-10 yrs)	€ 4.20

Oliva

Kiko Park Oliva

Ctra Assagador de Carro 2, E-46780 Oliva (Valencia) T: 962 850 905. E: kikopark@kikopark.com

alanrogers.com/ES86150

Kiko Park is a smart site nestling behind protective sand dunes alongside a Blue Flag beach. There are sets of tiled steps over the dunes or a long boardwalk near the beach bar to take you to the fine white sandy beach and the sea. From the central reception point, flat, fine gravel pitches and access roads are divided to the left and right. Backing onto one another, the 180 large pitches all have electricity and the aim is to progressively upgrade all these with full services. There are flowers, hedging and trees adding shade, privacy and colour. An outdoor pool complex provides a spa, whirlpool, solarium, gym and a pool bar. An award-winning restaurant and a tropical style beach bar both overlook the marina, beach and sea. A wide variety of entertainment is provided all year and Spanish lessons are taught along with dance classes and aerobics during the winter. The site is run by the second generation of a family involved in camping for 30 years. They are supported by a friendly, efficient team who speak many languages. The narrow roads leading to the site can be a little challenging for very large units.

Facilities

Four mature, heated sanitary blocks include facilities for babies and for disabled visitors. Laundry facilities. Gas. Motorcaravan services. Supermarket (closed Sundays). Restaurant. Bar with TV. Beach-side bar and restaurant. Swimming pools and gym. New spa with treatments and beauty programmes. Playground. Watersports facilities. Diving school in high season (from mid June). Internet. WiFi. Entertainment for children from mid June. Bicycle hire. Off site: Indoor pool 1 km. Golf 5 km. Riding 7 km.

Open: All year.

Directions

From AP7 take exit 61. From the toll turn right at T-junction and on to lights. Turn left then right at roundabout. At next roundabout take third exit (Platja and Alicante). Follow one way system to next roundabout then site signs. GPS: 38.9316, -0.0968

Charges guide

Per unit incl. 2 persons	€ 15.20 - € 34.00
extra person	€ 3.20 - € 6.40
electricity (per kWh)	€ 0.40

Oliva

Euro Camping

Partida Rabdells s/n, CN332 km210, E-46780 Oliva (Valencia) T: 962 854 098. E: info@eurocamping-es.com

alanrogers.com/ES86120

Approached through a new urbanisation, Euro Camping is a well maintained, British-owned site. Spacious and flat, it is set amidst many high trees, mainly eucalyptus, with its own access to a fine sandy beach. From reception with its helpful English speaking staff and aviary opposite, wide tarmac or paved roads lead to 315 large, gravel based pitches which are either marked or hedged (most are for touring units). The main site road leads down to a beachside restaurant with superb views and a supermarket.

Facilities

One newly built and two mature sanitary blocks are well maintained. British type WCs, preset hot water in the showers. Toilet facilities for disabled campers. Facilities for babies. Washing machines and dryer. Motorcaravan services. Well stocked supermarket and roast chicken takeaway. Restaurant/bar. Fridge hire. WiFi. Entertainment in high season. Gas. Bicycle hire. Communal barbecue. WiFi throughout (charged). Off site: Golf, riding and tennis 1 km. Oliva 3 km. with restaurants, cafés and supermarkets. Friday street market. Ideal area for cycling.

Open: All year.

Directions

From north on AP7 take exit 61 onto N332 and drive through Oliva. From south exit 62 and left for Oliva. Exit at km. 213 (south) or 210 (north) signed 'urbanisation'. At roundabout take fourth exit. Turn right immediately before narrow bridge. Continue on wide road, bear right at end (Carrer de Xeraco). Site on left at bottom of road. GPS: 38.905, -0.066

Charges guide

Per unit incl. 2 persons and electricity	€ 30.20 - € 47.80

Camping Cheques accepted.

Oliva

Camping Olé

Partida Aigua Morta s/n, E-46780 Oliva (Valencia) T: 962 857 517. E: campingole@hotmail.com

alanrogers.com/ES86130

Olé is a large, flat, seaside holiday site south of Valencia and close to the modern resort of Oliva. Its entrance is only 250 m. from the pleasant sandy beach. For those who do not want to share the busy beach, a large swimming pool is opened in July and August. There are 308 small pitches of compressed gravel and with 6/10A electricity. Many are separated by hedges with pruned trees giving good shade to those away from the beach. A bar and restaurant stands on the dunes overlooking the sea, together with a few unmarked pitches that are ideal for larger units. There are small groups of chalets and a few apartments to rent, all within their own areas. The site has a large terrace, part of which is given over to entertainment in high season. The town of Oliva is popular with British and Dutch holidaymakers.

Facilities

Three clean, well maintained sanitary blocks provide very reasonable facilities. The central one serves most of the touring pitches. Laundry facilities. Fridge rental. Well stocked supermarket (1/3-30/9). Various vending machines. Bar with TV and restaurant with daily menu, drinks and snacks (1/3-15/12). Takeaway. Swimming pool (1/7-1/9). Playground. Entertainment (July/Aug). Fishing off the beach. Off site: Golf 800 m. Bicycle hire. Oliva with shops, restaurants and bars.

Open: All year.

Directions

From the north on AP7 (Alicante - Valencia) take exit 61 on N332 through Oliva. From the south take exit 62 and turn left for Oliva. Exit at km. 213 (south) or 210 (north) signed 'urbanisation'. At roundabout take third exit following signs to site.
GPS: 38.8943, -0.0536

Charges guide

Per unit incl. 2 persons and electricity	€ 29.93 - € 42.85
extra person	€ 6.40

Pilar de la Horadada

Camping Lo Monte

Avenida Comunidad Valenciana, no 157, E-03190 Pilar de la Horadada (Alacant) T: 966 766 782.
E: info@campinglomonte-alicante.es **alanrogers.com/ES87400**

Lo Monte is a brand new all-year site which has been recommended by our Spanish agent. We plan to make a full inspection in 2012. There are 127 pitches here, of which the majority are available for tourers. All pitches have 16A electricity, water and drainage. Leisure facilities include an indoor pool (open all year) and an outdoor pool (open May to September) and a wellness centre. Lo Monte is located at Pilar de la Horadada, the most southerly town on the Costa Blanca. This is a popular holiday destination, with a fine beach and a good range of facilities. For nature lovers, the areas around the town are rich in flora and fauna, the tidal sections support an incredible variety of creatures, with species such as pipefish, seahorses and wrasse. The birdlife is varied too, you are likely to spot curlew, grey herons, egrets, turnstones and plovers. There are a number of excellent golf courses in the vicinity, notably the 3 courses of the Orihuela Costa.

Facilities

Outdoor swimming pool (1/6-15/9). Wellness centre, shop, bar, restaurant, takeaway food (all open all year). Children's play area. Tourist information. Mobile homes for rent. Bicycle hire. Off site: Pilar de la Horadada centre (shops and restaurants). Watersports. Fishing. Golf

Open: All year.

Directions

Head south on AP7 motorway beyond Torrevieja and take the exit to Pilar de la Horadada. The site is well signposted. GPS: 37.86964, -0.77248

Charges guide

Per unit incl. 2 persons and electricity	€ 28.00 - € 57.00
extra person	€ 5.50 - € 7.00
child (4-12 yrs)	€ 4.50 - € 5.00

Ribera de Cabanes

Camping Torre La Sal 2

Cami l'Atall, E-12595 Ribera de Cabanes (Castelló) T: 964 319 744. E: camping@torrelasal2.com

alanrogers.com/ES85700

Torre La Sal 2 is a very large site divided into two by a quiet road, with a reception on each side with friendly, helpful staff. There are three pool complexes (one can be covered in cooler weather and is heated) all of which are on the west side, whilst the beach is on the east. Both sides have a restaurant. The 530 flat pitches vary in size, some have their own sinks, and most have shade. All have 10A electricity and a few have a partial view of the sea. There are 85 bungalows around the two areas. This is a high quality site offering a great choice to campers.

Facilities

Toilet facilities are of a good standard in both sections. Facilities for disabled campers. Baby rooms. Hot water to some sinks. Washing machines. Motorcaravan services. Shop, bars, restaurants and takeaway. Swimming pools, one heated and covered (a large new pool complex should be ready for the season). Jacuzzi and sauna (winter). Play park. Disco. Sports centre. Tennis. Squash. Football pitches. Outdoor gym. Games room. Bullring. Hairdresser. Activities and entertainment. WiFi. Torches useful. Off site: Bicycle hire. Riding 10 km. Golf 20 km.

Open: All year.

Directions

From A7/E15 take exit 45 for Oropesa del Mar on N340. Follow road to Oropesa and then the many clear signs to the site. GPS: 40.127, 0.158

Charges guide

Per unit incl. 2 persons and electricity	€ 36.35
extra person	€ 6.80
child (2-9 yrs)	€ 6.25

Special prices for retired persons 1/9 - 30/6.

San Miguel de Salinas

Camping Florantilles

Ctra Torrevieja - San Miguel de Salinas, E-03193 San Miguel de Salinas (Alacant) T: 965 720 456.
E: camping@campingflorantilles.com **alanrogers.com/ES87410**

Florantilles is an excellent site situated 6 km. west of Torrevieja, 60 km. south of Alicante and occupying an elevated position overlooking orange groves and the famous salt lake nature reserve, Salinas de la Mata. The site is terraced and well lit, with gravel pitches of a good size and tarmac roads. All 262 pitches are separated by hedges and have 10A electricity (metered for long stays), water and waste water drainage. A third of the pitches are for touring, while the others are occupied by privately owned mobile homes or are seasonal pitches mainly used by retired British owners.

Facilities

Two, well kept toilet blocks (one heated), plus another smaller block on each level with WCs and handbasins but no private cubicles. Facilities for disabled visitors. Two laundry rooms. Shop (Mon-Sat), with freshly baked bread. Two unheated, linked swimming pools (15/6-30/9). Bar/café. TV room. Aerobics. Social evenings. Day trips. No vehicle movement on site between 23.00-07.00. Dogs are not accepted. WiFi. Off site: Restaurant and shops 3 km. Bicycle hire 4 km. Beach 5 km. Golf 6 km. Sailing and fishing (licence required) 7 km.

Open: All year.

Directions

From south, leave motorway AP7 at exit 758. At roundabout, go under motorway, take exit for CV95. In 300 m, take first right for CV942 (Los Montesinos). Site on left through archway. From north, leave AP7 at exit 758. Take first exit for CV95, then as above. New arrivals should park to left of entrance so you do not obstruct barrier. GPS: 37.97505, -0.75131

Charges guide

Per unit incl. 2 persons and electricity	€ 17.09 - € 30.05
extra person	€ 3.24 - € 6.48

Villajoyosa

Camping Playa Paraiso

Ctra Valencia - Alicante km 136, Partida Paraiso, 66, E-03570 Villajoyosa (Alacant) T: 966 851 838.
E: jacinto@playaparaiso.com **alanrogers.com/ES86880**

This site has been reopened by new owners who lost one of their other sites to housing developers. Major works are underway to provide modern facilities. When we visited work was being done on the upper levels of the site to provide serviced pitches and a fully refurbished toilet block. On the lower level, the main site road is of tarmac and the gravel pitches are on shallow terraces as the site slopes gently down to the sea which provides one of the boundaries. The views are pleasant and trees provide a degree of shade for some pitches, with overhead sunshades on others. Electricity is available (16A).

Facilities

Two toilet blocks are old but are well maintained and very clean. Spacious showers. Facilities for disabled visitors. Facilities for babies. Laundry facilities. Bar and restaurant with limited menu. Indoor games and TV. Swimming pool (Easter-Oct). Off site: Beach. Bus stop 100 m. Riding and bicycle hire 15 km. Villajoyosa with holiday attractions.

Open: 2 February - 31 December.

Directions

From the N332 take exit at km. 136 to Villajoysa Playa and site is 100 m. on the right.
GPS: 38.50005, -0.24905

Charges guide

Per unit incl. 2 persons and electricity	€ 26.35 - € 38.55

Villargordo del Cabriel

Kiko Park Rural

Ctra Embalse Contreras km 3, E-46317 Villargordo del Cabriel (Valencia) T: 962 139 082.
E: kikoparkrural@kikopark.com **alanrogers.com/ES86250**

alan rogers Runner up 2011 Awards

Approaching Kiko Park Rural, you will see a small hilltop village appearing in a landscape of mountains, vines and a jewel-like lake. Kiko was a small village and farm and the village now forms the campsite and accommodation. Amenities are contained within the architecturally authentic buildings, some old and some new. The 76 generous pitches (mainly hardstanding and with 6A electricity and water) have high hedges (as does the site) for privacy. Generous plantings have been made which already afford some privacy and hundreds of trees planted in 2003 are now providing shade. The restaurant provides extremely good food in a pleasant, spacious setting overlooking the pools and their surrounding immaculate lawns. Kiko Rural is run by cousins from a family with 30 years of camping experience – a passionate and enthusiastic team with a vision of excellence. Kiko Rural is an ideal site for those folk, young and old, who enjoy adventurous activities, communing with nature, or relaxing with an occasional sightseeing excursion. A sister site to Kiko Park in Oliva, Valencia (ES86150), old and new have combined here to create an environment that is, within its category, outstanding. The high speed Madrid-Valencia train line emerges from a tunnel approximately 500 m. from the site. However, noise-moderating banks should eliminate any possible problems.

Facilities

Three toilet blocks are well equipped (but have short timers for lighting and showers), including facilities for disabled campers. Motorcaravan services. Gas. Pleasant bar. Excellent restaurant. Takeaway (Easter-Oct). Swimming and paddling pools. Very good playground. Bicycle hire. Entertainment in high season. Many adventurous activities can be arranged, including white-water rafting, gorging, orienteering, trekking, bungee jumping and riding. Large families and groups catered for. Off site: Fishing, canoeing and windsurfing on the lake. Village 3 km.

Open: All year.

Directions

From autopista A7/E15 on Valencia ring road (near the airport) take A3 (E901) to the west. Villargordo del Cabriel is 80 km. towards Motilla. Take village exit 255 and follow signs through village and over a hill – spot the village on a hill 2 km. away. That is the campsite! GPS: 39.552176, -1.47456

Charges guide

Per unit incl. 2 persons and electricity	€ 20.15 - € 29.95
extra person	€ 5.00 - € 6.25
child (under 10 yrs)	€ 3.80 - € 4.30
dog	€ 0.70

Vinaros

Camping Vinaros

Ctra N340 km 1054, E-12500 Vinaros (Castelló) T: 964 402 424. E: info@campingvinaros.com
alanrogers.com/ES85580

Taking its name from the nearby seaside town with its fishing harbour and marina, this pleasant site has 258 flat numbered pitches of average size on flat ground. Mature trees provide shade and neat hedges separate the pitches, all of which have an individual sink. The site entrance is directly off the N340, with a restaurant outside the main boundary. There is a spacious entrance with lots of outside parking, but there is traffic noise. A swimming pool has a sunbathing area and a paddling pool and a pleasant snack bar serves snacks all year. Large blocks of natural stone have been used for decoration around the site. This theme is continued in the spotless sanitary block. This site is very popular as an all year stopover site and has several long stay British customers enjoying the good discounts in low season.

Facilities

Two exceptionally clean, fully equipped toilet blocks use marble and tiling to create a light environment enhanced by potted shrubs. Some washbasins are in cabins. Facilities for disabled campers. Laundry facilities. Motorcaravan services. Milk and bread delivered daily. Restaurant, snack bar and bar (all year). Play area. Swimming pool (1/4-30/10). Pétanque. Musical and other entertainment in season. Large aviary and terrapin pool. Children's club (high season) and artistic activities for adults (all year). Off site: Rail station nearby. Bus service and Vinaros 500 m. Beach and fishing 800 m. Golf 7 km.

Open: All year.

Directions

Take exit 43 (Ulldecona) from the A7 and head to Vinaros. At the junction with the N340, turn left and head towards Barcelona. Site is at 1054 km. marker directly off the N340, opposite a large garden centre. GPS: 40.4931, 0.4838

Charges guide

Per unit, all inclusive	€ 11.00 - € 16.00

Stay over 7 days in low season € 7.20.

In the province of Murcia you'll find sandy beaches, dunes and unspoilt coves along the coast; inland hills and valleys plus the regional parks of Sierra de Carche, Sierra de la Pila, Sierra de Espuña, and Carrascoy and El Valle.

THE CAPITAL OF THE REGION IS THE CITY OF MURCIA

Murcia, the capital of the region, was founded in the ninth century by the Moors on the banks of the Río Segura. The square of Cardinal Belluga houses two of the town's architectural gems, the Episcopal Palace and the Cathedral, and there is a range of museums and exhibitions to visit. With narrow medieval streets, the characterful town of Cartagena has lots of bars and restaurants plus two nautical museums: the National Museum of Maritime Archaeology and the Naval Museum. Also on a nautical theme, the International Nautical Week is celebrated here in June. Along the coast there are numerous beaches offering a wide range of watersports: sailing, windsurfing, canoeing, water skiing and diving. The area between the coastal towns of Águilas and Mazarrón is a breeding ground for tortoises and eagles. Inland are the historic towns of Lorca and Caravaca de le Cruz. The former is known as the 'baroque city' with its examples of baroque architecture, seen in the parish churches, convents, and houses; the latter too is home to beautiful churches, including El Santuario de Vera Cruz.

Places of interest

Águilas: seaside town with good beaches.

Moratalla: pretty village, castle offering stunning views of the surrounding countryside and forests.

Puerto de Mazarrón: Enchanted City of Bolnuevo - a small area of eroded rocks, nature reserve and lagoon at La Rambla de Moreras.

San Pedro del Pinatar: seaside resort, La Pagan beach is renowned for its therapeutic mud, which reputedly relieves rheumatism and is good for the skin.

Santiago de la Ribera: upmarket resort with sailing club.

Cuisine of the region

Vegetables are important and found in nearly every dish. Fish is also popular, cooked in a salt crust or *a la espalda* (lightly fried and baked), and usually accompanied by rice. Fig bread is a speciality of the region.

Bizcochos borrachos: sponge soaked in wine and syrup.

Cabello de Ángel: pumpkin strands in syrup.

Caldero: made of rice, fish and the hot ñora pepper.

Caldo con pelotas: stew made of turkey with meatballs.

Chuletas de cordero al ajo cabañil: suckling lamb chops served with a dressing of garlic and vinegar.

Tocino de cielo: dessert made with egg yolks and syrup.

Yemas de Caravaca: cake made with egg yolks.

Banos de Fortuna

Camping La Fuente

Camino de La Bocamina, E-30626 Baños de Fortuna (Murcia) T: 968 685 125. E: info@campingfuente.com

alanrogers.com/ES87450

Located in an area known for its thermal waters since Roman and Moorish times and with just 87 pitches and 14 bungalows, La Fuente is a gem. Unusually, winter is high season here. The main attraction here is the huge hydrotherapy centre where the water is a constant 36 degrees all year. The pool can be covered in inclement weather. The site is in two sections, one where pitches are in standard rows and the other where they are in circles around blocks. The hard, flat pitches are on shingle (rock pegs advised), have 10A electricity (Europlug) and 53 have their own mini sanitary unit. Some artificial shade has been added to 22 pitches. There is accommodation to rent on site but it is separate from the camping area. A daily charge applies for use of the pool and jacuzzis (€4.50 but well worth it). There is also a very good restaurant with terrace and separate bar.

Facilities

Some pitches have their own facilities including a unit for disabled campers. Washing machines and dryers. Supermarket. High quality restaurant shared with accommodation guests. Snack bar by pool. Jacuzzi. Bicycle hire. Communal barbecues only. WiFi (free). Off site: Spa town, massage therapies and hot pools 500 m. Fortuna with shops, bars and restaurants 3 km. Golf and riding 20 km.

Open: All year.

Directions

From A7/E15 Alicante - Murcia road take C3223 to Fortuna then follow signs to Baños de Fortuna. The site with its bright yellow walls can be easily seen from the road and is very well signed in the town. GPS: 38.20682, -1.10732

Charges 2012

Per unit incl. 2 persons and electricity	€ 16.74
with individual sanitary facility	€ 18.90
extra person	€ 3.51
child (3-12 yrs)	€ 1.35
dog	€ 1.08

Pitch prices discounted after five days.

Cartagena

Camping Naturista El Portus

El Portus, E-30394 Cartagena (Murcia) T: 968 553 052. E: elportus@elportus.com

alanrogers.com/ES87520

Set in a secluded south facing bay fringed by mountains, El Portus is a fairly large naturist site enjoying magnificent views and with direct access to a small sand and pebble beach. This part of Spain enjoys almost all-year-round sunshine. There are some 400 pitches, 300 for tourers, ranging from 60-100 sq.m, all but a few having electricity (6A). They are mostly on fairly level, if somewhat stony and barren ground. El Portus has a reasonable amount of shade from established trees and nearly every pitch has a view. Residential units are situated on the hillside above the site. In season, a large supervised swimming pool and paddling pool are sheltered with landscaping and grass areas for sunbathing. At other times there is a smaller heated pool above the camping area that has a retractable dome cover. One of the bar/restaurants is open all year. Mobile homes, chalets and new, fully equipped, modern studios with panoramic views are available for rent. El Portus has a positive Spanish atmosphere in high season and is extremely popular through the winter months with all nationalities including many British. This is a relaxed site with welcoming, English speaking reception staff.

Facilities

Five acceptable toilet blocks, all unisex, are of varying styles and fully equipped. Opened as required, they are clean and bright. Showers all with hot water. Unit for disabled visitors, key from reception. Washing machines. Motorcaravan services. Well stocked shop. Bar with TV and library. Restaurants. The beach restaurant is closed in low season. Swimming pools (June-Sept). Wellness centre. Play area. Tennis. Pétanque. Yoga. Scuba-diving club (high season). Windsurfing. Spanish lessons. Small boat moorings. Entertainment programme all season. WiFi throughout (charged). Off site: Fishing from beach. Golf 28 km. Riding 40 km.

Open: All year.

Directions

Site is on the coast, 10 km. west of Cartagena. Follow signs to Mazarron then take E22 to Canteras. Site is well signed for 4 km. If approaching through Cartagena, exit the town on N332 following signs for Canteras. Site signed on joining the N332. GPS: 37.585, -1.06717

Charges guide

Per person	€ 7.00
child (3-9 yrs)	€ 5.00
pitch	€ 16.30
pitch incl. 6A electricity	€ 22.20
dog	€ 4.70

Isla Plana

Camping Los Madriles

Ctra de la Azohia km 4.5, E-30868 Isla Plana (Murcia) T: 968 152 151. E: camplosmadriles@terra.es

alanrogers.com/ES87480

An exceptional site with super facilities, Los Madriles is run by a hard working team, with constant improvements being made. Twenty kilometres west of Cartagena, the approach to the site and the surrounding area is fairly unremarkable, but the site is not. A fairly steep access road leads to the 313 flat, good to large sized terraced pitches, each having electricity, water and a waste point. Most have shade from large trees with a number benefiting from panoramic views of the sea or behind to the mountains. The site has huge rectangular and lagoon style pools with water sprays and jacuzzis. These are fed by the thermal waters first used by the ancient Romans and unbelievably are emptied every night after they close at 10 pm and are refilled by morning with fresh water, thus doing away with the need for chlorination. Simple snacks are served in the bar and attractive area near the pools. The campsite is immaculately clean and has excellent sports facilities. In between the popular winter season (50% British) and summer, through the months of May and June, the site is very peaceful, temperatures are in the mid-twenties, with spring flowers and other flora abundant.

Facilities

Four sanitary blocks and one small toilet block provide excellent facilities, including services in one block for disabled campers. Private wash cabins. Washing machines and dryers. Motorcaravan services. Car wash. Supermarket, restaurant/snack bar and bar (all open all season but hours are limited). Swimming pools with jacuzzi. Boules. Play areas. Animals are not accepted. Off site: Town close by. Beach and fishing (licence required, purchase in Puerto Mazarron) 800 m. Boat launching 3 km. Riding and bicycle hire 6 km. Golf 20 km.

Open: All year.

Directions

From E15/A7 take exit 845 and follow RM3 in direction of Cartagena, Fuente Alamo and Mazarron (do not turn into Mazarron). Continue towards Puerto Mazarron and take N332 (Cartagena). On reaching coast continue with N332 (Cartagena and Alicante). At roundabout turn right towards Isla Plana and La Azohia. Site is well signed and on the left in approx. 5 km. GPS: 37.3441N, -1.1147W

Charges guide

Per unit incl. 2 persons and electricity	€ 32.10

Large discounts for longer stays.

We can book this site for you! alan rogers travel
Call 01580 214000

La Manga del Mar Menor

Caravaning La Manga

Autovia Cartagena - La Manga, Salida 11, E-30386 La Manga del Mar Menor (Murcia) T: 968 563 014.
E: lamanga@caravaning.es **alanrogers.com/ES87530**

This is a very large, well equipped 'holiday style' site with its own beach and both indoor and outdoor pools. With a good number of typical Spanish long stay units, the length of the site is impressive (1 km) and a bicycle is very helpful for getting about. The 1,000 regularly laid out, gravel touring pitches (100 or 110 sq.m) are generally separated by hedges which also provide a degree of shade. Each has 10A electricity supply, water and the possibility of satellite TV reception. This site's excellent facilities are ideally suited for holidays in the winter when the weather is very pleasantly warm. November daytime temperatures usually exceed 20 degrees. La Manga is a 22 km. long narrow strip of land, bordered by the Mediterranean on one side and by the Mar Menor on the other. There are sandy bathing beaches on both sides and considerable development in terms of hotels, apartments, restaurants, night clubs, etc. in between – a little reminiscent of Miami Beach! The very end of the southern part is great for 'getting away from it all'. The campsite is situated on the approach to 'the strip', enjoying the benefit of its own semi-private beach with impressive tall palm trees alongside the Mar Menor, which provides shallow warm waters, ideal for families with children.

Facilities

Nine clean toilet blocks are well spaced around the site, include washbasins. Laundry. Gas. Large supermarket. Restaurant. Bar. Snack bar. Swimming pool complex (April-Sept). Indoor pool, gymnasium (April-Oct), sauna, jacuzzi and massage service. New outdoor fitness course for adults. Open air family cinema (July/Aug). Tennis. Pétanque. Minigolf. Play area. Watersports school. Internet café (also WiFi). Winter activities. Spanish classes. Max. 2 dogs. Off site: Golf, bicycle hire and riding 5 km.

Open: All year.

Directions

Use exit (Salida) 11 from MU312 dual carriageway towards Cabo de Palos, signed Playa Honda. Cross road bridge and double back on yourself. Site entrance is clearly visible beside dual carriageway with many flags flying. GPS: 37.62445, -0.74442

Charges guide

Per unit incl. 2 persons and electricity	€ 20.00 - € 35.00
extra person	€ 4.10 - € 5.10

Camping Cheques accepted.

Moratalla

Camping La Puerta

Ctra de La Puerta s/n, E-30440 Moratalla (Murcia) T: 968 730 008. E: info@campinglapuerta.com
alanrogers.com/ES87440

Camping La Puerta is part of the Camping La Manga group. It is a typical Spanish weekend and holiday site and advance booking is essential for high season and most weekends. Set in the secluded hills above Moratalla, it provides a rural base from which to explore the surrounding countryside or simply relax and enjoy the magnificent swimming pool complex. Most of the 159 touring pitches are rather small, so large units could have difficulty in manoeuvring due to randomly growing trees.

Facilities

Three fully fitted sanitary blocks provide toilets, washbasins and shower cubicles. Facilities for disabled visitors. Washing machines. Shop. Bar and terrace. Caféteria and restaurant serving a variety of local dishes. Play area. Tennis. Fishing. Barbecues are not permitted. Off site: Riding 5 km.

Open: All year.

Directions

From the A7 (Murcia - Lorca) exit at 651 km. onto the C415 in the direction of Mula and Caravaca. Follow signs to Moratalla and then on to site which is well signed. GPS: 38.20555, -1.91975

Charges guide

Per unit incl. 2 persons and electricity	€ 20.20 - € 23.20

Camping Cheques accepted.

Famous for its sun, its beautiful traditions, its poets, original folklore, age-old history and magnificent heritage left behind by the Moors, Andalucía is one of the most attractive regions in Spain.

THIS COMPRISES EIGHT PROVINCES: ALMERIA, CADIZ, CORDOBA, GRANADA, HUELVA, MALAGA, JAEN AND SEVILLE

THE REGIONAL CAPITAL IS SEVILLE

With the River Guadalquivir running through it, the charming city of Seville is one of the most visited places in the region. The old city, with its great monuments; the Giralda tower, cathedral and the Alcázar, plus the narrow, winding streets of Santa Cruz, is particularly popular. Also on the Guadalquivir, Cordoba is located northeast of Seville. It too has a picturesque Jewish Quarter along with a rich Moorish heritage. Indeed, the Mezquita is one of the grandest mosques ever built by the Moors in Spain. Located further east on the foothills of the Sierra Nevada mountain range, Granada is home to the impressive Alhambra, a group of distinct buildings including a Royal Palace, splendid gardens, and the fortress of Alcazaba. The Sierra Nevada, Spain's highest range, offers good skiing and trekking. Further south, you'll find the fine beaches and tourist areas of the Costa Tropical and the Costa del Sol, including the developed resort of Malaga. There are more beaches on the west coast plus one of the oldest settlements in Spain, the bustling port of Cádiz.

Places of interest

Almeria: preserved Moorish heritage with greatest purity. Located on a beautiful bay.

Casa-Museo Pablo Ruiz Picasso: art museum including collection of originals by Pablo Picasso.

Jaen: medieval fortress, Renaissance cathedral, 11th-century Moorish baths, Santa Catalina castle.

Jerez de la Frontera: birthplace of sherry and Spanish brandy, site of renowned equestrian school.

Mijas: enchanting village, with narrow streets bordered by brilliantly white-washed houses.

Parque Natural de las Sierras de Cazorla y Segura: largest park in Spain with mountains, river gorges, forests and wildlife.

Ronda: beautiful town on the edge of an abrupt rocky precipice.

Cuisine of the region

Andalucía has more tapas bars than anywhere else in Spain. Seafood in abundance, fresh vegetables and fruit: oranges from Cordoba; persimmons, pomegranates, figs, strawberries from Alpujarra; avocados, mangos, guavas, papayas from the coast of Granada and Malaga. Locally produced wine and sherry.

Alboronía: vegetable stew.

Alfajors: almond and nut pastry.

Gazpacho ajoblanco: cold soup with garlic and almond.

Gazpacho salmorejo: much thicker and made with tomatoes only.

Pestiños: honey coated pastries.

Tocinillo de cielo: pudding made with egg yolks and syrup.

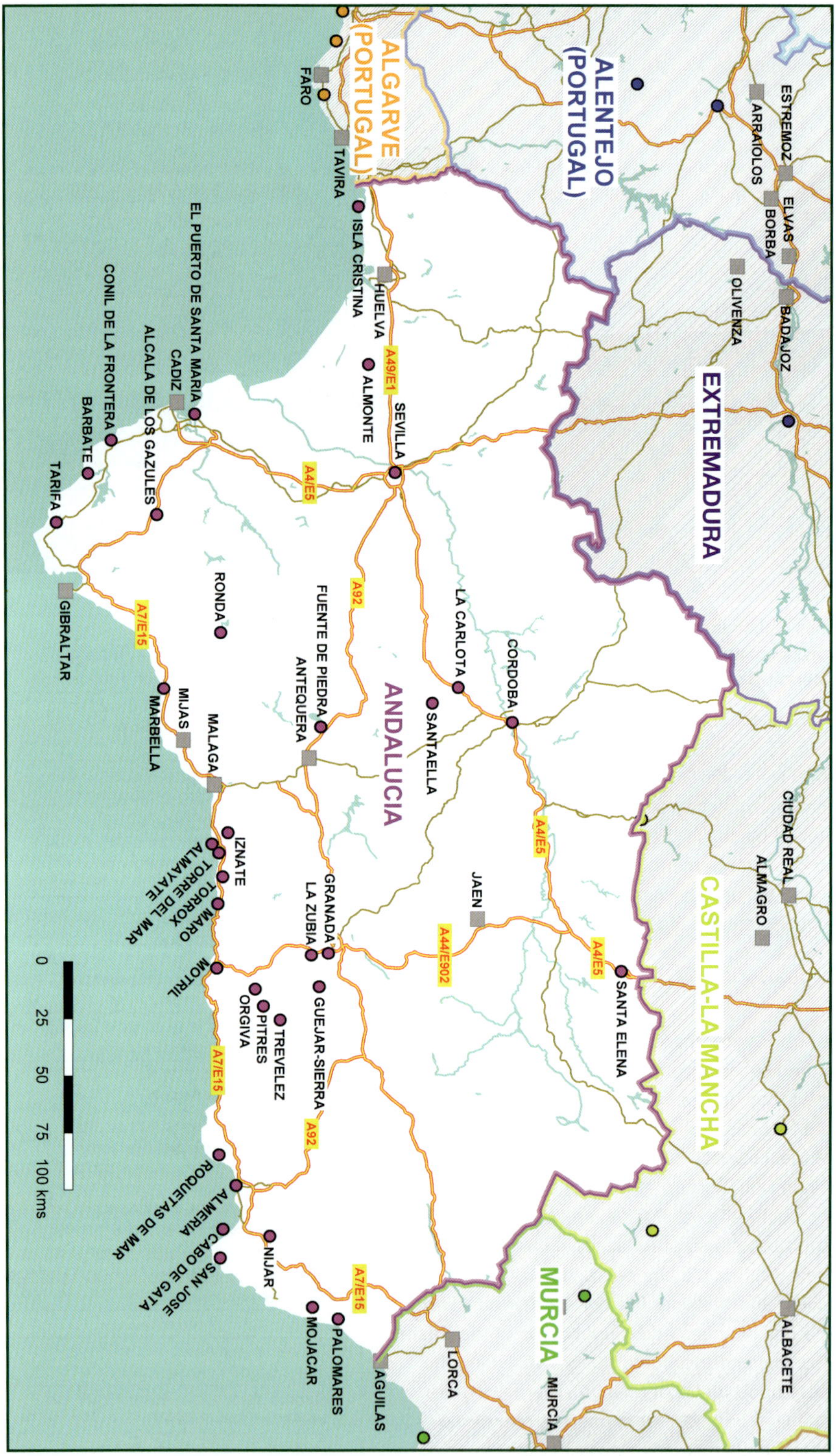
ANDALUCIA
EXTREMADURA
CASTILLA-LA MANCHA
MURCIA
ALGARVE (PORTUGAL)
ALENTEJO (PORTUGAL)
ESTREMOZ
ARRAIOLOS
ELVAS
BORBA
OLIVENZA
BADAJOZ
FARO
TAVIRA
ISLA CRISTINA
HUELVA
ALMONTE
SEVILLA
A49/E1
A4/E5
EL PUERTO DE SANTA MARIA
CADIZ
ALCALA DE LOS GAZULES
CONIL DE LA FRONTERA
BARBATE
TARIFA
GIBRALTAR
A7/E15
RONDA
A92
FUENTE DE PIEDRA
ANTEQUERA
LA CARLOTA
CORDOBA
SANTAELLA
MIJAS
MARBELLA
MALAGA
IZNATE
ALMAYATE
TORRE DEL MAR
TORROX
MARO
GRANADA
LA ZUBIA
JAEN
A44/E902
SANTA ELENA
CIUDAD REAL
ALMAGRO
MOTRIL
GUEJAR-SIERRA
ORGIVA
PITRES
TREVELEZ
ROQUETAS DE MAR
ALMERIA
CABO DE GATA
SAN JOSE
NIJAR
MOJACAR
PALOMARES
AGUILAS
LORCA
MURCIA
ALBACETE
0
25
50
75
100 kms

Alcalá de los Gazules

Camping Los Gazules

Ctra de Patrite km 4, E-11180 Alcalá de los Gazules (Cádiz) T: 956 420 486.
E: camping@losgazules.e.telefonica.net **alanrogers.com/ES88900**

The site is set in the beautiful surroundings of the Los Alcornocales Nature Park and has 135 touring pitches with 10A electricity. Although basic, this would make an ideal site for a quiet, relaxing holiday in the countryside. The main building complex, consisting of the shop and restaurant has been newly painted outside and improved and the well furnished restaurant/bar is a pleasant place to eat. The sanitary facilities have also been improved and there is a swimming pool, open from the end of June.

Facilities

A circular sanitary block offers clean facilities, including those for disabled campers. Washing machine in supervised room. Bar/restaurant. Shop in bar sells basic supplies. Swimming pool (June-Sept). Playground.
Off site: Site is well placed for exploring the local area and for excursions to Cádiz.

Open: All year.

Directions

From A381 Algecieras - Jerez road take exit to Alcalá de los Gazules onto A375 (C440). Continue around village on A375 to Ubrique and proceed to 42 km. marker. Then turn onto the road to Patrite, the site is on the right at the 4 km. marker.
GPS: 36.463, -5.664

Charges guide

Per unit incl. 2 persons and electricity	€ 18.00 - € 19.00
extra person	€ 4.50 - € 5.00

Almayate

Camping Naturista Almanat

Carril de la Torre Alta s/n, E-29749 Almayate (Málaga) T: 952 556 462. E: info@almanat.de
alanrogers.com/ES87830

With direct access to a one kilometre grey sand and shingle naturist beach, this established all year naturist site, set amongst agricultural land with mountain backdrop, is proving a firm favourite with many British seeking winter sun. The facilities on site are to a very high standard. The entire two-hectare site is flat with a fine shingle surface. A large number of mature trees provide much needed shade in the summer months. The 194 touring pitches with 16A electricity, vary in size and shape with the majority demanding physical manoeuvring of a touring caravan.

Facilities

The large, unisex toilet block is fully equipped, regularly cleaned and all under cover. Good facilities for disabled campers near reception. Small shop. Bar/restaurant with terrace. Large unheated swimming pool. New indoor pool with jacuzzi (closed 15/6-15/9). Sauna and gym. Cinema (56 seats). Social room. Play area. Minigolf. Weather permitting, one is expected to be nude which is obligatory in the pool area and bar during the day. Off site: Fishing, riding nearby. Bus service 1 km. Torre del Mar is 2 km.

Open: All year.

Directions

Approaching from the east (Torre del Mar) it is necessary to turn left to access the 600 m. single track access to the site. It is illegal to make that left turn. From east or west on N340 autovia take exit 265 signed Cajiz Iznate and Costa 340a. Follow Costa direction and on reaching the coast turn left on N340a toward Torre del Mar. Site well signed in 5 km. on right. GPS: 36.72703, -4.11334

Charges guide

Per unit incl. 2 persons and electricity	€ 32.14 - € 37.00

Almeria

Camping La Garrofa

Ctra N340 km 435,4, direccion a Aguadulce via Litoral, E-04002 Almeria (Almería) T: 950 235 770.
E: info@lagarrofa.com **alanrogers.com/ES87650**

One of the earliest sites in Spain (dating back to 1957), La Garrofa nestles in a cove with a virtually private beach accessed only by sea or through the campsite. It is rather dramatic with the tall mountain cliffs behind. Many of the rather small 100 flat and sloping sandy pitches are shaded, with some very close to the beach and sea. Eighty have 6/10A electricity. An old fortress looks down on the campsite – you can walk to it via a valley at the back of the site and across an old Roman bridge. Other walks directly from the site include a Roman road providing fine coastal views.

Facilities

Sanitary facilities are mature but clean. Facilities for disabled campers. Restaurant/snack bar. Shop. Play area. Fishing. Torches useful. WiFi. Off site: Town close by. Walks. Sub-aqua diving. Bicycle hire 2 km. Golf 8 km. Excursions – tickets to attractions sold. Bus stop nearby to Almeria and Aguadulce.

Open: All year.

Directions

Site is west of Almeria. Take 438 exit from the N340 and follow the Almeria/Puerto signs. Then take the Aguadulce direction, from where site is signposted. GPS: 36.8257, -2.5161

Charges guide

Per unit incl. 2 persons and electricity	€ 24.28 - € 27.90
extra person	€ 5.50

Almonte

Camping La Aldea

El Rocio, E-21750 Almonte (Huelva) T: 959 442 677. E: info@campinglaaldea.com

alanrogers.com/ES88730

This impressive site lies just on the edge of the Parque Nacional de Doñana, southwest of Sevilla on the outskirts of El Rocio. The town hosts a fiesta at the end of May with over one million people attending the local shrine. They travel for days in processions with cow-drawn or motorised vehicles to attend. If you want to stay this weekend book well in advance! The well planned, modern site is well set out and the 246 pitches have natural shade from trees or artificial shade and 10A electricity. There are 52 serviced pitches with water and sewerage. There are also pitches for tents and bungalows for rent. The facilities are new, large and very clean. A beautiful waiter service restaurant (where the Spanish eat) provides lovely local food. The staff are welcoming and helpful. Expeditions on horseback or by 4 x 4 vehicle can be arranged in the national park.

Facilities

Two sanitary blocks provide excellent facilities including provision for disabled visitors. Motorcaravan service point. Swimming pool (May-Oct). Restaurant and bar in separate new complex. Shop. Internet connection. Playground. Off site: Bus stop 5 minutes walk. Beach 15 km. Huelva and Sevilla are about an hour's drive.

Open: All year.

Directions

From the main Huelva - Sevilla road E1/A49 take exit 48 and drive south through Almonte to outskirts of El Rocio. Site is on left just past 25 km. marker. Go down to the roundabout and back up to be on the right side of the road to turn in.
GPS: 37.1428, -6.491164

Charges guide

Per unit incl. 2 persons and electricity	€ 23.00 - € 26.00
extra person	€ 5.50
child (0-10 yrs)	€ 4.50
dog	€ 3.00

Less 10-15% for low season stays over 3 days.

Barbate

Camping Pinar San José

Carretera de Vejer - Caños de Meca km 10,2, Los Caños de Meca, E-11159 Barbate (Cádiz) T: 956 437 030. E: info@campingpinarsanjose.com **alanrogers.com/ES88570**

Pinar San José is a new site, first opened in 2008. The site is located in the La Breña nature park and has been developed to reflect the natural beauty that surrounds it. The nearest beaches on the Costa de la Luz are around 1km. away. On site amenities are modern and well designed and include two swimming pools, tennis and a sports court. Pitches are grassy and all have electrical connections. There is a good provision of water points and many pitches also have drainage and Internet connections. A number of brick built chalets are available for rent. Cabo de Trafalgar (Cape Trafalgar) is very close and, of course, gave its name to the famous battle several kilometres to the west. The nearest village to the site is Zahora and the great cities of Cádiz and Jerez, as well as Gibraltar, are all accessible in less than an hour. The nature park is a large, forested area, criss-crossed with cycle tracks and footpaths.

Facilities

Bar. Restaurant. Shop. Two swimming pools. Tennis. Sports court. Play area. Games room. Chalets for rent. Dogs are not accepted in high season. Off site: Nearest beach 1 km. Cádiz 50 km. Fishing. Golf. Watersports.

Open: All year.

Directions

Heading south from Cádiz on the A48 motorway at the Vejer de la Frontera exit and head west on A2230 and then south on A2233 to Zahora. Site is well signed from here. GPS: 36.19998, -6.034627

Charges guide

Per unit incl. 2 persons and electricity	€ 21.50 - € 32.00
extra person	€ 4.50 - € 6.00

Cabo de Gata

Camping Cabo de Gata

Ctra Cabo de Gata s/n, E-04150 Cabo de Gata (Almería) T: 950 160 443. E: info@campingcabodegata.com **alanrogers.com/ES87630**

Cabo de Gata is situated on the Gulf of Almería, a pleasant, all-year campsite offering facilities to a good standard. Popular with British visitors through the winter, and within the Cabo de Gata-Nijar Nature Park and set amongst fruit farms, it is only a 1 km. walk to a fine sandy beach. The 250 gravel pitches are level and of a reasonable size, with 6/16A electricity and limited shade from maturing trees or canopies. There are specific areas for very large units with very high canopies for shade and seven chalets for rent. A modern, airy reception is adjacent to Internet facilities, whilst the nearby irregularly shaped swimming pool is in close proximity to the bar/restaurant with a very Spanish feel. To the west, Salinas de Acosta and the lighthouse at Faro de Gata (fine views). The salinas are renowned for their birdlife and from the hides you will see large flocks of pink flamingo and many other species. Almería has many quality shops.

Facilities

Two, well maintained, clean toilet blocks provide all the necessary sanitary facilities. including British type WCs, washbasins and free hot showers. Facilities for disabled campers. Restaurant, bar and shop (all year). Swimming pool. Football. Pétanque. Tennis. Small playground. Library. Bicycle hire. English spoken. Entertainment programme. Internet access (charged). WiFi throughout site. Off site: Bus from gate. Nearest beach and fishing 1 km. Golf 10 km. Riding 15 km.

Open: All year.

Directions

From A7-E15 take exit 460 or 467 and follow signs for Retamar via N344 and for Cabo de Gata. Site is on the right before village of Cabo de Gata. The final stretch of road is in a poor state of repair due to restrictions imposed within the natural park. GPS: 36.80188, -2.24471

Charges guide

Per unit incl. 2 persons and electricity	€ 29.45 - € 30.10
extra person	€ 5.95

Conil de la Frontera

Camping Roche

N340 km 19,5, Carril de Pilahito, E-11140 Conil de la Frontera (Cádiz) T: 956 442 216.

E: info@campingroche.com **alanrogers.com/ES88590**

Camping Roche is situated in a pine forest near white sandy beaches in the lovely region of Andalucia. It is a clean, tidy and welcoming site. English is spoken but try your Spanish, German or French as the staff are very helpful. A family site, it offers a variety of facilities including a sports area and swimming pools. The restaurant has good food and a pleasant outlook over the pool. Games are organised for children. A recently built extension provides further pitches, a new toilet block and a tennis court. There are 335 pitches which include 104 bungalows to rent. The touring pitches all have electricity (10A), and 76 also have water and waste water. There are pleasant paths in the area for mountain biking and this is an ideal base for visiting the cities of Seville and Cádiz.

Facilities

Three toilet blocks are traditional in style and provide simple, clean facilities. Washbasins have cold water only. Washing machine. Supermarket. Bar and restaurant. Swimming and paddling pools. Sports area. Tennis. Play area. Off site: Bus stops 3 times daily outside gates. Cádiz. Cape Trafalgar. Baelo Claudia archaeological site.

Open: All year.

Directions

From the N340 (Cádiz - Algeciras) turn off to site at km. 19.5 point. From Conil, take El Pradillo road. Keep following signs to site. From CA3208 road turn at km. 1 and site is 1.5 km. down this road on the right. GPS: 36.31089, -6.11268

Charges guide

Per unit incl. 2 persons and electricity	€ 18.81 - € 33.10
extra person	€ 3.71 - € 6.50
child	€ 3.14 - € 5.50
dog	€ 2.14 - € 3.75

Conil de la Frontera

Camping La Rosaleda

Ctra del Pradillo km 1,3, E-11140 Conil de la Frontera (Cádiz) T: 956 443 327.

E: info@campinglarosaleda.com **alanrogers.com/ES88580**

This excellent site in Andalucia was opened in 1999. Its owner has many years of experience and has listened to what campers want and has then delivered. Much money has been spent and will continue to be spent to make this an even better site. Great care has been taken with the planning to ensure campers have an enjoyable holiday, with many top class facilities and a first class service. There are 335 well kept pitches of three different sizes (70-120 sq.m), the smallest just for tents, the largest with electricity and water. This is an ideal place to experience the sunshine and culture of Spain.

Facilities

Four modern, fully equipped sanitary blocks include facilities for campers with disabilities and were spotless when seen. Motorcaravan services. Gas supplies. Excellent supermarket (all year). Bar/restaurant (all year). Swimming pool complex (large with stunning views). Large play area. Massage, sauna, gym, yoga room, hairdressing. Wooden bungalows with good facilities and own gardens. WiFi over site. No barbecues on pitches 15/6-15/10. Dogs are not accepted in high season. Off site: Conil town with bars restaurants and shops. Excursions. Bicycle hire 1 km. Beach 1.5 km. Riding 1.5 km. Golf 15 km.

Open: All year.

Directions

Follow signs to Conil from N340, then signs to site around several roundabouts. Site is 1 km. from centre on Ctra del Pradillo, on the side of this road with a car park in front and a large campsite sign high in the air. GPS: 36.29317, -6.09547

Charges guide

Per person	€ 4.72 - € 8.00
child (3-10 yrs)	€ 3.24 - € 5.50
pitch incl. electricity	€ 11.80 - € 21.00

Conil de la Frontera

Camping Fuente del Gallo

Apdo 48, E-11149 Conil de la Frontera (Cádiz) T: 956 440 137. E: camping@campingfuentedelgallo.com

alanrogers.com/ES88600

Fuente del Gallo is well maintained with 184 pitches allocated to touring units. Each pitch has 6A electricity and a number of trees create shade to some pitches. Although the actual pitch areas are generally a good size, the majority are long and narrow. This could, in some cases, prevent the erection of an awning and your neighbour may feel close. In low season it is generally accepted to make additional use of an adjoining pitch. The attractive pool, restaurant and bar complex with its large, shaded terrace, are very welcoming in the height of summer. Good beaches are within 300 m.

Facilities

Two modernised and very clean sanitary blocks include services for babies and disabled visitors. Laundry facilities. Motorcaravan services. Gas. Shop. Bar and restaurant (breakfast served). Swimming pool (1/6-30/9 with lifeguard) with paddling pool. Play area. TV and games machines. Excursions. Torches useful. Picnic area with playground. WiFi throughout (charged). Off site: Fishing 300 m. Riding 1 km. Bicycle hire 2 km. Golf 5 km.

Open: 23 March - 30 September.

Directions

From the Cadiz - Algeciras road (N340) at km. 23.00, follow signs to Conil de la Frontera town centre, then shortly right to Fuente del Gallo and 'playas', following signs. GPS: 36.2961, -6.1102

Charges 2012

Per unit incl. 2 persons and electricity	€ 24.50 - € 32.50
extra person	€ 5.50 - € 7.00

Córdoba

Camping Los Villares

Parque Periurbano, avenida de l Fuen Santa 8, E-14071 Córdoba (Córdoba) T: 957 330 145

alanrogers.com/ES90780

This is a site with a difference. Unusually, it is part of one of Spain's natural parks and the environmental rules must be strictly followed. For peaceful, simple camping with no frills, there is an area with electricity for 30 units about five minutes walk from a toilet block, restaurant and reception. The 170 tent pitches are delightfully informal. Trees provide shade and the setting is absolutely natural. Some natural stone tables and benches are scattered around. The bar and restaurant provide a simple menu and drinks.

Facilities

The single toilet facility is centrally located, provides free hot water and is of good quality. Washing machines. Shop. Restaurant/bar. Off site: Nature park (protected) with walks and wildlife.

Open: All year.

Directions

Site is 7 km. north of Córdoba on north side of river which bisects the city. It is simpler to go to centre to find small access road to Parque and site. Follow signs for Parador or Parque Periurbano, also signs for municipal camping (bringing you past the municipal camping). Look for major right turn and follow signs out of city. GPS: 37.95738, -4.81033

Charges guide

Per person	€ 3.75
pitch incl. car	€ 7.00 - € 8.00

No credit cards.

Córdoba

Camping Municipal El Brillante

Avenida del Brillante 50, E-14012 Córdoba (Córdoba) T: 957 403 836. E: elbrillante@campings.net

alanrogers.com/ES90800

Córdoba is one of the hottest places in Europe and the superb pool here is more than welcome. If you really want to stay in the city, then this large site is a good choice. It has 120 neat pitches of gravel and sand, the upper pitches covered by artificial and natural shade but the lower, newer area has little. The site becomes very crowded in high season. The entrance is narrow and may be congested so care must be exercised – there is a layby just outside and it is easier to walk in initially. All pitches have electricity (6/10A) plus the newer area has 32 fully serviced pitches and an area for a few large motorcaravans.

Facilities

The toilet blocks include facilities for babies and disabled visitors. Motorcaravan services. Gas supplies. Shop (all year). Bar and restaurant (1/7-15/9). Swimming pool (1/6-10/9). Play area. Off site: Bus service to city centre from outside site. Commercial centre 300 m. (left out of site, right at traffic lights).

Open: All year.

Directions

From the NIV/E25 road from Madrid, take exit at km. 403 (the middle of three for Córdoba). Follow signs for Mosque/Cathedral into city centre. Pass it (on right) and turn right onto main avenue. Continue and take right fork where road splits. Follow signs for site. Site on right. GPS: 37.899975, -4.787319

Charges guide

Per unit incl. 2 persons and electricity	€ 25.00 - € 28.00

No credit cards.

El Puerto de Santa Maria

Camping Playa Las Dunas

Paseo Maritimo, Playa de la Puntilla s/n, E-11500 El Puerto de Santa Maria (Cádiz) T: 956 872 210.
E: info@lasdunascamping.com **alanrogers.com/ES88650**

This site lies within the Parque Natural Bahia de Les Dunes and is adjacent to the long and gently sloping golden sands of Puntilla beach. This is a pleasant and peaceful site (though very busy in August) with some 539 separate marked pitches, 260 for tourers, with much natural shade and ample electrical connections (10A). Motorcaravans park in an area called the Oasis, which is very pretty. The tent and caravan pitches, under mature trees, are terraced and separated by low walls. This is a spacious site with a tranquil setting and it is popular with people who wish to 'winter over' in peace.

Facilities

Immaculate modern sanitary facilities with separate facilities for disabled campers and a baby room. Laundry facilities are excellent. Gas supplies. Bar/restaurant (all year). Supermarket (high season). Very large swimming pool and paddling pool (1/7-31/8). Night security all year. Barbecues are not permitted 15/5-15/10. WiFi throughout (charged). Off site: Beach 100 m. Fishing 500 m. Bicycle hire, riding and golf 2 km. Municipal sports centre. Local buses for town and city visits and a ferry to Cadiz.

Open: All year.

Directions

Site is 5 km. north of Cadiz off the N443. Take road to Puerto Santa Maria, site is very well signed throughout the town (small yellow signs high on posts). From south, turn left into town just after large bridge. Keeping sea inlet on your left, follow road for about 1 km. Site on right opposite beach.
GPS: 36.5890, -6.2384

Charges 2012

Per unit incl. 2 persons and electricity	€ 21.96 - € 27.11
extra person	€ 4.80 - € 5.33

Fuente de Piedra

Espacios Rurales Fuente de Piedra

Ctra La Rábita s/n, E-29520 Fuente de Piedra (Málaga) T: 952 735 294. E: info@camping-rural.com
alanrogers.com/ES87900

In a remote area of Andalucia, this tiny campsite with just 30 touring pitches looks over the salty lakes and marshes of the Laguna de Fuente. The average sized pitches are on a sloping, terraced hillside, with some having a view of the lake. With a gravel surface and good shade, many pitches slope so chocks would be useful. There is a separate grassy area for tents near the pool and bungalows (cars are not permitted here). Unusually for a site of this size, there is a pool and an excellent bar, snack bar and huge restaurant which serves delicious Spanish food. Try the excellent, inexpensive 'menu del dia'.

Facilities

Sanitary facilities are in one block and are looking a little tired. Facilities for disabled campers. Washing machines. Shop. Restaurant. Bar with TV. Snack bar. Swimming pool. Pool bar. Electronic games. Bicycle hire. Off site: Lake with flamingos. Bicycle hire 1 km. Fishing 5 km. Riding 10 km. Golf 40 km. Excursions organised in July/Aug.

Open: All year.

Directions

Site is 20 km. northwest of Antequera. From Antequera take A92 and exit at 132 km. point and follow road to the town. Site is well signed from the town but the signs are small. GPS: 37.1292, -4.7334

Charges guide

Per person	€ 5.40 - € 6.00
pitch	€ 3.60 - € 8.00
electricity	€ 5.00

Granada

Camping Suspiro del Moro

Ctra Bailén - Motril km 144, Puerto Suspiro del Moro, E-18630 Granada (Granada) T: 958 555 411.
E: campingsuspirodelmoro@yahoo.es **alanrogers.com/ES92700**

Suspiro del Moro is a small, family run site with 64 pitches, which packs a big punch with its associated Olympic-sized swimming pool and huge bar and restaurant. It is cool and peaceful with great views from the site perimeter. The flat pitches are shaded by mature trees and there are no statics here. The whole site is neat, clean and well ordered and great for chilling out while visiting the area and the famous Alhambra. The site also has its own small bar and restaurant serving snacks.

Facilities

Clean and tidy, the small toilet blocks are situated around the camping area with British style WCs and free hot showers. Laundry and dishwashing facilities. Small basic shop. Small simple restaurant/bar (high season). Small play area on gravel. WiFi. Off site: Swimming pool and restaurant adjacent. Sierra Nevada and Granada within reasonable distance to explore. Public transport 50 m. from gate.

Open: All year.

Directions

Leave Granada to Motril road (E902/A44) at exit 144 (from south) or 139 (from north) and follow unnamed campsite signs. At roundabout go towards Suspiro, then left (signed after turn). Site is about 600 m. on right on A4050. GPS: 37.0852, -3.6348

Charges guide

Per person	€ 4.00 - € 4.80
pitch incl. car	€ 9.00 - € 9.50
electricity	€ 3.00 - € 3.30

Granada

Camping Sierra Nevada

Avenida Juan Pablo II no.23, E-18014 Granada (Granada) T: 958 150 062. E: campingmotel@terra.es

alanrogers.com/ES92800

This is a good site either for a night stop or for a stay of a few days while visiting Granada, especially the Alhambra, and for a city site it is surprisingly pleasant. Quite large, it has an open feel and a smart, irregular shape pool with a smaller children's pool open in high season. There is some traffic noise around the pool as it is on the road boundary. With 148 pitches for touring units (10/20A electricity), the site is in two connected parts with more mature trees and facilities to the northern end.

Facilities

Two modern sanitary blocks, with good facilities, including cabins, very good facilities for disabled campers and babies. Washing machines. Motorcaravan services. Gas supplies. Shop (15/3-15/10). Swimming pools with lifeguards and charge of € 1.80 (15/6-15/9). Bar/restaurant by pool. Tennis. Pétanque. Large playground. Off site: Supermarket. Bus station 100 m. from site gate. Fishing 10 km. Golf 12 km. Riding 15 km.

Open: 1 March - 31 October.

Directions

Site is just outside the city to north, on road to Jaén and Madrid. From autopista, take Granada North - Almanjayar exit 123 (close to central bus station). Follow road back towards Granada and site is on the right, well signed. From other roads join the motorway to access the correct exit.
GPS: 37.20402, -3.61703

Charges guide

Per unit incl. 2 persons and electricity	€ 30.00
extra person	€ 6.00

Güéjar-Sierra

Camping Las Lomas

Ctra de Sierra Nevada, E-18160 Güéjar-Sierra (Granada) T: 958 484 742. E: laslomas@campingsonline.com

alanrogers.com/ES92850

This site is high in the Sierra Nevada natural park and looks down on the Patano de Canales reservoir. After a scenic drive to Güejar-Sierra, you are rewarded with a site boasting excellent facilities. It is set on a slope but the pitches have been levelled and are quite private, with high separating hedges and many mature trees giving good shade, (some pitches are fully serviced, with sinks and all but four have electricity). The large bar/restaurant complex and pools have wonderful views over the lake.

Facilities

Adequate sanitary blocks (heated in winter) provide clean facilities. First class facilities for disabled campers and well equipped baby room (key at reception). Motorcaravan services. Good supermarket. Restaurant/bar. Swimming pool. Play area. Minigolf. Barbecue. WiFi (charged). Torches useful. A no noise policy (including cars) is strictly enforced midnight-07.00. Off site: Buses to village and Granada (15 km). Bicycle hire 1.5 km. Fishing 3 km. Tours of The Alhambra and Granada organised. Useful site for winter skiing. Parascending and skiing nearby.

Open: All year.

Directions

Heading south towards Granada on A44 (E902 Jaén - Motril) take exit 132 onto A395 (Alhamba - Sierra Nevada). After 4 km. marker, exit 5B (Sierra Nevada). At 7 km. marker, exit right onto slip road. At (Cenes de la Vega - Güejar-Sierra) junction turn left. In 200 m. turn right on A4026. In 1.6 km. turn left (Güejar-Sierra). Drive uphill, past dam and site is on right in 2.8 km. GPS: 37.16073, -3.45388

Charges guide

Per person	€ 4.00 - € 6.00
pitch	€ 12.00 - € 14.00
electricity	€ 3.50

Isla Cristina

Camping Giralda

Ctra Provincial 4117, E-21410 Isla Cristina (Huelva) T: 959 343 318. E: recepcion@campinggiralda.com

alanrogers.com/ES88710

The fountains at the entrance and the circular thatched reception building set the tone for this very large site. The 587 pitches are quite spacious on sand, most benefiting from the attractive mature trees which abound on the site. Most pitches have electricity (142 are for tents). Access to the excellent beach is gained by a short stroll, crossing the minor road alongside the site and passing through attractive pine trees. This is a quiet site out of the main tourist areas, with good leisure and adventure facilities. The many additional activities are listed below.

Facilities

Four large, modern, semi-circular thatched sanitary blocks are clean and fully equipped. Laundry. Shop and bar (all year). Restaurant and snacks (June-Sept). Swimming pools. Archery. Mountain biking. Beach games. Watersports school. Play area. Activity area for groups low season. Excursions booked. Off site: Beach and fishing 200 m. Bicycle hire 1.5 km. Golf 4 km. Riding 7 km.

Open: All year.

Directions

Leave E1/A49 at exit 113 signed Lepe on N444. Turn right on N431, use Lepe bypass, then left to Le Antilla and then on to Isla Cristina. Site on right just as you reach Isla Christina (route avoids speed bumps). GPS: 37.19998, -7.30087

Charges guide

Per unit incl. 2 persons and electricity	€ 25.85 - € 27.80

Iznate

Camping Iznate

Ctra Benamocarra - Iznate km 2,7, E-29792 Iznate (Málaga) T: 952 535 613. E: info@campingiznate.com

alanrogers.com/ES87850

This new site is situated amid beautiful scenery 1 km. away from the picturesque village of Iznate. It is surrounded by avocado and olive trees and is on the wine route – the region is the centre of Spain's Muscadet production. The site is well thought out and immaculately maintained. The large swimming pool is an ideal spot for cooling off after a walk and the next door restaurant serves excellent food at very reasonable prices. This is a small new site and we would recommend booking during high season. There are wonderful views all round the site and eagles, wild boar and black squirrels can be seen.

Facilities

The modern toilet block has hot showers and facilities for disabled visitors. Laundry facilities under a covered area. Fridge hire. Small shop. Bar/restaurant with terrace adjoining the site. Swimming pool (15/5-15/9). Summer entertainment. Pétanque. Play area. TV room. WiFi. Barbecues not permitted in high season. Off site: Beach 20 minutes drive. Sayalonga and Frigeliana nearby.

Open: All year.

Directions

From A7/E15 take exit 265 and head towards Cajiz and Iznate. Site is on left after Iznate.
GPS: 36.79219, -4.17131

Charges guide

Per person	€ 4.30
child (2-10 yrs)	€ 3.70
pitch incl. car	€ 8.30 - € 9.30
electricity	€ 3.00 - € 3.50

La Carlota

Camping Carlos III

Ctra Madrid - Cadiz km 430, E-14100 La Carlota (Córdoba) T: 957 300 338.
E: camping@campingcarlosiii.com **alanrogers.com/ES90850**

This rural site lies 25 km. south of Córdoba, just off the main Córdoba - Sevilla road and may be a good alternative to staying in the city. A very large, busy site especially at weekends, it has many supporting facilities including a good swimming pool and a pool, play area and animal corner for children. With the catering services open all year, the site has a more open feel than the bustling municipal site in Córdoba. The touring areas are canopied by trees which offer considerable shade for the 338 separated pitches. On sandy, gently sloping ground, around two-thirds have 5/10A electricity.

Facilities

Modern toilet blocks provide a mix of British and Turkish WCs, with hot showers in the block near reception. Laundry service. Motorcaravan services. Bar/restaurant, shop (all year). Swimming pools (1/6-15/9). Aviary. Boules. Minigolf. Play area. Hairdressers. WiFi (free). Off site: Bus service outside site. Riding 200 m. Village 1 km.

Open: All year.

Directions

From NIV Córdoba-Seville motorway take La Carlota exit (at km. 429 point northbound or exit 432 southbound). Site is 500 m. and well signed.
GPS: 37.67664, -4.93329

Charges guide

Per unit incl. 2 persons and electricity	€ 24.50 - € 24.85
extra person	€ 5.35
child (3-12 yrs)	€ 4.00

La Zubia

Camping Reina Isabel

Laurel de la Reina 15, E-18140 La Zubia (Granada) T: 958 590 041. E: info@reinaisabelcamping.com

alanrogers.com/ES92760

Reina Isabel can be found just 3 km. from the centre of Granada and just 1 km. from the entrance to the spectacular Sierra Nevada National Park. The site is open for an extended season and is well located for winter sports holidays in the Sierra Nevada. There are 51 shady touring pitches here (each around 70 sq.m), all with electrical connections. There are also 11 bungalows available for rent. A regular bus service operates to the city centre and to other places of interest, notably the Alhambra Palace. The Sierra Nevada is made up of some of Spain's most stunning mountain scenery and is ideal walking and mountain biking country.

Facilities

The single toilet block is clean but the toilet and shower cubicles have large frosted glass panels which are revealing at night. Used paper goes into baskets and not into the toilet. Shop in reception, bar/restaurant/takeaway (all season). Outdoor swimming pool (15/5-30/9). Play area. Bungalows for rent. Excursions available. WiFi. Off site: Bus stop with regular service to the city centre. Sierra Nevada ski resort 29 km.

Open: All year.

Directions

Site is south of Granada. Leave A44 motorway at exit 132 and head east on A395. Follow signs to La Zubia, joining the southbound Calle de Laurel de la Reina. Site is clearly signed from here.
GPS: 37.12456, -3.58625

Charges guide

Per unit incl. 2 persons and electricity	€ 29.00
extra person	€ 5.90
child	€ 4.35

Marbella

Camping Marbella Playa

Ctra N340 km 192,8, E-29600 Marbella (Málaga) T: 952 833 998. E: recepcion@campingmarbella.com

alanrogers.com/ES88000

This large site is 12 kilometres east of the internationally famous resort of Marbella with public transport available to the town centre and local attractions. A sandy beach is about 150 metres away with direct access. There are 430 individual pitches of up to 70 sq.m. with natural shade (additional artificial shade is provided to some), and electricity (10/20A) available throughout. Long leads may be required for some pitches, and those next to the road can experience some noise from 6pm onwards. The site is busy throughout the high season but the high staff/customer ratio and the friendly staff approach ensures a comfortable stay. A large pool complex with a restaurant/bar provides a very attractive feature.

Facilities

Four sanitary blocks of mixed ages, are fully equipped and well maintained. Three modern units for disabled visitors. Laundry service. Large supermarket with butcher and fresh vegetable counter. Bar, restaurant and café (all open all year). Supervised swimming pool (free April-Sept). Playground. Children's activities. WiFi (charged). Torches advised. Off site: Fishing 100 m. Bus service 150 m. Beach 200 m. Golf and bicycle hire 5 km. Riding 10 km.

Open: All year.

Directions

Site is 12 km. east of Marbella with access close to the 193 km. point on the main N340 road. Signed Elviria, then follow camping signs.
GPS: 36.49127, -4.76325

Charges guide

Per person	€ 3.30 - € 5.75
child (1-10 yrs)	€ 2.55 - € 5.06
pitch	€ 4.60 - € 13.70
electricity	€ 4.10 - € 7.05

Reductions (up to 50%) for long stays and senior citizens outside 1/6-16/9.

Marbella

Kawan Village Cabopino

Ctra N340 km 194,7, E-29604 Marbella (Málaga) T: 952 834 373. E: info@campingcabopino.com

alanrogers.com/ES88020

This large, mature site is alongside the main N340/A7 Costa del Sol coast road, 12 km. east of Marbella and 15 km. from Fuengirola. The Costa del Sol is also known as the Costa del Golf and fittingly there is a major golf course alongside the site. The site is set amongst tall pine trees which provide shade for the sandy pitches (there are some huge areas for large units). The 300 touring pitches, a mix of level and sloping (chocks advisable), all have electricity (10A), but long leads may be required for some. There is a separate area on the western side for groups of younger guests. The upper areas of the site are filled with permanent pitches and bungalows. At the other side of the site you will find a fenced swimming pool with a grass sunbathing area and a new heated covered pool has been added. Close to the entrance is an Italian restaurant with a terrace that enjoys shade and is very pleasant. A short walk over the road and down the hill brings you to a restaurant on the beach and an unofficial naturist area.

Facilities

Five mature but very clean sanitary blocks provide hot water throughout (may be under pressure at peak times). Washing machines. Bar/restaurant and takeaway (all year). Shop. Outdoor pool (1/5-15/9) and indoor pool (all year). Play area. Adult exercise equipment. Some evening entertainment. Excursions can be booked. ATM. Torches necessary in the more remote parts of the site. Only gas or electric barbecues are permitted. Off site: Beach and golf 200 m. Fishing, bicycle hire and riding within 1 km.

Open: All year.

Directions

Site is 12 km. from Marbella. Approaching Marbella from the east, leave the N340/A7 at the 194 km. marker (signed Cabopino). Site is off the roundabout at the top of the slip road. GPS: 36.49350, -4.74383

Charges guide

Per unit incl. 2 persons and electricity	€ 23.11 - € 34.82
extra person	€ 4.55 - € 6.97
child (2-11 yrs)	€ 2.93 - € 5.80
dog	€ 1.72

Discounts outside high season and for over 7 days. Camping Cheques accepted.

Marbella

Camping La Buganvilla

Ctra N340 km 188,8, E-29600 Marbella (Málaga) T: 952 831 973. E: info@campingbuganvilla.com

alanrogers.com/ES88030

La Buganvilla is a large, uncomplicated site with mature trees providing shade to some of the 250 touring pitches. They all have 16A electricity and are mostly on terraces so there are some views across to the mountains and hinterland of this coastal area. The terrain is a little rugged in places and the buildings are older and in need of some attention, but all were clean when we visited. A pool complex near the bar and restaurant is ideal for cooling off after a day's sightseeing. This is an acceptable base from which to explore areas of the Costa del Sol and it is an easy drive to the picturesque Ronda Valley.

Facilities

Three painted sanitary blocks are clean and adequate. Laundry facilities (not all sinks have hot water). Outdoor pool (all year). Bar/restaurant with basic food. Well stocked small supermarket. Play area. Tennis (high season). WiFi (charged). Dogs are not accepted in July/Aug. Off site: Bus service close to site entrance. Fishing and watersports 400 m. Bicycle and scooter hire 1 km. Golf 5 km. Resort type entertainment close.

Open: All year.

Directions

Site is between Marbella and Fuengirola off the N340/A7. Access at 188.8 km. marker is only possible when travelling west, i.e. from Fuengirola. From the other direction, continue to the 'cambio de sentido' signed Elviria and turn back over the dual-carriageway. Site is signed. GPS: 36.5023, -4.804

Charges guide

Per unit incl. 2 persons and electricity	€ 22.82 - € 33.82
extra person	€ 5.50 - € 7.50

Maro

Nerja Camping

Ctra N340 km 297, E-29787 Maro (Málaga) T: 952 529 714. E: info@nerjacamping.com

alanrogers.com/ES87110

This site is set on the lower slopes of the Sierra Laminar, some five kilometres from Nerja and two kilometres from the excellent beaches. Nerja Camping is a small site of 55 pitches with impressive views of the surrounding mountains and the Mediterranean. There are 25 touring pitches (15A electricity) and four new mobile homes to rent. The pitches are on the small side and set on slopes with some terracing along with some artificial shade. The roads, although sloping, should present few problems for siting units. The small restaurant doubles as a bar and has a small terrace where you can order snacks.

Facilities

The single sanitary block has been refurbished and tiled; all washbasins and showers have hot water. Laundry facilities. Small restaurant/bar (Mar-Sept). Essentials from the bar. Small swimming pool (Mar-Sept). Accommodation to rent. WiFi. Off site: Nerja limestone caves 1 km. Beach 2 km. Fishing 3 km. Bicycle hire and riding 5 km. Sub-aqua diving, parascending and watersports. Day trips to Granada and Gibraltar. Sierra Nevada 100 km.

Open: All year excl. October.

Directions

Site signed from main N340 coast road about 5 km. east of Nerja after 296 km. marker. If coming from Nerja, go 200 m. past site entrance (opposite radio masts) to cross main road. GPS: 36.7605, -3.83475

Charges guide

Per unit incl. 2 persons and electricity	€ 20.00 - € 24.25
extra person	€ 5.50

No credit cards.

Mojacar

Camping Sopalmo

Apdo 761, Sopalmo, E-04638 Mojacar (Almería) T: 950 478 413. E: info@campingsopalmoelcortijillo.com

alanrogers.com/ES87490

This is a tiny, homely site run by the cheerful Simon and his charming wife Macu (both speaking some English) who are determined that you will enjoy your stay. The site is on three levels (with a slightly steep gravel track to the gates) with space for 29 tents, caravans or medium sized motorcaravans. All the pitches are marked, level and on gravel with electricity (6A). The site is unspoilt and has much rustic charm with the family house providing the focal point. Trees and shrubs include olives, figs and cacti.

Facilities

The small sanitary block is very clean and fully equipped. Hot showers assisted by solar power. Facilities for disabled campers. Basic laundry and dishwashing facilities. Bar. Breakfast available in summer and the baker calls at 10.30 daily. Torch useful. Internet access. Off site: Bus to Mojecar from site. Beach 1.5 km. Nearest serious shops 5 km. Riding 6 km. Golf 10 km.

Open: All year.

Directions

From the main coast road (N340) take exit 520 (northeast of Almeria). Take the AL152 (formerly A150) to Mojacar Playa and continue south towards Carboneras. Site is 6 km. south of Mojacar Playa, signed off the road. GPS: 37.06533, -1.86881

Charges guide

Per unit incl. 2 persons and electricity	€ 20.20
extra person	€ 3.95 - € 4.65

No credit cards.

Mojacar

Camping Cueva Negra

Camino Lotaza 2, Frenta - Playa Macenas, E-04638 Mojacar (Almería) T: 950 475 855.
E: info@campingcuevanegra.es **alanrogers.com/ES87560**

This tiny jewel of a site, just 9 km. south of Mojacar is approached by a short, steep and winding road with passing places. There are only 40 pitches, but they are all 100 sq.m. and 30 have electricity, water and drainage, with artificial shade provided in summer. The elevated site is attractively laid out with views to the nearby sea. The superb covered swimming pool has four jacuzzis and a large, partly covered terrace with an open-air shower for disabled campers. There are facilities for tennis and pétanque and a play area for children.

Facilities

Modern toilet block with facilities for disabled visitors. Laundry with washing machine and dryer. Well stocked shop and small bar (all year). Takeaway (high season). Covered swimming pool (1/5-31/10). Tennis. Play area. Apartment and bungalow for rent. Off site: Beach 400 m. Five golf courses nearby. The towns of Mojacar, Aguilas Nijar and Almeria within easy reach.

Open: All year.

Directions

Site is 9 km. south of Mojacar on the Mojacar - Carboneras road, on the right when travelling south. There is a small sign at the entry road.
GPS: 37.08674, -1.85396

Charges guide

Per unit incl. 2 persons and electricity	€ 19.19 - € 29.60
extra person	€ 3.41 - € 5.57

Motril

Camping Don Cactus

Ctra N340 km 343, Playa de Carchuna, E-18730 Carchuna-Motril (Granada) T: 958 623 109.
E: camping@doncactus.com **alanrogers.com/ES92950**

Situated between the main N340 and the beach, this family run campsite is pleasantly surprising with clever planning and ongoing improvements. It is a comfortable site of 320 pitches (280 for touring). The flat pitches vary in size with electricity (5/12A), some providing water and satellite TV connections, and are arranged along avenues with eucalyptus trees for shade. This quieter section of the coast is beautiful with coves and access to larger towns if wished. The friendly reception staff are very helpful with tourist advice and can arrange trips for you if needed.

Facilities

The large toilet block is dated but clean and provides British style WCs, showers and plenty of washbasins. Laundry facilities. Beach showers. Shop. Bar, restaurant and takeaway. Swimming pool (in high season € 1.50 per day). Tennis. Play area. Summer activities for children. Outdoor fitness centre for adults. Pets corner. Internet point. WiFi (charged; free in bar). Dogs are not accepted in July/Aug. Barbecues only in special area. Caravan storage. Car wash facility. Off site: Bus service 500 m.

Open: All year.

Directions

From Motril - Carchuna road (N340/E15) turn towards the sea at km. 343. (site signed, but look at roof level for large green tent on the top of the building!). Travel about 600 m. then turn east to site on left. GPS: 36.70066, -3.44032

Charges guide

Per person	€ 6.96
pitch	€ 15.75
electricity (5A)	€ 4.75

Nijar

Camping Los Escullos

Paraje de los Escullos s/n, E-04118 San Jose-Nijar (Almería) T: 950 389 811. E: info@losescullossanjose.com
alanrogers.com/ES87620

This efficient, well maintained, medium sized site has 171 pitches (60-80 sq.m). They are divided by hedges and trees and 100 pitches have 10A electric supply and some have artificial shading. Specific taps about the grounds provide drinking water. The pool has an overlooking bar and restaurant which is kept busy serving excellent typical Spanish 'menu del dia' food at very low prices. It is a popular site with British tourists seeking the sun. The salinas on the approach to Cabo de Gata are famous for bird life (including flocks of pink flamingo).

Facilities

The main sanitary block is large and clean with hot showers and facilities for disabled visitors. Second small sanitary block close to reception. Small supermarket. Bar/restaurant. Takeaway (15/6-15/9). Large outdoor pool (15/5-1/10) and jacuzzi (1/7-1/10). Hairdresser. Massage. Gym. Internet access. Multisports court. Scuba diving. TV room. Bicycle hire. No charcoal barbecues. Entertainment in high season. WiFi (free). Off site: No public transport (a vehicle is required here). Fishing 1 km. Walking track to the nearest (pebble) beach 1 km. Riding 7 km. Golf 25 km.

Open: All year.

Directions

From A7/E15 autovia exit at either exit 479 or 471 in direction of San Jose. On approach to San Jose left turn toward Los Escullos. Site is well signed.
GPS: 36.80288, -2.07756

Charges guide

Per unit incl. 2 persons and electricity	€ 23.50 - € 35.20
extra person	€ 5.50 - € 7.25
child (2-14 yrs)	€ 4.50 - € 6.25

Camping Cheques accepted.

Orgiva

Camping Puerta de La Alpujarra

Ctra Lanjarón - Orgiva (Las Barreras), E-18400 Orgiva (Granada) T: 958 784 450. E: puertalpujarra@yahoo.es

alanrogers.com/ES92920

You will receive a warm welcome from the family who run this site and nothing is too much trouble. The site overlooks the Sierra Nevada with lovely panoramic views. There are 60 touring pitches, terraced and with plenty of shade (all with electricity connections). This is an area that is becoming more popular with tourists and is an ideal spot from which to explore the mountain villages. Orgiva, steeped in history, is just 1.5 km. from the site and there are many interesting walks from here.

Facilities

Three central sanitary blocks are clean and provide open washbasins and roomy shower cubicles. Toilet for disabled visitors (no shower). Laundry facilities. Shop (baker delivers daily). Bar, restaurant and takeaway (closed Mon-Wed). Outdoor swimming and paddling pools (15/5-15/10). Play area. WiFi. Torches useful. Communal barbecues only. Off site: Bicycle hire 1 km. Orgiva 1.5 km. Pampaneria, Bubion and Capileira (steep and winding with many bends so take time and care).

Open: All year.

Directions

Head south from Granada on A44 (E902) and exit 164 signed Lanjaron onto A348. Alpujarra is signed with Orgiva. Site is on right on outskirts of Orgiva (signed). GPS: 36.90375, -3.43891

Charges guide

Per person	€ 4.00 - € 5.00
child	€ 3.00 - € 4.00
pitch	€ 7.50 - € 10.00
electricity	€ 3.00 - € 4.00

Orgiva

Camping Orgiva

Ctra A348 km 18,9, E-18400 Orgiva (Granada) T: 958 784 307. E: campingorgiva@descubrelaalpujarra.com

alanrogers.com/ES92930

Set in the high slopes of the Sierra Nevada and only 2 km. from Orgiva, this is a small and well managed site that offers the opportunity to escape into rural Spain. It is open all year and is an ideal place to relax. For those who feel more energetic, there are facilities for climbing, horse riding and canoeing, all within close proximity of the site. The 40 touring pitches are well defined and separated by shrubs and small trees and all have views of the surrounding countryside. Access to the site is good but being high in the mountains it is not suitable for large units. Good English is spoken on site.

Facilities

One centrally placed sanitary block provides toilets, washbasins and shower cubicles. Facilities for disabled visitors. Washing machine and dryer. Very good swimming pool with adjacent small pool for children (June-Sept). Shop. Terrace bar. No barbecues allowed on site. Off site: Fishing 10 km. Golf 35 km.

Open: All year.

Directions

From A44-E902 Granada - Motril road, exit at 164 km. and take A348 east to Lanjaron and Orgiva. Continue past Orgiva and the site is well signed on left. GPS: 36.88708, -3.41754

Charges guide

Per person	€ 4.74
pitch incl. car and electricity	€ 12.09

Palomares

Camping Cuevas Mar

Cuevas del Almanzora, E-04618 Palomares (Almería) T: 950 467 382. E: cuevasmar@arrakis.es

alanrogers.com/ES87510

This is a popular, well established and traditional campsite, busy during the warm winter months with 180 pleasant pitches with shrubs and trees providing pitch dividers and shade. A few pitches are quite close to the road but it is not busy with traffic. All the pitches are flat and are of an acceptable 80-100 sq.m. with a clean stone chip surface and 6/10A electricity supply. During the hot summer months overhead shade canopies are erected on several pitches. A pleasant and uncomplicated site with a peaceful atmosphere and a spa.

Facilities

The well designed sanitary blocks provide sufficient showers and toilets for all. Washing machines and dryer. Water to the taps is to European standard, however a single tap near reception provides high quality water from a nearby mountain spring source. Daily fresh bread, emergency provisions and gas from reception. Open-air unheated swimming pool and jacuzzi (May-Sept). Caravan storage. WiFi (weekly charge). Off site: Many restaurants in the vicinity. Public transport 100 m. from gate. Fishing 200 m. Beach 600 m. Naturist beach 800 m. Bicycle hire 3 km. Golf 4 km. Riding 12 km.

Open: All year.

Directions

From E15/A7 take exit 537 passing under autovia following signs in general direction of Cuevas Del Almanzora. At T-junction turn right (Palomares and Vera). In 1 km. on right hand bend turn left (Palomares). On to roundabout, first exit and site is on left in 2 km. To avoid left turn continue 500 m. to next roundabout and return. GPS: 37.237, -1.798

Charges guide

Per unit incl. 1 or 2 persons	€ 8.60 - € 17.90
extra person	€ 4.20
electricity (6A)	€ 3.00

No credit cards.

Pitres

Camping El Balcon de Pitres

Ctra Orgiva - Ugijar km 51, E-18414 Pitres (Granada) T: 958 766 111. E: info@balcondepitres.com

alanrogers.com/ES92900

A simple country site perched high in the mountains of Las Alpujarras, on the south side of the Sierra Nevada, El Balcon de Pitres has its own rustic charm. Hundreds of trees planted around the site provide shade. There are stunning views from some of the 175 level grassy pitches (large units may find pitch access difficult). The garden is kept green by spring waters, which you can hear and sometimes see, tinkling away in places. The Lopez family have built this site from barren mountain top to cool oasis in the mountains in just fifteen years.

Facilities

Two toilet blocks provide adequate facilities including some for disabled campers (but the steeply sloping site is unsuitable for visitors with mobility problems). Bar/snack bar (with TV and pool table). Swimming pools (charged: € 2.40 adult, € 1.50 child). Barbecues are not permitted. Torches useful. WiFi. Off site: Fishing. Canyoning. Trekking. Parascending. Quad bikes. Sports centre for football.

Open: All year.

Directions

Site is about 30 km. northeast of Motril. Heading south on A44 (E902) exit 164 (Lanjaron) onto E348 towards Orgiva. Fork left at sign (A4132) Pampaneira 8 km. Continue to Pitres (7 km). Site signed (steep and winding roads). GPS: 36.9323, -3.3334

Charges guide

Per unit incl. 2 persons and electricity	€ 26.75 - € 32.10
extra person	€ 5.35 - € 6.42

Ronda

Camping El Sur

Ctra Ronda - Algeciras km 1,5, Apdo 127, E-29400 Ronda (Málaga) T: 952 875 939.
E: info@campingelsur.com **alanrogers.com/ES88090**

The delightfully decorated entrance with generous manoeuvring area is a promise of something different, which is fulfilled in all respects. The friendly family who run the site have worked hard for many years combining innovative thinking with excellent service. The 125 terraced pitches have electricity (6/10A) and water, and are partially shaded by olive and almond trees. Levels vary so chocks are recommended. Most have relaxing views of the surrounding mountains but at an elevation of 850 m. the upper pitches (the very top 45 pitches are for tents only) allow a clear view of the fascinating town of Ronda.

Facilities

The immaculate sanitary block is fully equipped. Laundry facilities in a separate block. Gas supplies. Bar and very large, high quality restaurant (1/2-31/10). Kidney-shaped pool (1/6-30/9). Playground and adventure play area. Separate camping area for groups. Minigolf. Off road bicycle hire. Internet and WiFi (charged). Off site: Riding 1.5 km. Bicycle hire 2.5 km. The famous town of Ronda with all its attractions. The coast is about an hour's drive (50 km).

Open: All year.

Directions

Site is on the A369 Ronda - Algerciras road 3 km. south of Ronda and is well signed.
GPS: 36.7211, -5.1716

Charges guide

Per unit incl. 2 persons and electricity	€ 23.00 - € 28.00
extra person	€ 4.80
child (under 10 yrs)	€ 4.30
dog	€ 1.60

No credit cards (except in restaurant).

Roquetas de Mar

Camping Roquetas

Ctra Los Parrales s/n, E-04740 Roquetas de Mar (Almería) T: 950 343 809. E: info@campingroquetas.com

alanrogers.com/ES87680

This level, very well maintained site is conveniently situated 9 km. from the A7 motorway within easy reach of Roquetas de Mar and 400 m. from a stony beach. It is a family run site and English is spoken. There are excellent facilities including two swimming pools and the site is within easy reach of the popular resort of Almeria and the Cabo de Gata Nature Park. There are 731 quite small pitches (60 sq.m), although during the winter months two pitches are allocated for the price of one. There are 18 pitches for longer units with water, electricity and waste connections.

Facilities

Five well equipped toilet blocks spread throughout the site. Two units for disabled visitors are close to the pools, as is a baby room. Spanish restaurant with excellent menu and reasonable prices. Shop. Two swimming pools, one with paddling pool. Tennis. Pétanque. WiFi (charged; free by reception). Off site: Towns of Roquetas de Mar and Almeria nearby. Mojacar, Nijar, 'Mini Hollywood' and the Tabernas desert are within easy reach.

Open: All year.

Directions

From A7/E15 exit 429 head towards Roquetas de Mar. Site is well signed and is about 9 km. from the main road. GPS: 36.797814, -2.590992

Charges guide

Per unit incl. 2 persons and electricity	€ 30.32 - € 33.54
extra person	€ 4.87
child (1-12 yrs)	€ 4.76

San José

Camping Tau de San José

Cua de Cala Hibuera s/n, E-04118 San José (Almería) T: 950 380 166. E: tau@parquenatural.com

alanrogers.com/ES87580

This attractive and quiet site was originally part of an old farm, typical of this region. It is well shaded and is particularly suitable for tents and low units. There is limited space for caravans and motorcaravans and phoning ahead is strongly advised. Electricity hook-ups are provided (6/16A) but long leads may be required. A level site, it is set in a nature park and is about 300 m. from the beach and the unspoilt village of San José. There is a new toilet block and the small bar/restaurant has a Spanish atmosphere with a large shady terrace outside, ideal for that relaxing drink.

Facilities

Large modern toilet block with extra unisex showers. Facilities for disabled visitors. Laundry. Small, well stocked shop. Covered barbecue area. A further covered area has pool and electronic games. Play area. Dogs are not accepted. Off site: Village of San José where fish restaurants are a speciality, beach and harbour 300 m. Almeria, and the villages of Nijar and Mojacar are close by. Further afield is the Tabernas desert and 'Mini Hollywood'.

Open: Easter - 1 October.

Directions

From E15 exit 471 or 479 follow signs for San José. Site is north of the village on left hand side (keep the white buildings to your right). Follow made up road to site. GPS: 36.76757, -2.10532

Charges guide

Per person	€ 4.75
pitch incl. car	€ 9.50 - € 13.00
electricity	€ 3.50 - € 5.50

Credit cards accepted for a minimum €100.

Santa Elena

Camping Despeñaperros

Ctra Infanta Elena, E-23213 Santa Elena (Jaén) T: 953 664 192. E: info@campingdespenaperros.com

alanrogers.com/ES90890

This site is on the edge of Santa Elena in a natural park with shade from mature pine trees. This is a good place to stay en-route from Madrid to the Costa del Sol or to just explore the surrounding countryside. The 116 pitches are fully serviced including a satellite TV/Internet link. All rubbish must be taken to large bins outside the site gates (a long walk from the other end of the site). The site is run in a very friendly manner where nothing is too much trouble. Reception has a monitor link with tourist information and access to the region's sites of interest.

Facilities

Two traditional, central sanitary blocks have Turkish style WCs and well equipped showers. One washing machine (launderette in town). Shop. Excellent bar (all year) and charming restaurant (12/3-20/10). Swimming pools (15/6-15/9). Tennis. Caravan storage. Night security. Off site: Walking, riding and mountain sports nearby. The main road gives good access to Jaén and Valdepeñas.

Open: All year.

Directions

Travelling north towards Madrid on A4 (E5) take exit 259 (Santa Elena). Drive through town. Site on right up steep slope (alternative entrance for tall vehicles – ask reception). Travelling south towards Bailén take exit 257 and as above. GPS: 38.34307, -3.53528

Charges guide

Per unit incl. 2 persons and electricity	€ 20.90 - € 23.20
extra person	€ 4.10 - € 4.70

Santaella

Camping La Campiña

Ctra A379 km 46, 2 La Guijarrosa, E-14547 Santaella (Córdoba) T: 957 315 303.
E: info@campinglacampina.com **alanrogers.com/ES90840**

A charming site amongst the olive trees and set high on a hill to catch cool summer breezes. Matilde, the daughter of the Martin-Rodriguez family, runs this site with enthusiasm and hard work, making a visit here a delightful experience. Everything is immaculately kept and we rarely see sites of this size with such excellent amenities and standards. The 35 pitches are level and most have shade, the surface is gravel and there are views over the olive fields to the surrounding hills. There is a large pool in a garden setting and the restaurant has a menu of home made food. Breakfast is included in pitch prices.

Facilities

Two small traditional sanitary blocks (heated in winter) have clean services including facilities for disabled campers (key at reception). Washing machines. Restaurant. Snack bar. Shop. Outdoor swimming pool (Apr-Oct). Bicycle hire. Yoga lessons. Torches useful. Walks and excursions arranged. Free WiFi over site. Off site: Bus from gate to Córdoba. Town 2 km. Riding 15 km. Golf 40 km.

Open: All year.

Directions

From the NIV/A4 (Sevilla - Córdoba) take exit 441 (La Rambla - Montilla) or 424 (La Victoria). Continue past Santaella towards La Victoria. La Campiña is tucked off this road behind high hedging. From the A92 use exit 109 (Puente-genil) or from the A45 (Malaga - Córdoba), exit 27 (La Rambla) and on towards Santaella. GPS: 37.623, -4.8587

Charges 2012

Per unit incl. 2 persons and electricity	€ 19.00 - € 25.50
extra person	€ 5.00

Sevilla

Camping Villsom

Ctra Sevilla - Cadiz km 554,8, E-41700 Sevilla (Sevilla) T: 954 720 828

alanrogers.com/ES90810

This city site was one of the first to open in Spain and it is still owned by the same friendly family. The administrative building consists of a peaceful and attractive bar with patio and satellite TV (where breakfast is served) and there is a pleasant, small reception area. It is a good site for visiting Seville with a frequent bus service to the centre. Camping Villsom has around 180 pitches which are level and shaded. A huge variety of trees and palms are to be seen around the site and in summer the bright colours of the flowers are very pleasing. There are no static caravans here, although there is an area for groups. The site has a most inviting, palm surrounded pool which is quite secluded.

Facilities

Sanitary facilities have been modernised. Some washbasins have cold water only. Laundry facilities. Small shop selling basic provisions. Bar with satellite TV (open July/Aug). Swimming pool (June-Sept). Putting. Drinks machine. Off site: Bus stop close. Most town facilities including restaurant, supermarket, cinema and theatre.

Open: 10 January - 23 December.

Directions

On main Seville - Cadiz NIV road travelling from Seville take exit at km. 555 signed Dos Hermanos - Isla Menor. At the roundabout turn right (SE-3205 Isla Menor) to site 80 m. on right. GPS: 37.27735, -5.93683

Charges guide

Per person	€ 4.45
child	€ 4.01
pitch incl. car	€ 9.40 - € 11.50
electricity	€ 3.05

Tarifa

Camping Paloma

Ctra Cadiz - Malaga km 70, E-11380 Tarifa (Cádiz) T: 956 684 203

alanrogers.com/ES88500

This spacious, neat and tidy, family orientated site is popular with Spanish families and young people of all nations in high season. Paloma is well established and the many tall palms around the site remind one of the proximity of Africa and the romance of Tangier. The site has 337 pitches on mostly flat ground, although the westerly pitches are sloping. They are of average size with some places for extra large units, some are separated by hedges and most are shaded by mature trees; around 150 pitches have electrical connections (10A). Paloma is 700 m. from a fabulous beach with white sands and enormous dunes, great for beach-combing, fishing and old fashioned seaside games. The area is famous for its kite and windsurfing conditions.

Facilities

Two sanitary blocks, one of a good size, although a long walk from the southern end of the site. The other block is smaller and open plan. British style WCs with some Turkish, washbasins have cold water. Facilities for disabled visitors in the smaller block. Washing machine. Gas supplies. Shop. Busy bar and good restaurant. Swimming pool with adjacent bar (high season only). Play area. Excursions (June-Sept). Dogs are not accepted in high season. Off site: Beach 700 m. Bicycle hire 5 km. Riding 10 km. Tarifa 12 km. Golf 25 km.

Open: All year.

Directions

Site is signed off N340 Cadiz road at Punta Paloma, about 10 km. northwest of Tarifa, just west of km. 74 marker. Watch carefully for the site sign – no advance notice. Be sure to use the slip road to turn left if coming from Tarifa. Follow signs down the road for 300 m. GPS: 36.0776, -5.694

Charges guide

Per person	€ 3.30 - € 5.50
child	€ 2.70 - € 4.50
pitch	€ 5.00 - € 10.00
electricity	€ 3.00

Tarifa

Camping Tarifa

Ctra N340 km 78,87, E-11380 Tarifa (Cádiz) T: 956 684 778. E: camping-tarifa@camping-tarifa.com

alanrogers.com/ES88550

The long, golden sandy beach adjacent to this site is a good feature being ideal for windsurfing and also clean and safe for swimming. The site has a pleasant, open feel and is reasonably sheltered from road noise. It has been thoughtfully landscaped and planted out with an amazing variety of shrubs and flowers and is clean. The 265 level pitches are of varying sizes and are surrounded by pine trees, which provide ample shade. All have electricity (5/10A) and there are adequate water points. There is a smart, modern reception area with an attractive water feature close by. A pleasant restaurant/bar area provides fast food and drinks. The pool is rather small and crowded in summer but has pleasant views of the distant mountain range. Tarifa is a little over 5 km. and is well worth a visit, also a drive inland to the traditional Pueblo Blancos (white villages) is rewarding.

Facilities

Two modern, fully equipped sanitary blocks include facilities for campers with disabilities and baby room. All spotless when seen. Motorcaravan services. Gas supplies. Supermarket and excellent bar/restaurant – fast food only, all open as site with patio. Swimming pool complex with bar. Large play area. Dogs are not accepted. No charcoal barbecues. Off site: Fishing 100 m. Riding 300 m. Bicycle hire 5 km. Excursions.

Open: 28 February - 31 October.

Directions

Site is on main N340 Cádiz road at 78.87 km. marker, 7.5 km. northwest of Tarifa. Large modern signs well ahead of the site with a deceleration lane if approaching from the Tarifa direction.
GPS: 36.0613, -5.6692

Charges guide

Per unit incl. 2 persons and electricity	€ 26.50 - € 28.00
extra person	€ 7.50
child (under 10 yrs)	€ 6.00

Camping Cheques accepted.

Torre del Mar

Camping Caravaning Laguna Playa

Prolongacion Paseo Maritimo, E-29740 Torre del Mar (Málaga) T: 952 540 631. E: info@lagunaplaya.com

alanrogers.com/ES87820

Laguna Playa is a pleasant and peaceful site run by a father and son team (the son speaks excellent English) and they give a personal service, alongside one of the Costa del Sol beaches. Trips are organised to the famous Alhambra Palace in Granada on a weekly basis and the site is well placed for visits to Malaga and Nerja. The 142 touring pitches are flat, of average size and with good artificial shade supplementing that provided by the many established trees on site. All pitches have electricity (10A). The busy restaurant with a terrace offers good value for money and many locals use it. The site has a distinctly Spanish flavour in August but in low season you will find lots of European ‘snow birds’ enjoying the warmth here. Animation is organised for children in high season and there are films and other activities in the party room near reception. Various competitions including pétanque are organised in summer. Good off peak discounts are available.

Facilities

Two well equipped, modern, sanitary blocks, both recently refurbished, can be heated. Baby baths. Good facilities for disabled campers. Laundry facilities. Supermarket. Bar and busy restaurant also used by locals (closed for two weeks in both May and Oct). Swimming pools (high season). Play area. Children’s entertainment. Spanish classes in low season. Dancing classes. WiFi. Off site: Beach promenade 200 m. Bicycle hire 500 m. Regular bus service 700 m. outside site. Golf 1.5 km. Riding 2 km.

Open: All year.

Directions

Site is on the seafront (oeste) of the town of Torre del Mar. Heading for the costa, go to the end of the ‘paseo’. Site is on the right.
GPS: 36.72433, -4.10133

Charges guide

Per person	€ 5.55
child (2-10 yrs)	€ 4.50
pitch and car	€ 11.10 - € 11.85
electricity	€ 4.40

Special offers for longer stays in low season.

Torrox

Camping El Pino

Ctra Nacional 340 km 285, Urb. Torrox Park s/n, E-29793 Torrox-Costa (Málaga) T: 952 530 006.
E: info@campingelpino.com **alanrogers.com/ES87810**

El Pino is located in the Axarquia region of the Costa del Sol, east of Malaga and is surrounded by avocado groves. The site enjoys some fine views of the surrounding countryside. There are 425 pitches here, mostly well shaded, and a further 47 mobile homes and chalets for rent. Most pitches have electrical connections and vary in size from 60-100 sq.m. The site is open all year and has some impressive facilities including a swimming pool, supermarket and bar/restaurant. The nearest beach is 800 m. distant – a bus service runs there from the site. The site can be found close to Torrox Costa, an area claiming to have the best climate in Europe. The old village of Torrox, like many in the area, has traces of its Arabic origins, with narrow, winding streets and whitewashed houses. Torrox Costa is quite different and has been extensively but attractively developed with a lighthouse at one end and a fine sandy beach, the Playa Ferrara.

Facilities

Toilet block with hot showers and individual cabins. Facilities for disabled visitors. Laundry facilities. Bar, restaurant and shop (all year). Takeaway. Swimming pool with new children's pool (1/6-15/9). Play area. Games room. Pétanque. Children's club. WiFi (free). Mobile homes and chalets for rent. Communal barbecue (only gas or electric barbecues permitted on pitches).
Off site: Nearest beach 800 m. Fishing 1 km. Riding 8 km. Golf 9 km. Malaga 45 km.

Open: All year.

Directions

Leave the A7 Autovia del Mediterraneo at exit 285 (Torrox) and follow signs to Torrox Costa. Site is well signed from here. GPS: 36.739245, -3.949713

Charges guide

Per unit incl. 2 persons and electricity	€ 16.80 - € 21.80
extra person	€ 3.00 - € 4.25
child (under 10 yrs)	€ 2.00 - € 3.00
dog	€ 1.50 - € 2.50

Trevélez

Camping Trevélez

Ctra Trevélez - Orgiva km 1, E-18417 Trevélez (Granada) T: 958 858 735. E: info@campingtrevelez.net
alanrogers.com/ES92890

Set high up in the Alpujarras region of the Sierra Nevada, Camping Trevélez is a super site that was bought in 2005 by the resident owners, Richard and Alexandra. Since taking over they have worked tirelessly to improve the site and each year have made significant progress. The site, which is open all year, is reached via a narrow, winding road and is ideally suited to tents and smaller motorcaravans which are sited on terraced plots, each with spectacular mountain views. Sit outside at night and wonder at the stars above but make sure you have a torch; it gets very dark at night.

Facilities

One sanitary block, recently redecorated, provides toilets, washbasins and shower cubicles. Facilities for disabled visitors. Washing machine and dryer. Shop. Bar and restaurant. Play area. Swimming pool (1/6-15/9). Barbecues only allowed in designated areas and not at all 15/6-15/10. Fishing. Riding. WiFi area (free).

Open: All year.

Directions

From A44 (E902) Granada - Motril road, exit at 164 km. onto A348. At Orgiva take A4132 for 32 km. to Trevelez. Road is winding and very narrow in places and is not suitable for large units. GPS: 36.99181, -3.27753

Charges guide

Per unit incl. 2 persons and electricity	€ 18.27 - € 20.30
extra person	€ 4.05 - € 4.50
child (under 12 yrs)	€ 2.70 - € 3.00

This is one of the most beautiful, and perhaps least known, regions of inland Spain. Its beautiful cities, first Roman and Moorish, then medieval and aristocratic, gave birth to many of the conquistadors - conquerors of the New World.

EXTREMADURA HAS TWO PROVINCES: BADAJOZ AND CÁCERES

Extremadura is a large and sparsely populated region in the west of Spain, bordering central Portugal and consisting of two provinces, both of which bear the name of their main town. Cáceres, to the north, has a fascinating old quarter, ringed by old Moorish walls and superb watchtowers. Nearby Plasencia is home to a splendid Gothic cathedral, old medieval walls and beautiful Baroque and Renaissance palaces. And the attractive town of Trujillo, birthplace of Pizzaro, the conqueror of Peru, has palaces, churches and a bustling town square. To the south is Badajoz, the second province and the largest in Spain. With its fortified main town and Alcazaba (citadel), the city of Badajoz is located on the Vía de la Plata (Silver Route), an old pilgrimage route to Santiago de Compostela used during the Middle Ages. Located on this route, Mérida is one of the best preserved archaeological sites in Spain. Indeed, the city boasts more Roman remains than any other city, including a Roman theatre and amphitheatre, a Roman bridge spanning over 800 metres long, with 60 arches, Roman villas and the Museum of Roman Art.

Places of interest

Alcántara: six-arched Roman bridge, castle, mansions.

Corio: quiet old town enclosed by 4th-century Roman walls, cathedral.

Cuacos de Yuste: town with 15th-century Jeronimos Monastery.

Guadalupe: old pilgrimage centre, church and monastery.

Jerez de los Caballeros: birthplace of various conquistadors.

Olivenza: town with strong Portuguese influence, castle, ethnographic museum, 17th-century church.

Pedroso de Acim: Convento del Palancar – said to be the smallest monastery in the world.

Cuisine of the region

Local cuisine includes Iberian cured ham and a variety of cheeses; *Torta del Casar, La Serena, Ibores, Gata* and *Cabra del Tietar*. Game abounds in this region (partridge, pigeon, turtle dove, rabbit, hare, wild boar, deer) served with wild mushrooms, truffles or wild asparagus. Honey, thyme, heather, rosemary, lavender, lime and eucalyptus are used to prepare a great variety of desserts.

Alfeñiques: caramel dessert.

Nuégados: egg yolk and orange buns.

Perrunillas: small round cakes.

Rosquillas: ring-shaped biscuits.

Técula-mécula: cinnamon, almond and tea.

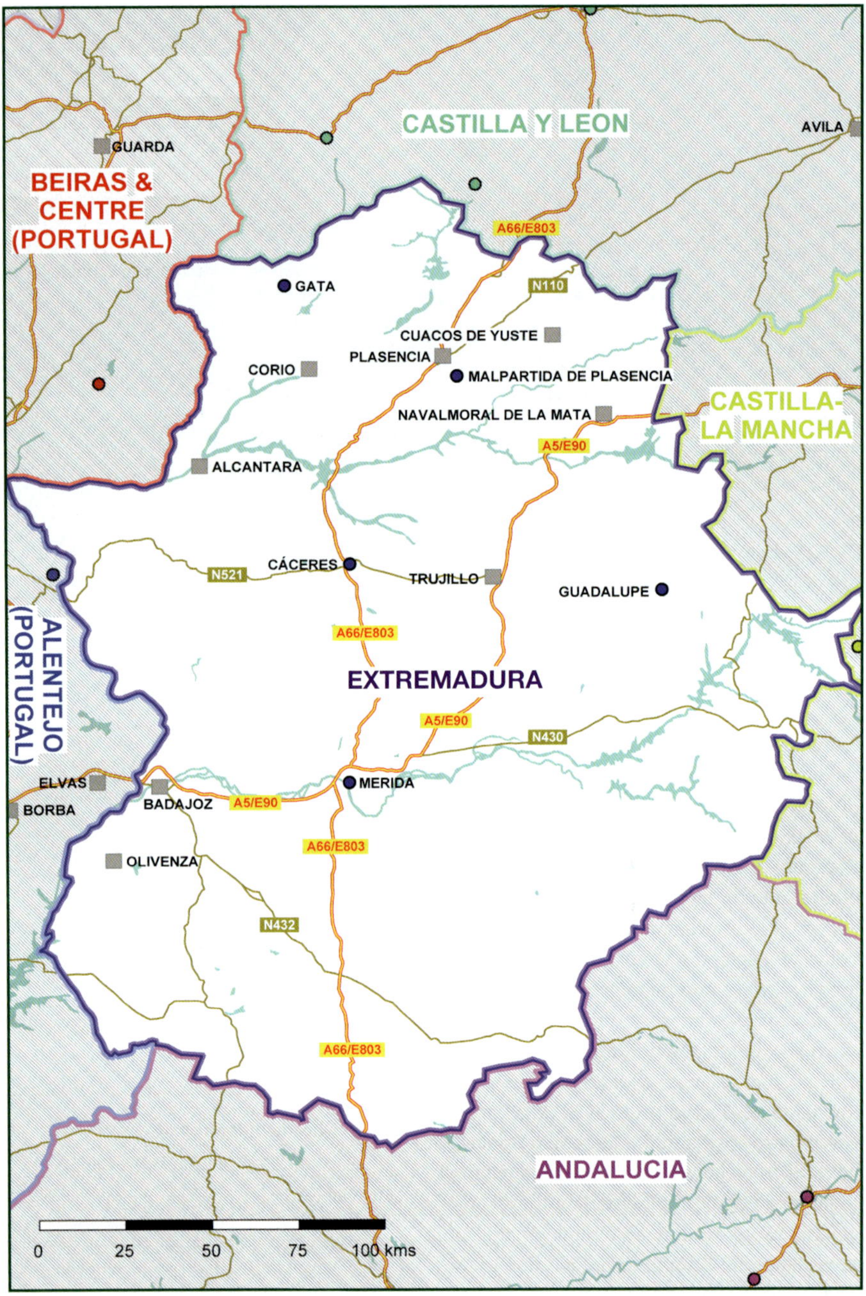
CASTILLA Y LEON
AVILA
GUARDA
BEIRAS & CENTRE (PORTUGAL)
A66/E803
N110
GATA
CUACOS DE YUSTE
PLASENCIA
CORIO
MALPARTIDA DE PLASENCIA
NAVALMORAL DE LA MATA
CASTILLA-LA MANCHA
A5/E90
ALCANTARA
CÁCERES
N521
TRUJILLO
GUADALUPE
ALENTEJO (PORTUGAL)
A66/E803
EXTREMADURA
A5/E90
N430
ELVAS
BORBA
BADAJOZ
A5/E90
MERIDA
A66/E803
OLIVENZA
N432
A66/E803
ANDALUCIA
0 25 50 75 100 kms

Cáceres

Cáceres Camping

Ctra N630 km 549,5, E-10005 Cáceres (Cáceres) T: 927 233 100. E: info@campingcaceres.com

alanrogers.com/ES90860

Cáceres Camping is quite a small site, located to the west of the interesting city of Cáceres, a World Heritage site. There are 130 pitches here, and, unusually, each has a chalet providing a shower, washbasin and toilet. The pitches are of a reasonable size (80 sq.m) and are well shaded. A range of leisure facilities is provided, including a swimming pool and a separate children's pool. Cáceres is a city with much interest, and a fascinating history. Cave paintings on the city outskirts date back 30,000 years! The city is capital of High Extremadura and close by, the Montanchez mountain range offers many opportunities for walking and cycling.

Facilities

Individual toilet blocks. Bar, restaurant, caféteria and takeaway meals. Supermarket. Swimming pool.
Off site: City centre 2 km. Golf, walking and cycling opportunities.

Open: All year.

Directions

From the east (E90 motorway) take the N521 to Cáceres. Continue on this road to the west of the city. At the large roundabout sign for 'Campo de Futbol Principe Felipe' is the entrance to the site. GPS: 39.489, -6.4128

Charges guide

Per unit incl. 2 persons and electricity	€ 20.00 - € 22.00
child	€ 3.00
extra person	€ 4.00 - € 4.50

Gata

Camping Sierra de Gata

Ctra Ex109 a Gata km 4,100, E-10860 Gata (Cáceres) T: 927 672 168. E: sierradegata@campingsonline.com

alanrogers.com/ES94000

For a taste of the real, rural Spain this very Spanish site (no English was spoken when we visited) is situated just before the tiny village of Sierra de Gata, south of Ciudad Rodrigo and northwest of Plasencia. Situated in beautiful countryside with a small stream alongside the site, the pitches are on grass with plenty of shade from trees. This site is undergoing refurbishment with the addition of 12 beautiful new bungalows to sleep four to six people. A special area with huts for groups of children to stay is positioned in one corner of the site. The village of Gata is small with only a few houses and if you continue along the road you will climb into the mountains and natural park, good for walks and picnics. The other side of the hill leads down into another town but this has very small streets and is probably best not driven through with a motorcaravan!

Facilities

Two toilet blocks with British style toilets also include child size toilets, a laundry room and dishwashing facilities. Medium sized shop for necessities in summer. Smart restaurant/bar complex provides good food.
Two swimming pools. Tennis. Play area. Fishing. Riding. Bicycle hire. Off site: Restaurant near site entrance.

Open: 18 March - 3 November.

Directions

Approach ONLY from the southwest from the 109 Ciudad Rodrico - Coria road. Where the 205 meets the 109 take turn 20-30 m. north signed Gata 10. Travel along this road until km. 4. Turn left (near restaurant and small bridge) and site is ahead through gate. GPS: 40.21195, -6.64224

Charges guide

Per person	€ 3.75 - € 4.25
pitch	€ 4.50 - € 8.00
electricity	€ 3.75 - € 4.25

Guadalupe

Camping Las Villuercas

Ctra Villanueva, E-10140 Guadalupe (Cáceres) T: 927 367 139

alanrogers.com/ES90280

This rural site nestles in an attractive valley northwest of Guadalupe. The 50 pitches (of which 25 have 10A electricity) are level and of a reasonable size; although large units may experience difficulty in getting into the more central pitches. With an abundance of mature trees most pitches offer some degree of shade. A river runs alongside the site and the ground can be muddy in very wet periods. The site is co-located with hostel accommodation. The restaurant provides excellent food at low prices.

Facilities

The single toilet block is older but very clean, with one area for women and one for men, providing British type WCs, washbasins and showers (hot water is from a 40-litre immersion heater which could be overwhelmed in busy periods). Facilities for disabled visitors. Laundry facilities. Restaurant. Bar. Swimming pools. Shop. Tennis. Small playground. Barbecue area. No English spoken. Off site: Riding 2 km. Fishing 3 km.

Open: 1 March - 30 November.

Directions

From NV/E90 Madrid - Mérida exit at Navelmoral de la Mata. Follow south to Guadalupe on the CC713 (83 km). Site is 2 km. from Guadalupe (near Monastery). From further southwest take exit 102 off main E90/NV (northeast of Mérida). Follow signs (Guadalupe). Go through a few villages and near 72 km. marker turn left to site, 100 m. on right. GPS: 39.441228, -5.322

Charges guide

Per person	€ 3.21
pitch	€ 4.28 - € 5.88
electricity	€ 2.67

No credit cards.

Malpartida de Plasencia

Camping Parque Natural de Monfrague

Ctra Plasencia - Trujillo km 10, E-10680 Malpartida de Plasencia (Cáceres) T: 927 459 233.

E: contacto@campingmonfrague.com **alanrogers.com/ES90270**

Situated on the edge of the Monfrague National Park, this well managed site owned by the Barrado family, has fine views to the Sierra de Mirabel and delightful surrounding countryside. Many of the 130 good sized grass pitches are on slightly sloping, terraced ground. Scattered trees offer a degree of shade, there are numerous water points and 10A electricity. On rare occasions, a goods train travels along the nearby railway line. Created as a national park in 1979, Monfrague is now recognised as one of the best locations in Europe for anyone interested in birdwatching.

Facilities

Large modern toilet blocks, fully equipped, are very clean. Facilities for disabled campers and baby baths. Laundry. Motorcaravan service point. Supermarket/shop. Restaurant, bar and coffee shop. TV room with recreational facilities. Swimming and paddling pools (June-Sept). Play area. Tennis. Entertainment for children in season. Barbecue areas. Free WiFi. Guided safaris into the Park for birdwatching. Off site: Large supermarket at Plasencia. Bicycle hire 2 km. Riding 6 km.

Open: All year.

Directions

On the N630, from the north take EX-208 (previously C524) Plasencia - Trujillo; site on left in 6 km. From the south turn right just south of Plasencia on EX-108 (previously C511) in direction of Malpartida de Plasencia. Right at main junction onto EX-208 to site. GPS: 39.9395, -6.084

Charges 2012

Per unit incl. 2 persons and electricity	€ 20.10 - € 20.40

Camping Cheques accepted.

Mérida

Camping Mérida

Ctra NV Madrid - Portugal km 336,6, E-06800 Mérida (Badajoz) T: 924 303 453. E: proexcam@jet.es

alanrogers.com/ES90870

Camping Mérida is situated alongside the main NV road to Madrid, the restaurant, café and pool complex separating the camping area from the road, where there is considerable noise. The site has 80 good sized pitches, most with some shade and on sloping ground, with ample electricity connections (long leads may be needed) and hedges. No English is spoken, but try out your Spanish. Camping Mérida is ideally located to serve both as a base to tour the local area and as an overnight stop en route.

Facilities

The central sanitary facility includes hot and cold showers, British style WCs. Gas supplies. Small shop for essentials. Busy restaurant/caféteria and bar, also open to the public. Medium sized swimming and paddling pools (May-Sept). Bicycle hire. Play area (unfenced and near road). Caravan storage. Torches useful. Off site: Town 5 km.

Open: All year.

Directions

Site is alongside NV road (Madrid - Lisbon), 5 km. east of Mérida, at km. 336.6. From east take exit 334 and follow camping signs (doubling back). Site is actually on the 630 road that runs alongside the new motorway. GPS: 38.9348, -6.3043

Charges guide

Per person	€ 4.06
pitch incl. car and electricity	€ 22.74

Castilla-La Mancha

This region is located south of Madrid and occupies what was the southern part of the ancient kingdom of Castille, including the area known as La Mancha, universally famous as the setting for Miguel de Cervantes great novel 'Don Quijote de la Mancha'.

CASTILLA-LA MANCHA HAS FIVE PROVINCES: ALBACETE, CIUDAD REAL, CUENCA, GUADALAJARA AND TOLEDO

THE CAPITAL OF THE REGION IS TOLEDO

The terrain can be divided into two distinct parts: the plateau, an extensive, flat land with very few mountains, and the mountainous areas, which encircle the plateau around the region's borders, including the foothills along the massifs of the Central mountain range, the Iberian mountain range and the Sierra Morena. Toledo is crammed with monuments and nearly all the different stages of Spanish art are represented with Moorish-Mudejar-Jewish buildings; Gothic structures, such as the splendid cathedral; and Renaissance buildings. Toledo was also home to El Greco and many of his paintings are displayed in the Museum of El Greco. The region of Cuenca is surrounded by mountainous, craggy countryside, with the city itself home to extraordinary houses which hang over the cliff tops of the deep gorges. One of these has been converted into the Museum of Abstract Art. In the heartland of La Mancha, through the region of Ciudad Real, you can follow the Ruta de Don Quijote and see the famous windmills at Campo de Criptana.

Places of interest

Almagro: home of international theatre festival.

Albacete: renowned for its knife-making industry, 16th-century cathedral.

Guadalajara: preserved Moorish walls, 10th-century bridge, Santa Maria la Mayor, 15th-century Duque del Infantado Palace.

Cuisine of the region

Local produce features heavily: aubergines, garlic, peppers, tomatoes, olive oil, meat, including both game and farm animals. Wine from La Mancha, Valdepeñas, Méntrida, Almansa, Dominio de Valdepusa and Finca de Elez.

Alajú: an almond and nut pastry.

Bizcochás de Alcázar: a tart soaked in milk with sugar, vanilla and cinnamon.

Caldereta manchega: lamb stew.

Morteruelo: pâté made of pork and game birds.

Pisto manchego: a type of ratatouille with tomatoes, red and green peppers, courgettes, served either hot or cold.

Tiznao: filleted cod which is flame-grilled in an earthenware dish with pepper, tomatoes, onions and garlic.

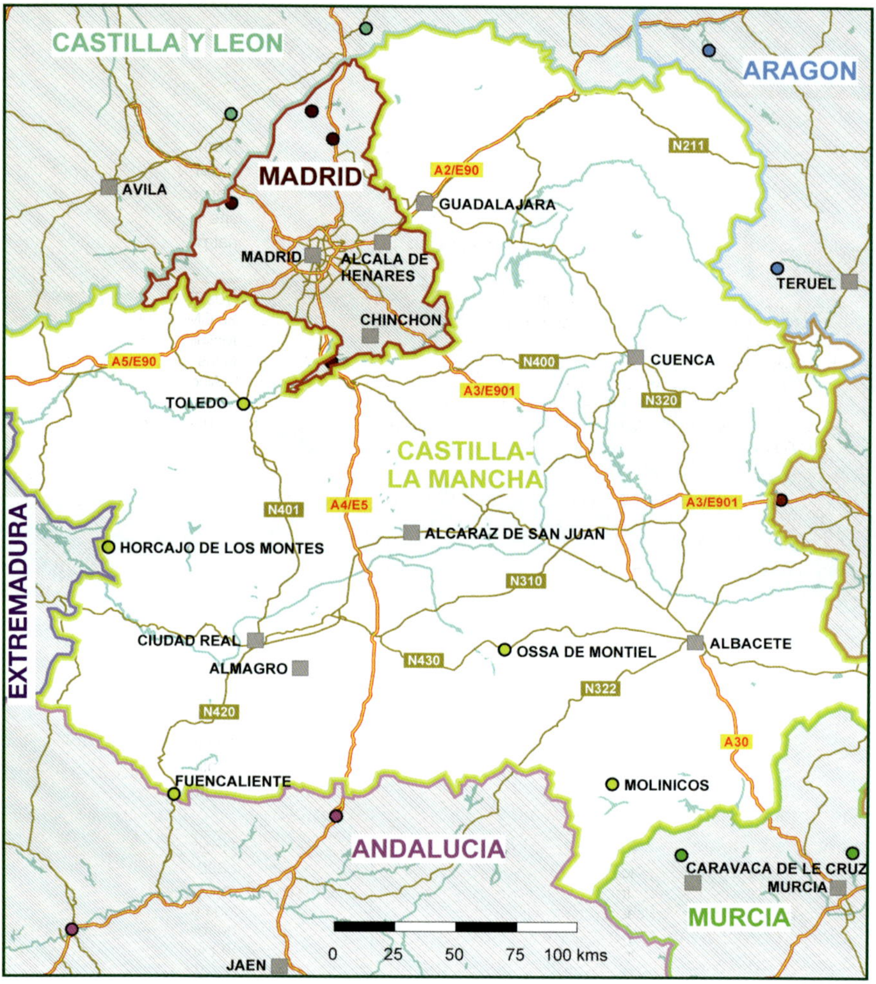

Fuencaliente

Camping de Fuencaliente

Ctra N420 km 105,8, E-13130 Fuencaliente (Ciudad Real) T: 926 698 170. E: raquel@campingfuencaliente.es

alanrogers.com/ES90880

This quiet site nestles in an attractive valley between the Sierra Modrona and the Sierra Morena. It is a site for getting away from it all and sampling the peaceful mountain beauty. It could be a useful stopover if crossing Spain coast to coast or if you wish to visit the fascinating historic town of Córdoba. With very few other desirable sites in this region of Castilla-La Mancha, this one is spacious with 91 generously sized pitches (over 100 sq.m) all with electricity (6A) and water. There is natural shade from pine trees and beautiful, restful views. Areas are also allocated for tents. The large swimming pool with a separate children's area is most welcome in summer as this part of Spain gets very hot. The site has a good restaurant overlooking the pools, with reasonable prices.

Facilities

The large, modern toilet block has reasonable facilities. Laundry sinks. Washing machine. Swimming pool (1/6-15/9; free). Restaurant/bar. Supermarket. Playground. Barbecue area with table and benches overlooking the countryside. Off site: Fuencaliente 5 km.

Open: Easter - 30 September.

Directions

From the N420 road (Cuidad Real - Córdoba) turn by 105 km. marker (about 5 km. north of Fuencaliente) onto unmade road signed Camping San Isidro to site. GPS: 38.442, -4.32

Charges guide

Per person	€ 4.00 - € 4.50
child (2-10 yrs)	€ 3.50 - € 4.00
pitch incl. electricity	€ 7.50 - € 11.00

Horcajo de Los Montes

Camping El Mirador de Cabaneros

Canada Real Segoviana s/n, E-13110 Horcajo de Los Montes (Ciudad Real) T: 926 775 439.

E: info@campingcabaneros.com **alanrogers.com/ES90960**

With panoramic views all around of the Sierra de Valdefuertes mountains, Camping El Mirador is set in the Cabaneros National Park. This is a well cared for, landscaped site with 80 terraced pitches on gravel and all with electricity. Although level once sited, the approach is via a steep slope which may cause difficulties for larger units. Run by a very helpful and friendly family, this site is in a peaceful location where you can just sit and relax or visit the many attractions that the national park has to offer.

Facilities

One spotlessly clean central toilet block with solar heating includes open washbasins and cubicle showers. Facilities for disabled visitors and babies. Laundry facilities. Motorcaravan services. No shop but bread and gas from reception. Bar and restaurant (15/6-15/9, weekends in low season). Outdoor swimming pool. Games room. Basic (unfenced) play area. Off site: Village of Horcajo de los Montes 200 m.

Open: All year.

Directions

From north head towards Toledo (southwest from Madrid). At Toledo, take CM4013 to Cuerva and pick up CM403 to El Molinillo. Turn right onto the CM4017 to Horcajo de los Montes. Through village onto CM4016 towards Alcoba de los Montes, past garage and up hill for 2 km. Site is on left (narrow approach). GPS: 39.3219, -4.6495

Charges guide

Per person	€ 4.80 - € 5.20
pitch incl. electricity	€ 11.90 - € 14.10

Molinicos

Camping Rio Mundo

Ctra Comarcal 412 km 205, Mesones, E-02449 Molinicos (Albacete) T: 967 433 230.

E: riomundo@campingriomundo.com **alanrogers.com/ES90980**

This uncomplicated and typically Spanish site is situated in the Sierra de Alcaraz (south of Albacete), just off the scenic route 412 between Elche de la Sierra and Valdepenas. The drive to this site is most enjoyable through beautiful scenery and from the west the main road is winding in some places. Shade is provided by mature trees for the 80 pitches and electricity (6/10A) is supplied to 70 (long leads are useful). It is in a beautiful setting with majestic mountains and wonderful countryside.

Facilities

One toilet block has been upgraded and provides clean modern facilities. Basic toilet facilities for disabled visitors. Washing machine. Small shop for basics. Outside bar serving snacks with covered seating area. Takeaway (all 15/3-12/10). Another bar by the swimming pool. Playground. Pétanque. WiFi. Only gas and electric barbecues permitted. Off site: Riding 7 km.

Open: 18 March - 12 October.

Directions

Site is just off the 412 road which runs west to east between the A30 and 322 roads south of Albacete. Turn at km. 205 on the 412, 5 km. east of village of Riopar and west of Elche de la Sierra. From here follow signs to site. The road narrows to one lane for a few hundred yards but keep straight on for 1-2 km. to site. GPS: 38.48917, -2.34639

Charges guide

Per person	€ 4.30 - € 5.90
pitch incl. electricity	€ 14.60 - € 19.80

Ossa de Montiel

Camping Los Batanes

Ctra Lagunas de Ruidera km 8, E-02611 Ossa de Montiel (Albacete) T: 926 699 076.

E: camping@losbatanes.com **alanrogers.com/ES90970**

This large campsite is in a lovely setting at the side of one of the many lakes in this area. The route to get here is beautiful and it is well worth the trip, but careful driving was necessary in parts with our large motorcaravan. A smaller, older part of the campsite houses reception, a small shop and a bar/restaurant. Here are medium sized pitches, shaded by pine trees with a small river running through. Over a wooden bridge is the main, newer part of the site with over 200 level, gravel and sand pitches of mixed sizes, shaded again by pine trees.

Facilities

One old toilet block and a newer, more spacious one. If cleaning is maintained they should cope in high season. Small shop. Simple restaurant, snacks and bar. Swimming pools (16/6-9/9). Play area. Children's activities. Off site: Beautiful walks and many lakes to explore. Watersports in summer. Tourist information either at reception or at nearest village 9 km. Bus stop in village.

Open: All year.

Directions

On E5/NIV Córdoba - Madrid road (south of Madrid) take 430 road towards Albacete. Coming into Ruidera turn right (just after lake on the right) signed Lagunas de Ruideria. Drive 8 km. along this country road to site on right. GPS: 38.93717, -2.84744

Charges guide

Per person	€ 4.60 - € 5.60
pitch	€ 18.50 - € 27.00
electricity (5A)	€ 3.40 - € 3.50

Toledo

Camping El Greco

Ctra CM4000 km 0,7, Puebla de Montalban, E-45004 Toledo (Toledo) T: 925 220 090.
E: campingelgreco@telefonica.net **alanrogers.com/ES90900**

Toledo was the home of the Grecian painter, El Greco, and the site that bears his name boasts a beautiful view of the ancient city from the restaurant, bar and superb pool. The friendly, family owners make you welcome and are proud of their site, which is the only one in Toledo (it can get crowded). The 150 pitches are of 80 sq.m. with electrical connections (5/10A) and shade from strategically planted trees. Most have separating hedges that give privacy, with others in herringbone layouts that make for interesting parking in some areas. The Tagus river stretches alongside the site which is fenced for safety. There is an attractive, tree-lined approach to the site. Ivy clad pergolas run down each side of the swimming pool (also fenced for safety) and a large shaded terrace offers shelter from the sun which can be very hot here. This site makes a relaxing base to return to after a hard day visiting the amazing sights of the old city of Toledo or for something different visit the Warner Brothers theme park.

Facilities

Two sanitary blocks, both modernised, one with facilities for disabled campers. Everything is of the highest standard and kept very clean. Laundry. Motorcaravan services. Swimming pool (15/6-15/9, charged). Restaurant/bar (1/4-30/9) with good menu and fair prices. Small shop in reception. Playgrounds. Ice machine.
Off site: Fishing in river. Golf 10 km. Riding 15 km. An hourly air-conditioned bus service runs from the gates to the city centre, touring the outside of the walls first.

Open: All year.

Directions

Site is on C4000 road on the edge of the town, signed towards Puebla de Montelban; site signs also in city centre. From Madrid on N401, turn off right towards Toledo city centre but turn right again at the roundabout at the gates to the old city. Site is signed from the next right turn. GPS: 39.865, -4.047

Charges 2012

Per unit incl. 2 persons and electricity	€ 30.60
extra person	€ 6.65
child (3-10 yrs)	€ 5.75

The region of Madrid lies right in the middle of the Spanish mainland bordering Castilla-La Mancha and Castilla and Leon. At the centre lies the city of Madrid, which since the 16th century has been the country's capital.

THE REGION OF MADRID IS A ONE PROVINCE AUTONOMY, ALSO CALLED MADRID

The mountainous region of Madrid can be divided into two areas: the Sierra, in the north and west of the region, which includes part of Somosierra and Guadarrama; and the central and southern parts, where the area is flatter and forms part of the plateau of La Mancha and La Alcarria. Founded by the Moors in the ninth century, Madrid is now a modern, vibrant city offering innumerable attractions to the visitor. Its architectural heritage is immense. Some of the oldest parts of Madrid lie around the Puerta del Sol, a good starting place for exploring the city. Full of outdoor restaurants and bars, Plaza Mayor is considered to be one of the finest in Spain, and in summer becomes an outdoor theatre and music stage. The city also has a large number of parks and gardens, among them El Retiro, the Botanical Gardens, the Parque del Oeste and the Casa de Campo; and numerous museums and art galleries. Outside the capital, the Sierra de Madrid is ideal for winter sports and the beautiful town of Aranjuez, home to the Royal Palace and glorious gardens, is a popular retreat from the city.

Places of interest

Alcala de Henares: university town, birthplace of Cervantes, author of Don Quijote, Cervantes House Museum, Archepiscopal Palace Cathedral.

Chinchón: 15th-century castle, beautiful medieval square, 19th-century church with painting by Goya, home of Alchoholera de Chinchón – aniseed liqueur!

Parque Natural de la Cumbre: mountain park, the highest mountains in the Madrid region.

San Lorenzo de El Escorial: town in heart of Guadarrama Mountains, Monastery of El Escorial, Royal Pantheon.

Cuisine of the region

Tapas is popular with typical dishes including seafood: steamed mussels, anchovies in vinegar and pickled bonito plus croquettes and mini-casseroles. Sea bream and cod are used a lot. Local produce includes beef from the Guadarrama Mountains, olives from Campo Real, aniseed from Chinchón and asparagus from Aranjuez. Madrid is also a good place to experience every regional style of Spanish cooking.

Buñuelos: a type of fritter which is filled with custard, chocolate and cream.

Cocido: meat, potato and chickpea stew.

Con gabardina: prawns cooked in beer.

Torrijas: bread pudding.

El Escorial

Caravanning El Escorial

184

Apdo 8, Ctra M600 km 3,5, E-28280 El Escorial (Madrid) T: 902 014 900. E: info@campingelescorial.com

alanrogers.com/ES92000

There is a shortage of good sites in the central regions of Spain, but this is one. El Escorial is very large, there are 1,358 individual pitches of which about 600 are for touring, with the remainder used for permanent or seasonal units, but situated to one side of the site. The pitches are shaded (ask for a pitch without a low tree canopy if you have a 3 m. high motorcaravan). There are another 250 pseudo 'wild' spaces for tourists on open fields, with good shade from mature trees (long cables may be necessary for electricity). The general amenities are good and include three swimming pools (unheated), plus a paddling pool in a central area with a bar/restaurant with terrace and plenty of grassy sitting out areas. At weekends in high season the site can be noisy. It is well situated for sightseeing visits especially to the magnificent El Escorial monastery (5 km). Also, the enormous civil war monument of the Valle de los Caidos is very close, while both Madrid and Segovia are 50 km. away.

Facilities

One large toilet block for the touring pitches, plus two smart, small blocks for the 'wild' camping area, are all fully equipped with some washbasins in cabins. Baby baths. Facilities for disabled campers. The blocks can be heated. Large supermarket, restaurant/bar and snack bar/takeaway (all year; w/ends only in low season). Disco-bar. Swimming pools (15/5-15/9). Three tennis courts. Two well equipped playgrounds on sand. ATM. Off site: Town 3 km. Riding and golf 7 km.

Open: All year.

Directions

From the south go through town of El Escorial, and follow M600 Guadarrama road. Site is between the 2 and 3 km. markers north of the town on the right. From the north use A6 autopista and exit 47 to M600 towards El Escorial town. Site is on the left. GPS: 40.62400, -4.099

Charges 2012

Per unit incl. 2 persons and electricity	€ 29.80 - € 36.20
extra person	€ 5.90 - € 7.10
child (3-10 yrs)	€ 4.00 - € 6.50

No credit cards.

Aranjuez

Camping Internacional Aranjuez

Soto del Rebollo, s/n antigua NIV km 46,8, E-28300 Aranjuez (Madrid) T: 918 911 395.
E: info@campingaranjuez.com **alanrogers.com/ES90910**

Aranjuez, supposedly Spain's version of Versailles, is worthy of a visit with its beautiful palaces, leafy squares, avenues and gardens. This useful, popular and unusually well equipped site is therefore excellent for enjoying the unusual attractions or for an en-route stop. It is 47 km. south of Madrid and 46 km. from Toledo. The site is alongside the River Tajo in a park-like situation with mature trees. There are 162 touring pitches, all with electricity (16A), set on flat grass amid tall trees. The site was bought by the owners of La Marina (ES87420) who have worked hard to improve the pitches and the site. Two little tourist road trains run from the site to the palaces daily. You can visit the huge, but slightly decaying, Royal Palace or the Casa del Labrador (translates as farmer's cottage) which is a small neo-classical palace in unusual and differing styles. It has superb gardens commissioned by Charles II. Canoes may be hired from behind the supermarket and there is a lockable moat gate to allow access to the river. There is good security backed up with CCTV around the river perimeter.

Facilities

The largest of three modern, good quality sanitary blocks is heated in winter and well equipped with some washbasins in cabins. Laundry facilities. Gas supplies. Small shop, bar and restaurant (all year) with attractive riverside patio (also open to the public). Takeaway. TV room. Swimming and paddling pools, (1/5-15/10). New play area. Pétanque. Bicycle hire. Canoe hire. WiFi (free). Torch useful. Off site: Within easy walking distance of palace, gardens and museums. Golf 2 km.

Open: All year.

Directions

From the M305 (Madrid - Aranjuez) look for 8 km. marker on the outskirts of town. Then follow campsite signs – these lead back onto the M305 (going north now) and the site is signed off right at 300 m. on the first left bend. Follow signs down the narrow road for 400 m. If coming from the south ensure that you have the M305 to Madrid (other roads are signed to Madrid). If in doubt ask as it is very confusing if the M305 road is missed.
GPS: 40.0426, -3.5995

Charges 2012

Per unit incl. 2 persons and electricity	€ 25.10 - € 35.10
extra person	€ 4.50 - € 6.00
child (3-10 yrs)	€ 3.25 - € 4.90

Gargantilla de Lozoya

Camping Monte Holiday

Ctra Rascafria - Lozoya km 9, Finca El Tercio Nuevo s/n, E-28739 Gargantilla de Lozoya (Madrid)
T: 918 695 278. E: monteholiday@monteholiday.com **alanrogers.com/ES92120**

The Somosierra offers spectacular scenery and is very popular with Spanish skiers. This site is situated in an open, sunny lower valley, in the Madrid area's only beech forest near a large nature reserve. The area is ideal for anglers and walkers and also offers many opportunities for outdoor sports enthusiasts. The site is on terraces and has 308 small pitches with 100 for touring (50 with electricity 5/7A Europlug; long leads required in some areas). These pitches are mainly flat with grass or gravel surfaces and shade from mature trees, but unfortunately are very uneven. The upper area is taken by permanent units. The site has an attractive swimming pool with sunbathing areas. The bar/restaurant offers a limited range of meals including some regional dishes. The strength of this site is the range of adventure and outdoor activities in the nearby mountains. There is horse riding in the area and skiing on the nearby slopes in winter. On site, less arduous activities are also organised for children (high season). From here it is possible to enjoy the wonderful Somosierra mountains or even to make a short trip to Spain's exciting capital, Madrid.

Facilities

The modern, heated and well equipped toilet block is well maintained. Facilities for disabled visitors and babies. Laundry facilities. Motorcaravan services. Shop. Bar and fair quality restaurant (15/6-15/9, bank holidays and weekends). Swimming pool (mid June-mid Sept). Multisports court. Tennis. Table-tennis. Beach volleyball. Play area. Gas supplies. Barbecues are not permitted 15/5-31/10. Bicycle hire. WiFi (free). Off site: Mountain trips, guided climbs. Fishing 1 km. Skiing 20 minutes. Boat launching and riding 8 km.

Open: All year.

Directions

From A1 motorway (Burgos - Madrid) take exit 69 towards Rascafria. Turn right after passing under a railway tunnel and site is on left after 800 m. GPS: 40.949917, -3.729267

Charges guide

Per unit incl. 2 persons and electricity	€ 27.10 - € 29.90
extra person	€ 6.40
child (3-10 yrs)	€ 5.90

Camping Cheques accepted.

La Cabrera

Camping Pico de la Miel

Ctra A1, Salida 57, E-28751 La Cabrera (Madrid) T: 918 688 082. E: info@picodelamiel.com
alanrogers.com/ES92100

Pico de la Miel is a very large site 60 km. north of Madrid. Mainly a long-stay site for Madrid, there are a huge number of very well established, fairly old statics. There is a small separate area with its own toilet block for the 80 touring units, all with electricity (8A Europlug). The pitches are on rather poor, sandy grass, but the artificial shade has been removed and trees planted. There are yet more pitches for tents (the ground could be hard for pegs). The noise level from the many Spanish customers is high and you will have a chance to practise your Spanish! Tall hedges abound and with the trees, make it resemble a giant maze. Internal signs are now provided, easing the long walk to the pool. The site is well signed and easy to find, two or three kilometres southwest off the main N1 road, with an amazing mountain backdrop.

Facilities

Dated but clean tiled toilet block, with some washbasins in cabins. It can be heated. En-suite unit with ramp for disabled visitors. Motorcaravan services. Gas supplies. Shop. Restaurant/bar and takeaway (1/6-30/9 and weekends rest of year). Excellent swimming pool complex (15/6-15/9). Tennis. Playground. WiFi throughout. Off site: Bicycle hire and riding 500 m. Fishing 6 km.

Open: All year.

Directions

Site is well signed from the N1. Going south or north use exit 57 and follow site signs. When at T-junction, facing a hotel, turn left. (Exit 57 is closer to site than exit 60). GPS: 40.85797, -3.6158

Charges guide

Per unit incl. 2 persons and electricity	€ 27.10 - € 29.75
extra person	€ 6.20
child (3-9 yrs)	€ 5.35

Less 10-25% for longer stays.

The large region of Castilla y León is located inland, bordering Portugal to the west. It has a rich legacy dating back to the Romans, with an extraordinary wealth of castles, cathedrals and mansions, historic cities and towns.

THE REGION IS MADE UP OF THE FOLLOWING PROVINCES: AVILA, BURGOS, LEON, PALENCIA, SALAMANCA, VALLADOLID, ZAMORA, SEGOVIA AND SORIA

Steeped in history and architectural sights, the major towns and cities of the provinces all have something to offer. In the south, the town of Ávila is set on a high plain, surrounded by 11th-century walls; and the graceful city of Salamanca was once home to one of the most prestigious universities in the world. Its grand Plaza Mayor is the finest in Spain. In the east, Segovia is well known for its magnificent Roman aqueduct, with 163 arches and 29 metres at its highest point; the cathedral; and the fairytale Alcazár, complete with turrets and narrow towers. And the attractive city of Soria still retains a Romanesque legacy in its network of medieval streets. Burgos in the north, is the birthplace of El Cid and has a Gothic cathedral of exceptional quality. The lively university city of Leon boasts a Royal Pantheon, decorated by Romanesque wall paintings, and also an impressive Gothic cathedral. There is also a Gothic cathedral in Palencia plus an archaeology museum. South of León, the old walled quarters of Zamora have a retained medieval appearance, with a dozen Romanesque churches. And in the centre of the region, Valladolid is famous for its extravagant and solemn processions during the Holy Week celebrations.

Places of interest

Astorga: city of Roman origin, chocolate museum, cathedral.

Ciudad Rodrigo: Renaissance mansions, cathedral, 12th-century walls.

Coca: impressive Mudejar castle, birthplace of the famous Roman emperor Theodosius the Great.

Pantano de Burgomillodo: reservoir, great for birdwatchers.

Parque Natural del Cañón del Río Lobos: park created around the canyon of the River Lobos with rock formations, cave and good walking tracks.

Parque Natural del Lago de Sanabria y alrededores: mountainous area with deep valleys and glacier lagoons, variety of flora and fauna including 76 types of birds and 17 large mammals.

Cuisine of the region

The region is best known for its roast pork and lamb which has earned it the nickname *España del Asado* (Spain of the Roast). Other local products include trout from León and Zamora, and a variety of pulses: white, red and black beans, Castilian and *Pedrosillano* chickpeas, and various types of lentils. Soups feature a lot in winter: trout soup, typical of Órbigo de León; garlic soup; Zamora soup, a garlic soup with ripe tomatoes and hot chilli peppers.

Bizcochos de San Lorenzo: sponge cakes.

Farinatos: sausages made from breadcrumbs, pork fat and spices.

Hornazos: sausage and egg tarts.

Judias del barco con chorizo: haricot beans with sausage.

Yemas: a sweet made with egg yolks and sugar.

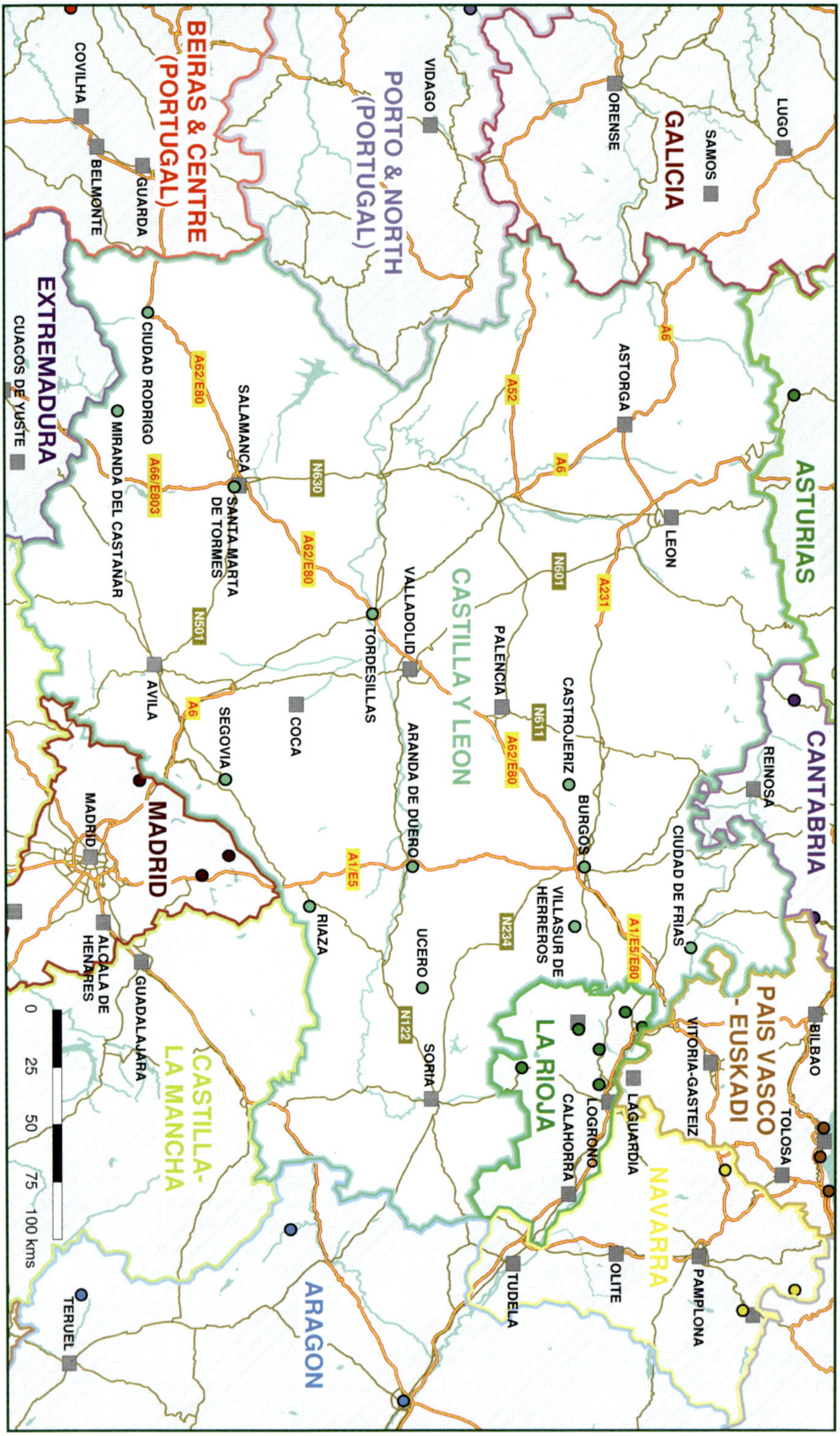
GALICIA
LUGO
SAMOS
ORENSE
ASTURIAS
CANTABRIA
REINOSA
PAIS VASCO - EUSKADI
BILBAO
TOLOSA
VITORIA-GASTEIZ
NAVARRA
PAMPLONA
OLITE
TUDELA
LA RIOJA
LAGUARDIA
LOGROÑO
CALAHORRA
PORTO & NORTH (PORTUGAL)
VIDAGO
BEIRAS & CENTRE (PORTUGAL)
COVILHA
BELMONTE
GUARDA
EXTREMADURA
CUACOS DE YUSTE
CASTILLA Y LEON
ASTORGA
LEON
PALENCIA
CASTROJERIZ
BURGOS
CIUDAD DE FRIAS
VILLASUR DE HERREROS
VALLADOLID
TORDESILLAS
ARANDA DE DUERO
UCERO
SORIA
SALAMANCA
SANTA MARTA DE TORMES
CIUDAD RODRIGO
MIRANDA DEL CASTAÑAR
AVILA
SEGOVIA
COCA
RIAZA
MADRID
ALCALA DE HENARES
GUADALAJARA
CASTILLA-LA MANCHA
ARAGON
TERUEL
A6
A52
A231
N601
N630
A62/E80
A66/E803
N501
N611
A1/E5
A1/E5/E80
N234
N122
0 25 50 75 100 kms

Aranda de Duero

Camping Costajan

Ctra NI E-5 km 164-165, E-09400 Aranda de Duero (Burgos) T: 947 502 070.
E: costajan@camping-costajan.com **alanrogers.com/ES92500**

This site is well placed as an en route stop for the ferries, being 80 km. south of Burgos. This is the capital of the Ribera del Duero wine region that produces many fine wines competing with the great Riojas. With 225 unmarked pitches, all with electricity available, there are around 100 for all types of tourer. Large units may find access to the 225 unmarked, variably sized pitches a bit tricky among dense olive and pine trees and on the slightly undulating sandy ground, but the trees provide good shade. There are 115 electricity connections. The welcome from Juan Carlos is warm and friendly.

Facilities

Good, heated, modern sanitary facilities. Facilities for disabled visitors. Washing machine. Gas supplies. Shop with essentials. Bar serving simple meals. Free access to adjacent large swimming pool (June-Sept). Tennis. Minigolf. WiFi throughout (charged). Torch useful. If reception is unmanned, choose a pitch and book in later. Off site: Riding 2 km. Fishing and river beach 3 km.

Open: All year.

Directions

From A1/E5 take exit at 164.5 km. and turn south on N1 towards Aranda de Duero. The site is on the right at the 162 km. mark. GPS: 41.702, -3.68803

Charges guide

Per person	€ 5.40 - € 5.60
pitch	€ 8.90 - € 11.50
electricity	€ 5.00

Burgos

Camping Municipal Fuentes Blancas

Ctra Cartuja - Miraflores km 3,5, E-09193 Burgos (Burgos) T: 947 486 016. E: info@campingburgos.com
alanrogers.com/ES90210

Fuentes Blancas is a comfortable municipal site on the edge of the historical town of Burgos and within easy reach of the Santander ferries. There are around 350 marked pitches of 70 sq.m. on flat ground, 250 with electrical connections (6A) and there is good shade in parts. The site has a fair amount of transit trade and reservations are not possible for August, so arrive early. Burgos is an attractive city, ideally placed for an overnight stop en-route to or from the south of Spain.

Facilities

Clean, modern, fully equipped sanitary facilities in five blocks with controllable showers and hot and cold water to sinks (not all are always open). Facilities for babies. Washing machine/dryer. Motorcaravan service point. Small shop (high season). Bar/snack bar and restaurant (high season). Swimming pool (1/7-30/8). Playground. English is spoken. Off site: Fishing and river beach 200 m. Bus service to city or a fairly shaded walk. Golf 30 km.

Open: All year.

Directions

From north (Santander) continue on the N623 through city centre to km. 0. Follow signs for the E5/A1 Madrid. After crossing river take slip road for N120/A231 Leon but then turn left towards Fuentes Blancas and Cartuja de Miraflores for 3 km. Site is well signed on left. From south on A1 and from all other motorways follow signs for Burgos and N623 Santander. At foot of hill, before river, take slip road for N120 (then as above). GPS: 42.34125, -3.65762

Charges guide

Per person	€ 4.65
pitch incl. electricity	€ 13.30

Castrojeriz

Camping Camino de Santiago

Avenida Virgen del Manzano s/n, E-09110 Castrojeriz (Burgos) T: 947 377 255. E: info@campingcamino.com
alanrogers.com/ES90230

This tranquil site lies to the west of Burgos on the outskirts of Castrojeriz, in a superb location, almost in the shadow of the ruined castle high on the hillside. The 50 marked pitches are level, grassy and divided by hedges, with electricity (10A). Mature trees provide shade and there is a pretty orchard in one corner of the site. This site is a birdwatchers' paradise. The owner takes visitors out on birdwatching trips currently on an ad hoc basis but he is considering making it a more formal affair.

Facilities

Older style sanitary block with hot showers, washbasin with cold water and British and Turkish style WCs. No facilities for disabled visitors. Washing machine. Bar/restaurant and takeaway with traditional cuisine. Bicycle hire. Library. WiFi (free). Games room. Tennis. Play area. Barbecue area. Ad hoc guided birdwatching. Off site: Fishing and riding 17 km.

Open: 1 March - 30 November.

Directions

Castrojeriz is 45 km. west of Burgos. From N120/A231 (Leon - Burgos), turn on Bu404 (Villasandino, Castrojeriz). Turn left at crossroads on southwest side of town, then left at site sign. From A62 (Burgos - Valladolid) turn north at Vallaquirán on Bu400/401 to Castrojeriz. Turn sharp right at filling station and as above. GPS: 42.2913, -4.1448

Charges guide

Per unit incl. 2 persons and electricity	€ 19.50 - € 24.00
extra person	€ 4.75 - € 5.00

Ciudad de Frias

Camping Frias

E-09211 Ciudad de Frias (Burgos) T: 947 357 198. E: info@campingfrias.com

alanrogers.com/ES92570

Located in a natural park northeast of Burgos, on the edge of the old, small Spanish town of Frias, much of this site is taken up with static units. However, an area at the end is reserved for touring caravans and motorcaravans. A beautiful river runs alongside, about 20 feet below the campsite but with access for fishing, and the level, numbered pitches (30 for touring) have views across the really beautiful scenery surrounding the campsite. A little shade is provided from a few trees. This is a very Spanish site.

Facilities

One toilet block provides basic facilities with British style WCs, washbasins with cold water only and coin operated showers. Washing machine and dryer. Shop with good range of produce (from 1/6). Bar and restaurant (from 1/6). Two swimming pools (22/6-15/9) and paddling pool. Off site: Transport would be needed to visit any interesting places.

Open: 1 April - 30 September.

Directions

Site is on the north side of Frias – approach only from this side. From A1 exit 5 onto A2122 (Quintana Martin Galindez), with a few tunnels, turn right on 625 then left to Quintana. After 16 km. turn left (Frias). Site is 3 km. on right. Or on A1 from exit 4 on N232 then 629 to Trespaderne. Turn right towards Miranda and drive east for 10 km. then turn right to Frias. GPS: 42.77098, -3.29686

Charges guide

Per person	€ 4.00
pitch incl. electricity	€ 11.00

Ciudad Rodrigo

Camping La Pesquera

Ctra de Caceres - Arrabal, E-37500 Ciudad Rodrigo (Salamanca) T: 923 481 348

alanrogers.com/ES90190

This modest site has just 54 pitches and is located near the Rio Agueda, looking up to the magnificent fortress ramparts of Ciudad Rodrigo. Entry to the site is through a municipal park with a large play area. Whilst the site is small it can take even the largest units, the centrally located facilities have all been refurbished to a high standard, the pitches are flat and grassy and the roads are well maintained gravel. The pitches are shaded by trees and there is site lighting at night, but you may find torches useful.

Facilities

Attractive ochre stone sanitary building with British WCs and free hot showers. Facilities for disabled campers. Washing machine. Basics sold from bar in high season. Bar/snacks (all season). Playground and barbecue area. Torches useful. Off site: River fishing 1 km. Riding 5 km. Superb walking area.

Open: 13 January - 13 December.

Directions

Site is southwest of Salamanca close to Ciudad Rodrigo. From the E80 N260, any direction, take the 526 to Coria. Site is alongside river directly off the road and well signed. GPS: 40.591965, -6.534301

Charges guide

Per unit incl. 2 persons and electricity	€ 13.00 - € 16.40

Miranda del Castañar

Camping El Burro Blanco

Camino de las Norias s/n, E-37660 Miranda del Castañar (Salamanca) T: 626 227 646.
E: camping.elburroblanco@gmail.com **alanrogers.com/ES90260**

Set on a hillside, within the Sierra Peña de Francia and with views of the romantic walled village of Miranda del Castañar and its charming, crumbling castle, this site is run by a Dutch couple, Jeff and Yvonne. You are welcomed at the gate and are walked around the facilities. In total, there are 30 level touring pitches, all between 80 and 120 sq.m. and 25 have electricity. The pitches are beautifully set in 3.5 hectares of the most attractive natural woodland. Owners of large caravans and motorcaravans should contact the site first due to the restricted number of suitable pitches.

Facilities

One central, modern and fully equipped sanitary facility includes a baby bath. Two washbasins have hot water. Out of season part of the unit is closed and therefore facilities are unisex. Launderette. Gas supplies. Library with book exchange and small bar. Off site: Restaurants, bars, shops and ATM in village 600 m. Municipal swimming pool nearby. Bicycle hire 1 km. River swimming and fishing 1.5 km. Riding 15 km.

Open: 1 April - 1 October.

Directions

From north - south direction take Salamanca - Coria road southwest for about 70 km. through Vecinos, Linares de Rio Frio towards Coria (keep on this main road). From east - west direction take Bejar - Ciudad Rodrigo road south towards Cepeda/Coria. Road to Miranda del Castañar is 7 km. northeast of Cepeda. Turn off main road (Miranda). After 1.2 km. downhill towards town look for left turn on concrete road. In 1.1 km. and site is on right. GPS: 40.4748, -5.99885

Charges guide

Per unit incl. 2 persons and electricity	€ 20.63 - € 24.19

No credit cards.

Riaza

Camping Riaza

Ctra de la Estacion s/n, E-40500 Riaza (Segovia) T: 921 550 580. E: info@camping-riaza.com

alanrogers.com/ES90245

This beautiful site is situated in the province of Segovia, a hundred or so kilometres north of Madrid, making it an ideal spot for a few days rest en route north or south. Of the 350 spacious pitches 213 are for touring, all with electricity (8A), water, and drainage. The pitches are divided by hedges and oak trees giving some shade. The buildings on the site are built of local stone housing a large clubroom, bar and welcoming restaurant lit by chandeliers, a good place to relax and enjoy the excellent menu.

Facilities

Two excellent, centrally located toilet blocks with underfloor heating. Shop. Bar, restaurant and clubroom. Swimming pool (1/6-31/8). Two natural pools in the river bordering site. Large play area. Wellness centre with heated indoor pool, gym, massage room, jacuzzi and sauna. Minigolf. New sports area. Tennis. Archery. Children's club (summer). WiFi throughout. Off site: Riding and Riaza with restaurant 2 km. Golf 9 km.

Open: All year.

Directions

From the A1 (Burgos - Madrid) take exit 104 and the N110 towards Soria. Leave the N110 signed Riaza and follow camping signs. At roundabout follow signs for 'Estacion' and site is 50 m. on left.
GPS: 41.26944, -3.49749

Charges guide

Per unit incl. 2 persons and electricity	€ 26.90 - € 29.50
extra person	€ 6.10

Santa Marta de Tormes

Camping Regio

Ctra de Madrid km 4, E-37900 Santa Marta de Tormes (Salamanca) T: 923 138 888.
E: recepcion@campingregio.com **alanrogers.com/ES90250**

Salamanca is one of Europe's oldest university cities, and this beautiful old sandstone city has to be visited. This is also a useful staging post en route to the south of Spain or central Portugal. The site is 7 km. outside the city on the old road to Madrid, behind the Hôtel Regio where campers can take advantage of the hotel facilities. The 129 pitches (with a large area for tents) are clearly marked on slightly sloping ground, with some shade in parts and plentiful electricity points (10A). Access to those pitches not on the wide central road can be difficult for caravans.

Facilities

Very large, fully equipped sanitary block is very clean. Good facilities for disabled campers. Washing machines. Gas supplies. Motorcaravan services. Bar. Supermarket (1/6-30/9). The hotel restaurant, café and swimming pool may be used by campers (discounts at the café and restaurant). Play area. Tennis. Internet and WiFi (both within hotel area). English is spoken. Off site: Bus to town terminates at hotel car park. Fishing 2 km. Bicycle hire 4 km. Town centre 7 km. Golf 14 km.

Open: All year.

Directions

Take the main N501 route from Salamanca towards Avila, then to St Marta de Tormes 7 km. east of the city. Hôtel Regio is on the right just outside the town at the 90 km. marker. There are yellow hotel and camping signs through the city and on the roads to the east. GPS: 40.9471, -5.614

Charges guide

Per unit incl. 2 persons and electricity	€ 19.40 - € 21.70

Segovia

Camping El Acueducto

Carretera de San Ildefonso la Granja, km 112, E-40004 Segovia (Segovia) T: 921 425 000.
E: informacion@campingacueducto.com **alanrogers.com/ES92420**

Located right on the edge of the interesting city of Segovia with lovely views across the open plain to the mountains beyond, this is a family run, typically Spanish site. The grass pitches are mostly of medium size, although a few pitches near the gate would have room for larger motorcaravans. An uncomplicated site, reception is small, but efficient and the owner is helpful and speaks good English. El Acueducto is about 5 km. from the city. Segovia is deeply and haughtily Castilian, with plenty of squares and mansions from its days of Golden Age grandeur, when it was a royal resort.

Facilities

Two traditional style toilet blocks provide simple, clean facilities. Laundry room. Motorcaravan services. Small shop for essentials. Bar. Two swimming pools. Large play area. Bicycle hire. WiFi in reception (charged). Car wash. Off site: Large restaurant nearby. Fishing, golf, riding and boat launching all 5 km. Bus service into city centre. Madrid is within reasonable driving distance.

Open: 1 April - 30 September.

Directions

From north on N1 (Burgos - Madrid) take exit 99 on N110 (Segovia). On outskirts of city take third exit onto N603 (Madrid). Pass one exit to Segovia and take second (Segovia and La Granja). At roundabout turn right (Segovia). Site is 500 m. on right beside the dual carriageway. GPS: 40.93125, -4.09243

Charges guide

Per person	€ 5.00 - € 6.00
pitch	€ 16.60 - € 17.00
electricity (5A)	€ 4.50 - € 5.00

Tordesillas

Kawan Village Camping El Astral

Camino de Pollos 8, E-47100 Tordesillas (Valladolid) T: 983 770 953. E: info@campingelastral.es

alanrogers.com/ES90290

The site is in a prime position alongside the wide River Duero (safely fenced). It is homely and run by a charming man, Eduardo Gutierrez, who speaks good English and is ably assisted by brother Gustavo and sister Lola. The site is generally flat with 154 pitches separated by thin hedges. The 144 touring pitches, 132 with electricity (6/10A), vary in size from 60-200 sq.m. with mature trees providing shade. The new toilet block has been designed with environmental sustainability in mind, including solar heated water. This is a friendly site ideal for exploring the area as you move through Spain.

Facilities

One new sanitary block designed to include energy saving measures and to be easily cleaned. Showers for children and baby room. Facilities for disabled visitors. Washing machines. Motorcaravan services. Supermarket. Bar and restaurant plus takeaway service. Swimming and paddling pools (1/6-15/9). Playground. Tennis (high season). Minigolf. Internet point and WiFi throughout (charged). English spoken. Torches useful. No charcoal barbecues. Off site: River fishing 100 m. Golf 10 km. Riding 20 km.

Open: 1 April - 30 September.

Directions

Tordesillas is 28 km. southwest of Valladolid. From all directions, leave the main road towards Tordesillas and follow signs to campsite or 'Parador' (a hotel opposite the campsite). GPS: 41.495305, -5.005222

Charges 2012

Per unit incl. 2 persons and electricity	€ 21.40 - € 31.30
extra person	€ 4.60 - € 6.85

Camping Cheques accepted.

Ucero

Camping Cañon del Rio Lobos

Ctra Burgos de Osma - San Leonardo, E-42317 Ucero (Soria) T: 975 363 565

alanrogers.com/ES92510

This is a delightful site with 83 neat pitches and vast amounts of flowers, set among attractive limestone cliffs of the Burgos canyons. The site is pricey but facilities are excellent and there are few others in the area. Reception is purpose built and control of the security barrier is from within – everything here is very organised. The very attractive swimming pool is within a secure walled area, which again has many flowers and shrubs and is private from the road that runs alongside the site (some traffic noise).

Facilities

Two fully equipped toilet blocks (only one opened when site is quiet). Bar serving a 'menu del día' and a smart restaurant. Basic shopping from bar. Swimming pool (charge). Two excellent free tennis courts. Play area. Fishing. Football pitch. Torch useful. Dogs are not accepted. Off site: Local bus service for town (Wed/Sat) 1 km. Walking, climbing, caving, fishing in nearby Parque Natural. Riding 10 km. Golf 35 km.

Open: Easter - 30 September.

Directions

From N234 (Burgos - Soria) turn south in San Leonado de Yagüe on SO690. Turn left after village on SO920 (El Burgo de Osma). Site on left in 18 km. just before Ucero. From N122/A11 (Valladolid - Soria) turn north in El Burgo de Osma on SO920 signed San Leonardo, 16 km. to Ucero. From San Leonardo cross Rio Lobo on El Burgo de Osma road and site is 400 m. on the left. GPS: 41.7293, -3.0475

Charges guide

Per person	€ 5.00
pitch	€ 18.60

Villasur de Herreros

Camping Puerta de la Demanda

Ctra de Pineda km 2, E-09199 Villasur de Herreros (Burgos) T: 983 796 819.
E: info@puertadelademanda.com **alanrogers.com/ES92540**

This site on flat ground, is overlooked on three sides by the hills and mountains of the Sierra de la Demanda which give the site its name. There is little shade over 50 well marked large pitches, all of which have electricity (3-6A) and drainage. The modern buildings are of local stone and wood in sympathy with the quiet surroundings, yet providing an excellent set of facilities. The whole site is securely fenced. Just 300 m. away is a dam which may provide non-powered watersports and a river is very close for swimming and fishing. Nearby is the trail of the pilgrims to Santiago de Compostella.

Facilities

Sanitary building with British WCs and free hot showers. Washing machine. Facilities for disabled campers. Shop (April-Sept). Bar serving meals and selling basics (all season). Bicycle hire. Torches useful. Pets are not accepted. Off site: Sailing on nearby reservoir. River fishing 1 km. Shop, restaurants and bars in attractive village 1 km. Superb walking area.

Open: 1 February - 30 November.

Directions

From the N120 (Burgos - Logroño), turn east at Ibeas de Juarros (about 13 km. east of Burgos) on Bu-P8101/Bu820 through Arlanzon to Villasur de Herreros. Site is beyond village after km. 13. GPS: 42.306, -3.375

Charges guide

Per person	€ 3.70
pitch incl. electricity	€ 9.50 - € 10.40

With a coastline of inlets and wide, rocky estuaries, sheltering traditional old fishing villages and fine beaches, Galicia is perhaps best known for Santiago de Compostela, the place where the famous pilgrims' route comes to an end.

THIS REGION IS MADE UP OF FOUR PROVINCES: OURENSE, LUGO, A CORUÑA AND PONTEVEDRA

The obvious highlight in the region has to be the beautiful medieval city of Santiago de Compostela, capital of Galicia and world famous centre of the old European pilgrimage. Now a World Heritage Site, the city boasts an impressive Romanesque cathedral with more churches, convents and monasteries dotted around. One of the best times to go to Santiago de Compostela is during the Festival of St James on 25 July, which has also been designated Galicia Day. Following the route into the city, are the towns of Portomarín and Samos. Near Samos, the Lóuzara valley and the Sierra do Oribio are ideal for those interested in hiking and wildlife. The Galician coastline is characterised by high cliffs and estuaries collectively known as the Rías Atlas and Rías Baixas with the Costa da Morte or Coast of Death separating them, so called because of the hundreds of shipwrecks that litter the cliffs and rocks. It was also once considered by the pilgrimages to be the 'end of the world'. Along the coast are medieval towns and villages including Noia, Muros, A Coruña and Finisterre. Corcubión, Camariñas and Corme-Laxe are other rias with fishing villages and home to some of the best barnacles in the region.

Places of interest

A Coruña: medieval quarters, Romanesque churches, Roman lighthouse.

Baiona: one of the region's best resorts.

Camariñas: town at the 'end of the world', good barnacle hunting ground, lacemaking traditions.

Lugo: town completely enclosed within preserved Roman walls, along which are 85 towers.

Malpica: seaside harbour, jumping off point for nearby islands.

Pontevedra: picturesque old town with lively atmosphere.

Vigo: fishing port, beaches.

Viveiro: beaches, old town surrounded by Renaissance walls.

Cuisine of the region

Local cuisine features heavily in fiestas and throughout the region are numerous markets. Good quality seafood is found in abundance; *percebes* (barnacles) are a favourite. *Pulpo* (octopus) is also popular and special *pulperías* will cook it in the traditional way. Vegetable dishes include the Galician broth made with green beans, cabbage, parsnip, potatoes and haricot beans. *Aguardiente gallego*, a regional liqueur, is used to make the traditional mulled drink known as *queimada*, where fruit, sugar and coffee grains are added and then set alight.

Caldeirada: fish soup.

Caldo gallego: thick potato and cabbage stew.

Empanada: light-crusted pastries often filled with pork, beef, tuna or cod.

Lacon con grelos: ham boiled with turnip greens.

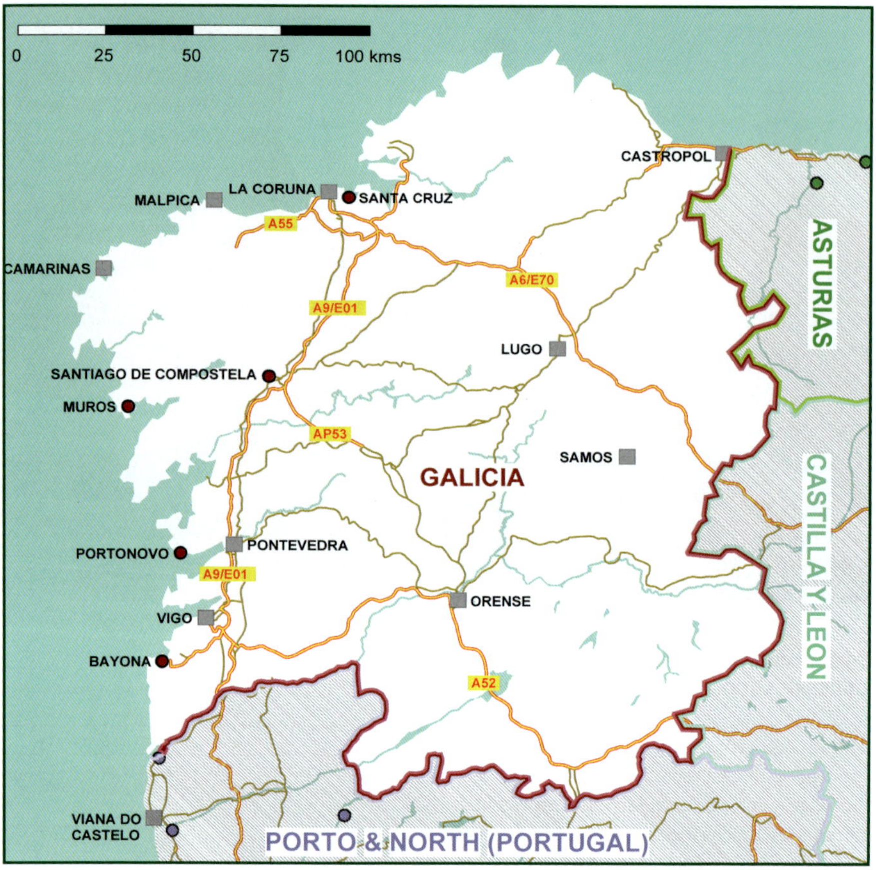

Bayona

Camping Bayona Playa

Ctra Vigo - Bayona km 19, E-36393 Bayona (Pontevedra) T: 986 350 035.
E: campingbayona@campingbayona.com **alanrogers.com/ES89360**

Situated on a narrow peninsula with the sea and river estuary all around it, this large and well maintained campsite is great for a relaxing break. The 450 pitches, 358 for touring, benefit from the shade of mature trees whilst still maintaining a very open feel. All have 5A electricity and 50 are fully serviced. It is busy here in high season so advance booking is recommended. Sabaris is a short walk away and Bayona is a 20-minute walk along the coast, where you can find a variety of shops, supermarkets, banks, bars and eating places. Maximum unit length is 7.5 m. From the moment you arrive at the well appointed reception, the staff, all of whom speak good English, make every effort to ensure that you have a memorable stay. You can also visit a replica of the Pinta, the ship that bought back the news of Christopher Columbus' discovery of America, which is moored here. The surrounding countryside has plenty of attractions and a variety of watersports is available, including the site's own school of windsurfing. Buses run from Sabaris to Vigo and to A Guarda.

Facilities

Three well maintained modern toilet blocks (one open low season), washbasins and shower cubicles. No washing machines but site provides a service wash. Facilities for visitors with disabilities. Large well stocked supermarket and gift shop (June-Sept). Terrace bar, caféteria, restaurant. Excellent pool complex with slide (small charge, redeemable in shop and restaurant). Play area. Organised activities July/Aug. Off site: Fishing 100 m. Bicycle hire 5 km. Riding 8 km. Golf 20 km.

Open: All year.

Directions

From Vigo leave AG57, exit 5 Bayona North. Follow signs to site at Sabaris, 2 km. east of Bayona.
GPS: 42.113978, -8.826013

Charges guide

Per person	€ 6.30
child (3-12 yrs)	€ 3.95
pitch	€ 3.95 - € 13.05
electricity	€ 3.95

Muros

Camping San Francisco

Camino do Convento 21, Louro, E-15291 Muros (A Coruña) T: 981 826 148. E: ofmlouro@yahoo.es

alanrogers.com/ES89300

Situated 400 m. from the coast, this small and attractive touring site with 104 small pitches occupies a clearing on a hillside that is undoubtedly a magnet for Spanish holidaymakers. Advance booking is recommended. The neatly laid out and numbered pitches are on level grass, divided by trees but with little shade. All have 10A electricity and 74 pitches are fully serviced. The surrounding countryside is scenic and unspoilt by development and the superb white sandy beaches and rocky coves provide endless hours of fun or relaxation for the whole family. The small town of Muros is only 3.5 km.

Facilities

One modern and spotlessly clean toilet block is centrally positioned. A family shower room with facilities for disabled visitors is provided in both male and female areas. Laundry facilities. First aid point. Shop. Café/bar. Restaurant with terrace. Play area. Tennis and multisports court. Off site: Sandy beach and fishing 400 m. Bicycle hire 500 m. Boat launching and sailing 3.5 km.

Open: 21 June - 7 September.

Directions

From Santiago de Compostela take AC543 to Noia. Just before Noia turn right onto road (Muros) and continue on AC550. Site signed 3.5 km. past Muros on right (narrow road). GPS: 42.761975, -9.072701

Charges guide

Per person	€ 5.50
pitch incl. car	€ 10.75 - € 11.25
electricity	€ 3.90

Portonovo

Camping Paxarinas

Ctra San Xenxo - O'Grove, E-36979 Portonovo (A Coruña) T: 986 723 055. E: info@campingpaxarinas.com

alanrogers.com/ES89380

Paxarinas is a family owned and managed coastal site open all year, set on a gently sloping area of hillside overlooking Ria de Pontevedra. Of the 260 very small pitches only 60 are for touring, in the centre of the site. All pitches are numbered and have 3A electricity, there is very little shade. It gets very busy in high season and advance booking is recommended. Care is needed with larger units at busy times. The site is situated in a most attractive area of Galicia and with access to two excellent beaches it makes a good stopover whilst visiting the area. Although open all year, facilities are very limited in low season.

Facilities

Two well maintained modern sanitary blocks. Private cabins. Facilities for visitors with disabilities. Washing machine and dryer. Play area. Shop, bar and snacks (20/6-5/9). Separate restaurant in adjacent hotel. Off site: Two beaches adjacent. Riding 4 km. Golf 8 km.

Open: All year.

Directions

Exit AP9, junction 129 Pontevedra. Follow signs to Sanxenxo. Follow coast road PO308 for 22 km. Site poorly signed on left hand side, behind hotel, 3 km. past Sanxenxo and just before a bend. GPS: 42.392481, -8.844069

Charges guide

Per unit incl. 2 persons and electricity	€ 26.95 - € 31.05
extra person	€ 6.20
child (2-7 yrs)	€ 4.95

Santa Cruz

Camping Los Manzanos

Avenida de Emilia Pardo Bazan, E-15179 Puerto de Santa Cruz (A Coruña) T: 981 614 825.
E: informacion@campinglosmanzanos.com **alanrogers.com/ES89420**

Los Manzanos has a steep access drive down to the site, which is divided by a stream into two sections linked by a bridge. Pitches for larger units are marked and numbered, 85 with electricity (12A) and, in one section, there is a fairly large, unmarked field for tents. Some aircraft noise should be expected as the site is under the flight path to La Coruña (but no aircraft at night). The site impressed us as being very clean, even when full, which it tends to be in high season. Some interesting huge stone sculptures create focal points and conversation pieces.

Facilities

One good toilet block provides modern facilities including free hot showers. Small shop with fresh produce daily (limited outside June-Sept). High quality restaurant/bar (July/Aug). Swimming pool with lifeguard, free to campers (15/6-30/9). Playground. Barbecue area. Bungalows for rent. Off site: Bus service at end of entrance drive. Beach and fishing 800 m. Bicycle hire 2 km. Golf and riding 8 km.

Open: April - 30 September.

Directions

From western end of the AP9 take exit 3, signed. GPS: 43.34908, -8.33567

Charges guide

Per unit incl. 2 persons and electricity	€ 29.20 - € 29.90
extra person	€ 6.00
child	€ 5.00

Santiago de Compostela

Camping As Cancelas

Rue do 25 de Xullo 35, E-15704 Santiago de Compostela (A Coruña) T: 981 580 476.
E: info@campingascancelas.com **alanrogers.com/ES90240**

The beautiful city of Santiago has been the destination for European Christian pilgrims for centuries and they now follow ancient routes to this unique city, the whole of which is a national monument. The As Cancelas campsite is excellent for sharing the experiences of these pilgrims in the city and around the magnificent cathedral. It has 125 marked pitches (60-90 sq.m), arranged in terraces and divided by trees and shrubs. On a hillside overlooking the city, the views are very pleasant, but the site has a steep approach road and access to most of the pitches can be a challenge for large units. Electrical hook-ups (5A) are available, the site is lit at night and a security guard patrols. There are many legendary festivals and processions here, the main one being on 25 July, especially in holy years (when the Saint's birthday falls on a Sunday). Examine for yourself the credibility of the fascinating story of the arrival of the bones of St James at Compostela (Compostela translates as 'field of stars'), and also discover why the pilgrims dutifully carry a scallop shell on their long journey. There are many pilgrims' routes, including one commencing from Fowey in Cornwall.

Facilities

Two modern toilet blocks are fully equipped, with ramped access for disabled campers. The quality and cleanliness of the fittings and tiling is good. Laundry with service wash for a small fee. Small shop. Restaurant. Bar with TV. Well kept, unsupervised swimming pool and children's pool. Small playground. Internet access. Off site: Regular bus service into city from near football ground 200 m. Huge commercial centre (open late and handy for off season use) 20 minutes walk downhill (uphill on the return!).

Open: All year.

Directions

From motorway AP9-E1 take exit 67 and follow signs for 'Casco Historico' and 'Centro Ciudad' then follow site signs. GPS: 42.88939, -8.52418

Charges guide

Per person	€ 4.50 - € 5.90
child (up to 12 yrs)	€ 2.70 - € 4.50
pitch	€ 4.50 - € 19.00
electricity	€ 4.10

Like its neighbouring province, Cantabria, Asturias also has a beautiful coastline, albeit more rugged and wild, with the Picos range separating them. In the south the Cantabrian mountains form a natural border between Asturias and Castilla-León.

THIS IS A ONE PROVINCE REGION

THE CAPITAL IS OVIEDO

Situated between the foothills of the Picos mountains and the coast is the seaside town of Llanes, in the east. It has several good beaches, beautiful coves and, given its location, is a good base for exploring the Picos del Europa. Along the coast towards Gijón are more seaside resorts including Ribadesella, with its fishing harbour and fine beach. The cities of Gijón and, in particular, Avilés are renowned for their carnival festivities, a national event which takes place in late February. This week-long party involves dancing, live music, fireworks and locals who dress up in elaborate costumes. South of here, towards the centre of the province, is the capital, Oviedo. The city boasts a pedestrian old quarter with numerous squares and narrow streets, a cathedral, palaces, a fine arts museum, an archaeological museum plus various remarkable churches that date from the ninth century. There are also plenty of sidrerías (cider houses). The west coast of Asturias is more rugged. One of the most attractive towns along here is Luarca, built around a cove surrounded by sheer cliffs. With a fishing harbour and an array of good restaurants and bars, the town's traditional character is reflected in its chigres – old Asturian taverns – where visitors learn the art of drinking cider.

Places of interest

Avilés: 14th- and 15th-century churches and palaces.

Cudillero: small, charming fishing port.

Gijón: 18th-century palace, beaches, museums.

Villahormes: seaside town with excellent swimming coves.

Villaviciosa: atmospheric old town, 13th-century church, cider factory.

Cuisine of the region

Local specialities include *fabada,* a type of stew made with haricot beans called *fabes*, *potes* (soups) and of course cider, which can be drunk in *sidrerías.* The customary way to serve cider is to pour it from a great height, a practice known as *escanciar*, into a wide-mouthed glass only just covering the *culín* or bottom. Rice pudding is the traditional dessert and *frixuelos* (crepe), *huesos de santo* (made from marzipan) and *tocinillo de cielo* (syrup pudding) are eaten during festivals.

Brazo de gitano: a type of Swiss roll.

Carne gobernada: beef in white wine with bacon, eggs, peppers and olives.

Fabada asturiana: haricot beans, chorizo, cabbage, cured pork shoulder and potatoes.

Pastel carbayón: almond pastry.

Arbón

Camping La Cascada

Arbón Villayón, E-33718 Arbón (Asturias) T: 985 625 081. E: campinglacascada@hotmail.com

alanrogers.com/ES89440

Located in a clearing of the attractive Arbon Valley this friendly, family run site offers the chance to experience the delights of rural Spain. There are 74 very small pitches (60 for touring units), all sited on gently sloping grass with electricity (4A), long leads are required. The beaches and small villages of the Costa Verde are only 12 km. away and the site has information about this spectacular region. Access to the site is not difficult but a 3,500 kg. weight restriction on the small bridge at the site entrance makes it unsuitable for larger units. The focal point of this small and well maintained site is its traditional style restaurant. It is open during July and August and serves a variety of home cooked, locally grown produce. The unheated, fenced swimming pool is open all season and provides a good sunbathing area. Open from Easter to the end of September, this is a quiet site but it can get busy in high season and advance booking is advised.

Facilities

Well maintained and modern toilet block. No specific facilities for visitors with disabilities. No washing machine. Shop, bar and snacks (all season). Restaurant (July/Aug). Swimming pool with sun terrace (all season). Play area. Fishing. Off site: Bicycle hire 500 m. Beaches 12 km.

Open: Easter - September.

Directions

From A8 (direction of La Coruna), exit, Navia onto N634. Turn left, AS25 (direction of Arbon). Site is 10 km. on right, well signed. Note: sign at site entrance refers to it as Camping Arbon.
GPS: 43.47993, -6.70261

Charges guide

Per person	€ 3.21
child	€ 3.00
caravan and car	€ 7.50
electricity	€ 2.68

Avín-Onís

Camping Picos de Europa

E-33556 Avín-Onís (Asturias) T: 985 844 070. E: info@picos-europa.com

alanrogers.com/ES89650

This delightful site is, as its name suggests, an ideal spot from which to explore these dramatic limestone mountains on foot, by bicycle or on horseback. The site itself is continuously developing and the dynamic owner, José, and his nephew who helps out when he is away, are both very pleasant and nothing is too much trouble. The site is in a valley beside a pleasant, fast flowing river. The 160 marked pitches are of varying sizes and have been developed in three avenues, on level grass mostly backing on to hedging, with 6A electricity. An area for tents and apartments is over a bridge past the fairly small, but pleasant, round swimming pool. Local stone has been used for the L-shaped building at the main entrance which houses reception and a very good bar/restaurant. The site can organise caving activities, and has information about the Cares gorge along with the many energetic ways of exploring the area, including by canoe and quad-bike! The Bulnes funicular railway is well worth a visit.

Facilities

Toilet facilities include a new fully equipped block, along with new facilities for disabled visitors and babies. Pleasant room with tables and chairs for poor weather. Washing machine and dryer. Shop (July-Sept). Swimming pool (Feb-Sept). Bar and caféteria style restaurant serves a good value 'menu del dia' and snacks. WiFi in restaurant area. Play area. Fishing. Torches necessary in the new tent area. Off site: Riding 12 km. Bicycle hire 15 km. Golf and coast at Llanes 25 km.

Open: All year.

Directions

Avín is 15 km. east of Cangas de Onís on the AS114 road to Panes and is probably best approached from this direction especially if towing. From A8 (Santander - Oviedo) use km. 326 exit and N634 northwest to Arriondas. Turn southeast on N625 to Cangas and join AS114 (Covodonga/Panes) bypassing Cangas. Site is just beyond Avín after 16 km. marker. GPS: 43.3363, -4.94498

Charges guide

Per person	€ 5.02
child (under 14 yrs)	€ 4.01
pitch incl. car	€ 8.57 - € 9.64
electricity	€ 3.75

Caravia Alta

Camping Caravaning Arenal de Moris

A8 Salida 337, E-33344 Caravia Alta (Asturias) T: 985 853 097. E: camoris@desdeasturias.com

alanrogers.com/ES89550

This smart, well run site is close to three fine sandy beaches so gets very busy at peak times. It has a backdrop of the mountains in the nature reserve known as the Sueve which is important for a breed of short Asturian horse, the Asturcone. The site has 330 grass pitches (269 for touring units) of 40-70 sq.m. and with 200 electricity connections available (10A). There are some shady, terraced pitches while others are on an open, slightly sloping field with limited views of the sea. The restaurant with a terrace serves local dishes and overlooks the pool with hills and woods beyond. The mountains of 'Picos de Europa' are only 35 km. away, Covadonga and its lakes are near and Ribadesella is 12 km. It is an ideal area for sea and mountain sports, horse riding, walking, birdwatching and cycling. A new motorway viaduct curves its way across the valley inland from the site and there was some traffic noise when we visited.

Facilities

Three sanitary blocks provide comfortable, controllable showers (no dividers) and vanity style washbasins, laundry facilities and external dishwashing (cold water). Supermarket. Bar/restaurant. Swimming pool. Tennis. Play area in lemon orchard. English is spoken. WiFi in the restaurant area. Off site: Beach and fishing 200 m. Bus 1 km. from gate. Bar and restaurants in village 2 km. Golf 5 km. Riding, bicycle hire and sailing 10 km.

Open: 1 June - 17 September.

Directions

Caravia Alta is 50 km. east of Gijón. Leave the A8 Santander - Oviedo motorway at km. 337 exit, turn left on N632 towards Colunga and site is signed to right in village, near 16 km. marker. GPS: 43.47248, -5.18332

Charges guide

Per person	€ 5.50
child	€ 4.40
pitch incl. car	€ 9.70 - € 14.00
electricity	€ 4.50

Colunga

Camping Costa Verde

Playa de la Griega, E-33320 Colunga (Asturias) T: 985 856 373

alanrogers.com/ES89500

This uncomplicated coastal site has a marked Spanish flavour and is just 1.5 km. from the pleasant town of Colunga. Although little English is spoken, the cheerful owner and his helpful staff will make sure you receive a warm welcome. The great advantage for many is that, 200 m. from the gate, is a spacious beach by a low tide lagoon with a recently constructed marine parade. Some of the 200 pitches are occupied on a seasonal basis, but there are 155 for tourers. These are flat but with little shades and electricity (6A) is available (long leads needed in places). The site gets very busy in high season.

Facilities

The single toilet block is of a high standard with a mixture of British and Turkish style toilets (all British for ladies), large showers and free hot water throughout. Laundry. Well stocked shop. Bar/restaurant is traditional and friendly. Play area. Torches needed. Off site: Fishing in river alongside site. Nearby towns of Ribadesella, Gijón and Oviedo. Excellent beaches. Bicycle hire 2 km. Sailing 4 km. Golf and riding 18 km.

Open: Easter - 1 October.

Directions

Colunga is 45 km. east of Gijón. Leave the A8 Santander - Oviedo motorway at km. 345 exit and take N632 towards Colunga. In village, turn right on As257 towards Lastres; site is on right after 1 km. marker. GPS: 43.49662, -5.26447

Charges guide

Per person	€ 4.70
pitch incl. car	€ 8.50 - € 9.85
electricity	€ 3.50 - € 5.20

Cudillero

Camping l'Amuravela

El Pito, E-33150 Cudillero (Asturias) T: 985 590 995

alanrogers.com/ES89480

This very well maintained, family run site, is close to the quaint old town of Cudillero and it is an ideal stopover when visiting 'green Spain'. Nearby is some of the most attractive mountain scenery in the region and if you stay here for one night it can easily extend to a much longer visit. There are 70 good sized touring pitches on level or gently sloping grass with easy access. Some pitches can accommodate large units. Mature trees give some shade and all pitches have 5A electricity. The excellent swimming pool provides an area for relaxation.

Facilities

One modern and very well maintained toilet block is close to all pitches and includes washbasins and shower cubicles. Facilities for visitors with disabilities. Washing machines and dryers. Well stocked shop. Café/bar and restaurant area (20/6-10/9). Swimming pool (June-Sept). Play area. Very little English is spoken. Off site: Fishing and beach 2 km. Golf 28 km.

Open: June - September.

Directions

From A8 take N632 towards Cudillero. After 120 km. marker turn right onto CU2 signed El Pito. Site is well signed on right in 2 km. On no account take caravans into Cudillero. GPS: 43.554391, -6.144581

Charges guide

Per unit incl. 2 persons and electricity	€ 21.80 - € 27.00
extra person	€ 4.90 - € 5.50

Luarca

Camping Los Cantiles

Ctra N634 km 502,7, E-33700 Luarca (Asturias) T: 985 640 938. E: cantiles@campingloscantiles.com

alanrogers.com/ES89400

Luarca is a picturesque little place with a pretty inner harbour and two sandy beaches, and Los Cantiles is two kilometres to the east of town on a cliff top that juts out into the sea, giving excellent views from some pitches and the sound of the waves to soothe you to sleep. The site is well maintained and is a pleasant place to stop along this under-developed coastline. The 150 pitches, 105 with electricity, are mostly on level grass, divided by huge hedges of hydrangeas and bushes. Some pitches have gravel surfaces. There is a separate area for late arrivals in high season.

Facilities

Two modern, fully equipped sanitary blocks (one in low season which is heated in winter) are kept very clean. Facilities for disabled campers and babies. Laundry. Freezer service. Gas. Small shop for basics. Bar with hot snacks (1/7-15/9). Day room for backpackers with tables, chairs and cooking facilities (own gas). Communal barbecue. Small playing field. Torches useful. WiFi (on payment). Off site: Indoor swimming pool, sauna and fitness centre, plus a bar/restaurant and shop 300 m. Beach and fishing 700 m. Luarca 2 km. Riding 4 km.

Open: All year.

Directions

Luarca is 85 km. west of Gijón. From A8 Oviedo - La Coruña exit at 467 onto N634 for Luarca. After km. 502 east of Luarca, turn right at petrol station and follow signs to site for 2.5 km. Last 150 m. is narrow. GPS: 43.54998, -6.51665

Charges 2012

Per unit incl. 2 persons and electricity	€ 19.30 - € 21.50
extra person	€ 4.30

No credit cards.

Somiedo

Camping Lagos de Somiedo

Valle de Lago, E-33840 Somiedo (Asturias) T: 985 763 776. E: campinglagosdesomiedo@hotmail.com

alanrogers.com/ES89450

This is a most unusual site in the Parque Natural de Somiedo. Winding narrow roads with challenging rock overhangs, hairpin bends and breathtaking views (for 8 km) finally bring you to the campsite at an elevation of 1,200 m. This is a site for 4x4s, powerful small campervans and cars – not for medium or large motorcaravans, and caravans are not accepted. It is not an approach for the faint hearted! The friendly Lana family make you welcome at their unique site, which is tailored for those who wish to explore the natural and cultural values of the park without the usual campsite amenities. There are 210 pitches (just four with electric hook-up), undefined in two open meadows. In this extraordinary glacial valley you can leave reality behind in the exploration of the marvels of nature including bears, wolves, capercailles and a unique wild goat which frequent these mountains.

Facilities

There are British style toilets and free hot water to clean hot showers and washbasins. Facilities for babies and children, and for disabled visitors. Washing machine. Combined reception, small restaurant with takeaway food, bar and reference section. Shop for bread, milk and other essentials, plus local produce and crafts. Horses for hire, trekking. Lectures on flora, fauna, history and culture. Fishing (licence required). Barbecue area. Small play area. Gas supplies. Off site: The very small village, which maintains the Spanish customs and traditions of this area 500 m.

Open: 1 April - 30 September.

Directions

From N634 via Oviedo turn left at 442 km. marker on AS-15 signed Parque Natural de Somiedo. At 9 km. marker past village of Longoria, turn left on AS-227. At 38 km. marker, turn left into Pol de Somiedo, signed Centro Urbano. Follow signs for Valle de Lago and El Valle; 8 km. of hairpin bends from Pola, passing Urria on the left, brings you to the valley. Site is signed on the right. GPS: 43.072018, -6.198885

Charges guide

Per person	€ 5.35
child	€ 4.28
tent and car	€ 11.23
motorcaravan with electricity	€ 11.77
dog	€ 3.35

Vidiago-Llanes

Camping La Paz

Ctra N634 Irun - Coruna km 292, E-33597 Vidiago-Llanes (Asturias) T: 985 411 235.
E: delfin@campinglapaz.com **alanrogers.com/ES89600**

This site occupies a spectacular location. The reception building is opposite a solid rock face and many hundred feet below the site and the climb to the upper part of the site is quite daunting but staff will place your caravan for you, although motorcaravan drivers will have an exciting drive to the top, especially to the loftier pitches. Once there, the views are absolutely outstanding, both along the coast and inland to the Picos de Europa mountains. There are 434 pitches, 350 with 10/15A electricity. There is also a lower section in a shaded valley to which access is easier, if rather tight in places. The upper area is arranged on numerous terraces, many of which require you to park your car by the roadside and climb the hill to your tent. The way down to the attractive beach is quite steep; from the lower area there is an easy walk to a smaller beach. The cliff-top restaurant and bar has commanding views over the ocean and beach. The site is very popular in high season so it does get crowded.

Facilities

Four good, modern toilet blocks are well equipped and include an interesting mix of electronic hot water and cold water from a tap for the showers. They are kept very clean even at peak times. Baby bath. Full laundry facilities. Motorcaravan services. Restaurant and bar/snack bar with small shop (all season). Watersports. Games room. Fishing. Torches useful in some areas. English spoken. WiFi in the restaurant. Off site: Shop, bar and restaurant in nearby village. Golf, riding, sailing and boat launching all 8 km.

Open: Easter - 30 September.

Directions

Vidiago is 85 km. west of Santander. Site is signed from A8/N634 Santander - Oviedo/Gijón road near km. 292 marker (on non-motorway section). Site approach road is just east of the village of Vidiago, marked by campsite signs (not named) and flags. Cross the railway track and exercise caution on bends. GPS: 43.39957, -4.65149

Charges guide

Per person	€ 6.15
child	€ 5.55
pitch incl. car	€ 13.20 - € 15.95
electricity	€ 4.25

The region of Cantabria in the north of Spain offers the best of both worlds. On the one hand there is the glorious coastline with beautiful beaches and pretty fishing villages; while inland there are a number of national parks including the mountainous, Picos de Europa.

CANTABRIA IS A ONE PROVINCE REGION

THE CAPITAL IS SANTANDER

The capital, Santander, is an elegant city which extends over a wide bay with views of the Cantabrian Sea. Its historic quarter is situated against a backdrop of sea and mountains, although the town is best known for its beaches; the Playa de la Magdalena, which has a summer windsurfing school, and the popular El Sardinero beach. There is also a Maritime Museum and Museum of Prehistory and Archaeology, plus a small zoo housed in the gardens of the old royal palace. A short distance from the city is the pretty medieval village of Santillana del Mar and the prehistoric caves of Altamira. The adjacent Altamira Museum houses a replica of these caves and their impressive prehistoric drawings. Also on the outskirts of the capital is the Cabárceno Nature Park with more protected areas scattered around the region, including those at Oyambre, Peña Cabarga and Saja-Besaya. The largest is the mountain range of Picos de Europa, a national park which shares its territory with Asturias and Castilla-León. With river gorges, valleys, woodlands and an abundance of wildlife, it is popular with walkers, trekkers and climbers.

Places of interest

Castro Urdiales: beaches, Gothic church, Roman bridge, old quarter.

Comillas: rural town, beaches, Gaudí-designed villa.

Laredo: lively seaside resort, 13th-century church, 5 km. long sandy beach.

Lienganes: 17th- and 18th-century architecture, spa.

Potes: on east side of Picos de Europa, mountain bike hire, paragliding available.

San Vicente de la Barquera: picturesque fishing port.

Cuisine of the region

Seafood is used a lot, including fresh shellfish, sardines, *rabas* (fried squid), *bocartes rebozados* (breaded whitebait). Cheese is produced throughout the region; *queso de nata* (cream cheese), *picón* from Treviso Bejes, and smoked cheeses from Áliva and Pido. A typical dish of the region is the Cantabrian stew, which contains haricot beans, cabbage, rice and sausage. Desserts include the traditional cheesecakes of the Pas Valley and pastries. The local tipple is *orujo*, a strong liquor.

Maganos encebollados: squid with onion.

Quesada: cheesecake.

Sobaos pasiegos: sponge cakes.

Sorropotún: type of fish stew.

Cabuérniga

Camping El Molino de Cabuérniga

Sopeña de Cabuérniga, Ctra C625 km 42, E-39510 Cabuérniga (Cantabria) T: 942 706 259.

E: cmcabuerniga@campingcabuerniga.com **alanrogers.com/ES89640**

Located in a peaceful valley with magnificent views of the mountains, beside the Saja river and only a short walk from the picturesque and unspoiled village of Sopeña, this gem of a site is on an open, level, grassy meadow with trees. Wonderful stone buildings and artefacts are a feature of this unique site. There are 102 marked pitches, all with 6A electricity, although long leads may be needed in places. This comfortable site is very good value and ideal for a few nights (or you may well choose to stay longer once there) whilst you explore the Cabuérniga Valley which forms part of the Reserva Nacional del Saja. The area is great for just relaxing or for indulging in active pursuits with opportunities for mountain biking, climbing, walking, swimming or fishing in the river, horse riding, hunting, paragliding and 4x4 safaris. Although little English is spoken, you will receive a warm welcome here with friendly advice on how best to enjoy your stay. Sopeña Fiesta is in mid-July each year.

Facilities

A superb, spotless sanitary block provides spacious, controllable showers and hot and cold water to washbasins. Washing machines and free ironing. Unit for disabled campers. Baby and toddler room. Bar serving breakfasts and 'bocadillos' (sandwiches) includes small shop section. Wonderful playground in rustic setting – supervision recommended. Fishing. Bicycle hire. Attractive stone cottages and apartments for rent. Off site: Bus service 500 m. Restaurant in village 1 km. Riding and bicycle hire 3 km. Beach and golf 20 km. Skiing 50 km.

Open: All year.

Directions

Sopeña is 55 km. southwest of Santander. From A8 (Santander - Oviedo) take km. 249 exit and join N634 to Cabezón de la Sal. Turn southwest on CA180 towards Reinosa for 11 km. to Sopeña (site signed to left). Turn into village (watch out for low eaves/gutters on buildings), continually bearing right following small site signs. GPS: 43.22594, -4.29034

Charges guide

Per unit incl. 2 persons and electricity	€ 26.00 - € 34.00
extra person	€ 6.00
child	€ 5.00

Isla

Camping Playa de Isla

Ctra Arnadal no. 1, E-39195 Isla (Cantabria) T: 942 679 361. E: bernac@teleonica.net

alanrogers.com/ES89980

This well maintained site is set on a headland, overlooking the sea on one side and the village of Quejo on the other. The 200 well defined small pitches (100 for touring) with little shade are on two levels. All have 6A electricity and some have sea views. Large units may experience difficulty accessing some pitches. There is direct access via a short flight of steps to the superb beach with its golden sand and rocky pools. The site has an illuminated 500 m. footpath to the village where there are restaurants, shops and bars. Since its opening in 1979 this site has undergone continuous improvement.

Facilities

One modern spotless toilet block is centrally positioned. Family shower room. Washing machines and dryers. Well stocked shop (Easter-Sept). Café/bar (July-Sept), with terrace overlooking the sea. Play area. Fishing from adjacent beach. Dogs are not accepted. Off site: Boat launching 500 m. Golf and bicycle hire 5 km. Riding 6 km.

Open: Easter - 30 September.

Directions

From A8 (Santander - Bilbao) take exit at 185 km. marker onto N634 (Beranga). Almost immediately turn right, CA147 (Noja). Left at roundabout, CA141 (Somo/Santander). Turn right, CA449 (Isla). Site is 5 km. through village. GPS: 43.5016, -3.54292

Charges guide

Per person	€ 5.13 - € 5.35
pitch	€ 11.55 - € 12.30
electricity	€ 4.28

Isla

Camping Punta Marina

Playa de la Arena s/n, E-39195 Isla (Cantabria) T: 942 679 349. E: puntamarina@ceoecant.es

alanrogers.com/ES89990

This well maintained site is open from Easter to the end of September. It has 98 pitches with only 28 for touring, on grass with little shade and all with 3A electricity, water and drainage. Most have sea views. The site comes alive at weekends and in the high season, when it can become very busy. Advanced booking is advisable. The small holiday village of Isla, with its many shops, restaurants and bars is only 1 km. away, and here there is also an excellent beach, rocky coves and a boat launching slipway. Care is needed with large units when approaching the site.

Facilities

One modern, very clean toilet block with family shower room and good facilities for visitors with disabilities. Washing machine and dryers. Well stocked shop (July/Aug). Separate restaurant, bar and takeaway (June-Sept). Swimming pools (July/Aug). Play area. Children's club (July/Aug). Tennis. Bicycle hire. Games room. TV room. Dogs are not accepted. Off site: Fishing and boat launching 1 km. Golf 5 km. Riding 6 km.

Open: Easter - 30 September.

Directions

Exit A8 at 185 km. marker and take N634 towards Beranga. Turn right, CA147, in towards Noja. At roundabout turn left, CA141 (Somo/Santander). Turn right, CA449 to Isla. Turn left CA448 to Playa la Arena. In 1.6 km. turn right to site. GPS: 43.49741, -3.57631

Charges guide

Per person	€ 4.00 - € 4.30
pitch incl. car	€ 13.40 - € 14.50
electricity	€ 2.70 - € 3.00

Laredo

Camping Playa del Regaton

El Regaton 8, E-39770 Laredo (Cantabria) T: 942 606 995. E: recepcion@campingplayaregaton.com

alanrogers.com/ES89930

Situated a short distance from the bustling seaside town of Laredo and easily accessible from Santander and Bilbao, Camping Playa del Regaton is an ideal stopover for those en route to the ferries. The site has direct access to the beach and the estuary of the Ria del Ason and is an important marsh area for migrating birds. Of the 128 small pitches, 100 are for touring and have 6/10A electricity and a sink. All are on level grass, with mature trees providing separation and a degree of shade. The site is popular with Spanish holidaymakers. The owners and their staff are keen to ensure you enjoy your stay.

Facilities

One modern, heated toilet block. Baby bath. Facilities for visitors with disabilities. Washing machine and dryer. Small shop (1/4-25/9) sells most essentials. Café/bar (1/4-25/9) with snacks (1/7-31/8). Play area. Children's club in high season. Games room. WiFi. Bicycle hire. Dogs are not accepted. Off site: Fishing 200 m. Riding 500 m. Boat launching 3 km. Golf 20 km. Beaches in Larado.

Open: 30 March - 30 September.

Directions

From the A8 (Santander - Bilbao) take exit 172 to Laredo. Straight on at roundabout signed hospital and beaches. Do not go into Laredo. At traffic lights turn left, site is well signed on left, 500 m. past hospital. GPS: 43.41319, -3.45039

Charges guide

Per unit incl. 2 persons and electricity	€ 18.70 - € 24.05
extra person	€ 3.25 - € 4.20

Noja

Camping Los Molinos

Ctra La Ria s/n, E-39180 Noja (Cantabria) T: 942 630 426. E: losmolinos@ceoecant.es

alanrogers.com/ES89950

Camping Los Molinos is close to the village of Noja, a seaside resort that gets very busy in high season. It is on the coast of Cantabria, a ten minute walk from the Playa del Ris beach which has fine sand and clear water. The site is divided into two main areas, both with a large number of permanent units, some of which look a little run down. There are 100 (60 sq.m) touring pitches, on level ground, but with little shade; 42 have 3A electricity. A separate large area without electricity is used for tents.

Facilities

Six fully equipped toilet blocks, two new and two recently refurbished, are kept clean. Facilities for disabled campers. Washing machines. Supermarkets and butcher. Restaurant (July/Aug). Bars and café bar serving tapas and pizzas. Swimming and paddling pools with lifeguard (20/6-7/9). Play area. ATM. Torch useful. WiFi (charged). Off site: Beach and fishing 400 m. Indoor pool and bicycle hire 500 m. Golf 9 holes 1 km, 18 holes 20 km. Boat launching 7 km. Riding 10 km.

Open: Easter, then 1 June - 30 September.

Directions

From A8 (Bilbao - Santander) take exit at km. 185 and join N634 (Beranga) and almost immediately turn right on CA147 to Noja. In 10 km. turn left down through town. At beach roundabout turn left and then left again just before Camping Playa Joyel at large sign for site. GPS: 43.48516, -3.53807

Charges 2012

Per unit incl. 2 persons and electricity	€ 22.60 - € 31.60

No credit cards.

Noja

Camping Playa Joyel

Playa de Ris, E-39180 Noja (Cantabria) T: 942 630 081. E: playajoyel@telefonica.net

alanrogers.com/ES90000

This very attractive holiday and touring site is some 40 kilometres from Santander and 80 km. from Bilbao. It is a busy, high quality, comprehensively equipped site by a superb beach providing 1,000 well shaded, marked and numbered pitches with 6A electricity available. These include 80 large pitches of 100 sq.m. Some 250 pitches are occupied by tour operators and seasonal units. This well managed site has a lot to offer for family holidays with much going on in high season when it gets crowded.

Facilities

Six excellent, spacious toilet blocks include baby baths. Laundry. Motorcaravan services. Gas. Supermarket. Shop. Kiosk. Restaurant and takeaway (1/7-31/8). Bar and snacks. Swimming pools, bathing caps compulsory (20/5-15/9). Entertainment. Soundproofed pub/disco (July/Aug). Gym park. Tennis. Playground. Riding. Fishing. Nature animal park. Hairdresser (July/Aug). Torches necessary in some areas. Animals are not accepted. WiFi (charged). Off site: Bicycle hire and sports complex 1 km. Sailing and boat launching 10 km. Riding and golf 20 km.

Open: 30 March - 30 September.

Directions

From A8 (Bilbao - Santander) take km. 185 exit and N634 towards Beranga. Almost immediately turn right on CA147 to Noja. In 10 km. turn left at multiple campsite signs and go through town. At beach follow signs to site. GPS: 43.48948, -3.53700

Charges guide

Per unit incl. 2 persons and electricity	€ 28.20 - € 47.40
extra person	€ 4.40 - € 6.70

Low season discounts.

Pechón

Camping Las Arenas-Pechón

Ctra Pechón - Unquera km 2, E-39594 Pechón (Cantabria) T: 942 717 188. E: info@campinglasarenas.com

alanrogers.com/ES89700

This site is in a very quiet, but rather spectacular location bordering the sea and the Tina Mayor estuary, with views to the mountains and access to an attractive little beach. Taking 350 units, half the site has grassy pitches (60 sq.m) in bays or on terraces with stunning sea and mountain views, with electricity available (5A) and connected by asphalted roads. There are some quite steep slopes to tackle – reception is at the top, as are the bar and restaurant; the latter has a terrace with fantastic views.

Facilities

Clean, well tiled sanitary facilities are in the older, simple style. Various blocks include showers (no divider; add hot water to the cold by pushing a switch). Washing machines. Well stocked supermarket. Restaurant/bar and snack bar (all season). Small playground. Riding arranged (collected from site). River and sea fishing and swimming. Torches helpful. English is spoken. Off site: Shops, bars and restaurants in Pechón, plus a disco/bar 1 km. Golf 28 km.

Open: 1 June - 30 September.

Directions

On A8 from Santander, take km. 272 exit for Unquera (N621) at end of motorway section. Take first exit CA380 (Pechón) and site which is 2 km. on left. From Oviedo/Gijón on A8/N634 at km. 272 take N621 slip-road for Unquera (do not join motorway), then as above. There are other roads to Pechón - ensure you take the 380! GPS: 43.39093, -4.5106

Charges guide

Per person	€ 6.25
pitch incl. car	€ 11.00 - € 14.30
electricity	€ 3.60

Potes

Camping La Isla Picos de Europa

Picos de Europa, E-39570 Potes-Turieno (Cantabria) T: 942 730 896. E: campicoseuropa@terra.es

alanrogers.com/ES89620

La Isla is beside the road from Potes to Fuente Dé, with many trees giving good shade and glimpses of the mountains above. Established for over 25 years, a warm welcome awaits you from the owners (who speak good English) and a most relaxed and peaceful atmosphere exists here. The 106 unmarked pitches are arranged around an oval gravel track under a variety of fruit and ornamental trees. Electricity (6A) is available to all pitches, although some need long leads. A river runs through the site.

Facilities

Single, clean and smart sanitary block retains the style of the site. Washbasins with cold water. Washing machine. Gas supplies. Small shop and restaurant/bar (1/4-30/9). Small swimming pool (caps compulsory; 1/5-30/9). Play area. Barbecue area. Fishing. Bicycle hire. Riding. WiFi. Off site: Bus from gate in high season. Shops, bars and restaurants in Potes 2.5 km. Riding 10 km. Fuente Dé and its spectacular cable car ride 18 km. Beach 40 km.

Open: 1 April - 15 October.

Directions

From A8/N634 (Santander - Oviedo) take km. 272 exit for Unquera (end of motorway section). Take N621 south to Panes and up spectacular gorge (care needed if towing) to Potes. Take CA165 to Fuente Dé and site is on the right, 2.5 km. beyond Potes. GPS: 43.14999, -4.69997

Charges guide

Per person	€ 4.15 - € 4.50
pitch	free - € 11.50
electricity	€ 3.60

Potes

Camping La Viorna

Ctra Santo Toribio, E-39570 Potes (Cantabria) T: 942 732 021. E: info@campinglaviorna.com

alanrogers.com/ES89630

The wonderful views of the valley below from the open terraces, with its spectacular backdrop of mountains, make this smart and sophisticated site an attractive base from which to tour this region or to relax by the swimming pool. There are beds of flowers everywhere and the trees provide shade on many pitches. Access is good for all sizes of unit to the 115 pitches of around 70 sq.m, all of which have electricity (6A). In high season, however, tents may be placed on less accessible, steeply sloping areas.

Facilities

Single, neat sanitary block of very high standard, clean and modern. Washbasins have cold water only. Facilities for disabled visitors double as unit for babies (key). Laundry facilities. Shop. Restaurant/bar with terrace. Swimming pool (23x13 m) and paddling pool (25/6-30/9; caps compulsory). Play area. Games room. Many sporting activities can be arranged such as parascending, mountain biking, trekking, rafting and canoeing. WiFi. Off site: Bicycle hire 1 km. Fishing, riding and Potes with shops, restaurants and bars 1.5 km. Beach 40 km.

Open: Easter/1 April - 31 October.

Directions

From A8/N634 (Santander - Oviedo) take km. 272 exit for Unquera (end of motorway section). Take N621 south to Panes and up spectacular gorge (care needed if towing) to Potes. After town take left fork signed Toribio de Liébana and site is on right after 800 m. GPS: 43.15435, -4.64348

Charges guide

Per person	€ 3.90 - € 4.40
pitch	€ 10.00 - € 11.50
electricity (3/6A)	€ 3.00 - € 3.20

Ramales de la Victoria

Camping La Barguilla

E-39800 Ramales de la Victoria (Cantabria) T: 942 646 586

alanrogers.com/ES89910

Located in a rural setting on the outskirts of the small Spanish town of Ramales de la Victoria, this small site provides an opportunity to sample traditional Spanish life. Access to the town is via an easy 1 km. walk. There are 79 small pitches with 50 for touring, all with 3/6A electricity. Some pitches have shade, whilst others enjoy views of the nearby Sierra del Hornijo mountains. Facilities are minimal but the site is well maintained. Advance booking in high season is recommended.

Facilities

One heated toilet block provides WCs, washbasins and shower cubicles. No facilities for visitors with disabilities. Washing machines. Shop. Terrace bar, caféteria, restaurant (all season). Fenced play area. Games room. Barbecues are not permitted. Off site: Fishing 200 m. Riding 10 km. Golf 20 km. Beaches in Laredo.

Open: All year (except November).

Directions

From A8, take exit 173 and N629 to Ramales de la Victoria. At entry to town, turn right, CA261 signed Arredondo. In 1.6 km. turn left over bridge into Parque Publico. Campsite is on right behind Restaurant Perigena. Sharp incline to site so care is needed for those with larger units. GPS: 43.25918, -3.47151

Charges guide

Per person	€ 4.82
pitch	€ 4.82 - € 9.10
electricity	€ 2.68

Ruiloba

Camping El Helguero

Ctra Santillana - Comillas, E-39527 Ruiloba (Cantabria) T: 942 722 124. E: reservas@campingelhelguero.com

alanrogers.com/ES89610

This site, in a peaceful location surrounded by tall trees and impressive towering rock formations, caters for 240 units (of which 100 are seasonal) on slightly sloping ground. There are many marked pitches on different levels, all with access to electricity (6A), but with varying amounts of shade. There are also attractive tent and small camper sections set close in to the rocks and 22 site owned chalets. The site gets very crowded in high season, so it is best to arrive early if you have not booked.

Facilities

Three well placed toilet blocks, although old, are clean and all include controllable showers and basins. Facilities for children and disabled visitors. Laundry facilities. Motorcaravan services. Small supermarket (July/Aug). Bar/snack bar. Restaurant. Swimming pool and children's pool with access lifts for disabled visitors (caps compulsory). Playground. Activities and entertainment (high season). Torches useful in some places. WiFi over site (charged by card). Off site: Bar/restaurants in village. Beach, fishing, sailing, golf and riding all 3 km.

Open: 1 April - 30 September.

Directions

From A8 (Santander - Oviedo) take km. 249 exit (Cabezón and Comillas) and turn north on CA135 towards Comillas. At km. 7 turn right on CA359 to Ruilobuca and Barrio la Iglesia. After village turn right up hill on CA358 to site on right (note: signs refer to 'Camping Ruiloba'). GPS: 43.38288, -4.24800

Charges 2012

Per unit incl. 2 persons and electricity	€ 24.10 - € 28.95
extra person	€ 4.55 - € 5.50

Camping Cheques accepted.

San Vicente de la Barquera

Camping Caravaning Playa de Oyambre

Finca Pe–a Guerra, E-39547 San Vicente de la Barquera (Cantabria) T: 942 711 461.

E: camping@oyambre.com **alanrogers.com/ES89710**

This exceptionally well managed site is ideally positioned to use as a base to visit the spectacular Picos de Europa or one of the sandy beaches along this northern coast. Despite its name, it is one kilometre from the beach on foot. The 100 touring pitches all have 10A electricity (long leads needed in places). The fairly flat central area is allocated to tents while caravans are mainly sited on wide terraces (access to some could be a little tight for larger units) and there is some shade. There may be some traffic noise.

Facilities

Good, clean sanitary facilities are in one, well kept block. Showers are spacious but have a frustrating mixture of pushbutton hot and ordinary cold controls. Facilities for babies and disabled visitors. Washing machines. Motorcaravan services. Shop in bar (all season). Restaurant. Takeaway. Swimming pools with lifeguard (1/6-15/9). Playground. WiFi. Off site: Bus service at site entrance. Fishing and superb beach 1 km. Golf 2 km. Riding 5 km. San Vicente de la Barquera 5 km.

Open: Easter/1 April - 30 September.

Directions

From A8 (Santander - Oviedo) take exit at km. 258 (Caviedes) and join N634. Turn towards San Vicente. Site signed at junction to Comillas, at km. 265 on the E70, 5 km. east of San Vicente de la Barquera. The entrance is quite steep. Another 'Camping La Playa' at Oyambre within 500 m. (on the beach) is not recommended. GPS: 43.385268, -4.33814

Charges guide

Per person	€ 5.08
pitch incl. electricity	€ 14.70

Santillana del Mar

Camping Santillana

Ctra de Comilias s/n, E-39330 Santillana del Mar (Cantabria) T: 942 818 250.

E: complejosantillana@cantabria.com **alanrogers.com/ES89730**

This is an attractive site on a hill above the charming medieval village of Santillana del Mar and five to ten kilometres from some of Costa Verde's good beaches. There are 400 pitches, all with access to electricity (5A), some primarily for tents, informally arranged on a slope, with others for caravans and motorcaravans on the lower part of the site. Where the pitches are numbered but unmarked some overcrowding may occur in high season, and those alongside the road will experience some noise.

Facilities

Modern toilet blocks (only one open in low season), with facilities for disabled visitors. Laundry facilities. Souvenir shop. Supermarket. Bar/restaurant and self-service café. Swimming and paddling pools (1/5-30/9). Play areas. Minigolf. Games room. Tennis. Bicycle hire. Library. Entertainment in high season. Chalets and mobile homes to rent. Off site: Short, if rather steep, walk to centre of village with shops, bars and restaurants. Riding 300 m. Fishing 5 km. Boat launching 16 km. Golf 20 km.

Open: All year.

Directions

Santillana is 30 km. west of Santander. From the A8 (Santander - Oviedo) take km. 234 exit west of Torrelavega and follow CA133 north to Santillana. Turn left at T-junction (busy) towards Comillas and site is on right in 300 m. GPS: 43.39258, -4.11334

Charges guide

Per person	€ 5.00 - € 5.61
pitch incl. electricity	€ 10.00 - € 18.04

No credit cards.
Camping Cheques accepted.

Located in northern Spain, this is a region steeped in Basque traditions, which is reflected in the architecture, native language, local sports and cuisine.

THERE ARE THREE PROVINCES: ALAVA, GIPUZKOA AND BIZKAIA

THE REGIONAL CAPITAL IS VITORIA

The province of Gipuzkoa adjoins France in the east. Its capital, San Sebastián, is a bustling, picturesque seaside town with a strong Basque identity. Overlooking La Concha Bay and enclosed by rolling low hills, this popular resort boasts four good beaches, including the celebrated La Concha Beach. As cider production is one of the oldest traditions in Basque country there are also plenty of sidrerías (cider houses) to visit. Heading along the rocky fringe of Costa Vasca towards Bilbao in Bizkaia are more excellent beaches and pretty fishing villages including Orio, Zarautz and Getaria. The biggest attraction in Bilbao is the famous Guggenheim Museum. Opened in 1997 this spectacular building is completely covered with titanium sheets and houses a collection of modern and contemporary art from around the world. The city also boasts a beautiful old quarter with a Gothic cathedral, the Plaza Nueva and a museum. Further inland in Alava is Vitoria, the region's capital. Its medieval streets intermingle with Renaissance Palaces and fine churches and are lined with lively bars and tavernas. In the summer, the city plays host to a jazz festival. Elsewhere in the province are several nature reserves.

Places of interest

Encartanciones: one of the world's largest cave chambers Torca del Carlista, wildlife sanctuary.

Hondarribia: fishing port, beaches, charming walled old town.

Laguardia: old walled town with cobbled streets, historic buildings, in wine-growing district of Rioja Alavesa.

Oñati: Baroque architecture, old university.

Tolosa: impressive old town square, carnival in February.

Zarautz: seaside town, famous for production of *txakoli.*

Zumaia: beaches, good coastal walks, July fiesta with Basque sports, dancing and bull racing.

Cuisine of the region

Basque cuisine is considered to be the finest in Spain. Tapas or *pintxos* is readily available in bars, served with the local white wine *txakolí*. Fish is popular, especially *bacalao* (cod) and seafood is often used to make casseroles and sauces. Lots of milk based desserts. Founded in the 19th century, the tradition of dining clubs or *txokos* are unique to the Basque country.

Alubias pochas: white haricot bean stew.

Chipirones en su tinta: squid cooked in its ink.

Goxua: sponge cake with whipped cream and caramel.

Intxaursalsa: milk pudding with cinnamon and walnuts.

Marmitaco: fish and potato stew.

Pantxineta: custard slice.

Itziar-Deba

Camping Itxaspe

Ctra Nacional 634 km 38, E-20829 Itziar-Deba (Bizkaia) T: 943 199 377. E: itxaspe@hotmail.es

alanrogers.com/ES90380

Set on a hill, surrounded by farmland and with views of the mountains, this site is ideal for a stopover or a couple of days rest. A fifteen minute walk through the woods leads to a rocky beach and the sea. Most of the 100 pitches are for tourers and are of medium size, flat and on grass, with plenty of water and electrical connections (6A, some Europlugs). Comfortable bar, restaurant and swimming pool open in July and August. Offering plenty of rural walks, this site will appeal to those wanting peace and quiet, but with little entertainment and some unfenced areas, children will need supervision. Eight extremely well presented, self-contained apartments above the bar/restaurant are roomy and decorated to a high standard. One has been specifically adapted for those with disabilities.

Facilities

The single traditional style sanitary block is basic but clean. Recently refurbished, new showers have been installed and more modernisation is gradually being undertaken. Facilities for disabled visitors. Washing machine. Well stocked shop. Restaurant and bar. Swimming pool (1/7-31/8). WiFi. Toddlers' play area. Barbecue and solarium area. Covered tables.
Off site: Beach and fishing 1 km. Riding and bicycle hire 7 km. Golf 15 km.

Open: 1 April - 30 September.

Directions

From the A8 take exit 13 and follow signs for Itziar. At junction turn left. In 150 m. take right slip road for immediate turn left onto GI3291 (i.e. to cross main road). Site is signed and at end of road.
GPS: 43.29398, -2.32978

Charges guide

Per unit incl. 2 persons and electricity	€ 26.60
extra person	€ 5.30
child (under 10 yrs)	€ 4.60
dog	free

Mendexa

Camping Leagi

Calle Barrio Leagi s/n, E-48289 Mendexa (Bizkaia) T: 946 842 352. E: leagi@campingleagi.com

alanrogers.com/ES90340

This site is perched high above Lekeitio and has commanding views of the town, sea and surrounding areas. A steep road leads up to the site, but upon arriving at the car park and reception, the area becomes flat. There are 111 touring pitches on open, level grass with good mountain views. All have electricity (5A). There is little shade and the pitches are not defined. This is a quiet site, suitable for couples and families with small children and for those wishing to explore the attractive local towns or the many rural walks in the area. Transport is essential.

Facilities

Two modern, clean sanitary blocks are well equipped and there are separate facilities for disabled visitors. Excellent laundry. Motorcaravan services. Shop (1/7-10/9). Restaurant, bar and takeaway (all year, closed Tues/Wed). Swimming pool (1/7-10/9). Dog washing area. Small toddlers' play area in car park. Free WiFi throughout. Off site: Fishing, sailing and beach 1.5 km.

Open: All year.

Directions

From Lekeitio cross bridge heading east. Immediately turn right onto BI4449 to Mendexa. Continue up hill for 800 m. Site is signed on bend. Immediately turn sharp right and access is via a steep and narrow road. GPS: 43.35163, -2.49203

Charges guide

Per person	€ 4.70 - € 5.70
pitch	€ 11.00 - € 15.00
electricity	€ 3.90

Mundaka

Camping Portuondo

Ctra Gernika - Bermeo, E-48360 Mundaka (Bizkaia) T: 946 877 701. E: recepcion@campingportuondo.com

alanrogers.com/ES90350

This site has a lovely restaurant, bar and terrace taking full advantage of the wonderful views across the ocean and estuary. Set amongst gardens, the 72 touring pitches are mainly for tents and smaller vans, but there are eight large pitches for caravans and motorcaravans. Access to these is a little difficult as the road is steep and there is no turning space. The site is mostly terraced, with tent pitches split, one section for your unit, the other for your car and there is some shade. Most are slightly sloping and all have electricity (6A, some may need long leads). In high season it is essential to ring to book your space.

Facilities

Two toilet blocks include mostly British WCs and a baby room. One new block has facilities for disabled visitors. A reader reports poor cleaning and maintenance during their visit. Laundry facilities. Motorcaravan service point. Shop (15/6-15/9). Bar and two restaurants, all open to public (28/1-14/12). Takeaway (15/6-15/9). Swimming pools (15/6-15/9). WiFi over part of site. Barbecue area. Torches may be useful. Off site: Fishing 100 m. Surfing on Mundaka beach 500 m. Bicycle hire 1 km. Shops, bars and restaurants 2 km. Sailing 3 km. Riding 8 km.

Open: 23 January - 9 December.

Directions

From the A8 (San Sebastián - Bilbao) take exit 18 and follow signs for Gernika on BI635. Continue on BI2235 (Bermeo). Site is on right approaching Mundaka. Care needed as a wide approach may be necessary (sharp right turn with a steep access). No left to site. GPS: 43.39918, -2.69610

Charges 2012

Per unit incl. 2 persons and electricity	€ 30.05 - € 34.50
extra person	€ 6.35 - € 8.00

San Sebastián

Camping Igueldo

Paseo Padre Orkolaga no. 69, Barrio de Igueldo, E-20008 San Sebastián (Gipuzkoa) T: 943 214 502.
E: info@campingigueldo.com **alanrogers.com/ES90300**

A five kilometre drive from the city takes you to this terraced campsite, high above San Sebastián, between the mountains and the sea. It offers mostly level, shaded, small (max. 70 sq.m) grass pitches with electricity (5/10A) and drainage. The restaurant and bar are open all year and a sun terrace looks toward the mountains. An excellent bus service to and from San Sebastián runs every 30 minutes (all year). There are 25 attractive chalets to rent at the entrance to the site. With few sporting facilities, this site is for those wishing to mix quiet surroundings with city life. English is spoken in reception.

Facilities

Three traditional toilet blocks are clean and light. Facilities for disabled campers and babies (key). Adequate covered dishwashing and laundry facilities. Motorcaravan service point. Shop for basics (all year). Bar/restaurant (all year, Wed-Sun in early/late season, daily in summer). Play area. Off site: The town of Igueldo within walking distance with shops, restaurants and bars. Bicycle hire, beach and fishing 5 km. Golf 9 km.

Open: All year.

Directions

From A8 take exit 8 for San Sebastián West (oeste). Head for Ondarreta. At Playa de Ondarreta, follow beach road on Avda de Satrustegui. At T-junction turn left. Keep right on Pase O De Igueldo. Continue for 5 km. Site on left. GPS: 43.304583, -2.045889

Charges 2012

Per unit incl. 2 persons and electricity	€ 22.10 - € 33.20
extra person	€ 4.30 - € 5.40

Zarautz

Gran Camping Zarautz

Monte Talai-Mendi, Ctra N634 San Sebastián - Bilbao, E-20800 Zarautz (Gipuzkoa) T: 943 831 238.
E: info@grancampingzarautz.com **alanrogers.com/ES90390**

This friendly site sits high in the hills to the east of the Basque town of Zarautz and has commanding views over the bay and the island of Getaria. Of the 400 pitches, 300 are for touring units, with 5A electricity; ten also have water and drainage. The remaining pitches are for tents and seasonal caravans. The grass pitches are of average size, shaded by mature trees and are reasonably level; those on the perimeter have superb sea views. Between the site and the sea is a protected public area where flora and fauna flourish and you can enjoy watching the birds and wildlife. The ruins of a once busy iron ore works on the shore and the adjacent small island of Mollarri are to be explored. A 'bodega' adjacent to the site produces the local white wine, Txakoli (pronounced Char-coal-lee). The town of Zarautz offers a cultural programme in summer and the pedestrian promenade with modern sculptures is a good vantage point to enjoy the beach and watch the surfers.

Facilities

Three well equipped toilet blocks. Facilities for disabled campers. Washing machines. Bar/snack bar with TV plus terrace. Play area. Restaurant with 'menu del día' and à la carte meals. Well stocked shop (all facilities open all year). Off site: Beach, fishing and golf (9 holes) 1 km. Bicycle hire 2 km. Shops, restaurants, bars, indoor pool plus bus/train services in Zarautz 2 km. Boat launching 4 km.

Open: All year.

Directions

Zarautz is 20 km. west of San Sebastián. From the A8 (San Sebastián - Bilbao) take exit 11 for Zarautz and straight on through two roundabouts and follow signs to site. If using the N634 coast road, site is signed near km. 17 marker.
GPS: 43.28958, -2.14603

Charges guide

Per unit incl. 2 persons and electricity	€ 26.10
extra person	€ 5.40
child (under 12 yrs)	€ 3.95

Camping Cheques accepted.

La Rioja

This small region located in the north eastern part of the country is the most outstanding wine-growing area in Spain. Its production, Rioja wine, figures among the finest wines in the world.

THIS IS A ONE PROVINCE REGION

THE CAPITAL IS LOGROÑO

The capital of the region, Logroño, did not gain importance till the 11th century, when the rise in popularity of the Pilgrims' Route to Santiago de Compostela attracted people. Indeed the 12th-century Codex Calixtinus, the first guide to the route, mentions the city. And throughout the region, every town along the way has a church dedicated to the saint. Pilgrimages aside, La Rioja is best known for its wine. At the centre of the region's wine production is Haro, a stately town northwest of Logroño, and obviously a good place to stock up on a bottle or two! For those interested in the wine processes the Museum of Wine is worth a visit; admission includes cheese and wine tasting. During the last week of June the town comes alive with festivities. With free outdoor concerts, costumed characters on giant stilts, wine tastings and bargain buys, the climax of these fiestas is the Battle of the Wine, where thousands of people happily gather to be drenched in wine.

Places of interest

Calahorra: main town in Lower Rioja, Cathedral Museum.

Ezcaray: in the Sierra de la Demanda mountains, the surrounding area is made up of streams, forests and peaks over 2,000 metres high.

Nájera: monastery of Santa María la Real, built in 1032, History and Archaeological Museum.

San Millán de la Cogolla: traditional town, Monasteries of Suso and Yuso where the first texts written in Spanish are preserved.

Santo Domingo de la Calzada: last great staging post of the Pilgrims' Route in La Rioja, Cathedral of San Salvador.

Cuisines of the region

Asparagus, beans, peppers, garlic, artichokes and other vegetables and pulses are the basic ingredients of a long list of dishes such as vegetable stew, potatoes a la riojana, lamb cutlets with vine shoots or stuffed peppers. Traditional desserts include pears in wine, almond pastries from Arnedo and marzipan from Soto.

Camerano Cheese: cheese made from goat's milk, typical of La Rioja, usually eaten as a dessert with honey.

Fardelejo: pastry cake filled with marzipan.

Riojan-style potatoes: prepared with chorizo, peppers, garlic and lamp chops (optional).

Berceo

Camping Berceo

Ctra de Nájera - Sto Domingo dir. San Millán, E-26227 Berceo (La Rioja) T: 941 373 227

alanrogers.com/ES92280

Camping Berceo would ideally suit those looking for a quiet break at a site with limited facilities. It sits low in the San Millan valley in the heart of the Sierra de la Demanda and a steep walk of about 20 minutes will take you into the village. Here you will find several bars and restaurants, but little English is spoken. The 30 touring pitches are varied in size and separated by hedges. Some have shade and there are views of the green valley and mountains. Apart from the swimming pool which is open in peak season, there are few activities provided.

Facilities

One main toilet block providing sufficient facilities, but none for disabled visitors. Laundry area. Shop for basic supplies. Bar/restaurant. Takeaway on request. TV in bar and games area. Swimming and paddling pools. Play area. Off site: Berceo village 20 minute uphill walk. San Millan monasteries.

Open: All year.

Directions

From the A68 head west until N120 exit. Turn left onto the N120 signed Najera. Turn left onto the LR113 (Bobadilla). Within 5 km. turn right onto the 205 (Cárdenas) until Berceo village. In village centre follow site arrow down steep hill. Site is on left within 500 m. GPS: 42.33497, -2.85328

Charges guide

Per person	€ 4.28 - € 4.81
child	€ 3.75 - € 4.30
pitch	€ 3.00 - € 9.50
electricity	€ 4.17

Castanares de Rioja

Camping de La Rioja

Ctra de Haro - Sto Domingo de la Calzada, E-26240 Castanares de Rioja (La Rioja) T: 941 300 174.
E: info@campingdelarioja.com **alanrogers.com/ES92250**

This site is situated just beyond the town of Castanares de Rioja. This is a busy site during the peak season with many sporting activities taking place. In low season it becomes rather more quiet with limited facilities available. There are 30 level, grass touring pitches, out of a total of 250, and these are separated by hedges and trees allowing privacy. Each has their own water, drainage and electricity connection. To the rear of the site is the Oja River which is ideal for fishing and there are views of the Obarenes mountains in the distance. Some noise from the main road is possible. There are many historic places worth visiting and naturally, being in Rioja, plenty of local wine to taste. A walk or cycle into the town of Castanares will enable you to sample the local cuisine.

Facilities

The central sanitary facilities are old and traditional in style but clean. Open style washbasins and controllable showers. Laundry and dishwashing facilities. Shop, bar, restaurant, takeaway (on request) all open 20/6-20/9. Outdoor swimming pool (20/6-20/9 supervised). Multisports court. Football. Tennis. River fishing. Riding. Children's cycle circuit. Play area. No individual barbecues. Off site: Town centre 1.5 km. The Guggenheim Museum in Bilbao. City of San Sebastian with beaches and aquarium.

Open: 1 January - 9 December.

Directions

Head west on N120. Turn right onto LR111 signed Castanares de Rioja. Continue through town towards Haro. Site is on left, 800 m. after leaving town speed restriction. GPS: 42.52911, -2.92243

Charges guide

Per person	€ 4.60 - € 5.75
child	€ 4.00 - € 5.00
pitch	€ 10.00 - € 12.50
electricity	€ 3.60

Haro

Camping de Haro

Avenida Miranda 1, E-26200 Haro (La Rioja) T: 941 312 737. E: campingdeharo@fer.es
alanrogers.com/ES90400

This quiet riverside site is on the outskirts of Haro, the commercial centre for the renowned Rioja wines. It is a family run site with excellent pools. Staff in the modern reception are helpful and you may well get a cheery welcome from Carlos, the owner's son, who speaks excellent English. All 236 pitches are on level ground and of reasonable size. Approximately 50% are occupied on a seasonal basis. Many of the touring pitches have some shade, a few have a great deal. Electricity connections (6A) are provided, although long leads may be required on some pitches. The River Tirón running alongside the site can provide fishing, and there is secure fencing. Reception provides information on the jewel of a town, and on tastings at the 'Bodegas' close by – CUNE and Muga are just two of those within easy walking distance. The famous Paternina is a few minutes drive away.

Facilities

Two toilet blocks, one heated in winter, the other with facilities for disabled campers. Laundry. Bar/snack bar with small counter selling basic provisions and adjacent swimming pool (15/6-15/9). Play area and entertainment for children in season. WiFi over part of site (charged). Torch useful. Charcoal barbecues are not permitted. Off site: Large municipal pool complex nearby. Shops, bars, restaurants within walking distance. Bicycle hire 1 km. Boat launching 6 km. Riding 24 km. Golf 25 km.

Open: All year excl. 9 December - 19 January.

Directions

Haro is between Miranda de Ebro and Logroño. From AP68 (Bilbao - Logroño) take exit 9 to Haro. Keep to LR111 (Vitoria) bearing left, crossing lights and over river where site is signed to left. From the N124 (Vitoria - Logroño) leave at exit north of Haro onto LR111 towards town and turn right before bridge (site signed). Avoid other turnings into town centre! GPS: 42.57894, -2.85157

Charges 2012

Per unit incl. 2 persons and electricity	€ 21.35 - € 26.95
extra person	€ 4.30 - € 5.70
child (3-10 yrs)	€ 3.35 - € 4.20
dog	€ 2.15 - € 2.85

Camping Cheques accepted.

Najera

Camping El Ruedo

Paseo San Julián 24, E-26300 Najera (La Rioja) T: 941 360 102.

alanrogers.com/ES92290

Camping El Ruedo is situated 500 m. from the town of Najera and the River Rio Najerilla runs close by. There are numerous walks possible and seating provided along the riverbank. This is a small site with a total of 20 touring pitches on level ground, unmarked and with no separation. You can pitch at your own discretion. The traditional style sanitary block is kept clean and tidy with ample provision for the small amount of visitors. Extremely quiet and with very basic facilities, this site would suit those looking for peace and tranquillity. The site is not suitable for large units. No English is spoken.

Facilities

One immaculate toilet block with washbasins and showers. No facilities for disabled visitors. Washing machines (rather old). No shop, but provisions in town. Swings. No site lighting so torches useful.
Off site: Town 500 m. (10 minutes walk).

Open: 1 April - 10 September.

Directions

From Logroño head west on AP68 until sign for N120 Najera. Turn left onto LR113 signed Najera. At traffic lights turn sharp left immediately before cobbled bridge. Site on left within 500 m. It is poorly signed after the A12. GPS: 42.41068, -2.73284

Charges guide

Per unit incl. 2 persons and electricity	€ 22.80
extra person	€ 4.00
child (under 10 yrs)	€ 4.80 - € 13.00

Navarrete

Camping Navarrete

Ctra de Entrena km 1, E-26370 Navarrete (La Rioja) T: 941 440 169. E: campingnavarrete@fer.es

alanrogers.com/ES92270

Camping Navarrete is a spotlessly clean site in which the owners take great pride. Ideal as a base for exploring the surrounding countryside and sampling wonderful wines as it is located in the heart of La Rioja. Many of the 180 pitches are taken up by static caravans but a designated grassy area has been set aside for 40 unmarked, spacious touring pitches with 5A electricity. Some have shade and there are good views of the Rioja valley. Facilities on site are limited until the height of the season but the area is surrounded by many villages and places of artistic and historical importance. Expect some road noise.

Facilities

One modern central sanitary block with heating is clean and provides communal washbasins and separate shower cubicles. Facilities for disabled visitors, one unisex cabin. Laundry facilities. Motorcaravan services. Shop (15/6-15/9). Bar, restaurant and takeaway (weekends only in low season). Outdoor swimming and paddling pools (15/6-15/9). Games machines. Tennis. Bicycle hire. Unfenced play area. Barbecues are allowed in special area. WiFi (free). Off site: Large town of Logroño 10 km.

Open: 12 January - 10 December.

Directions

From Logroño proceed west along AP68. Take exit 11 signed Navarrete. At town centre turn left onto LR137 signed Entrena. Site is on the right in 800 m. GPS: 42.41614, -2.55172

Charges guide

Per unit incl. 2 persons and electricity	€ 22.00 - € 26.40
extra person	€ 4.60 - € 5.50
child (under 10 yrs)	€ 4.25 - € 5.00

Villoslada de Cameros

Camping Los Cameros

Ctra de la Virgen de Lomos de Orios km 3, E-26125 Villoslada de Cameros (La Rioja) T: 941 747 021.

E: info@camping-loscameros.com **alanrogers.com/ES92260**

Situated 3 km. from the small town of Villoslada de Cameros, this site is in a quiet location, in a valley surrounded by tree covered mountains. The area provides the opportunity for plenty of hill walking and a footpath from the site takes you into the town. Of the 173 pitches, 146 are available for touring. They are open with some shade and have 5/10A electricity. This is a simple site with limited facilities available but it is well kept and has character; ideal for relaxation. A large playing field allows children to play ball games and bicycles can be hired from reception.

Facilities

One heated sanitary block provides WCs, washbasins with cold water only (one with hot water) and cubicle showers. No facilities for disabled visitors. Cold water only for washing machine and dishwashing. Shop. Bar with games. Restaurant with comprehensive menu and takeaway to order. Playing field and play area. Picnic area. Only gas barbecues permitted on pitches. Off site: Town 3 km. with shops, bars and restaurants and swimming pool.

Open: 20 January - 20 December.

Directions

From Logroño (AP68) turn left onto N111 heading south towards Soria and Madrid. At sign for Villoslada de Cameros turn right, pass the centre and turn left by camping sign (LR448). Site on left in 3 km. Road bumpy and uneven, drive with care and watch for animals on road. GPS: 42.08068, -2.67723

Charges 2012

Per unit incl. 2 persons and electricity	€ 22.80 - € 25.20

The region of Navarra lies in the north of Spain, separated from France by the Pyrenees. With mountain retreats, beautiful valleys and an array of attractive towns and historic buildings, it is also popular for those wishing to follow the Pilgrims' Route to Santiago de Compostela.

THERE IS ONLY ONE PROVINCE ALSO KNOWN AS NAVARRA

THE CAPITAL IS PAMPLONA

Founded by the Roman general Pompey in 75 BC, the region's capital, Pamplona, is perhaps best known for the Fiestas de San Fermín (July), when the encierro takes place, a tradition which involves people running through the streets in front of bulls. The city also boasts its fair share of sights including the old town, with its ancient churches and elegant buildings. Outside the city is the Sierra de Aralar, with well marked paths of all grades. A wander through here will take you past waterfalls and caves and in Excelsis you'll come across Navarra's oldest church, the Sanctuario de San Miguel, a popular pilgrimage destination. In the south, the historic medieval town of Olite is home to an outstanding 15th-century castle, with turrets galore, and a Romanesque and Gothic church. To the west is the Urbasa and Andía Nature Reserve. Further north and in the east, the villages and valleys of the Pyrenees provide some of the most beautiful landscapes in the province and offer the perfect place to relax. Of particular note are the Valle de Baztán and the Valle de Salazar. For the more active, the Valle de Roncal is a good place to explore the mountains, as is the Pirenaico National Park.

Places of interest

Andía Nature Reserve: forests, ponds, wildlife including the golden eagle, wild boar and wildcat.

Camino de Santiago: ancient Pilgrims' route. There are variants but the most popular point of entry into Spain was the pass of Roncesvalles, in the Pyrenees. It then continues south through Navarra via Sangüesa, Puente La Reina and Estella, then west through the provinces of La Rioja and Castilla-León till it reaches Santiago in the Galicia province.

Orreaga-Roncesvalles: a town established as a sanctuary and hospital in 1132 and first staging post for pilgrims, museum with exhibition on Pilgrims' Route.

Sangüesa: small town, 14th-century churches, medieval hospital.

Ujué: medieval defensive village, Romanesqe church.

Cuisine of the region

Typical products found in abundance in this area include asparagus grown on the river banks, small red peppers and artichokes from Tudela, pork from Estella, cherries from Ciriza, cheese made in the Roncal Valley and *chorizo* from Pamplona.

Ajoarriero: cod cooked with garlic, potato, 'choricero' peppers and tomatoes.

Canutillos de Sumbilla: sweet pastry made with aniseed, filled with lemon flavouring.

Chorizo: shaped like a candle, stuffed in thick tripe with pork and beef, seasoned with salt, paprika, garlic and sugars.

Cordero al chilindrón: lamb stew.

Cuajada: made from sheep's milk and natural curd, sweetened by honey or sugar.

Pacharán: traditional aniseed liquor.

Erratzu

Camping Baztan

Ctra Francia s/n, E-31714 Erratzu (Navarra) T: 948 453 133. E: campingbaztan@campingbaztan.com

alanrogers.com/ES90490

When driving through the small town of Erratzu extreme caution is required due to the narrowness of the streets and it is not advised at all for large units. This site's rural setting and the mountain views make this a retreat for those who enjoy camping in quiet surroundings. It consists of a main building housing reception, a shop, bar and a small restaurant and above, 14 tidy apartments. There are also ten timber cottages for rent. Tarmac roads lead to the grass touring pitches which are supplied with water and electricity (10A). Shady and of a good size, most of the pitches are level. In early and late season the campsite is open, but a telephone call is necessary to gain access. You may be the only occupants. The one toilet block is open and cleaned but facilities are minimal.

Facilities

The single sanitary block is clean and has facilities for disabled visitors. Shop, bar and restaurant (weekends only outside 1/6-20/9). Swimming pool (1/6-20/9). Squash court. Only charcoal barbecues permitted. In April, May and 20/9-1/11 the site is only open at weekends. If you wish to stay on weekdays, entry can be obtained by dialling a number displayed at reception (sanitary block will be open). Off site: River fishing 50 m. Village (5 mins walk) with a small supermarket, bars and restaurant. Riding 2 km. Excursions arranged to activity centre (riding, kayaking, rafting) 15 km. away. Buses run to Pamplona and San Sebastian (3 per day, all year). Bicycle hire 15 km. Golf (in France) 20 km.

Open: 10 March - 9 December.

Directions

From Hendaye head south on the N121A. Turn east on N121B. Continue north to the junction with NA2600. Turn right to Erratzu. Proceed through village, bear left at sign 'Francia NA2600' and site is on the right. GPS: 43.18067, -1.45139

Charges guide

Per unit incl. 2 persons and electricity	€ 23.90 - € 34.50

Espinal

Camping Urrobi

Ctra Pamplona - Valcarlos km 42 N135, E-31694 Espinal (Navarra) T: 948 760 200.
E: info@campingurrobi.com **alanrogers.com/ES90480**

This large site is in a beautiful location with mountain views. At the entrance is a lively bar, a reasonably priced restaurant and a well stocked shop. The site is popular with Spanish families and there are many mobile homes, so it can be busy at holiday times and weekends. However, there is plenty of room on the 150 unmarked grass pitches. All have electricity points (6A) and there are plenty of water taps. Water activities of all types are catered for with both a swimming pool and an area of the river sectioned off for safe bathing and paddling. This is a suitable site for families. With many walks and bicycle tracks, there is plenty of scope for discovering this delightful area.

Facilities

Clean sanitary blocks include facilities for disabled visitors (key from reception). Laundry facilities. Motorcaravan service point. Shop, bar and restaurant (all season). Swimming pool. Games room with TV (Spanish). Internet access. Minigolf. Tennis. Playing field. Play area. Off site: Village 1 km. with shops, restaurant and bars. Forest of Irati 15 mins. Bicycle hire 15 km. Golf and riding 40 km. Beach 70 km. One bus per day to and from Pamplona.

Open: 1 April - 31 October.

Directions

From Pamplona take N135 northeast for 42 km. After village of Auritzberri turn right onto NA172. Site is on the left. GPS: 42.97315, -1.351817

Charges guide

Per unit incl. 2 persons and electricity	€ 24.00 - € 25.50
extra person	€ 5.00
child (2-12 yrs)	€ 4.00

Etxarri-Aranatz

Camping Etxarri

Paraje Dambolintxulo s/n, E-31820 Etxarri-Aranatz (Navarra) T: 948 460 537. E: info@campingetxarri.com
alanrogers.com/ES90420

Situated in the Valle de la Burundi, this site is a peaceful oasis with superb views of the 1,300 m. high San-Donator Mountains. The approach to this improving site is via a road lined by huge 300-year-old oak trees, which are a feature of the site. Reception is housed in the main building beside the pool with a restaurant above (access also by lift). There are 108 pitches of average size on flat ground (50 for tourers) with 6A electricity to all and water to 25. The site is well placed for fascinating walks in unspoilt countryside and is close to three recognised nature walks. The site gets very crowded during the Fiestas de San Fermín (bull running) in Pamplona early in July. It is essential to make a reservation if you wish to stay. A visit to Pamplona is recommended. Parking is difficult – try to the west of the bullring, then wander down to Plaza de Toros (renamed Plaza Hemingway), to savour the atmosphere. It is common to use dual naming of places and roads (one in the Spanish language, the other in Basque and it can be confusing) – ask for advice if in doubt.

Facilities

Toilet facilities are good and include a baby bath and facilities for disabled visitors. Laundry. Motorcaravan service point. Gas supplies. Essential supplies kept in high season. Bar (1/4-30/9). Restaurant and takeaway (1/6-15/9). Swimming and paddling pools (15/6-15/9) also open to the public and can get crowded. Bicycle hire. Minigolf. Play area. Entertainment for children in high season. WiFi (charged). Fishing. Tennis and squash courts have been added. No charcoal barbecues. Off site: Buses and trains nearby to Pamplona. Bars, restaurants and shops 2 km. Golf, fishing and riding all 20 km. Pamplona 40 km. Beach 60 km.

Open: 1 April - 3 October.

Directions

Etxarri-Aranatz is 40 km. northwest of Pamplona. From A8 (San Sebastian - Bilbao) take A15 towards Pamplona, then 20 km. northwest of Pamplona, take A10 west towards Vitoria/Gasteix. At km. 19 take NA120 to and through town following site signs. Turn left after crossing railway to site at end of road. GPS: 42.913031, -2.079924

Charges guide

Per unit incl. 2 persons and electricity	€ 23.60 - € 27.60

Mendigorría

Camping Caravanning Errota el Molino

E-31150 Mendigorría (Navarra) T: 948 340 604. E: info@campingelmolino.com

alanrogers.com/ES90430

This is an extensive site set by an attractive weir near the town of Mendigorría, alongside the River Arga. It takes its name from an old disused water mill (molino) close by. The site is split into separate permanent and touring sections. The touring area is a new development with good sized flat pitches with electricity and water for tourers, and a separate area for tents. Many trees have been planted around the site but there is still only minimal shade. The friendly owner Anna Beriain will give you a warm welcome. Reception is housed in the lower part of a long building along with the bar/snack bar which has a cool shaded terrace, a separate restaurant and a supermarket. The upper floor of this building is dormitory accommodation for backpackers. The site has a sophisticated dock and boat launching facility and an ambitious watersport competition programme in season with a safety boat present at all times. There are pedaloes and canoes for hire. The site is very busy during the festival of San Fermín (bull running) in July in Pamplona (28 km). Tours of the local bodegas (groups of ten) to sample the fantastic Navarra wines can be organised by reception.

Facilities

The well equipped toilet block is very clean and well maintained, with cold water to washbasins. Facilities for disabled campers. Washing machine. Large restaurant, pleasant bar. Supermarket. Superb new swimming pools for adults and children (1/6-15/9). Bicycle hire. Riverside bar. Weekly entertainment programme (July/Aug) and many sporting activities. Squash courts. Internet access. River walk. Torches useful. Off site: Bus to Pamplona 500 m. Riding 15 km. Golf 35 km.

Open: All year (excl. 23 December - 4 January).

Directions

Mendigorría is 30 km. southwest of Pamplona. From A15 San Sebastian - Zaragoza motorway, leave Pamplona bypass on A12 towards Logon. Leave at km. 23 on NA601 to hilltop town of Mendigorría. At crossroads turn right towards Larraga and down hill to site. GPS: 42.62423, -1.84259

Charges guide

Per person	€ 4.70 - € 5.00
child	€ 3.95 - € 4.22
pitch incl. car and electricity	€ 12.90 - € 13.80

Discounts outside high season.

In the north eastern part of Spain, Aragón borders France with the Pyrenees lying between them. It is a region rich in folklore, with rural, mountainside villages renowned for their Romanesque architecture, beautiful valleys and awe-inspiring peaks.

ARAGÓN IS MADE UP OF THREE PROVINCES: HUESCA, ZARAGOZA AND TERUEL

THE CAPITAL OF THE REGION IS ZARAGOZA

The region can be separated into three different areas: the central area consisting of the Ebro basin, a vast flat lowland, the northern Pyrenees, and the area made up of the Iberian mountain range in the northwest and southeast of the region. The northernmost province of Huesca is located in the foothills of the Pyrenees mountains, a beautiful area with plenty of picturesque towns and villages to visit. It is also good walking country with numerous trails offering anything from short day-walks in the valleys to long-distance treks in the mountains. Skiing is popular too. Bordering Huesca, the province of Zaragoza is home to the region's capital, also of the same name. Zaragoza is a lively town with plenty of bars and restaurants, plus numerous museums and architectural treasures. Outside the capital you'll find more villages, countryside, and vineyards where the best of the region's wine is produced; the mapped out Ruta del Vino will take you through the area. The third province of Teruel is largely comprised of the Iberian mountain range, with attractive towns, medieval sights and more dramatic scenery to admire.

Places of interest

Aljafería Palace: spectacular Moorish monument.

Basílica de Nuestra Señora del Pilar: Baroque temple from the 17th and 18th centuries.

Benasque: attractive alpine town, gateway to the Pyrenees.

Casa-Museo de Goya: art museum, including engravings by Goya.

Jaca: home of the country's oldest Romanesque cathedral.

Monasterio de San Juan de la Peña: 17th-century Baroque monastery and 10th-century monastery in Romanesque style.

Parque Nacional de Ordesa y Monte Perdido: alpine national park.

Cuisine of the region

Specialities include lamb, locally produced ham and sausages; fruit is also used a lot in desserts.

Chilindrones: sauce of tomato and pepper.

Frutas de Aragón: sugar-candied fruits covered in chocolate.

Pollo al chilindrón: chicken (or lamb) stew with onions, tomatoes and red peppers.

Salmorrejos: cold soup.

Suspiros de amante: dessert with cheese and egg.

Ternasco: roast lamb.

Tortas de alma: dessert made with pumpkin, honey and sugar.

Trenza de Almudévar: dessert with nuts and raisins soaked in liqueur.

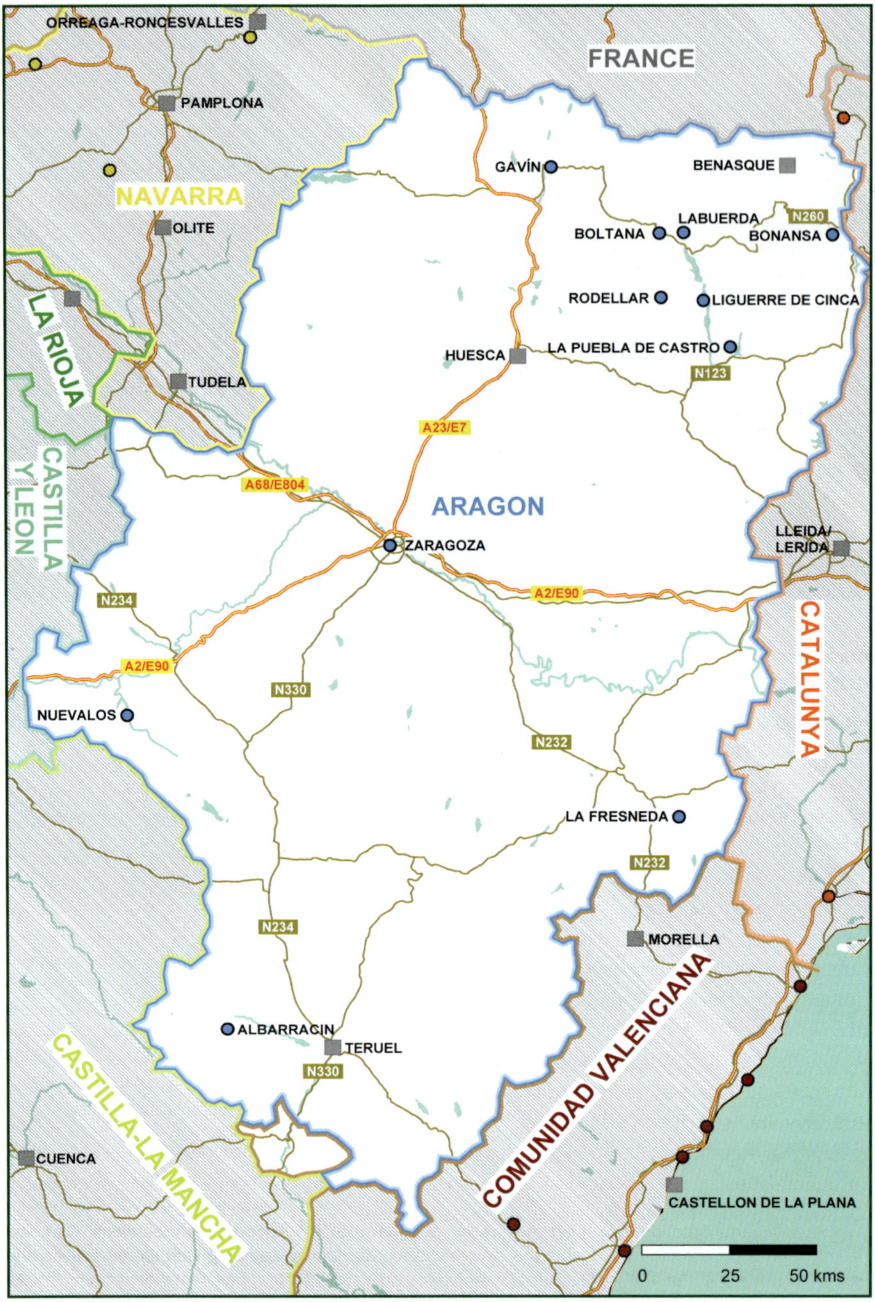
ORREAGA-RONCESVALLES
FRANCE
PAMPLONA
GAVÍN
BENASQUE
NAVARRA
N260
LABUERDA
OLITE
BOLTANA
BONANSA
RODELLAR
LIGUERRE DE CINCA
LA RIOJA
HUESCA
LA PUEBLA DE CASTRO
N123
TUDELA
A23/E7
CASTILLA Y LEON
A68/E804
ARAGON
LLEIDA/ LERIDA
ZARAGOZA
A2/E90
N234
CATALUNYA
A2/E90
N330
NUEVALOS
N232
LA FRESNEDA
N232
N234
MORELLA
COMUNIDAD VALENCIANA
ALBARRACIN
TERUEL
N330
CASTILLA-LA MANCHA
CUENCA
CASTELLON DE LA PLANA
0
25
50 kms

Albarracin

Camping Ciudad de Albarracin

Junto al Polideportivo, Camino de gea, E-44100 Albarracin (Teruel) T: 978 710 197

alanrogers.com/ES90950

Albarracin, in southern Aragon, is set in the Reserva Nacional de los Montes Universales and is a popular and fascinating town with a Moorish castle. The old city walls towering above date from its days when it attempted to become a separate country within Spain. This neat and clean family site is set on three levels on a hillside behind the town, with a walk of 1 km. to the centre. It is very modern and has high quality facilities including a superb building for barbecuing (all materials provided). There are 140 pitches (70 for tourers), all with electricity and separated by trees. Some require cars to be parked separately.

Facilities

The two spotless, modern sanitary buildings provide British style WCs, quite large showers and hot water throughout. Baby bath. Washing machines. Bar/restaurant (all season). Essentials from bar. Special room for barbecues with fire and wood provided. Play area. Torches required in some areas. Off site: Municipal swimming pool 100 m. (high season). Town shops, bars and restaurants 500 m. Fishing 1 km.

Open: 1 March - 2 November.

Directions

From Teruel north on the N330 for about 8 km. then west onto A1512 for 30 km. From the A23 use exit 124 then the A1512, from the N235 take exit for Albarracin and the A1512. Site is well signed in the town. GPS: 40.41655, -1.43332

Charges guide

Per unit incl. 2 persons and electricity	€ 18.05 - € 18.75
extra person	€ 3.80

Boltaña

Camping Boltaña

Ctra N260 km 442, E-22340 Boltaña (Huesca) T: 974 502 347. E: info@campingboltana.com

alanrogers.com/ES90620

Nestled in the Rio Ara valley, surrounded by the Pyrenees mountains and below a tiny but enchanting, historic, hill top village, is the very pretty, thoughtfully planned Camping Boltaña. Generously sized, 190 grassy pitches (all with 10A electricity) have good shade from a variety of trees and a stream meanders through the campsite. The landscaping includes ten charming rocky water gardens and a covered pergola doubles as an eating and play area. A stone building houses the site's reception, social room and supermarket. Angel Moreno, the owner of the site, is a charming host and has tried to think of everything to make his guests comfortable.

Facilities

Two modern sanitary blocks include facilities for disabled visitors and laundry facilities. Supermarket. Bar, restaurant and takeaway (1/7-31/8). Swimming pools (15/6-15/9). Playground. Entertainment for children (high season). Pétanque. Guided tours, plus hiking, canyoning, rafting, climbing, mountain biking and caving. Bicycle hire. WiFi. No charcoal barbecues. Torches useful in some parts. Off site: Local bus service. Fishing 1 km.

Open: 15 January - 15 December.

Directions

South of the Park Nacional de Ordesa, site is about 50 km. from Jaca near Ainsa. From Ainsa travel northwest on N260 toward Boltaña (near 443 km. marker) and 1 km. from Boltaña turn south toward Margudgued. Site is well signed and is 1 km. along this road. GPS: 42.43018, 0.07882

Charges guide

Per unit incl. 2 persons and electricity	€ 35.40

Camping Cheques accepted.

Bonansa

Camping Baliera

Ctra N260 km 355,5, E-22486 Bonansa (Huesca) T: 974 554 016. E: info@baliera.com

alanrogers.com/ES90580

With its wonderful location in a quiet river valley with views of the surrounding mountains, Camping Baliera is an excellent site for enjoying this beautiful area. Combining camping with timber chalets and apartments, the site has 133 well kept grass touring pitches (80-120 sq.m) all with electricity (5/7/10A). The pitches are mostly located close to the attractive, stone built reception building which also houses a comfortable bar and shop. The approach to this site is by narrow and winding mountain roads and it is 5 km. from the nearest village. However, for all but the largest units, the trip is well worth making.

Facilities

Two toilet blocks, one part of the apartment block near the entrance, the other in the reception building (closed in low season). Heated, they are good with well equipped showers, vanity style washbasins. Laundry room and drying room. Motorcaravan services. Shop (1/7-31/8). Bar (automatic). Takeaway (1/7-31/8). Swimming pool (15/7-15/9). Fitness equipment. Play area. Entertainment (high season). Communal barbecue. WiFi. Off site: National parks and outdoor activities. Nearest village 5 km.

Open: All year excl. November.

Directions

On N230, 34 km. south of Vielha, turn on N260 for 2-3 km, then onto A1605 signed Graus for 100 m. to site on left. Reception is 200 m. through the site. Approach roads are narrow and winding, but navigable. GPS: 42.43958, 0.69918

Charges guide

Per unit incl. 2 persons and electricity	€ 29.00 - € 30.00

Camping Cheques accepted.

Gavín

Camping Gavín

Ctra N260 km 503, E-22639 Gavín (Huesca) T: 974 485 090. E: info@campinggavin.com

alanrogers.com/ES90640

Camping Gavín is set on a terraced, wooded hillside and you will find a friendly welcome. The site offers 150 pitches of 90 sq.m. in size and with electricity available to all (10A). In some areas the terracing means that some pitches are quite small. The main site buildings have been constructed using natural stone. There are also 13 bungalows and 11 superb, balconied apartments. At about 900 m. the site is surrounded by towering peaks at the portal of the Tena Valley. One can enjoy the natural beauty of the Pyrenees and venture near or far along the great Pyrenean footpaths.

Facilities

Excellent shower and toilet facilities in three main buildings with subtle, tasteful décor include facilities for babies and disabled visitors. Laundry facilities. Bar and snacks. Well stocked supermarket. Swimming pools (15/6-15/9) and paddling pools (all year). Tennis. Playground. Bicycle hire. Barbecues are not permitted at some times of the year. Off site: Windsurfing, rafting, fishing, walking and climbing in the vicinity. Riding 6 km. Golf 15 km. Day excursions to the Monastery of San Juan de la Peña.

Open: All year.

Directions

Site is off the N260, 2 km. from Biescas at km. 503. GPS: 42.61940, -0.30408

Charges guide

Per unit incl. 2 persons and electricity	€ 29.92 - € 37.37
extra person	€ 4.97 - € 6.80

Camping Cheques accepted.

La Fresneda

Camping La Fresneda

Partida Vall del Pi, E-44596 La Fresneda (Teruel) T: 978 854 085. E: info@campinglafresneda.com

alanrogers.com/ES91100

La Fresneda is a great little campsite, situated on three terraces at the foot of a wooded escarpment and overlooking the huge valley of the National Reserve of Los Puertos de Beceite. Everything is in line with the natural beauty of the area and the very clean, very well equipped, toilet block is partly underground. There are 25 pitches with grass and gravel surfaces, all used for touring and with 6A electricity. The site is quite new and the enthusiastic Dutch owners, Jet Knijn and her partner, Joost Leeuwenberg, built it from scratch, recently adding a shady garden atrium with a terrace and plunge pool for guests to relax in and enjoy the views.

Facilities

Toilet block with hot water throughout. Washing machine. Bar with terrace where meals are served a few times a week. Fresh bread daily. Garden atrium with terrace and plunge pool. Bicycle hire. Information on walking and cycling routes. Pets are not accepted. WiFi throughout (free). Off site: Baker, grocer and butcher in the village. Supermarkets at Alcañiz 30 minutes drive. Fishing 10 km.

Open: 1 April - 1 October.

Directions

From the N232 (Alcañiz - Vinaros/Castellón) turn off just east of Valdealgorfa (at Restaurant Las Ventas) onto A231 to Valjunquera/Valderrobres, then La Fresneda. GPS: 40.90695, 0.061667

Charges guide

Per unit incl. 2 persons and electricity	€ 22.00
extra person	€ 5.00
child (0-1 yrs)	free

La Puebla de Castro

Camping Barasona

Ctra N123a km 25, E-22435 La Puebla de Castro (Huesca) T: 974 545 148. E: info@lagobarasona.com

alanrogers.com/ES91250

This site, alongside its associated ten room hotel, is beautifully positioned on terraces across a road from the shores of the Lago de Barasona (a large reservoir), with views of hills and the distant Pyrenees. The very friendly, English-speaking owner is keen to please and has applied very high standards throughout the site. The grassy, fairly level pitches are generally around 100 sq.m. with 35 high quality pitches of 110 sq.m. for larger units. All have electricity (6/10A), many are well shaded and some have great views of the lake and/or hills. Water skiing and other watersports are available in July and August.

Facilities

Two toilet blocks in modern buildings have high standards and hot water throughout including cabins (3 for women, 1 for men). Bar/snack bar and two excellent restaurants (all season). Shop (1/4-30/9). Swimming pools (1/6-30/9). Tennis. Mountain bike hire. Canoe, windsurfing, motor boat and pedalo hire. Miniclub (high season). Lake swimming, fishing, canoeing, etc. Walking (maps provided). Money exchange. Minidisco. WiFi. Wellness centre with sauna, jacuzzi and gym. Off site: Riding 4 km.

Open: All year.

Directions

Site is on the west bank of the lake, close to km. 25 on the N123A, 6 km. south of Graus (about 80 km. north of Lleida/Lerida). Travelling from the south, the site is on the left from a newly-built roundabout and slip road. GPS: 42.14163, 0.31525

Charges guide

Per unit incl. 2 persons and electricity	€ 23.00 - € 35.00
extra person	€ 4.50 - € 6.50

Camping Cheques accepted.

Labuerda

Camping Peña Montañesa

Ctra Ainsa - Francia km 2, E-22360 Labuerda (Huesca) T: 974 500 032. E: info@penamontanesa.com

alanrogers.com/ES90600

A large site situated quite high up in the Pyrenees near the Ordesa National Park, Peña Montañesa is easily accessible from Ainsa or from France via the Bielsa Tunnel (steep sections on the French side). The site is essentially divided into three sections opening progressively throughout the season and all have shade. The 288 pitches on fairly level grass are of about 75 sq.m. and 10A electricity is available on virtually all. Grouped near the entrance are the facilities that make the site so attractive, including a fair sized outdoor pool and a glass-covered indoor pool with jacuzzi and sauna. Here too is an attractive bar/restaurant with an open fire and a terrace, a supermarket and takeaway are opposite. There is an entertainment programme for children (21/6-15/9 and Easter weekend) and twice weekly for adults in July and August. This is quite a large site which has grown very quickly and as such, it may at times be a little hard pressed, although it is very well run. The site is ideally situated for exploring the beautiful Pyrenees. The complete town of Ainsa is listed as a national monument of Spain and should be explored while you are here, along with the national park.

Facilities

A newer toilet block, heated when necessary, has free hot showers but cold water to open plan washbasins. Facilities for disabled visitors. Small baby room. An older block has similar provision. Washing machine and dryer. Bar, restaurant, takeaway and supermarket (all 1/1-31/12). Outdoor swimming pool (1/4-31/10). Indoor pool (all year). Playground. Boules. Bicycle hire. Riding. Rafting. Only gas barbecues are permitted. Torches required in some areas. Off site: Fishing 100 m. Skiing in season. Canoeing nearby.

Open: All year.

Directions

Site is 2 km. from Ainsa, on the road from Ainsa to France. GPS: 42.4352, 0.13618

Charges guide

Per unit incl. 2 persons and electricity	€ 24.60 - € 33.30

Ligüerre de Cinca

Camping Ligüerre de Cinca

Ctra A138 km 28 de Barbastro a Ainsa, E-22393 Ligüerre de Cinca (Huesca) T: 974 500 800.
E: info@liguerredecinca.com **alanrogers.com/ES90610**

Ligüerre de Cinca, a medieval village abandoned when the El Grado reservoir was constructed, is now being regenerated for tourism. It is situated near the Ordesa National Park in a beautiful region of the Pyrenees mountains and has the advantage of being open all year. Attractive traditional style buildings house the reception, bar, restaurant and takeaway. The swimming and paddling pools are surrounded by grass sunbathing areas with wonderful mountain views. There are 150 small, terraced, level pitches marked out and shaded by tall trees. These include 110 for touring units, all with 10A electricity. Access is easy for large outfits.

Facilities

Adequate central toilet block, heated in winter, with smaller one on periphery. No facilities for disabled campers. Shop (July/Aug). Bar, restaurant, takeaway (all year). Swimming and paddling pools (July/Aug). Miniclub (July/Aug). Multisports court. Tennis. Boules. Playground. Fishing and watersports, boat storage. Organised watersports including courses. Internet access. ATM. Barbecues are not allowed. Off site: Bus to Huesca. Rafting, canyoning, climbing, biking, hiking. Ancient villages and wonderful area for lovers of mountains. Riding 18 km.

Open: All year.

Directions

Site is between El Grado and Ainsa on the N138. From the Tunnel de Bielsa at the French/Spanish border, go south on N138, through Ainsa. Site is on left in about 20 km. GPS: 42.28111, 0.19638

Charges guide

Per person	€ 4.85
child (2-10 yrs)	€ 4.25
pitch	€ 5.75 - € 7.05

Low season and long stay discounts.

Nuevalos

Camping Lago Park

Ctra Alhama de Aragon - Nuevalos, E-50210 Nuevalos (Zaragoza) T: 976 849 038

alanrogers.com/ES91050

Lago Park is situated in an attractive area which receives many visitors for the Monasterio de Piedra just 3 km. distant and it enjoys pleasant views of the surrounding mountains. This site is suitable for transit stops or if you wish to visit the monasterio as it is the only one hereabouts and appears to make the most of that fact. It is not recommended for extended stays. Set on a steep hillside, the 280 pitches (260 for tourers) are on terraces. Only the lower rows are suitable for large caravans. These pitches are numbered and marked by trees, and most have electricity (10A).

Facilities

The single very clean sanitary block has British style WCs. Washbasins with hot water and controllable hot showers (no dividers). Restaurant/bar (June-Sept). Shop (all season). Swimming pool (late June-Sept). Play area. Gas supplies. Torches needed in some areas. Off site: Fishing 300 m. Riding 2 km.

Open: 1 April - 30 September.

Directions

From Zaragoza (120 km) take fast A2/N11/E90 road and turn onto C202 road beyond Calatayud to Nuévalos (25 km). From Madrid, exit A2 at Alhama de Aragón (13 km). Follow signs for Monasterio de Piedra from all directions. GPS: 41.21800, -1.792

Charges guide

Per unit incl. 2 persons and electricity	€ 19.00

Rodellar

Camping El Puente

Ctra NZ40, E-22144 Rodellar (Huesca) T: 974 318 312. E: info@campingelpuente.com

alanrogers.com/ES90630

Situated in the world famous Parc de la Sierra y los Canyons de Guara in Aragon, this specialised site is a must for those who wish to experience canyoning and climbing. There are 78 rather dusty pitches which are shaded by mature trees, just 12 with 6A electricity. The site is set on a hillside although any views are restricted by trees. A pleasant restaurant serves excellent food at no nonsense prices. A professional team of guides is here to hire, as is all the necessary equipment for you to experience the thrills of around 100 superb canyons in the area.

Facilities

One sanitary block with mature but clean facilities. Hot showers. Cold water at sinks, hot for dishwashing. Motorcaravan service point. Washing machines. Well stocked shop. Restaurant. Snack bar. Barbecue areas. River swimming. Fishing. Canyon guides and canyoning and climbing equipment for hire. Tourist information. Off site: Village of Rodella with all facilities 1 km. Adventure sports (canyoning, swimming, hiking, climbing, caving, cycling, riding and river crossing by horse), 'Route Ferrata' climbing. Historical architecture and local festivals. Raptors, bearded vultures and other animals abound.

Open: Easter - 1 November.

Directions

From the N240 (Lleida - Huesca), 15 km. west of Barbastro take the A1229 towards Abiego, then the A1227 to Abiego and Bierge. Finally take the HU341 to Las Aluminas and continue to Rodellar. Site is well signed 1 km. before the village. Do not try to take caravans and motorcaravans into the village as the roads are too narrow, park outside and walk. GPS: 42.274104, -0.073222

Charges guide

Per unit incl. 2 persons	€ 19.20 - € 19.60
extra person	€ 4.80 - € 5.00
child (2-10 yrs)	€ 4.40 - € 4.60

Zaragoza

Camping Ciudad de Zaragoza

Ctra San Juan Bautista de la Salle s/n, E-50012 Zaragoza (Zaragoza) T: 876 241 495.

E: info@campingzaragoza.com **alanrogers.com/ES91040**

Zaragoza is a popular en route stop between the ports of Santander and Bilbao and the beaches of the Costa Brava. The city, however, has much more to offer as the former capital of Aragon and now Spain's fifth largest city. Primarily for short stay, transit visitors, this all year site gives impressions of concrete, metal and plastic, although it will soften in time. There are 103 touring pitches with electricity and water, which are mostly of gravel and without shade as yet. A modern bar/restaurant serves good food at reasonable prices, there are good facilities for children and the very pleasant swimming and paddling pools are welcome as it gets very hot here.

Facilities

Modern toilet blocks include good facilities for disabled visitors. Motorcaravan services. Bar and restaurant (all year). Swimming and paddling pools (30/5-30/9). Tennis. Pétanque. Multisports pitch. Play areas. Bungalows for rent. Hostel. Club and TV room. Internet access and free WiFi. Off site: Zaragoza city centre 4 km. (regular bus service 100 m. from gate). Golf 5 km. Tours available.

Open: All year.

Directions

Follow the Autovia del Nordeste (Zaragoza ring road) southwest to leave at junction with N11a. Follow signs to the city centre (Autovia de Madrid) and the site is signed to the right. GPS: 41.63766, -0.94273

Charges 2012

Per unit incl. 2 persons and electricity	€ 18.37 - € 25.90

Menorca, steeped in history and blanketed by mystery, is an enchanting island of roughly 270 square miles in area. The C721 highway provides the backbone to the island, connecting modest market towns to Mahon (the main town) in the east and Ciutadella in the west.

Mahon's classic Georgian-style buildings, complete with sash windows, will endear them to the British traveller. Its impressive harbour was captured by the British in 1708 during the Spanish War of Succession. In complete contrast, Ciutadella has a more Gothic feel to it. A labyrinth of tiny streets entwine the 'little city', most of which can only be accessed on foot. Monte Toro stands proudly at the centre of the island surveying all. To the south a greener lush terrain exists with long, luxurious beaches, while to the north a giant rockery erupts riddled with caves and prehistoric finds.

Alaior

Camping Son Bou

Ctra de San Jaime km 3,5, Apdo 85, Alaior, E-07730 Menorca (Menorca) T: 971 372 727.
E: info@campingsonbou.com **alanrogers.com/ES80000**

Camping Son Bou was opened in 1996 and has been purpose built in local style providing a large, irregular shaped pool with marvellous views across to Monte Toro and overlooked by a pine shaded, terraced bar and restaurant. The 313 large pitches, 143 for tourers with 10A electricity, are arranged in circles radiating out from the main facilities and clearly edged with stones. Natural pine tree shade covers most but the outer ring. Drinking water and refuse points are well placed. The ground is hard and devoid of grass except where sprinklers operate. The beautiful island of Menorca cries out to be explored. It is peaceful and tranquil, with its characteristic dry stone walls, its low white buildings with terracotta tiled roofs, its beautiful coastline, ancient monuments and pretty villages with their cycle of fiestas of religious origin with the noble horse as the central element. The site gets very busy with Spanish people from the mainland in high season. Earlier in the year it is quieter and greener. If you do not fancy the ferry crossings the site has some neat wooden chalets and ready erected tents. The site is happy to arrange the overnight ferry crossing from Barcelona or Valencia (discounts available).

Facilities

Well designed toilet block of good quality, open plan in places. Some washbasins in cabins (cold water). Bathrooms and shower. Baby room. Facilities for disabled visitors. Service wash. Shop, bar, restaurant, takeaway and outdoor pool (all open all season). Tennis. Play area. Bicycle hire. Open-air cinema. Occasional barbecue with guitarist. Comprehensive activity programme. English spoken. Dogs are not accepted. Off site: Village 3 km. with sandy beach. Riding 4 km.

Open: 16 April - 16 October.

Directions

From Mahon (Mao) follow main road to Ciutadella. Go past Alaior (bypassed) and watch for restaurant on left and sign for 3.5 km. Torre Soli Nou and campsite sign. GPS: 39.92199, 4.09114

Charges guide

Per unit incl. 2 persons and electricity	€ 29.10 - € 34.32
extra person	€ 6.56 - € 7.94
child (3-13 yrs)	€ 4.87 - € 5.34

Portugal is a relatively small country occupying the southwest corner of the Iberian peninsula, bordered by Spain in the north and east, with the Atlantic coast in the south and west. In spite of its size, the country offers a tremendous variety in both its way of life and traditions.

Tourist Office

Portuguese National Tourist Office
11 Belgrave Square
London SW1X 8PP

Tel: 0845 355 1212
E-mail: tourism.london@icep.pt
Fax: 020 7201 6633
Internet: www.visitportugal.com

Most visitors looking for a beach type holiday head for the busy Algarve, with its long stretches of sheltered sandy beaches, and warm, clear Atlantic waters, great for bathing and watersports. With its monuments and fertile rolling hills, central Portugal adjoins the beautiful Tagus river that winds its way through the capital city of Lisbon, on its way to the Atlantic Ocean.

Lisbon city itself has deep rooted, cultural traditions, coming alive at night with buzzing cafés, restaurants and discos. Moving south east of Lisbon the land becomes rather impoverished, consisting of stretches of vast undulating plains, dominated by cork plantations. Most people head for the walled town of Evora, an area steeped in two thousand years of history. The Portuguese consider the Minho area in the north to be the most beautiful part of their country, with its wooded mountain and wild coastline, a rural and conservative region with picturesque towns.

Population

10.7 million

Capital

Lisbon

Climate

The country enjoys a maritime climate with hot summers and mild winters with comparatively low rainfall in the south, heavy rain in the north.

Language

Portuguese, but English is widely spoken in cities, towns and larger resorts. French can be useful.

Telephone

The country code is 00 351.

Currency

The Euro (€)

Banks

Mon-Fri 08.30-11.45 and 13.00-14.45. Some large city banks offer a currency exchange 18.30-23.00.

Shops

Mon-Fri 09.00-13.00 and 15.00-19.00. Sat 09.00-13.00.

Public Holidays

New Year; Carnival (Shrove Tues); Good Fri; Liberty Day 25 Apr; Labour Day; Corpus Christi; National Day 10 June; Saints Days; Assumption 15 Aug; Republic Day 5 Oct; All Saints 1 Nov; Immaculate Conception 8 Dec; Christmas 24-26 Dec.

The Algarve, Portugal's southernmost province, is a true sunseekers' paradise, offering all-year-round sunshine and over 150 miles of beautiful sandy beaches.

THE ALGARVE HAS ONE DISTRICT: FARO

The coast of the Algarve offers mile after mile of golden beaches and small sandy coves with interesting rock formations, interspersed with busy fishing ports. The capital, Faro, boasts excellent beaches, while the thriving fishing port and market centre of Lagos is one of the most popular destinations in the Algarve. Although the earthquake of 1755 caused great damage to Lagos, the streets and squares of the town have retained much of their charm. Within walking distance are some superb beaches, including Praia de Dona Ana, which is considered to be the most picturesque of all, and the smaller coves of Praia do Pinhão and Praia Camilo. Further inland and to the north, the hills mark the edge of a greener and more fertile region, brilliantly coloured by fig trees, orange groves and almond trees that come into blossom in the winter. Here you will also find a series of typical villages that have successfully preserved their ancestral traditions. The walled town of Silves has a Moorish fortress, 13th-century cathedral and archaeology museum. Nearby, the narrow streets of the old spa town of Monchique wind up a steep hillside, revealing magnificent views.

Places of interest

Albufeira: popular resort, daily market, good nightlife.

Cape São Vicente: south westernmost point of Europe.

Faro: monuments, churches, museums, Gothic cathedral, good shopping centre.

Sagres: 17th-century fortress.

Tavira: picturesque town, 17th- and 18th-century architecture.

Vilamoura: good sporting facilities including golf courses.

Cuisine of the region

Fresh fish and seafood are popular; the local speciality is *Ameijoas na Cataplana* (clams steamed in a copper pan). One of the most traditional dishes is *caldeiradas* (stew made with all kinds of different fish) and *sardinha assada* (grilled sardines). Given the abundance of trees in the region, figs and almonds are used a lot in desserts including *bolinhos de amêndoa* (small cakes made with almond paste), which are moulded into the shape of fruits and vegetables in all kinds of different sizes.

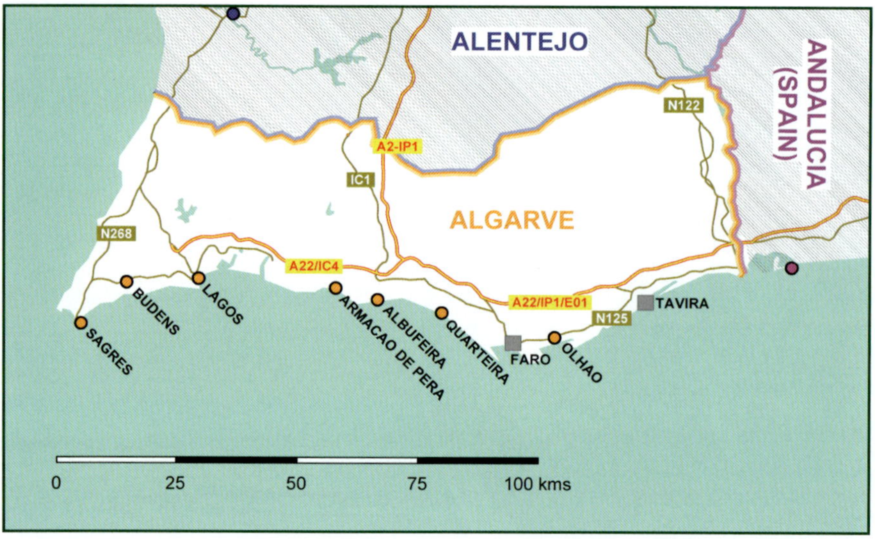

Albufeira

Parque de Campismo Albufeira

N395 Ferreiras - Albufeira, P-8200-555 Albufeira (Faro) T: 289 587 629. E: campingalbufeira@mail.telepac.pt

alanrogers.com/PO8210

The spacious entrance to this site will accommodate the largest of units (watch for severe speed bumps at the barrier). One of the better sites on the Algarve, it has pitches on fairly flat ground with some terracing, trees and shrubs giving reasonable shade in most parts. There are some marked and numbered pitches of 50-80 sq.m. Winter stays are encouraged with many facilities remaining open including a pool. An attractively designed complex of traditional Portuguese style buildings on the hill, with an unusually shaped pool and two more for children, forms the central area of the site. It has large terraces for sunbathing with pleasant views and is surrounded by a variety of flowers, shrubs and well watered lawns, complete with a fountain. The à la carte restaurant, impressive with its international cuisine, and the very pleasant self-service one; both have views across the three pools. A pizzeria, bars and a soundproofed disco are great for younger campers.

Facilities

Very clean toilet blocks include hot showers. Launderette. Very large supermarket. Tabac (English papers). Waiter- and self-service restaurants. Pizzeria. Bars. Satellite TV. Soundproofed disco. Swimming pools. Tennis. Playground. Internet access. First aid post with doctor nearby. Car wash. ATM. Car hire. Off site: Site bus service from gate to Albufeira every 45 minutes (2 km). Theme parks nearby. Beaches.

Open: All year.

Directions

From N125 coast road or N264 (from Lisbon) at new junctions follow N395 to Albufeira. Site is about 2 km. on the left. GPS: 37.10639, -8.25361

Charges guide

Per unit incl. 2 persons	€ 23.50 - € 24.65
extra person	€ 5.50
child (4-10 yrs)	€ 2.70
electricity	€ 3.00

Armação de Pera

Parque de Campismo de Armação de Pera

P-8365 Armação de Pera (Faro) T: 282 312 260. E: camping_arm_pera@hotmail.com

alanrogers.com/PO8410

A pleasant site with a wide attractive entrance and a large external parking area, the 1,200 pitches at ths site are in zones on level grassy sand. They are marked by trees that provide some shade, and are easily accessed from tarmac and gravel roads. Electricity is available for most pitches. The facilities are good and the self-service restaurant, bar and well stocked supermarket should cater for most needs. You can relax around the swimming pools. The disco near the entrance and café complex is soundproofed which should ensure a peaceful night for non-revellers. The site is within easy reach of Albufeira and Portimão.

Facilities

Three modern sanitary blocks provide British and Turkish style WCs and showers with hot water on payment. Facilities for disabled campers. A reader reports that maintenance can be variable. Laundry. Supermarket. Self-service restaurant. Three bars (one all year). Swimming and paddling pools (May-Sept; daily charge; no lifeguard). Games and TV rooms. Tennis. Well maintained play area. ATM. Internet access. Off site: Bus to town from gate. Fishing, bicycle hire and watersports nearby.

Open: All year.

Directions

Site is west of Albufeira. Turn off N125/IC4 road in Alcantarilha, taking EN269-1 towards coast. Site is second 'campismo' left on roundabout just before Armação de Pêra. N.B: there are other sites with similar names! GPS: 37.10947, -8.35329

Charges guide

Per unit incl. 2 persons and electricity	€ 10.50 - € 24.50

Min. stay 3 nights 1/6-31/8.

Lagos

Yelloh! Village Turiscampo

N125, Espiche, Luz, P-8600 Lagos (Faro) T: 282 789 265. E: info@turiscampo.com

alanrogers.com/PO8202

This good quality site has been thoughtfully refurbished and updated since it was purchased by the friendly Coll family, who are known to us from their previous Spanish site. The site provides 206 pitches for touring units, mainly in rows of terraces, all with electricity (6/10A) and some with shade. Twelve pitches have water and waste water. They vary in size (70-120 sq.m). The upper areas of the site are mainly used for bungalow accommodation (and are generally separate from the touring areas). A new, elevated Californian style pool plus a children's pool have been constructed. The supporting structure is a clever water cascade and surround, with a large sun lounger area on astroturf. One side of the pool area is open to the road. The restaurant/bar has been tastefully refurbished and Roberto and his staff, who speak excellent English, provide good fare at very reasonable prices. The restaurant has two patios, one used for live entertainment and discos in season, the other for dining out. The sea is 2 km. away and the city of Lagos 4 km. with all the attractions of the Algarve within easy reach.

Facilities

Two toilet blocks have been refurbished, the other two are new and contain modern facilities for disabled campers. Hot water throughout. Facilities for children. Washing machines. Shop. Gas supplies. Restaurant/bar. Swimming pool (Mar-Oct). Bicycle hire. Entertainment in high season on the bar terrace. Two children's playgrounds. Adult art workshops. Aqua gymnastics. Miniclub (5-12 yrs) in season. Boules. Archery. Cable TV. Internet. WiFi (charged). Bungalows to rent. Off site: Beach 2 km.

Open: All year.

Directions

Take exit 1 from the N125 Lagos - Vila do Bispo. The impressive entrance is about 3 km. on the right. GPS: 37.10111, -8.73278

Charges guide

Per unit incl. 2 persons and electricity	€ 16.20 - € 28.83
extra person	€ 3.28 - € 6.56
child (3-10 yrs)	€ 1.77 - € 3.28

Camping Cheques accepted.

Budens

Parque de Campismo Quinta dos Carriços

Praia da Salema, Vila do Bispo, P-8650-196 Budens (Faro) T: 282 695 201. E: quintacarrico@oninet.pt

alanrogers.com/PO8440

This is an attractive and peaceful, valley site with a separate naturist area. A traditional tiled Portuguese style entrance leads you down a steep incline into this excellent and well maintained site which has a village atmosphere. With continuing improvements, the site has been developed over the years by the Dutch owner. It is spread over two valleys (which are real sun traps), with the 300 partially terraced pitches marked and divided by trees and shrubs (oleanders and roses). A small stream (dry when seen) meanders through the site. The most remote part, 250 m. from the main site, is dedicated to naturists.

Facilities

Four modern, spacious sanitary blocks, well tiled with quality fittings, are spotlessly clean. Washbasins with cold water, hot showers on payment. Washing machine. Excellent facility for disabled campers. Gas supplies. Well stocked shop. Restaurant (1/3-15/10). Bar (daily in season, once weekly 1/3-15/10). TV (cable). WiFi. Games room. Bicycle, scooter, moped and motorcycle hire. Off site: Fishing, golf and beach 1 km. Riding 8 km. Bus service to town (not beach) from site.

Open: All year.

Directions

Turn off RN125 (Lagos - Sagres) road at junction to Figuere and Salema (17 km. from Lagos); site is signed. GPS: 37.075427, -8.831338

Charges guide

Per person	€ 5.65
child	€ 2.60
pitch and electricity	€ 12.15 - € 15.75
dog	€ 2.50

Lagos

Orbitur Camping Valverde

Estrada da Praia da Luz, Valverde, P-8600-148 Lagos (Faro) T: 282 789 211. E: infovalverde@orbitur.pt

alanrogers.com/PO8200

A little over a kilometre from the village of Praia da Luz and its beach and about 7 km. from Lagos, this large, well run site is certainly worth considering for your stay in the Algarve. It has 650 numbered pitches, of varying sizes, which are enclosed by hedges. All are on flat ground or broad terraces with good shade in most parts from established trees and shrubs. The site has a swimming pool with a long curling slide and a paddling pool (under tens free, adults charged). This is an excellent site with well maintained facilities and good security. It attracts a good number of long-term winter visitors and is one of the better Orbitur sites.

Facilities

Six large, clean, toilet blocks have some washbasins and sinks with cold water only, and hot showers. Units for disabled campers. Laundry. Motorcaravan services. Supermarket, shops, restaurant and bar complex with both self-service and waiter service in season (closed November). Takeaway. Coffee shop. Swimming pool (Apr-Sept) with slide and paddling pool (June-Sept). Playground. Tennis. Satellite TV in bar. Disco. Pub. WiFi throughout (free). Excursions. Off site: Bus service from site gate. Beach and fishing 1.5 km. Bicycle hire 3 km. Golf 10 km.

Open: All year.

Directions

From Lagos on N125 road, after 7 km. turn south to Praia da Luz. At the town follow signs for campismo. The beach road is narrow and cobbled and is very challenging in a large unit. GPS: 37.09973, -8.71744

Charges guide

Per person	€ 5.80
child (5-10 yrs)	€ 3.00
pitch	€ 11.50 - € 12.50
electricity	€ 2.90 - € 3.50

Off season discounts (up to 70%).

Olhão

Camping Olhão

Pinheiros de Marim, P-8700 Olhão (Faro) T: 289 700 300. E: parque.campismo@sbsi.pt

alanrogers.com/PO8230

This site, with around 800 pitches, is open all year. It has many mature trees providing good shade. The pitches are marked, numbered and in rows divided by shrubs, although levelling will be necessary and the trees make access tricky on some. There is electricity for 102 pitches (6A) and a separate area for tents. Permanent and long stay units take 20% of the pitches, the touring pitches filling up quickly in July and August, so arrive early. There is some noise nuisance from an adjacent railway. The site has a relaxed, casual atmosphere. Amenities include very pleasant swimming pools and tennis courts, a reasonable restaurant/bar and a café/bar with TV and games room. All are very popular with the local Portuguese who pay to use the facilities. The large, sandy beaches in this area are on offshore islands reached by ferry and are, as a result, relatively quiet; some are reserved for naturists. This site can get very busy in peak periods and maintenance can be variable. There was a large, low season British contingent when we visited, enjoying the low prices.

Facilities

Eleven sanitary blocks are adequate, clean when seen, and are specifically sited to be a maximum of 50 m. from any pitch. One block has facilities for disabled visitors. Laundry. Excellent supermarket. Kiosk. Restaurant/bar. Café and general room with cable TV. Playgrounds. Swimming pools (all year) and tennis courts (fees for both). Bicycle hire. Internet at reception. Off site: Bus service to the nearest ferry at Olhão 50 m. from site. Riding 1 km. Indoor pool and fishing 2 km.

Open: All year.

Directions

Just over 1 km. east of Olhão, on EN125, take turn to Pinheiros de Marim. Site is back off the road on the left. Look for very large, white, triangular entry arch as the site name is different on the outside wall. GPS: 37.03528, -7.8225

Charges guide

Per person	€ 2.30 - € 4.70
child (5-12 yrs)	€ 1.30 - € 2.30
pitch	€ 3.45 - € 12.80
electricity	€ 1.80

Less for longer winter stays.

Quarteira

Orbitur Camping Quarteira

Estrada da Fonte Santa, avenida Sá Cameiro, P-8125-618 Quarteira (Faro) T: 289 302 826.
E: infoquarteira@orbitur.pt **alanrogers.com/PO8220**

This is a large, busy, attractive site on undulating ground with some terracing, taking 795 units. On the outskirts of the popular Algarve resort of Quarteira, it is 600 m. from a sandy beach which stretches for a kilometre to the town centre. Many of the unmarked pitches have shade from tall trees and there are a few small individual pitches of 50 sq.m. with electricity and water. There are 659 electrical connections. Like others along this coast, the site encourages long winter stays. There is a large restaurant and supermarket which have a separate entrance for local trade. The swimming pools (free for campers) are excellent, featuring pools for adults (with a large flume) and children (with fountains).

Facilities

Five toilet blocks provide British and Turkish style toilets, washbasins with cold water, hot showers plus facilities for disabled visitors. Washing machines. Motorcaravan services. Gas supplies. Supermarket. Self-service restaurant (closed Nov). Separate takeaway (from late May). Swimming pools (Apr-Sept). General room with bar and satellite TV. WiFi. Tennis. Open-air disco (high season). Off site: Bus from gate to Faro. Fishing and bicycle hire (summer) 1 km. Golf 4 km.

Open: All year.

Directions

Turn off N125 for village of Almancil. In the village take road south to Quarteira. Site is on the left 1 km. after large, official town welcome sign.
GPS: 37.06666, -8.08333

Charges guide

Per person	€ 5.90
child (5-10 yrs)	€ 3.00
pitch	€ 12.70 - € 13.70
electricity	€ 2.90 - € 3.50

Off season discounts (up to 70%).

Sagres

Orbitur Camping Sagres

Cerro das Moitas, P-8650-998 Sagres (Faro) T: 282 624 371. E: infosagres@orbitur.pt
alanrogers.com/PO8430

Camping Sagres is a pleasant site at the western tip of the Algarve, not very far from a lighthouse in the relatively unspoilt southwest corner of Portugal. With 960 pitches for tents and 120 for tourers, the sandy pitches, some terraced, are located amongst pine trees that give good shade. There are some hardstandings for motorcaravans and electricity throughout. The fairly bland restaurant, bar and café/grill provide a range of reasonably priced meals. This is a reasonable site for those seeking winter sun, or as a base for exploring this 'Land's End' region of Portugal. It is away from the hustle and bustle of the more crowded resorts. The beaches and the town of Sagres (the departure point of the Portuguese navigators) with its fort, are a short drive.

Facilities

Three spacious toilet blocks are showing some signs of wear but provide hot and cold showers and washbasins with cold water. Washing machines. Motorcaravan services. Supermarket. Restaurant/bar and café/grill (all Easter and June-Oct). TV room. Satellite TV in restaurant. Bicycle hire. Barbecue area. Playground. Fishing. Medical post. Car wash. WiFi (free). Off site: Buses from village 1 km. Beach and fishing 2 km. Boat launching 8 km. Golf 12 km.

Open: All year.

Directions

From Sagres, turn off the N268 road west onto the EN268. After about 2 km. the site is signed off to the right. GPS: 37.02278, -8.94583

Charges guide

Per person	€ 4.90
child (5-10 yrs)	€ 2.50
caravan and car	€ 9.90 - € 10.90
electricity (6A)	€ 2.90 - € 3.50

Off season discounts (up to 70%).

With huge, sparsely populated plains dominated by vast cork plantations, which provide nearly half of the world's cork, Alentejo's main attractions include the historic city of Évora and the coastal resorts with their fine, sandy beaches.

ALENTEJO IS MADE UP OF FOUR DISTRICTS: BEJA, ÉVORA, SETÚBAL AND PORTALEGRE

One of the most impressive cities in Portugal, Évora lies on a gently sloping hill rising out of the huge Alentejo plain. A city steeped in history, it was occupied by the Romans and Moors for centuries. With its narrow streets, of Moorish origin, and white-washed houses, it also boasts one of the best-preserved Roman temples in the country plus various palaces and monuments, the majority dating from the 14th-16th centuries. One of the more extraordinary sights can be found in the Capela dos Ossos in the church of São Francisco; adorning the walls and pillars of this chamber are the bones of more than 5,000 monks. On the Alentejo coast is the small, peaceful town of Santiago do Cacém, which has two of the best beaches in Portugal. The nearby archaeological site at Miróbriga includes ruins of a hippodrome, several houses (some of which have mural paintings) and a clearly defined acropolis. Further south along the coast is Porto Côvo and the larger, popular resort of Vila Nova de Milfontes, which has a little castle and ancient port.

Places of interest

Arraiolos: ancient town, 17th-century castle, famous for its carpets.

Beja: provincial town founded by Julius Caesar, 13th-century castle.

Borba: pretty town, noted for its marble and wine.

Elvas: ancient fortress town, 15th-century aqueduct.

Estremoz: market town, medieval castle.

Odemira: quiet, characterful country town.

Reguengos de Monsaraz: charming, unspoiled village with white-washed houses.

Vila Viçosa: attractive hillside town, 16th-century convent.

Cuisine of the region

Alentejo was traditionally an important wheat-growing region (it is frequently referred to as the 'granary of Portugal'). Local specialities include *sopa de cação* (skate soup), made from fish and bread, and *ensopado de borrego* (lamb stew). Cheeses of the region include *queijo de Serpa* and *queijos de Niza*, made from goats' milk. The *queijos de Évora*, made from ewes' milk, is smaller in size with a strong, spicy flavour. *Arroz Doce* (rice pudding topped with cinnamon) is the traditional dessert for festivals and parties and is to be found all over the country.

FATIMA
TOMAR
BEIRAS & CENTRE
SAO MARTINHO DO PORTO
SANTO ANTONIO DAS AREIAS
SANTAREM
PORTALEGRE
N245
E802
LISBON & VALE DO TEJO
CORUCHE
ESTREMOZ
ELVAS
BORBA
ARRAIOLOS
A6/E802,E90
A6,IP7
SETUBAL
EVORA
SESIMBRA
N256
IP2/E802
A2/E01
ALVITO
ALENTEJO
SANTIAGO DO CACEM
N121
BEJA
N260,IP8
PORTO COVO
N120,IC4
VILA NOVA DE MILFONTES
N122
N263
ODEMIRA
A2/E01
ANDALUCIA (SPAIN)
ALGARVE
0
25
50
75 kms

Alvito

Camping Markádia

Barragem de Odivelas, Apartado 17, P-7920-999 Alvito (Beja) T: 284 763 141. E: markadia@hotmail.com

alanrogers.com/PO8350

A tranquil, lakeside site in an unspoilt setting, this will appeal most to those nature lovers who want to 'get away from it all' and to those who enjoy country pursuits such as walking, fishing and riding. There are 130 casual unmarked pitches on undulating grass and sand with ample electricity connections (16A). The site is lit but a torch is required. The friendly Dutch owner has carefully planned the site so each pitch has its own oak tree to provide shade. The open countryside and lake provide excellent views and a very pleasant environment. The lake is in fact a 1,000 hectare reservoir, and more than 150 species of birds can be found in the area. The stellar views in the very low ambient lighting are wonderful at night. The bar/restaurant with a terrace is open daily in season but weekends only during the winter. One can swim in the reservoir and canoes, pedaloes and windsurfers are available for hire.

Facilities

Four modern, very clean and well equipped toilet blocks are built in traditional Portuguese style with hot water throughout. Washing machines. Motorcaravan services. Bar and restaurant (1/4-30/9). Shop (all year, bread to order). Lounge. Playground. Fishing. Boat hire. Tennis. Riding. Medical post. Car wash. Dogs are not accepted in July/Aug. Facilities and amenities may be reduced outside the main season. Off site: Swimming and boating in the lake.

Open: All year.

Directions

From A2 between Setubal and the Algarve take exit 10 on IP8 signed Ferreira and Beja. Take road to Torrao and 13 km. later, 1 km. north of Odivelas, turn right towards Barragem and site is 3 km. after crossing head of reservoir following small signs (400 m. section of poor road).
GPS: 38.1812, -8.10293

Charges guide

Per unit incl. 2 persons and electricity	€ 25.70
extra person	€ 5.80
child (5-10 yrs)	€ 2.90

Discounts of 10-20% outside June - Aug, and for longer stays. No credit cards.

Évora

Orbitur Camping Évora

Estrada de Alca Covas, Herdade Esphrragosa, P-700-703 Évora (Evora) T: 266 705 190.
E: infoevora@orbitur.pt **alanrogers.com/PO8340**

Situated some 1.5 km. from the historic former provincial capital, this site is well located for an overnight stop. There is a small swimming pool and a simple small bar where snacks may be served. Most of the 285 sandy and good sized touring pitches have 15A electricity and those in the older part of the site have well developed shade. The ground is probably not suitable for visitors using wheelchairs. The historic walled town and its castle (on the World Heritage list) and the surrounding area with its megalithic monuments are well worth visiting.

Facilities

Two toilet blocks are just acceptable. Free hot showers and British style WCs. Laundry. Motorcaravan services. Gas supplies. Bar and snacks (May-Oct). Bread to order. Swimming pool (June-Sept). Tennis. Mature play area (supervision necessary). Off site: Bicycle hire 2 km. Riding and golf 5 km. Supermarkets in the town.

Open: All year.

Directions

Site is 1.5 km. southwest of the town on the N380 road to Alcácovas. GPS: 38.557294, -7.925863

Charges guide

Per person	€ 5.10
child (5-10 yrs)	€ 2.60
pitch	€ 10.90 - € 11.90
electricity	€ 2.90 - € 3.50

Off season discounts (up to 70%).

Odemira

Parque de Campismo São Miguel

São Miguel, Odeceixe, P-7630-592 Odemira (Beja) T: 282 947 145. E: camping.sao.miguel@mail.telepac.pt

alanrogers.com/PO8170

Nestled in green hills near two pretty white villages, 4 km. from the beautiful Praia Odeceixe (beach) is the attractive camping park São Miguel. Unusually, the site works on a maximum number of 700 campers, you find your own place (there are no defined pitches) under the tall trees, there are ample electrical points, and the land slopes away gently. Wooden chalet style accommodation to rent is in a separate area, but some mobile homes share the two traditional older style but clean sanitary blocks. The main building with its traditional Portuguese architecture is built around two sides of a large square.

Facilities

Two older style toilet blocks with British style WCs and free hot showers. Washing machines. Toilets and basins for disabled campers but no shower. Shop (June-Sept). Self-service restaurant (Mar-Oct). Bar, snacks and pizzeria (June-Sept). Satellite TV. Playground. Tennis (charged). Swimming pool (charged). Dogs are not accepted. Torches useful. Off site: Bus service from gate. Historic village of Odeceixe 2 km. Beach, fishing and sailing 4 km. Riding 20 km. Site is inside the Alentejo nature park.

Open: All year.

Directions

Between Odemira and Lagos on the N120 just before the village of Odeceixe on the main road well signed. GPS: 37.43868, -8.75568

Charges guide

Per unit incl. 2 persons and electricity	€ 17.40 - € 27.40
extra person	€ 4.20 - € 6.40
child (5-10 yrs)	€ 2.50 - € 3.70

Odemira

Zmar-Eco Camping Resort

Herdade A de Mateus E.N. 393/1, San Salvador, P-7630 Odemira (Beja) T: 707 200 626. E: info@zmar.eu

alanrogers.com/PO8175

Zmar is an exciting new project which should be fully open this year. The site is located near Zambujeira do Mar, on the Alentejo coast. This is a highly ambitious initiative developed along strict environmental lines. For example, renewable resources such as locally harvested timber and recycled plastic are used wherever possible and solar energy is used whenever practicable. Public indoor spaces have no air conditioning, but there is adequate cooling through underfloor ventilation and electric fans where possible. Pitches are 100 sq.m. and benefit from artificial shade. Caravans and wood-clad mobile homes are also available for rent. Swimming pool complex features a large outdoor pool and an indoor pool area with a wave machine and a wellness centre. The very large and innovative children's play park has climbing nets, labyrinths and caves. There is also a children's farm and a large play house. For adults, many sporting amenities will be available around the resort's 81 hectare park.

Facilities

Eight toilet blocks provide comprehensive facilities, including those for children and disabled visitors. Bar. Restaurant. Crêperie. Takeaway food. Large supermarket. Swimming pool. Covered pool. Wellness centre. Sports field. Games room. Play area, farm and play house. Tennis. Bicycle hire. Activity and entertainment programme. Mobile homes and caravans for rent. Caravan repair and servicing. The site's own debit card system is used for payment at all facilities. Off site: Vicentina coast and the Alentejo Natural Park. Sines (birthplace of Vasco de Gama). Cycle and walking tracks. Sea fishing.

Open: All year.

Directions

From the N120 from Odemira to Lagos, at roundabout in the centre of Portas de Transval turn towards Milfontes. Take turn to Cabo Sardão and then Zambujeira do Mar. Site is on the left. GPS: 37.60422, -8.73142

Charges guide

Per unit incl. up to 4 persons and electricity	€ 20.00 - € 50.00
extra person	€ 5.00 - € 10.00
child (4-12 yrs)	€ 5.00

Camping Cheques accepted.

Porto Covo

Parque de Campismo Porto Covo

Estrada Municipal 554, P-7520-437 Porto Covo (Setubal) T: 269 905 136. E: camping.portocovo@gmail.com

alanrogers.com/PO8160

This is a site in a popular, small seaside resort where a fairly large proportion of the pitches are occupied by Portuguese units. However, it has a reasonable sense of space as you pass the security barrier to reception which is part of an uncluttered and attractively designed village square area with some well established apartments for rent. The pitches are somewhat small but are hedged, reasonably level, all have electricity (5A), and are shaded. The beaches are a short walk and feature steep cliffs and pleasant sandy shores. If you do not want to venture out to the beach then the site has a swimming pool located behind the restaurant and with areas for sunbathing. Dedicated barbecue areas are close to the pools. A mini market stocks the essentials and some souvenirs. A jolly bar and restaurant with terrace cleverly operates across the boundary of the site and it offers a varied Portuguese menu (popular with the locals) at very reasonable prices. A second smaller restaurant operates in the site in low season.

Facilities

The toilet blocks are clean with the usual amenities including hot showers. Motorcaravan services (outside gate). Restaurant (10/6-30/9). Bar with satellite TV. Shop in season. Recreation room with games and a TV. Play area. Swimming pools (10/6-30/9). Tennis. Barbecue areas. Boat trips and fishing trips organised. Off site: The village is a short walk with shops, bars and restaurants. Bus service to Lisbon 300 m. from site. Fishing 500 m. Riding 20 km. Golf 25 km.

Open: All year.

Directions

From E120-1 Cercal - Sines road (the road changes from the E120 at Tanganheira). Turn left (southwest) to Porto Covo and follow site signs. Do not be surprised to be led through a new housing estate. Look for large white-water tower with site logo. GPS: 37.85269, -8.78806

Charges guide

Per person	€ 2.50 - € 3.55
child (5-10 yrs)	€ 1.75
pitch	€ 5.25 - € 10.80
electricity	€ 2.65 - € 3.30

Reductions in low season.

Santo Antonio das Areias

Camping Asseiceira

Caixa Postal 2, P-7330-204 Santo Antonio das Areias (Portalegre) T: 245 992 940.
E: gary-campingasseiceira@hotmail.com **alanrogers.com/PO8355**

Set amongst unspoilt mountain scenery in the spectacular national park of Serra de São Mamede, Camping Asseiceira is a British owned site offering visitors a warm welcome. The Spanish border is just 8 km. away. Arranged in a small olive grove are 12 pitches with views rising up to the spectacular medieval castle and town of Marvão. This a pleasant, well looked after small site with few facilities, although the village of Santo António das Areias is only a few minutes walk with shops, restaurants and a bank. Access to the site is from a tarmac road suitable for most units. The site has a small swimming pool with a bar service from nearby and the owners are working hard to improve the facilities. There is some cultural and historical sightseeing to be done in Portalegre or the nearby town of Marvão but the site is an ideal place to relax after a long drive on your way to or from the Algarve. The British owner, Gary Chuwen, oversees every aspect of the site personally.

Facilities

A small clean and well equipped toilet block, built in wood, with hot water throughout. Small swimming pool with adjacent bar and terrace (June-Oct). WiFi. Off site: Village with shops, restaurants and bank 3 km. Daily train or bus to Lisbon. Golf 4 km. Riding 7 km. Fishing 8 km.

Open: All year.

Directions

From the IP1 take exit 7 onto the A6/IP7 towards Estremoz, then the IP2/E802 towards Portalegre. Continue past Portalegre to right turn for Marvão and Spain. Follow signs for Marvão and after roundabout at Portagem take first right and follow road to Santo António das Areias. At petrol station turn right down the hill and site is 400 m. on left. GPS: 39.41225, -7.35236

Charges guide

Per person	€ 3.00
pitch	€ 2.00 - € 6.00
awning	€ 3.00
electricity (16A)	€ 4.00

With its deep-rooted cultural traditions, range of leisure activities, year-round sunshine, sandy beaches, historic towns and villages, Lisbon and Vale do Tejo has something for everyone. It is also the centre of Fado, the traditional haunting folk song of Portugal.

THIS REGION IS DIVIDED INTO FOUR DISTRICTS: LEIRIA, LISBON, SANTARÉM AND SETÚBAL

(PART OF SETÚBAL ALSO FEATURES IN THE ALENTEJO REGION)

Standing on the banks of the river Tagus, Lisbon has been the capital of Portugal since 1255. Places of interest in the city include the medieval quarters of Alfama and Mouraria, with their cobbled streets and alleys, colourful buildings, markets and castles, and Belém, with its tower and the 16th-century Jerónimos monastery. Lisbon also boasts an assortment of museums. Not far from the capital lies the romantic town of Sintra, which has an array of cottages, manor houses and palaces. Its mountains also form part of the Sintra-Cascais Natural Park. Along the Atlantic coast, high sweeping cliffs lead down to white sandy beaches, backed by lagoons. Europe's westernmost point, Cabo da Roca, is found here as are plenty of coastal towns and villages including Peniche, Nazaré and Óbidos, a small medieval walled town with cobbled streets, tiny white-washed houses and balconies brimming with flowers. Further inland, at Alcobaça, Tomar and Batalha, are ancient monasteries, with castles in Leiria, Tomar and Santarém. Recreational pursuits include watersports, fishing and golf. In summer there are open-air music festivals.

Places of interest

Estoril: casino, golf course and racing track.

Fátima: one of the most important centres of pilgrimage in the Catholic world.

Leiria: medieval royal castle, 16th-century cathedral, Romanesque church.

Mafra: 18th-century Palace-Convent, the largest Portuguese religious monument.

Santarém: castle, archaeology museum, Gothic convent and churches.

Sesimbra: picturesque small fishing town, medieval castle, the Lagoa de Albufeira is a favourite spot for windsurfers.

Setúbal: nature reserve, beaches, golf courses.

Tomar: 12th-century Templars' Castle, Gothic and Renaissance churches, 15th-century synagogue.

Cuisine of the region

Fish soups, stews and seafood are popular, including *sardinha assada* (grilled sardines) and *Bifes de Espardarte* (swordfish steaks). Sintra is famed for its cheesecakes which, according to ancient documents, were already being made in the 12th century and were part of the rent payments. Wine-producing regions include Azeitão, Bucelas, Carcavelos and Colares.

Caldeiradas: fish stews.

Queijadas: cheese tarts.

Pastéis de Belém: custard tarts.

Travesseiros: puff pastries stuffed with a sweet eggy mixture.

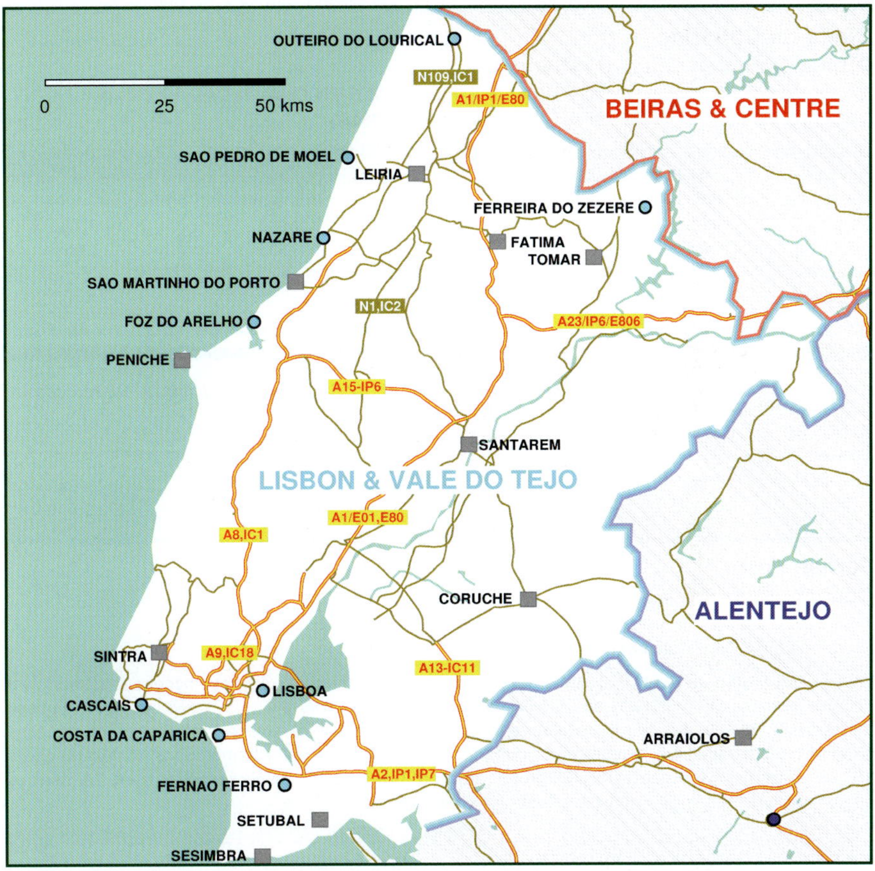

Cascais

Orbitur Camping Guincho

EN247, Lugar da Areia - Guincho, P-2750-053 Cascais (Lisbon) T: 214 870 450. E: infoguincho@orbitur.pt

alanrogers.com/PO8130

Although this is a popular site for permanent Portuguese units with 1,295 pitches, it is nevertheless quite attractively laid out among low pine trees and with the A5 autostrada connection to Lisbon (30 km), it provides a useful alternative to sites nearer the city. This is viewed as an alternative for visiting Lisbon, not a holiday site. There is a choice of pitches (small – mainly about 50 sq.m) mostly with electricity, although siting amongst the trees may be tricky, particularly when the site is full. Located behind sand dunes and a wide, sandy beach, the site offers a wide range of facilities. These include a fairly plain bar/restaurant, supermarket (all year), general lounge with pool tables, electronic games, TV room and a good laundry.

Facilities

Three sanitary blocks, one refurbished, are in the older style but are clean and tidy. Washbasins with cold water but hot showers. Facilities for disabled visitors. Washing machines and dryers. Motorcaravan services. Gas. Supermarket. Restaurant, bar and terrace. General room with TV. Tennis. Playground. Entertainment in summer. WiFi. Chalets to rent. Off site: Bus service from gate. Excursions. Riding 500 m. Beach 800 m. Fishing 1 km. Golf 3 km.

Open: All year.

Directions

Approach from either direction on N247. Turn inland 6.5 km. west of Cascais at site sign. Travelling direct from Lisbon, the site is well signed as you leave the A5 at exit 12 and follow directions for Birre.
GPS: 38.72117, -9.46667

Charges guide

Per person	€ 5.10
child (5-10 yrs)	€ 2.60
pitch	€ 10.90 - € 11.90
electricity	€ 2.90 - € 3.50

Off season discounts (up to 70%).

Costa da Caparica

Orbitur Camping Costa da Caparica

Avenida Alfonso de Albuquerque, Quinta de Ste Antonio, P-2825-450 Costa da Caparica (Setubal)
T: 212 901 366. E: infocaparica@orbitur.pt **alanrogers.com/PO8150**

This site has relatively easy access to Lisbon (just under 20 km) via the motorway, by bus or even by bus and ferry if you wish. It is situated near a small resort, favoured by the Portuguese themselves, which has all the usual amenities plus a good sandy beach (200 m. from the site) and promenade walks. An area for touring units includes some larger pitches for motorcaravans. There are 240 pitches with electricity connections (long electricity leads may be needed). In addition, there are 140 permanent caravans. We see this very much as a site to visit Lisbon rather than for prolonged stays.

Facilities

The three toilet blocks have mostly British style toilets, washbasins with cold water and some hot showers – they are under pressure when the site is full. Facilities for disabled visitors. Washing machine. Motorcaravan services. Supermarket. Large bar/restaurant (not Nov). Satellite TV. Playground. Gas supplies. Off site: Bus from site gate. Fishing 1 km. Riding 4 km. Golf 5 km.

Open: All year.

Directions

Cross the Tagus bridge (toll) on A2 motorway going south from Lisbon, immediately take the turning for Caparica and Trafaria. At 7 km. marker on IC20 turn right (no sign) – the site is at the second roundabout. GPS: 38.65595, -9.24107

Charges guide

Per person	€ 5.10
pitch	€ 10.90 - € 11.90
electricity	€ 2.90 - € 3.50

Fernão Ferro

Camping Parque Verde

Avenida do Casal Sapo, Fontainhas, P-2685-065 Fernão Ferro (Setubal) T: 212 108 999.
E: info@parqueverde.pt **alanrogers.com/PO8155**

This is very much a site for 812 permanent caravans but it has relatively easy access to Lisbon (just under 20 km) via the motorway and the impressive bridge. It is very much favoured by the Portuguese themselves. The site has all the usual amenities and a village-like central bar and restaurant complex. Most of the amenities are open all year round. There is a small area for touring units containing about 18 pitches and some larger pitches for motorcaravans. There are 20 mobile homes for rent. We see this site as useful for visiting Lisbon rather than for prolonged stays.

Facilities

The single toilet block for the touring units provides acceptable facilities. Washing machines. Supermarket. Bar, restaurants and snack bar (all year). Swimming pool and children's pool (1/5-30/9). Fitness facilities. Play area. Disco and other entertainment. Off site: Trains for Lisbon 4 km. Golf 5 km. Riding 12 km. Fishing 15 km.

Open: All year.

Directions

From A2 toll road take exit 2 onto N378 towards Sesimbra. Pass through Fernão Ferro and at roundabout follow for Coina into Fontainhas. Stay on tarred road through Fontainhas (rua 25 de Abril) and site is on the right. GPS: 38.55056, -9.07167

Charges guide

Per unit incl. 2 persons and electricity	€ 16.00
extra person	€ 2.00 - € 3.00

Ferreira do Zêzere

Camping Quinta da Cerejeira

P-2240-333 Ferreira do Zêzere (Santarem) T: 249 361 756. E: info@cerejeira.com
alanrogers.com/PO8550

This is a delightful, small, family owned venture run by Gert and Teunie Verheij, assisted by Catarina and Rodrigo Santos. It is a converted farm (quinta) and has been coaxed into a very special campsite. The pitches are on flat grass or on long terraces under fruit and olive trees. There are 30 pitches of which 18 have access to 6A electricity (long leads may be needed). There is some shade and the site is full of rustic charm and craft works. It is very peaceful with views of the surrounding green hills from the charming vine-covered patio above a small swimming pool. You will notice the working well, no longer powered by a donkey but you can see where he used to circle to pump water.

Facilities

The single rustic sanitary building has British style WCs with hot showers. It could be busy at peak periods. Washing machine. No facilities for disabled campers. No shop but just ask and the baker calls daily. Bar with snacks and restaurant. Children's club room. Separate games and rest room with satellite TV. Artistic workshops. Internet terminals and WiFi. Swing for children. Torches useful. Off site: Town with shops, bars and restaurants and bus service 1 km. Fishing and watersports 5 km.

Open: 1 February - 30 November.

Directions

From Lisbon take A1/A23 to Torres Novas then IC3 to Tomar and N238 to Ferreira do Zêzere. Take road N348 to Vila de Rei and the site is 1 km. from Ferreira do Zêzere to the eastern side of town (do not go into the town). From Coimbra use the N238 road at an earlier exit. GPS: 39.70075, -8.2782

Charges guide

Per unit incl. 2 persons and electricity	€ 16.25 - € 18.25
extra person	€ 3.50 - € 4.00

Foz do Arelho

Orbitur Camping Foz do Arelho

Rua Maldonado Freitas, P-2500-516 Foz do Arelho (Leiria) T: 262 978 683. E: infofozarelho@orbitur.pt

alanrogers.com/PO8480

This is a large and roomy ex-municipal site and improvements are still taking place. It is 2 km. from the beach and has a new central complex with a most impressive swimming pool and separated children's pool with lifeguard. Pitches are generally sandy with some hardstandings. They vary in size and are unmarked on two main levels with wide tarmac roads. There is some shade and all touring pitches have electricity (5/15A). The large two storey, brick-faced building contains all the site's leisure facilities but has no ramped access.

Facilities

Four identical modern sanitary buildings (solar heating) with seatless British and Turkish style WCs and free showers. Washing machine in one. Facilities for disabled campers at the block near reception. Supermarket. Bar/snacks and restaurant (closed Nov). Bread to order (1/9-30/6). Children's club. Games room. Small new amphitheatre. Playground – supervision needed. Bus service. Doctor's room. Torches useful. Off site: Bus 500 m. Beach and fishing 2 km. Supermarkets in Foz do Arelho.

Open: All year.

Directions

Site is north of Lisbon and west of Caldos la Rainha. From the A8 take N360 to Foz do Arelho. Site is well signed. GPS: 39.43067, -9.20083

Charges guide

Per person	€ 5.10
child (5-10 yrs)	€ 2.60
pitch	€ 10.90 - € 11.90
electricity	€ 2.90 - € 3.50

Lisboa

Lisboa Camping-Parque Municipal de Monsanto

Estrada da Circunvalacão, P-1400-061 Lisboa (Lisbon) T: 217 628 200. E: info@lisboacamping.com

alanrogers.com/PO8140

This very large site is professionally operated by many uniformed staff, providing a quality service at a good price. The wide entrance with its ponds, fountains and the trees, lawns and flowering shrubs leading up to the two swimming pools, is a most attractive feature. On sloping ground, the site's many terraces are well shaded by trees and shrubs. The 400 good pitches include 170 serviced pitches on concrete hardstandings. There is a huge separate area for tents, and 70 chalet style bungalows are for hire. Central Lisbon is 8 km. away with two bus routes giving a regular service from the gate.

Facilities

Eight solar-powered toilet blocks contain quality facilities, including those for disabled visitors. Launderette. Motorcaravan service point. Shops, bar and restaurants. Two swimming pools (with lifeguard; May-Sept). Tennis. Minigolf. Sports field. Playgrounds. Roman theatre. Entertainment in high season. General and TV (cable) rooms. Internet. Organised excursions. Off site: Excellent bus service from site gate. Lisbon city. Bicycle hire 2 km. Golf 5 km. Beaches 10 km. Riding 16 km.

Open: All year.

Directions

From Lisbon take A5 motorway towards Estoril and site is signed from junction 4 onto the 1C17 (huge site signs at first exit to Buraca). Site is immediately on the right. Enter to the right of the fountain on the tiled road. GPS: 38.72477, -9.20737

Charges guide

Per unit incl. 2 persons and electricity	€ 20.00 - € 30.00
extra person	€ 5.50 - € 7.00

Nazaré

Orbitur Camping Valado

Rua dos Combatentes do Ultramar 2, Valado, P-2450-148 Nazaré (Leiria) T: 262 561 111.
E: infovalado@orbitur.pt **alanrogers.com/PO8110**

This popular site is close to the old, traditional fishing port of Nazaré which has now become something of a holiday resort and popular with coach parties. The large sandy beach in the town (about 2 km. steeply downhill from the site) is sheltered by headlands and provides good swimming. The campsite is on undulating ground under tall pine trees. There are said to be 503 pitches and, although some smallish individual pitches with electricity and water can be reserved, the bulk of the site is not marked out and units are close together during July/August. About 420 electrical connections are available.

Facilities

The three toilet blocks have British and Turkish style WCs, washbasins (some cold water) and 17 hot showers, all very clean when inspected. Laundry. Motorcaravan services. Gas supplies. Supermarket. Bar, snack bar and restaurant with terrace (Easter and June-Oct). TV/general room. Playground. Tennis. WiFi. Off site: Bus service 20 m. Fishing and bicycle hire 2 km.

Open: 30 December - 16 October.

Directions

Site is on the Nazaré - Alcobaca N8-5 road, 2 km. east of Nazaré. GPS: 39.5934, -9.02783

Charges guide

Per person	€ 4.30
child (5-10 yrs)	€ 2.20
pitch	€ 8.60 - € 9.60
electricity	€ 2.90 - € 3.50

Off season discounts (up to 70%).

Nazaré

Camping Caravaning Vale Paraiso

EN242, P-2450-138 Nazaré (Leiria) T: 262 561 800. E: info@valeparaiso.com

alanrogers.com/PO8460

A pleasant, well managed site, Vale Paraiso improves every year, with the latest additions being new reception buildings and pool areas. The owners are keen to welcome British visitors and English is spoken. The site is by the main N242 road in eight hectares of undulating pine woods. There are 650 shady pitches, many on sandy ground only suitable for tents. For other units there are around 250 individual pitches of varying size on harder ground with electricity available. A large range of sporting and leisure activities includes a good outdoor pool and paddling pool with sunbathing areas.

Facilities

Spotless sanitary facilities have hot water throughout. Nearly all WCs are British style. Modern facilities for disabled visitors. Baby baths. Washing machine and dryers. Motorcaravan services. Supermarket (1/5-30/9). Restaurant (15/5-15/9). Café/bar with satellite TV. Takeaway. Tabac. Swimming and paddling pools (Mar-Sept; free for under 11s). Pétanque. Leisure games. Amusement hall. Bicycle hire. Safety deposit. Gas supplies. E-mail and fax facilities. WiFi (free). Apartments, tents and mobile homes to rent. Off site: Bus service from gate. Fishing and boat launching 2 km. Riding 6 km.

Open: All year except 19-27 December.

Directions

Site is 2 km. north of Nazaré on the EN242 Marinha Grande road. GPS: 39.62028, -9.05639

Charges guide

Per unit incl. 2 persons and electricity	€ 21.20 - € 26.70
extra person	€ 3.25 - € 4.85
child (3-10 yrs)	€ 1.60 - € 2.40
dog	€ 2.90

Credit cards accepted for amounts over € 150. Camping Cheques accepted.

Outeiro do Louriçal

Campismo O Tamanco

Rua do Louriçal 11, Casas Brancas, P-3105-158 Outeiro do Louriçal (Leiria) T: 236 952 551.

E: tamanco@me.com **alanrogers.com/PO8400**

O Tamanco is a peaceful countryside site, with a homely almost farmstead atmosphere; you will have chickens and ducks wandering around and there is a Burro here. The young Dutch owners, Irene and Hans, are sure to give you a warm welcome at this delightful little site. The 65 good sized pitches are separated by cordons of all manner of fruit trees, ornamental trees and flowering shrubs, on level grassy ground. There is electricity (6/16A) to all the pitches and 5 pitches are suitable for large motorcaravans. The site is lit and there is nearly always space available.

Facilities

The single toilet block provides very clean and generously sized facilities including washbasins in cabins. No easy access for disabled visitors. As facilities are limited they may be busy in peak periods. Hot water throughout. Washing machine. Bar/restaurant. Roofed patio with fireplace. TV room/lounge (satellite). Internet access. Swimming pool. Yurts for hire. Off site: Bus service 1 km. Lake 2 km. Beach 11 km. Sun. market in nearby Lourical.

Open: All year.

Directions

From the A17 (Lisboa - Porto), take exit 5 for Carrico, turn right at the roundabout and O Tamanco is on the left. GPS: 39.99455, -8.78584

Charges 2012

Per unit incl. 2 persons and electricity	€ 18.55

Winter discounts up to 40%. No credit cards. Special prices low season for self-contained motorcaravans.

São Pedro de Moel

Orbitur Camping São Pedro de Moel

Rua Volta do Sete, P-2430 São Pedro de Moel (Leiria) T: 244 599 168. E: infospedro@orbitur.pt

alanrogers.com/PO8100

This quiet and very attractive site is situated under tall pines, on the edge of the rather select small resort of São Pedro de Moel. This is a shady site which can be crowded in July and August. The 525 pitches are in blocks and unmarked (cars may be parked separately) with 404 electrical connections. A few pitches are used for permanent units. Although there are areas of soft sand, there should be no problem in finding a firm place. The large restaurant and bar are modern as is the superb swimming pool, paddling pool and flume (there is a lifeguard).

Facilities

Four clean toilet blocks have mainly British style toilets (some with bidets), some washbasins with hot water. Hot showers are mostly in one unisex block. Laundry. Motorcaravan services. Gas supplies. Supermarket. Large restaurant and bar with terrace (closed in November). Swimming pools (1/3-30/9). Satellite TV. Games room. Playground. Tennis. WiFi. Off site: Beach 500 m.

Open: All year.

Directions

Site is 9 km. west of Marinha Grande, on the right as you enter São Pedro de Moel. GPS: 39.75883, -9.02229

Charges guide

Per person	€ 5.10
pitch	€ 10.90 - € 11.90
electricity	€ 2.90 - € 3.50

Beiras is the traditional name for the strip of land flanked by Portugal's two main rivers – the Douro and the Tagus. This region is made up of two contrasting areas: white sandy beaches, fishing villages and pine forests lie along the coast, while inland the mountains dominate the landscape.

BEIRAS HAS FIVE DISTRICTS: AVEIRO, COIMBRA, CASTELO BRANCO, GUARDA AND VISEU

One of Europe's oldest university towns, Coimbra was Portugal's capital from 1143 to 1255. The university, founded in 1290, has kept its academic traditions, as seen in the black-capped students, in the soulful tones of the fado de Coimbra (a traditional song sung to the sound of guitars by the students) and in the Queima das Fitas (Burning of the Ribbons), a boisterous celebration of graduating students. Coimbra also boasts a Romanesque cathedral, and south of the town lies Conímbriga, with the most important Roman remains in Portugal. Surrounded by the original walls, the archaeological site features an early Christian burial ground, hot springs and a museum. Further north lies Aveiro. Famous for its lagoon, the town is criss-crossed by canals where colourfully-painted moliceiro boats sail. To the east lies the Serra de Estrela, the highest mountain range in the country. It is home to the textile town of Covilha, attractive villages including Gouveia, Manteigas and Seia, plus the mountain resort of Guarda. Along the coast, the pretty seaside resorts of São Martinho do Porto, Nazaré and Figueira da Foz offer fine sandy beaches, good seafood restaurants and watersports facilities.

Places of interest

Belmonte: hilltop town, castle, Romanesque-Gothic church.

Bussaco: national park founded by monks in the 6th century.

Castelo Branco: 13th-century castle, medieval quarter, 16th- and 18th-century churches.

Curia and *Luso:* spa towns.

Monsanto: historic village, 12th-century castle, 18th-century manor houses.

Viseu: remains of Gothic walls, cathedral.

Cuisine of the region

Roast pork, lamb stew, seafood and fresh fish are popular, including *truta* (trout) from the mountains of Serra da Estrela. The famous ewes' milk cheese *Queijo da Serra*, is also produced in the mountains, and can be bought at cheese fairs held in villages and towns throughout the region during February and March. Regional desserts include hard and sweet biscuits, pancakes and sponge cake (*ovos-moles*, *pão-de-ló*).

Chanfana: lamb stewed in red wine.

Leitão assado da Bairrada: roast pork.

Arganil

Camping Municipal Arganil

EN17 km 5, Sarzedo, P-3300 Arganil (Coimbra) T: 235 205 706. E: camping@cm-arganil.pt

alanrogers.com/PO8330

This peaceful, inland site is attractively located in the hamlet of Sarzedo, some 2 km. from the town of Arganil. A spacious and well planned site, it is of a high quality for a municipal and prices are very reasonable! Delightfully situated among pine trees above the River Alva where one can swim, fish or canoe. The 150 pitches, most with electricity (15A), are of a reasonable size, mainly on flat sandy grass terraces and most shaded by tall trees. The site is kept beautifully clean and neat and access roads are tarmac. An excellent, small restaurant has an unusual attached bar with terrace.

Facilities

Sanitary facilities are clean and well maintained, with Turkish and British style WCs, controllable hot showers, washbasins in semi-private partitioned cabins and a hairdressing area. Ramped entrances make it suitable for disabled visitors. Washing machines. Bar, restaurant and snacks. Shop (July-Sept). TV room. Tennis. Free WiFi over part of site. Off site: Bus service 50 m. River beach and fishing 100 m. Watersports 200 m. Swimming pool in nearby Arganil. Golf 25 km.

Open: All year.

Directions

From Coimbra on the IC2 take exit 8 onto the IP3 towards Viseu. Take exit 13 onto the IP6 (N17) towards Arganil and onto the N324-4 to Sarzedo (site signed). Ignore the first site sign in Avelar as there is better access 500 m. further up the road on the right, also signed. GPS: 40.23333, -8.08333

Charges guide

Per unit incl. 2 persons and electricity	€ 8.30 - € 13.00
extra person	€ 1.60 - € 1.80
child (5-10 yrs)	€ 1.10 - € 1.30

Aveiro

Orbitur Camping São Jacinto

EN327 km 20, São Jacinto, P-3800-909 Aveiro (Aveiro) T: 234 838 284. E: infosjacinto@orbitur.pt

alanrogers.com/PO8050

This small site is in the São Jacinto Nature Reserve, on a peninsula between the Atlantic and the Barrinha, with views to the mountains beyond. The area is a weekend resort for locals and can be crowded in high season – it may therefore be difficult to find space in July and August, particularly for larger units. This is not a large site, taking 169 units on unmarked pitches, but in most places trees provide natural limits and shade. Swimming and fishing are both possible in the adjacent Ria, or the sea, a 20 minute walk from a guarded back gate.

Facilities

Two toilet blocks, very clean when inspected, contain the usual facilities. Dishwashing and laundry sinks. Washing machine and ironing board in a separate part of the toilet block. Motorcaravan services. Shop. Restaurant, bar and snack bar (Easter, June-Oct). Attractive new playground. Five bungalows to rent. Off site: Bus service 20 m. Fishing 200 m. Bicycle hire 10 km.

Open: 30 December - 16 October.

Directions

Turn off N109 at Estarreja to N109-5 to cross bridge over Ria da Gosta Nova and on to Torreira and São Jacinto. From Porto go south N1/09, turn for Ovar on the N327 which leads to São Jacinto.
GPS: 40.67497, -8.72295

Charges guide

Per person	€ 4.30
pitch	€ 11.40
electricity	€ 2.90 - € 3.50

Figueira da Foz

Orbitur Camping Gala

EN109 km 4 Gala, P-3080-458 Figueira da Foz (Coimbra) T: 233 431 492. E: infogala@orbitur.pt

alanrogers.com/PO8090

One of the best Orbitur sites, Gala has around 450 pitches on sandy terrain under a canopy of pine trees and is well cared for. Some pitches near the road are rather noisy. One can drive or walk the 300 m. from the back of the site to a private beach; you should swim with caution when it is windy – the warden will advise. The site fills up in July/August and units may be very close together, but there should be plenty of room at other times. Besides the beach, Coimbra and the Roman remains are worth visiting.

Facilities

The three toilet blocks have British and Turkish style toilets, individual basins (some with hot water) and free hot showers. Laundry. Motorcaravan services. Gas supplies. Supermarket and restaurant/bar with terrace. Lounge. Open-air pool (June-Sept). Playground. Tennis. TV. WiFi throughout. Doctor visits in season. Car wash area. Off site: Beach 300 m. Fishing 1 km. Bicycle hire and riding 3 km.

Open: All year.

Directions

Coming from the north, the site is 4 km. south of Figueira da Foz beyond the two rivers; turn off the N109 1 km. from bridge on southern edge of Gala, look for Orbitur sign on roundabout it is then 600 m. to site. GPS: 40.11850, -8.85683

Charges guide

Per person	€ 5.10
pitch	€ 10.90 - € 11.90
electricity	€ 2.90 - € 3.50

Idanha-a-Nova

Orbitur Camping Idanha-a-Nova

Barragem Marechal Carmona, P-6060-192 Idanha-a-Nova (Castelo Branco) T: 277 202 793.

E: infoidanha@orbitur.pt **alanrogers.com/PO8360**

This attractive and well laid out site is located in quiet, unspoilt countryside close to a reservoir near the small town of Idanha-a-Nova. The site has around 500 spacious unmarked pitches on wide grassy terraces and there is a little shade from young trees. Electricity (16A) is included in the price. Amenities include tennis courts with stadium-style spectator seating and a medium sized swimming pool with paddling pool, together with several playgrounds. A good supermarket, restaurant, bar and terrace complex is located centrally on site but these are only open in high season.

Facilities

Four large toilet blocks, built in the traditional Portuguese style, provide quality installations with some washbasins in private cabins, hot showers with dividers, foot baths and facilities for disabled visitors. Laundry. Supermarket (1/7-30/9). Café and bar (1/6-30/9). Restaurant (1/7-20/9). Swimming pool. Tennis. TV room. Vending machines. Medical post. Car wash. Canoe hire. Off site: Small town of Idanha-a-Nova.

Open: All year.

Directions

Using the N240, turn off at Ladoeiro onto the N354 (32 km. east of Castelo Branco) and follow signs to Idanha. After 16 km. follow signs for 'Campismo'. Do not turn towards Idanha-a-Nova or approach via this town. GPS: 39.950485, -7.187011

Charges guide

Per unit incl. 2 persons and electricity	€ 15.60 - € 26.00
extra person	€ 2.58 - € 4.30
child (5-10 yrs)	€ 1.32 - € 2.20

Ilhavo

Camping Costa Nova

Quinta dos Patos, Costa Nova do Prado, P-3830 Gafanha da Encarnação - Ilhavo (Aveiro)

T: 234 393 220. E: info@campingcostanova.com **alanrogers.com/PO8060**

Camping Costa Nova is situated between a river (Ria de Aveiro) and the sea in a protected natural reserve. There is direct access to a large sandy beach via a wooden walkway over the dunes. The 300 grassy pitches are provided with electricity hook ups (10A). This site is ideal for those who enjoy watersports and the surroundings offer plenty of sites of interest for exploration. The site boasts a large bar/restaurant and a café with TV and Internet access. English speaking visitors are welcomed and this sheltered site also attracts many for winter stays. Apartments are available for let.

Facilities

Three toilet blocks are well spaced around the site and offer adequate facilities with free hot water. Laundry room. Supermarket. Bar (all season). Restaurant (1/7-31/8). Takeaway. Snack bar. Shop. Games room. Disco. TV. Play area. Football field. Internet access. Off site: Beach 500 m. Fishing. Golf 600 m.

Open: 2 February - 31 December.

Directions

On the IP5 travelling from Aveiro east towards Barra, cross the bridge. At roundabout take third exit and site is well signed. GPS: 40.59972, -8.75139

Charges guide

Per unit incl. 2 persons and electricity	€ 12.70 - € 16.40
extra person	€ 2.50 - € 3.80
child (5-10 yrs)	€ 1.25 - € 1.90
dog	€ 1.50 - € 1.70

Praia de Mira

Orbitur Camping Mira

Estrada Florestal no 1, km 2, Dunas de Mira, P-3070-792 Praia de Mira (Coimbra) T: 231 471 234.

E: infomira@orbitur.pt **alanrogers.com/PO8070**

A small, peaceful seaside site set in pinewoods, Orbitur Camping Mira is situated to the south of Aveiro and Vagos, in a quieter and less crowded area. It fronts onto a lake at the head of the Ria de Mira, which eventually runs into the Aveiro Ria. A back gate leads directly to the sea and a wide quiet beach 300 m. away. A road runs alongside the site boundary where the restaurant complex is situated resulting in some road noise. The site has around 225 pitches on sand, which are not marked but have trees creating natural divisions. Electricity and water points are plentiful. The site provides an inexpensive restaurant, snack bar, lounge bar and TV lounge. A medium sized supermarket is well stocked, with plenty of fresh produce. The Mira Ria is fascinating, with the brightly painted, decorative 'moliceiros' (traditional fishing boats).

Facilities

The modern toilet blocks are clean, with 14 free hot showers and washing machines. Facilities for disabled visitors. Motorcaravan services. Gas supplies. Shop. Restaurant, bar and snack bar (Easter, June-Oct). TV room. Play area. Bicycle hire. WiFi at the bar. Bungalows (7) to rent. Off site: Bus service 150 m. (summer only). Fishing 500 m. Indoor pool, lake swimming and riding at Mira 7 km.

Open: 30 December - 16 October.

Directions

Take the IP5 (A25) southwest to Aveiro then the A17 south to Figuera da Foz. Then take the N109 north to Mira and follow signs west to Praia (beach) de Mira. GPS: 40.4533, -8.79902

Charges guide

Per person	€ 4.90
child (5-10 yrs)	€ 2.50
pitch	€ 8.60 - € 11.90
electricity	€ 2.90 - € 3.50

Off season discounts (up to 70%).

Sátão

Camping Quinta Chave Grande

Casfreires, Ferreira d'Aves, P-3560-043 Sátão (Viseu) T: 232 665 552. E: chave-grande@sapo.pt

alanrogers.com/PO8335

Quinta Chave Grande is a good quality campsite with friendly Dutch owners. It is set in a rural valley, close to many charming old villages, yet also only 25 km. from the provincial capital of Viseu, with its museums, churches and beautiful old town centre. The site occupies a large area and there are 150 unmarked touring pitches, although some are defined by trees. Electricity (6A) is available to all but long leads may be required. Larger units can be accommodated and there is a separate terraced area for tents. Torches are essential. For those who enjoy walking there are eight marked walking tours starting from the campsite. They take between 90 minutes and four hours, and each tour provides an opportunity to see some magnificent scenery with the occasional glimpse of wildlife. Excursions are organised and themed evenings are held in the welcoming bar area, including a Portuguese night, a Dutch night and a barbecue.

Facilities

Three modern toilet blocks, one with private en-suite cubicles for use by families and for visitors with disabilities. Service wash available. No shop but local tradesmen visit the site. Bar (all season). Swimming pool and children's pool (15/5-1/10). Fenced play area. Organised events for children and teenagers in July/Aug. Tennis. Boules. Off site: Fishing and bicycle hire 4 km. Riding 25 km. Golf 40 km. Marked walks. Good touring area.

Open: 1 April - 15 October.

Directions

From A25 Guarda - Viseu road take exit 19, than at the IP5 take exit 17 to Sátão. Take the N229 northeast to Sátão. Site is very well signed along road and is 12 km. northeast of Sátão.
GPS: 40.8227, -7.69609

Charges guide

Per unit incl. 2 persons and electricity	€ 22.50
extra person	€ 5.00
child (2-15 yrs)	€ 3.00

Vagos

Orbitur Camping Vagueira

Gafanha da Vagueira, Gafanha da Boa Hora, P-3840-254 Vagos (Aveiro) T: 234 797 526.
E: infovagueira@orbitur.pt **alanrogers.com/PO8040**

This is a large site set 1.5 km. from the beach and 500 m. from the Ria da Gosta Nova river. It is shaded under tall pine trees and has comprehensive facilities and reasonable prices. The 800 pitches are unmarked, on sand and pine needles with a large number of permanent Portuguese units, which are here in high season and weekends at other times. Groups are taken in high season. All touring pitches have electricity (6A). In sympathy with the surroundings, the modern buildings have clean lines and include a restaurant and bar with a disco area outside where music is played at weekends. This complex extends into a large rectangle holding the extremely large supermarket and facilities listed below. The whole site is securely fenced and is kept remarkably clean. The rules of peace between 23.00-07.00 are firmly applied. This is a good family site if you do not need a pool and have transport to get you to the beach. The seaside town here is a mixture of buildings and services which seem to be unsure of which future direction to take, but the beach is excellent.

Facilities

Seven modern sanitary buildings with British and Turkish style WCs and free showers. Facilities for disabled campers (unlocked). Washing machines. Bar/snacks and separate restaurant (June-Sept). Large supermarket. Children's club. Outdoor disco. Games room. Playground. Tennis (charge). Satellite TV. Internet room and WiFi. Torches useful. Off site: Seaside town has shops, bars and restaurants. Bus 500 m. River fishing 500 m. Golf and riding 1 km. Watersports at beach 1.5 km.

Open: All year.

Directions

Site is south of Aveiro. Take N109 south from Aveiro towards Mira. At Vagos take the N333 right turn towards Vagueira. Site is well signed at this turn and is just off the roundabout you arrive at on the beach road. GPS: 40.55792, -8.74517

Charges guide

Per person	€ 1.83 - € 3.65
child	€ 0.95 - € 1.85
pitch and car	€ 3.25 - € 8.50
electricity	€ 2.00

Camping Cheques accepted.

Originally inhabited by Celtics, Romans and Moors, the North is a region steeped in history. Renowned for its beautiful countryside, the River Douro winds its way past mountains, valleys, vineyards and cliffs until it reaches the sandy beaches of the Atlantic coast near the city of Porto.

THE REGION COMPRISES FIVE DISTRICTS: BRAGA, BRAGANÇA, PORTO, VIANA DO CASTELO AND VILA REAL

Situated in the north western corner of Portugal, the Costa Verde boasts lush green pine forests and unspoilt sandy beaches, dotted with picturesque seaside villages, including Caminha and Vila Nova de Cerveira. It is also renowned for its wine, being the home of Port and Vinho Verdo. Located on the banks of the River Douro, the attractive city of Porto is the centre of the Port wine trade – free tastings are offered at the wine cellars in Vila Nova de Gaia – and terraced vineyards can be found across the Douro Valley. The region is also a perfect place for walking, mountain trekking, canoeing or simply relaxing in the spa towns of Carvalhelhos, Chaves and Pedras Salgadas. Vidago has a magnificent park with swimming pools and a golf course, while the mountains of Peneda, Soajo and Gerês form the Peneda Geres National Park, an area covering 170,000 acres, with an abundance of wildlife. Vila Nova de Foz is the centre for visits to the Côa Archaeological Park, which houses one of the world's largest collections of outdoor Palaeolithic rock art, dating back 22,000 years.

Places of interest

Barcelos: medieval walled town with dungeon, ceramics museum, archaeology museum.

Bragança: medieval castle and walls, 16th-century cathedral, railway museum with 19th-century locomotives and carriages.

Chaves: Roman bridge, 14th-century castle with Archaeology and Epigraphy Museum.

Guimarães: medieval castle and walls, palace.

Lamego: medieval castle, 12th-century fortress.

Ponte de Lima: beautiful small town, Roman bridge, medieval towers, manor houses.

Viana do Castelo: town famous for its handicrafts and colourful regional costumes.

Vila do Conde: ancient medieval shipyard, famous for its manufactured lace.

Cuisine of the region

Typical dishes include *bacalhau* (dried and salted cod), *rabanadas*, *papos-de-anjo* and *barrigas-de-freiras* (sweetmeats). Porto has its own tripe dish, *Tripas à moda do Porto*.

The Minho region is renowned for its *Vinhos Verdes*, whose vines are grown on trellises (suspended high in the air on special frames). In the Douro region, the vines are grown on terraces, giving the impression of huge, natural staircases leading down to the banks of the river. Both red and white wines are produced here including the famous *Vinho do Porto* (Port wine).

Caldo verde: thick soup made with green cabbage, potatoes and spicy sausage.

Feijoada à transmontana: bean stew.

Caminha

Orbitur Camping Caminha

EN13 km 90, Mata do Camarido, P-4910-180 Caminha (Viana do Costelo) T: 258 921 295.
E: infocaminha@orbitur.pt **alanrogers.com/PO8010**

In northern Portugal, close to the Spanish border, this pleasant site is just 200 m. from the beach. It has an attractive and peaceful setting in woods alongside the river estuary that marks the border with Spain and on the edge of the little town of Caminha. The site is shaded by tall pines with other small trees planted to mark large sandy pitches. The main site road is surfaced but elsewhere take care not to get trapped in soft sand. Pitching and parking can be haphazard. Static units are grouped together on one side of the site. Water points, electrical supply and lighting are good. With a pleasant, open feel about the setting, fishing is possible in the estuary, as is swimming, and from the rather open, sandy beach.

Facilities

The clean, well maintained toilet block has British style toilets, washbasins (cold water) and hot showers, plus beach showers, extra dishwashing and laundry sinks (cold water). Laundry. Motorcaravan services. Supermarket. Small restaurant/bar with snacks (all Easter and 1/6-15/9). Bicycle hire. Off site: Beach and fishing 200 m. Bus service 800 m.

Open: All year.

Directions

From the north, turn off the main coast road (N13-E50) just after camping sign at the end of the embankment alongside estuary, about 1.5 km. south of ferry. From the south on N13 turn left at Hotel Faz de Minho at start of estuary and follow for 1 km. through woods to site. GPS: 41.86635, -8.85844

Charges guide

Per person	€ 2.50 - € 4.50
child (5-10 yrs)	€ 1.30 - € 2.50
caravan and car	€ 5.60 - € 10.20
electricity	€ 2.50 - € 3.10

Off season discounts (up to 70%).

Campo do Gerês

Parque de Campismo de Cerdeira

Rua de Cerdeira 400, P-4840 Campo do Gerês (Braga) T: 253 351 005. E: info@parquecerdeira.com

alanrogers.com/PO8370

Located in the national park of Peneda-Gerês, amidst spectacular mountain scenery, this excellent site offers modern facilities in a truly natural area. The national park is home to all manner of flora, fauna and wildlife, including the roebuck, wolf and wild boar. The well fenced, professional and peaceful site has some 600 good sized, unmarked, mostly level, grassy pitches in a shady woodland setting. Electricity is available for most pitches, though some long leads may be required. A very large timber complex, tastefully designed with the use of noble materials – granite and wood – provides a superb restaurant with a comprehensive menu.

Facilities

Four very clean sanitary blocks provide mixed style WCs, controllable showers and hot water. Laundry. Gas supplies. Shop. Restaurant/bar (1/4- 6/10, plus weekends and holidays). Playground. Bicycle hire. TV room (satellite). Medical post. Good tennis courts. Minigolf. Car wash. Barbecue area. Torches useful. English spoken. Attractive bungalows to rent. Dogs are not accepted June-Aug. Off site: Fishing and riding 800 m.

Open: All year.

Directions

From north, N103 (Braga - Chaves), turn left at the N205 (7.5 km. north of Braga). Follow N205 to Caldelas Terras de Bouro and Covide where site is clearly marked to Campo do Geres. An eastern approach from the N103 is for the adventurous but affords magnificent views. GPS: 41.7631, -8.1905

Charges guide

Per unit incl. 2 persons and electricity	€ 15.75 - € 24.45
extra person	€ 3.20 - € 4.60

Darque

Orbitur Camping Viana do Castelo

Rua Diogo Alvares, Cabadelo, P-4900-161 Darque (Viana do Costelo) T: 258 322 167. E: infoviana@orbitur.pt

alanrogers.com/PO8020

This site in northern Portugal is worth considering as it has the advantage of direct access, via a gate in the fence (locked at night), to a large and excellent soft sand beach (400 m.) which is popular for windsurfing. There are 225 pitches on undulating sand, most with good shade from pine trees and with electricity in all areas (long leads may be needed). Some flat, good sized pitches are reserved for caravans and motorcaravans. As usual with Orbitur sites, most pitches are not marked and it could be crowded in July/August. A pleasant restaurant terrace overlooks the pool.

Facilities

Toilet facilities are in two blocks, both with washbasins with cold water and hot showers. Facilities for disabled campers. Laundry. Motorcaravan services. Gas supplies. Supermarket. Small restaurant with terrace and bar (all Easter and 1/6-30/9). Open-air pool (June-Sept). Reading room with TV, video and fireplace. Playground. Tennis. Medical post. Off site: Beach 50 m. Fishing 100 m.

Open: All year.

Directions

On N13 coast road driving north to south, go through Viana do Castelo and over estuary bridge. Turn immediately right off N13 towards Cabedelo and sea. Site is third campsite signed, the other two are not recommended. GPS: 41.67866, -8.82637

Charges guide

Per unit incl. 2 persons and electricity	€ 14.60 - € 24.00

Póvoa de Varzim

Orbitur Camping Rio Alto

EN13 km 13 Rio Alto-Est, Estela, P-4570-275 Póvoa de Varzim (Porto) T: 252 615 699.
E: inforioalto@orbitur.pt **alanrogers.com/PO8030**

This site makes an excellent base for visiting Porto which is some 35 km. south of Estela. It has around 700 pitches on sandy terrain, next to what is virtually a private beach. There are some hardstandings for caravans and motorcaravans and electrical connections to most pitches (long leads may be required). The area for tents is furthest from the beach and windswept, stunted pines give some shade. There are arrangements for car parking away from camping areas in peak season. There is a quality restaurant, a snack bar and a large swimming pool across the road from reception.

Facilities

Four refurbished and well equipped toilet blocks have hot water. Laundry facilities. Facilities for disabled campers. Gas supplies. Shop (1/6-31/10). Restaurant, bar, snack bar (1/5-31/10). Swimming pool (1/6-30/9). Tennis. Playground. Games room. Surfing. TV. Medical post. Car wash. Evening entertainment twice weekly in season. Off site: Fishing. Golf. Bicycle hire. Riding (all within 5 km).

Open: All year.

Directions

From A28 in direction of Porto, leave at exit 18 (Fao/Apuila). At roundabout take N13 in direction of Pavoa de Varzim/Porto for 2.5 km. At Hotel Contriz, turn right onto narrow cobbled road. Site well signed in 2 km. GPS: 41.44504, -8.75767

Charges guide

Per person	€ 2.90 - € 5.40
caravan and car	€ 6.80 - € 12.00
electricity (5/15A)	€ 2.50 - € 3.10

Accommodation

Over recent years many of the campsites featured in this guide have added large numbers of high quality mobile homes and chalets. Many site owners believe that some former caravanners and motorcaravanners have been enticed by the extra comfort they can now provide, and that maybe this is the ideal solution to combine the freedom of camping with all the comforts of home.

Quality is consistently high and, although the exact size and inventory may vary from site to site, if you choose any of the sites detailed here, you can be sure that you're staying in some of the best quality and best value mobile homes available.

Home comforts are provided and typically these include a fridge with freezer compartment, gas hob, proper shower – often a microwave and radio/cassette hi-fi too, but do check for details. All mobile homes and chalets come fully equipped with a good range of kitchen utensils, pots and pans, crockery, cutlery and outdoor furniture. Some even have an attractive wooden sundeck or paved terrace – a perfect spot for outdoors eating or relaxing with a book and watching the world go by.

Regardless of model, colourful soft furnishings are the norm and a generally breezy décor helps to provide a real holiday feel.

Although some sites may have a large number of different accommodation types, we have restricted our choice to one or two of the most popular accommodation units (either mobile homes or chalets) for each of the sites listed.

The mobile homes here will be of modern design, and recent innovations, for example, often include pitched roofs which substantially improve their appearance.

Design will invariably include clever use of space and fittings/furniture to provide for comfortable holidays – usually light and airy, with big windows and patio-style doors, fully equipped kitchen areas, a shower room with shower, washbasin and WC, cleverly designed bedrooms and a comfortable lounge/dining area (often incorporating a sofa bed).

In general, modern campsite chalets incorporate all the best features of mobile homes in a more traditional structure, sometimes with the advantage of an upper mezzanine floor for an additional bedroom.

Our selected campsites offer a massive range of different types of mobile home and chalet, and it would be impractical to inspect every single accommodation unit. Our selection criteria, therefore, primarily takes account of the quality standards of the campsite itself.

However, there are a couple of important ground rules:

- Featured mobile homes must be no more than 5 years old
- Chalets no more than ten years old
- All listed accommodation must, of course, fully conform with all applicable local, national and European safety legislation.

For each campsite we have given details of the type, or types, of accommodation available to rent, but these details are necessarily quite brief. Sometimes internal layouts can differ quite substantially, particularly with regard to sleeping arrangements, where these include the flexible provision for 'extra persons' on sofa beds located in the living area. These arrangements may vary from accommodation to accommodation, and if you're planning a holiday which includes more people than are catered for by the main bedrooms you should check exactly how the extra sleeping arrangements are to be provided!

Charges

An indication of the tariff for each type of accommodation featured is also included, indicating the variance between the low and high season tariffs. However, given that many campsites have a large and often complex range of pricing options, incorporating special deals and various discounts, the charges we mention should be taken to be just an indication. We strongly recommend therefore that you confirm the actual cost when making a booking.

We also strongly recommend that you check with the campsite, when booking, what (if anything) will be provided by way of bed linen, blankets, pillows etc. Again, in our experience, this can vary widely from site to site.

On every campsite a fully refundable deposit (usually between 150 and 300 euros) is payable on arrival. There may also be an optional cleaning service for which a further charge is made. Other options may include sheet hire (typically 30 euros per unit) or baby pack hire (cot and high chair).

Mobile homes & chalets

ES81400 Camping Treumal

see report page 26

Ctra 253 km 47.5, E-17250 Calonge

AR1 – MB6 – Mobile Home	AR2 – MT6 – Mobile Home
Sleeping: 2 bedrooms, sleeps 4: 1 double, 2 singles, sofa bed, pillows and blankets provided	**Sleeping:** 2 bedrooms, sleeps 4: 1 double, 2 singles, sofa bed, pillows and blankets provided
Living: living/kitchen area, heating, shower, WC	**Living:** living/kitchen area, heating, shower, WC, seperate WC
Eating: fitted kitchen with hobs, coffee maker, fridge, freezer	**Eating:** fitted kitchen with hobs, coffee maker, fridge, freezer
Outside: table & chairs, parasol	**Outside:** table & chairs, parasol
Pets: not accepted	**Pets:** not accepted

Other (AR1 and AR2): bed linen to hire

Open: 31 March - 30 September

Weekly Charge	AR1	AR2
Low Season (from)	€ 512	€ 603
High Season (from)	€ 854	€ 1008

ES82330 Camping La Tordera

see report page 37

Cami de la Tordera s/n, E-08380 Malgrat de Mar

AR1 – BUNGALOW 3 PERSONS – Bungalow	AR2 – BUNGALOW 5 PERSONS – Bungalow
Sleeping: 1 bedroom, sleeps 3, 2 doubles, 1 single, bunk bed, sofa bed	**Sleeping:** 2 bedrooms, sleeps 5: 2 doubles, 1 single, bunk bed, sofa bed
Living: living/kitchen area, heating, TV, air conditioning, shower, seperate WC	**Living:** living/kitchen area, heating, TV, air conditioning, shower, seperate WC
Eating: fitted kitchen with microwave, grill, coffee maker, fridge, freezer	**Eating:** fitted kitchen with microwave, grill, coffee maker, fridge, freezer
Outside: table & chairs, barbecue	**Outside:** table & chairs, barbecue
Pets: not accepted	**Pets:** not accepted

Other (AR1 and AR2): bed linen, highchair to hire

Open: 3 June - 2 October

Weekly Charge	AR1	AR2
Low Season (from)	€ 413	€ 553
High Season (from)	€ 833	€ 1113

ES85400 Camping La Torre del Sol

see report page 40

Ctra N340 km 1136, E-43300 Montroig

AR1 – PAGAN – Bungalow Tent

Sleeping: 2 bedrooms, sleeps 5: 3 singles, bunk bed, pillows and blankets provided

Living: living/kitchen area, shower, WC, seperate WC

Eating: fitted kitchen with hobs, coffee maker, fridge

Outside: table & chairs, parasol, 2 sun loungers

Pets: not accepted

Open: 1 April - 30 September

Weekly Charge	AR1
Low Season (from)	€ 161.5
High Season (from)	€ 586.5

ES84800 Camping Resort Sangulí Salou

see report page 46

Passeig miramar - Pl. Venus, Apdo 123, E-43840 Salou

AR1 – VILLA PARADISE – Chalet	AR2 – LOUISIANE – Mobile Home
Sleeping: 2 bedrooms, sleeps 6: 1 double, 2 singles, sofa bed, pillows and blankets provided	**Sleeping:** 2 bedrooms, sleeps 6: 1 double, 2 singles, sofa bed, pillows and blankets provided
Living: living/kitchen area, TV, air conditioning, shower, seperate WC	**Living:** living/kitchen area, air conditioning, shower, WC
Eating: fitted kitchen with hobs, microwave, dishwasher, fridge, freezer	**Eating:** fitted kitchen with hobs, oven, microwave, fridge
Outside: table & chairs, 2 sun loungers	**Outside:** table & chairs
Pets: not accepted	**Pets:** not accepted

Open: 19 March - 1 November

Weekly Charge	AR1	AR2
Low Season (from)	€ 399	€ 308
High Season (from)	€ 1470	€ 1155

ES80600 Camping La Ballena Alegre

see report page 52

Ctra Sant Marti d'Empuries s/n, E-17470 Sant Pere Pescador

AR1 – TAMARIU – Bungalow	AR2 – MEDITERRANI – Mobile Home
Sleeping: 2 bedrooms, sleeps 5: 1 double, 1 single, bunk bed, sofa bed, pillows and blankets provided	**Sleeping:** 2 bedrooms, sleeps 5: 2 singles, bunk bed, sofa bed, pillows and blankets provided
Living: living/kitchen area, heating, TV, air conditioning, shower, seperate WC	**Living:** living/kitchen area, heating, air conditioning, shower, seperate WC
Eating: fitted kitchen with microwave, dishwasher, coffee maker, fridge, freezer	**Eating:** fitted kitchen with microwave, dishwasher, coffee maker, fridge, freezer
Outside: table & chairs, 2 sun loungers	**Outside:** table & chairs, 2 sun loungers
Pets: not accepted	**Pets:** not accepted

Other (AR1 and AR2): bed linen, highchair to hire

Open: 12 May - 24 September

Weekly Charge	AR1	AR2
Low Season (from)	€ 420	€ 355
High Season (from)	€ 1148	€ 994

ES83900 Vilanova Park

see report page 59

Ctra de l'Arboc km 2.5, E-08800 Vilanova i la Geltru

AR1 – BUNGALOW SERIE 950 – Bungalow	AR2 – BUNGALOW SERIE 540 – Bungalow
Sleeping: 2 bedrooms, sleeps 6: 1 double, 3 singles, sofa bed, pillows and blankets provided	**Sleeping:** 2 bedrooms, sleeps 6: 1 double, 2 singles, sofa bed, pillows and blankets provided
Living: living/kitchen area, heating, TV, air conditioning, shower, WC	**Living:** living/kitchen area, heating, TV, air conditioning, shower, WC
Eating: fitted kitchen with hobs, microwave, coffee maker, fridge	**Eating:** fitted kitchen with hobs, microwave, coffee maker, fridge
Outside: table & chairs	**Outside:** table & chairs
Pets: not accepted	**Pets:** not accepted

Other (AR1 and AR2): bed linen to hire

Open: All year

Weekly Charge	AR1	AR2
Low Season (from)	€ 714	€ 637
High Season (from)	€ 1155	€ 1057

ES92000 Caravanning El Escorial

see report page 110

Apdo 8, Ctra M600 km 3,5, E-28280 El Escorial

AR1 – ESPECIAL – Bungalow	AR2 – CLASICO – Bungalow
Sleeping: 4 bedrooms, sleeps 5: 4 singles, sofa bed, pillows and blankets provided	**Sleeping:** 3 bedrooms, sleeps 5: 1 double, bunk bed, pillows and blankets provided
Living: living/kitchen area, heating, TV, shower, WC	**Living:** living/kitchen area, heating, TV, shower, WC
Eating: fitted kitchen with hobs, microwave, coffee maker, fridge, freezer	**Eating:** fitted kitchen with hobs, microwave, coffee maker, fridge, freezer
Outside: table & chairs	**Outside:** table & chairs
Pets: not accepted	**Pets:** not accepted

Open: All year

Weekly Charge	AR1	AR2
Low Season (from)	€ 791	€ 749
High Season (from)	€ 903	€ 847

Travelling in Europe

When taking your car (and caravan, tent or trailer tent) or motorcaravan to the continent you do need to plan in advance and to find out as much as possible about driving in the countries you plan to visit. Whilst European harmonisation has eliminated many of the differences between one country and another, it is well worth reading the short notes we provide in the introduction to each country in this guide in addition to this more general summary.

Of course, the main difference from driving in the UK is that in mainland Europe you will need to drive on the right. Without taking extra time and care, especially at busy junctions and conversely when roads are empty, it is easy to forget to drive on the right. Remember that traffic approaching from the right usually has priority unless otherwise indicated by road markings and signs. Harmonisation also means that most (but not all) common road signs are the same in all countries.

Your vehicle

Book your vehicle in for a good service well before your intended departure date. This will lessen the chance of an expensive breakdown. Make sure your brakes are working efficiently and that your tyres have plenty of tread (3 mm. is recommended, particularly if you are undertaking a long journey).

Also make sure that your caravan or trailer is roadworthy and that its tyres are in good order and correctly inflated. Plan your packing and be careful not to overload your vehicle, caravan and trailer – this is unsafe and may well invalidate your insurance cover (it must not be more fully loaded than the kerb weight of the insured vehicle).

CHECK ALL THE FOLLOWING:

- GB sticker. If you do not display a sticker, you may risk an on-the-spot fine as this identifier is compulsory in all countries. Euro-plates are an acceptable alternative within the EU (but not outside). Remember to attach another sticker (or Euro-plate) to caravans and trailers. Only GB stickers (not England, Scotland, Wales or N. Ireland) stickers are valid in the EU.
- Headlights. As you will be driving on the right you must adjust your headlights so that the dipped beam does not dazzle oncoming drivers. Converter kits are readily available for most vehicles, although if your car is fitted with high intensity headlights, you should check with your motor dealer. Check that any planned extra loading does not affect the beam height.
- Seatbelts. Rules for the fitting and wearing of seatbelts throughout Europe are similar to those in the UK, but it is worth checking before you go. Rules for carrying children in the front of vehicles vary from country to country. It is best to plan not to do this if possible.
- Door/wing mirrors. To help with driving on the right, if your vehicle is not fitted with a mirror on the left hand side, we recommend you have one fitted.
- Fuel. Leaded and Lead Replacement petrol is increasingly difficult to find in Northern Europe.

Compulsory additional equipment

The driving laws of the countries of Europe still vary in what you are required to carry in your vehicle, although the consequences of not carrying a required piece of equipment are almost always an on-the-spot fine.

To meet these requirements we suggest that you carry the following:

- FIRE EXTINGUISHER
- BASIC TOOL KIT
- FIRST AID KIT
- SPARE BULBS
- TWO WARNING TRIANGLES – two are required in some countries at all times, and are compulsory in most countries when towing.
- HIGH VISIBILITY VEST – now compulsory in France, Spain, Italy and Austria (and likely to become compulsory throughout the EU) in case you need to walk on a motorway.

Insurance and Motoring Documents

Vehicle insurance

Contact your insurer well before you depart to check that your car insurance policy covers driving outside the UK. Most do, but many policies only provide minimum cover (so if you have an accident your insurance may only cover the cost of damage to the other person's property, with no cover for fire and theft).

To maintain the same level of cover abroad as you enjoy at home you need to tell your vehicle insurer. Some will automatically cover you abroad with no extra cost and no extra paperwork. Some will say you need a Green Card (which is neither green nor on card) but won't charge for it. Some will charge extra for the Green Card. Ideally you should contact your vehicle insurer 3-4 weeks before you set off, and confirm your conversation with them in writing.

Breakdown insurance

Arrange breakdown cover for your trip in good time so that if your vehicle breaks down or is involved in an accident it (and your caravan or trailer) can be repaired or returned to this country. This cover can usually be arranged as part of your travel insurance policy (see below).

Documents you must take with you

You may be asked to show your documents at any time so make sure that they are in order, up-to-date and easily accessible while you travel.

These are what you need to take:

- Passports (you may also need a visa in some countries if you hold either a UK passport not issued in the UK or a passport that was issued outside the EU).
- Motor Insurance Certificate, including Green Card (or Continental Cover clause)
- DVLA Vehicle Registration Document plus, if not your own vehicle, the owner's written authority to drive.
- A full valid Driving Licence (not provisional). The new photo style licence is now mandatory in most European countries.

Personal Holiday insurance

Even though you are just travelling within Europe you must take out travel insurance. Few EU countries pay the full cost of medical treatment even under reciprocal health service arrangements. The first part of a holiday insurance policy covers people. It will include the cost of doctor, ambulance and hospital treatment if needed. If needed the better companies will even pay for English language speaking doctors and nurses and will bring a sick or injured holidaymaker home by air ambulance.

Personal Holiday insurance (continued)

An important part of the insurance, often ignored, is cancellation (and curtailment) cover. Few things are as heartbreaking as having to cancel a holiday because a member of the family falls ill. Cancellation insurance can't take away the disappointment, but it makes sure you don't suffer financially as well. For this reason you should arrange your holiday insurance at least eight weeks before you set off.

Whichever insurance you choose we would advise reading very carefully the policies sold by the High Street travel trade. Whilst they may be good, they may not cover the specific needs of campers, caravanners and motorcaravanners.

Telephone 01580 214000 for a quote for our Camping Travel Insurance with cover arranged through leading leisure insurance providers.
Alternatively visit our website at: alanrogers.com/insurance

European Health Insurance Card (EHIC)

Make sure you apply for your EHIC before travelling in Europe. Eligible travellers from the UK are entitled to receive free or reduced-cost medical care in many European countries on production of an EHIC. This free card is available by completing a form in the booklet 'Health Advice for Travellers' from local Post Offices. One should be completed for each family member. Alternatively visit www.ehic.org.uk and apply on-line. Please allow time to send your application off and have the EHIC returned to you.

The EHIC is valid in all European Community countries plus Iceland, Liechtenstein, Switzerland and Norway. If you or any of your dependants are suddenly taken ill or have an accident during a visit to any of these countries, free or reduced-cost emergency treatment is available – in most cases on production of a valid EHIC.

Only state-provided emergency treatment is covered, and you will receive treatment on the same terms as nationals of the country you are visiting. Private treatment is generally not covered, and state-provided treatment may not cover all of the things that you would expect to receive free of charge from the NHS.

Remember an EHIC does not cover you for all the medical costs that you can incur or for repatriation - it is not an alternative to travel insurance. You will still need appropriate insurance to ensure you are fully covered for all eventualities.

Travelling with children

Most countries in Europe are enforcing strict guidelines when you are travelling with children who are not your own. A minor (under the age of 18) must be accompanied by a parent or legal guardian or must carry a letter of authorisation from a parent or guardian. The letter should name the adult responsible for the minor during his or her stay. Similarly, a minor travelling with just one of his/her parents, must have a letter of authority to leave their home country from the parent staying behind. Full information is available at www.fco.gov.uk

Open All Year

The following sites are understood to accept caravanners and campers all year round. It is always wise to phone the site to check as the facilities available, for example, may be reduced.

SPAIN

Cataluña-Catalunya

ES85360	Ametlla	21
ES91240	Bedurà Park	35
ES82280	Blanes	23
ES82350	Bon Repos	54
ES82400	Bona Vista Kim	24
ES85350	Cala d'Oques	33
ES81300	Calonge	25
ES80360	Esponellà	31
ES91190	Frontera	32
ES84770	La Llosa	27
ES84820	Pineda de Salou	36
ES85080	Poboleda	44
ES85060	Serra de Prades	58
ES91225	Vall de Camprodon	28
ES83900	Vilanova Park	59

Comunidad Valenciana

ES86200	Alqueria	67
ES85850	Altomira	72
ES86830	Benisol	63
ES85800	Bonterra	63
ES86900	Costa Blanca	67
ES86850	El Raco	64
ES86120	Euro (Oliva)	73
ES87410	Florantilles	75
ES87540	Javea	68
ES86150	Kiko	73
ES86250	Kiko Rural	76
ES87400	Lo Monte	74
ES87420	Marina	71
ES86450	Mariola	65
ES87430	Marjal Camping	68
ES87435	Marjal C. Blanca	66
ES85900	Monmar	70
ES87550	Moraira	70
ES86130	Olé	74
ES85600	Playa Tropicana	62
ES85610	Ribamar	62
ES85700	Torre La Sal 2	75
ES86750	Vall de Laguar	65
ES86810	Villasol	64
ES85580	Vinaros	76

Murcia

ES87520	El Portus (Naturist)	79
ES87450	Fuente	78
ES87480	Madriles	79
ES87530	Manga	80
ES87440	Puerta	80

Andalucia

ES88730	Aldea	84
ES87830	Almanat (Naturist)	83
ES88030	Buganvilla	92
ES87630	Cabo de Gata	85
ES88020	Cabopino	91
ES90840	Campiña	96
ES90850	Carlos III	90
ES87560	Cueva Negra	93
ES87510	Cuevas Mar	94
ES90890	Despeñaperros	96
ES92950	Don Cactus	93
ES92900	El Balcon	95
ES90800	El Brillante	87
ES87810	El Pino	99
ES88090	El Sur	95
ES87620	Escullos	93
ES87900	Fuente de Piedra	88
ES87650	Garrofa	83
ES88900	Gazules	83
ES88710	Giralda	89
ES87820	Laguna Playa	98
ES92850	Lomas	89
ES88000	Marbella Playa	91
ES92930	Orgiva	94
ES88500	Paloma	97
ES88570	Pinar San José	85
ES88650	Playa Las Dunas	88
ES92920	Puerta La Alpujarra	94
ES92760	Reina Isabel	90
ES88590	Roche	86
ES87680	Roquetas	95
ES88580	Rosaleda	86
ES87850	Rural Iznate	90
ES87490	Sopalmo	92
ES92700	Suspiro-Moro	88
ES92890	Trevélez	99
ES90780	Villares	87

Extremadura

ES90860	Cáceres	103
ES90870	Merida	104
ES90270	Monfrague	104

Castilla La-Mancha

ES90970	Batanes	107
ES90900	El Greco	108
ES90960	Mirador	107

Madrid

ES90910	Aranjuez	111
ES92000	El Escorial	110
ES92120	Monte Holiday	112
ES92100	Pico-Miel	112

Castilla y León

ES92500	Costajan	115
ES90210	Fuentes Blancas	115
ES90250	Regio	117
ES90245	Riaza	117

Galicia

ES90240	As Cancelas	122
ES89360	Bayona Playa	120
ES89380	Paxarinas	121

Asturias

ES89400	Cantiles	126
ES89650	Picos-Europa	125

Cantabria

ES89640	Molino	130
ES89730	Santillana	134

Pais Vasco-Euskadi

ES90390	Gran Zarautz	138
ES90300	Igueldo	137
ES90340	Leagi	137

La Rioja

ES92280	Berceo	140

Aragón

ES91040	Ciudad de Zaragoza	152
ES90640	Gavín	150
ES91250	Lago Barasona	150
ES90610	Ligüerre de Cinca	151
ES90600	Peña Montañesa	151

PORTUGAL

Algarve

PO8210	Albufeira	156
PO8410	Armacao-Pera	157
PO8230	Olhão	159
PO8220	Quarteira	160
PO8440	Quinta	158
PO8430	Sagres	160
PO8202	Turiscampo	157
PO8200	Valverde	158

Alentejo

PO8355	Asseiceira	165
PO8340	Évora	163
PO8350	Markádia	163
PO8160	Porto Covo	165
PO8170	São Miguel	164
PO8175	Zmar	164

Lisbon & Vale do Tejo

PO8150	Caparica	168
PO8480	Foz do Arelho	169
PO8130	Guincho	167
PO8140	Monsanto	169
PO8400	O Tamanco	170
PO8155	Parque Verde	168
PO8100	Sao Pedro-Moel	170

Beiras & Centre

PO8330	Arganil	172
PO8090	Gala	173
PO8360	Idanha-a-Nova	173
PO8040	Vagueira	175

Porto & North

PO8010	Caminha	177
PO8370	Cerdeira	178
PO8030	Rio Alto	178
PO8020	Viana-Castelo	178

Dogs

For the benefit of those who want to take their dogs with them or for people who do not like dogs at the sites they visit, we list here the sites that have indicated to us that they do not accept dogs. If you are, however, planning to take your dog we do advise you to contact them first to check – there may be limits on numbers, breeds, etc. or times of the year when they are excluded.

Never – these sites do not accept dogs at any time

SPAIN

Cataluña-Catalunya

ES91240	Bedurà Park	35
ES84810	Cambrils	28
ES80900	Cypsela	43
ES81030	El Maset	21
ES80700	Escala	34
ES91430	Pirineus	32
ES81010	Playa Brava	43
ES85300	Playa Montroig	39
ES91230	Solsones	54
ES84200	Stel (Roda)	44
ES85370	Templo del Sol (Nat)	33
ES85400	Torre del Sol	40
ES81400	Treumal	26

Comunidad Valenciana

ES87410	Florantilles	75
ES85900	Monmar	70
ES86810	Villasol	64

Murcia

ES87480	Madriles	79

Andalucia

ES88550	Tarifa	98
ES87580	Tau de San José	96

Castilla y León

ES92540	Demanda	118
ES92510	Rio Lobos	118

Cantabria

ES89980	Playa de Isla	131
ES90000	Playa Joyel	132
ES89990	Punta Marina	131

Aragón

ES91100	Fresneda	150

Balears

ES80000	Son Bou	153

PORTUGAL

Alentejo

PO8170	São Miguel	164

Maybe – not accepted in high season

SPAIN

Cataluña-Catalunya

ES82320	Bella Terra	24
ES81600	Cala Gogo	26
ES80800	Delfin Verde	57
ES80720	Medes	35
ES84820	Pineda de Salou	36
ES80090	Salatà	45

Comunidad Valenciana

ES85800	Bonterra	63

Andalucia

ES88030	Buganvilla	92
ES92950	Don Cactus	93
ES88500	Paloma	97
ES88570	Pinar San José	85
ES88580	Rosaleda	86

Cantabria

ES89930	Playa del Regaton	131

PORTUGAL

Alentejo

PO8350	Markádia	163

Fishing

We are pleased to include details of sites which provide facilities for fishing on site. However, it is always best to contact sites directly to check that they provide for your individual requirements.

SPAIN

Cataluña-Catalunya

ES85360	Ametlla	21
ES80350	Amfora	49
ES80500	Aquarius	53
ES80600	Ballena Alegre	52
ES82320	Bella Terra	24
ES82280	Blanes	23
ES82350	Bon Repos	54
ES82380	Caballo de Mar	40
ES85350	Cala d'Oques	33
ES81600	Cala Gogo	26
ES82000	Cala Llevadó	58
ES80100	Castell Mar	30
ES82340	Del Mar	37
ES80800	Delfin Verde	57
ES80400	Dunas	50
ES82300	El Pinar	23
ES85330	Els Prats Village	38
ES80360	Esponellà	31
ES91190	Frontera	32
ES80310	Gaviota	47
ES84780	Joan	27
ES84770	La Llosa	27
ES80150	Laguna	29
ES80300	Nautic Almata	30
ES84850	Palmeras	55
ES85300	Playa Montroig	39
ES80320	Riu	50
ES91420	Solana del Segre	22
ES84200	Stel (Roda)	44
ES84830	Tamarit	56
ES85370	Templo del Sol (Nat)	33
ES82330	Tordera	37
ES84860	Torre de la Mora	55
ES85400	Torre del Sol	40
ES81400	Treumal	26
ES91225	Vall de Camprodon	28

Fishing continued

Comunidad Valenciana

ES86115	Azul	72
ES86120	Euro (Oliva)	73
ES86150	Kiko	73
ES87430	Marjal Camping	68
ES86130	Olé	74
ES86880	Playa Paraiso	75
ES85600	Playa Tropicana	62
ES85610	Ribamar	62
ES85700	Torre La Sal 2	75

Murcia

ES87520	El Portus (Naturist)	79
ES87530	Manga	80
ES87440	Puerta	80

Andalucia

ES87830	Almanat (Naturist)	83
ES92950	Don Cactus	93
ES87650	Garrofa	83
ES87820	Laguna Playa	98
ES88550	Tarifa	98
ES92890	Trevélez	99

Castilla La-Mancha

ES90900	El Greco	108
ES90980	Rio Mundo	107

Madrid

ES90910	Aranjuez	111

Castilla y León

ES92570	Frias	116
ES92510	Rio Lobos	118

Galicia

ES89360	Bayona Playa	120
ES89380	Paxarinas	121

Asturias

ES89440	Cascada	124
ES89500	Costa Verde	126
ES89450	Lagos-Somiedo	127
ES89600	Paz	127
ES89650	Picos-Europa	125

Cantabria

ES89700	Arenas-Pechon	132
ES89910	Barguilla	133
ES89620	Isla	133
ES89640	Molino	130
ES89980	Playa de Isla	131
ES89930	Playa del Regaton	131
ES90000	Playa Joyel	132

Pais Vasco-Euskadi

ES90350	Portuondo	137

La Rioja

ES92260	Cameros	142
ES92250	Rioja	141

Navarra

ES90430	Errota el Molino	146
ES90420	Etxarri	145
ES90480	Urrobi	145

Aragón

ES90580	Baliera	149
ES90610	Ligüerre de Cinca	151
ES90600	Peña Montañesa	151
ES90630	Puente	152

PORTUGAL

Alentejo

PO8350	Markádia	163

Beiras & Centre

PO8060	Costa Nova	174
PO8360	Idanha-a-Nova	173
PO8070	Mira	174

Porto & North

PO8010	Caminha	177

Bicycle Hire

We understand that the following sites have bicycles to hire on site or can arrange for bicycles to be delivered. However, we would recommend that you contact them directly to check as the situation can change.

SPAIN

Cataluña-Catalunya

ES85360	Ametlla	21
ES80350	Amfora	49
ES80500	Aquarius	53
ES80600	Ballena Alegre	52
ES82450	Barcelona	38
ES80640	Bassegoda	20
ES82320	Bella Terra	24
ES81600	Cala Gogo	26
ES80900	Cypsela	43
ES80800	Delfin Verde	57
ES84790	Don Camilo	27
ES80400	Dunas	50
ES83920	El Garrofer	54
ES85330	Els Prats Village	38
ES80360	Esponellà	31
ES85550	Eucaliptus	21
ES80310	Gaviota	47
ES81000	Inter-Pals	42
ES84780	Joan	27
ES84770	La Llosa	27
ES80150	Laguna	29
ES81750	Mas Sant Josep	53
ES80720	Medes	35
ES85020	Montblanc Park	39
ES80300	Nautic Almata	30
ES80690	Neus	34
ES81500	Palamos	40
ES80330	Palmeras	48
ES84850	Palmeras	55
ES91400	Pedraforca	45
ES84820	Pineda de Salou	36
ES81010	Playa Brava	43
ES85300	Playa Montroig	39
ES80320	Riu	50
ES85060	Serra de Prades	58
ES91230	Solsones	54
ES91440	Stel (Puigcerdá)	44
ES84200	Stel (Roda)	44
ES84830	Tamarit	56
ES85370	Templo del Sol (Nat)	33
ES82330	Tordera	37
ES85400	Torre del Sol	40
ES82100	Tucan	36
ES81700	Valldaro	42
ES83900	Vilanova Park	59

Comunidad Valenciana

ES86115	Azul	72
ES85800	Bonterra	63
ES86120	Euro (Oliva)	73
ES86150	Kiko	73
ES86250	Kiko Rural	76
ES87400	Lo Monte	74
ES87420	Marina	71
ES87430	Marjal Camping	68
ES87435	Marjal C. Blanca	66
ES85600	Playa Tropicana	62
ES85610	Ribamar	62
ES86220	Santa Marta	66

Bicycle Hire continued

Murcia

ES87440 Puerta 80

Andalucia

ES87830 Almanat (Naturist) 83
ES87630 Cabo de Gata 85
ES90840 Campiña 96
ES92950 Don Cactus 93
ES87620 Escullos 93
ES87900 Fuente de Piedra 88
ES88900 Gazules 83
ES92930 Orgiva 94
ES87580 Tau de San José 96
ES92890 Trevélez 99

Extremadura

ES90870 Merida 104

Castilla La-Mancha

ES90970 Batanes 107
ES90980 Rio Mundo 107

Madrid

ES90910 Aranjuez 111
ES92120 Monte Holiday 112

Castilla y León

ES92420 Acueducto 117
ES92540 Demanda 118
ES90230 Santiago 115

Galicia

ES90240 As Cancelas 122
ES89380 Paxarinas 121

Cantabria

ES89910 Barguilla 133
ES89620 Isla 133
ES89930 Playa del Regaton 131
ES89730 Santillana 134

La Rioja

ES90400 Haro 141

Navarra

ES90430 Errota el Molino 146
ES90420 Etxarri 145

Aragón

ES90620 Boltana 149
ES91100 Fresneda 150
ES90640 Gavín 150
ES91250 Lago Barasona 150
ES90610 Ligüerre de Cinca 151
ES90600 Peña Montañesa 151
ES90630 Puente 152

Balears

ES80000 Son Bou 153

PORTUGAL

Algarve

PO8210 Albufeira 156
PO8230 Olhão 159
PO8440 Quinta 158
PO8430 Sagres 160
PO8202 Turiscampo 157

Alentejo

PO8355 Asseiceira 165
PO8160 Porto Covo 165
PO8175 Zmar 164

Lisbon & Vale do Tejo

PO8480 Foz do Arelho 169
PO8550 Quinta Da Cerejeira 168
PO8460 Vale Paraiso 170

Beiras & Centre

PO8360 Idanha-a-Nova 173
PO8070 Mira 174
PO8040 Vagueira 175

Porto & North

PO8010 Caminha 177

Horse Riding

We understand that the following sites have horse riding stables on site. Where facilities are within easy reach and we have been given details, we have included this information in the individual site reports. However, we recommend that you contact the site to check that they meet your requirements.

SPAIN

Cataluña-Catalunya

ES80150 Laguna 29
ES80300 Nautic Almata 30
ES85060 Serra de Prades 58
ES91225 Vall de Camprodon 28

Comunidad Valenciana

ES85600 Playa Tropicana 62

Andalucia

ES92890 Trevélez 99

Asturias

ES89450 Lagos-Somiedo 127

Cantabria

ES89700 Arenas-Pechon 132
ES89620 Isla 133

La Rioja

ES92250 Rioja 141

Aragón

ES90600 Peña Montañesa 151
ES90630 Puente 152

PORTUGAL

Alentejo

PO8350 Markádia 163

Been to any good campsites lately?

We have

You'll find them here...

The UK's market leading independent guides to the best campsites

Also available on iPad alanrogers.com/digital

GO THERE NOW!

HOLIDAY OFFERS
£536
£543
CALL NOW 01580 214 000
Family camping holidays in France, Spain, Italy & more...
Map Search
yelloh!

2012 warms up at ExCeL...
The ONLY SHOW in the spring where the leading caravan and motorhome manufacturers will be displaying their NEW 2012 SEASON MODELS.
The MOTORHOME CARAVAN & CAMPING SHOW
14-19 FEB 2012 • EXCEL LONDON
OFFICIAL PARTNER:
THE CARAVAN CLUB
SUPPORTER:
The Camping and Caravanning Club
The Friendly Club
WWW.MOTORHOMECARAVANANDCAMPING.CO.UK
The NATIONAL SHOW at the NEC where you'll see the NEW 2013 SEASON caravan and motorhome models from all the leading manufacturers.
...and Autumn's looking hot too.
The MOTORHOME & CARAVAN SHOW
16-21 OCT 2012 • NEC BIRMINGHAM
SUPPORTERS:
THE CARAVAN CLUB
The Camping and Caravanning Club
The Friendly Club
WWW.MOTORHOMEANDCARAVANSHOW.CO.UK
ORGANISED BY:
NCC events

Regions of Spain & Portugal

Town & Village Index

SPAIN

Town & Village Index continued

PORTUGAL

Index by Campsite Number

SPAIN

Index by Campsite Number continued

Index by Campsite Number continued

PORTUGAL

Index by Campsite Region & Name

SPAIN

Cataluña-Catalunya

Index by Campsite Region & Name continued

Index by Campsite Region & Name continued